D1378134

When Government Speaks

When Government Speaks

Politics, Law, and Government Expression in America

Mark G. Yudof

University of California Press
Berkeley / Los Angeles / London

University of California Press
Berkeley and Los Angeles, California
University of California Press, Ltd.
London, England
© 1983 by
The Regents of the University of California
Printed in the United States of America

1 2 3 4 5 6 7 8 9

Library of Congress Cataloging in Publication Data
Yudof, Mark G.
   When government speaks.
   Includes index.
   1. Government information—United States. 2. Freedom
of information—United States. 3. Government publicity
—United States. 4. Liberty of speech—United States.
I. Title.
KF5753.Y83   342.73′0853   81-1965
ISBN 0-520-04254-9 347.302853   AACR2

To my colleagues on the University
of Texas Law School faculty, who
intellectually sustained me throughout the writing of this book.

Not the gun but the word is the symbol of authority.

—CHARLES LINDBLOM

A legitimate government is one whose authority citizens can recognize while still regarding themselves as equal, autonomous, rational agents.

—THOMAS SCANLON

Contents

Acknowledgments xiii
Preface xv

Part I. Government Expression in a Democracy
  Introduction 3

1. The Nerves of Government:
   Government Communication,
   the Welfare State, and Technology 5
     Sins of Commission 6
     Sins of Omission 9
     The Exacerbating Effects of Technology 10
     Majority Will in the Twentieth Century 12
     Social Change and the Rigidity of Law 15

2. Government Communication and the
   "Self-Controlled Citizen" 20
     Democratic and Authoritarian Ideals 20
     The Mutually Affecting Relationship Between Government
       and Nongovernment Expression 22
     Communications "Overload," Selectivity, and Power
       Configurations in the Private Sector 31

3. Communication and the Polity: Legitimacy, Policy,
   and Government "Rights" of Expression 38
     The Legitimacy of Government Speech 38
     Beyond Legitimacy: Policy 41
     A Government Right of Expression? 42

4. The Opportunity for Abuse of
   Government Communication 51
     Public Education and Indoctrination 52
     Federal Executive Department Speech 55
     Propaganda in Wartime 62

Part II. Limits on Government Expression

Introduction 69

5. The Indeterminate Impact of
    Mass Communications 71

6. Government Expression and the Pluralist Faith 90

Introduction 90
Critiques of Pluralism 92
Living with Pluralism 108

7. Nonjudicial Restraints on
    Government Expression 111

Attitudes 111
Structural Limits 114
Implementation 116
The Office of War Information 121
Public Broadcasting 124
Delegation of Special Functions and
    the "Morality of Consent" 135

Part III. Government Expression and First Amendment Theory

Introduction 141

8. The Majoritarian Underpinnings of the First
    Amendment: Verifying and Falsifying Consent 145

The Countermajoritarian Difficulty 145
The Difficulty Reconsidered 152

9. The First Amendment as a Constraint on Government
    Expression: Arguments from History and Structure 158

Constitutionalizing the Arguments 158
Implications for First Amendment Analysis: Recent
    Controversies in Perspective 161
Preliminary Caveats 164

10. Verifying and Falsifying Majorities: Legislative
    and Judicial Competence 174

Introduction 174
Verifying Majorities 176
Falsifying Majorities 178

11. Government Expression, the First Amendment,
and the Courts **200**

> The Relationship Between Government Expression and the
> Vindication of Individual First Amendment Claims 200
> Direct Controls on Government Expression 203

Part IV. Limiting Government Expression Through the First Amendment
> Introduction 211

12. The First Amendment and Public Schooling **213**

> The School Prayer Cases 214
> The Academic Freedom Cases 215
> School Newspaper Cases 218
> Selection of Teachers 220
> Students' Rights 224
> The Schools as Public Forums 225
> Private Schooling 227
> Releasing the Captive Audience 231

13. Government Subsidies of Private Speech, the
Public-Forum Doctrine, and Government as Editor **234**

> Government Subsidies 234
> Government Financing of Election Campaigns:
>   A Brief Note 237
> Government as Editor: Reconsidering the
>   Delegation Doctrine 240

14. Rights to Gather State-Held Information
and Freedom of Association **246**

> Introduction 246
> Rights to Gather Information 246
> Countering Government Expression: Pluralism and
>   Freedom of Association 255

15. Direct Judicial Controls on
Government Expression **259**

> Government Incitement of Unconstitutional or
>   Unlawful Behavior 259
> Stigmatizing Government Expression and the
>   Due Process Clause 263
> The Speech or Debate Clause 280

Enjoining Government Expression: Legislative and
Administrative Investigations   286
Wickard v. *Filburn*: Misleading Speech by an
Executive Officer   290
Government Speech and the "Right of Reply"   292
Captive Audiences and Enjoining Government Expression:
Bonner-Lyons Reconsidered   299

Conclusion: Enjoining Government Expression
under an *Ultra Vires* Doctrine   301
Index   307

Acknowledgments

The research for this book was funded through grants from the Spencer Foundation, the Ford Foundation, and the University of Texas Law School Foundation. An abbreviated version of portions of the book appeared as an article in the August 1979 issue of the *Texas Law Review*. The author wishes to thank the following persons for their many helpful criticisms and suggestions: Professors David Anderson, Philip Bobbitt, Sanford Levinson, Robert Means, Robert Mnookin, Scot Powe, William Powers, George Schatzki, Laurence Tribe, William Van Alstyne, and Jerre Williams. I am particularly grateful to Professors David Filvaroff and David Kirp for their close reading of the manuscript and their many suggestions for improvement. Roy Mersky and his staff at the University of Texas Law Library were immensely helpful in obtaining research materials. My research assistants, Danna Fischer, Douglas Gordon, David Jameson, and Matt Johnson, did yeoman's service in assisting my efforts. Olin McGill edited an early version of the manuscript and made innumerable and creative suggestions for revising the book. Alyce Lottman typed the manuscript, graciously enduring my endless modifications and redrafts. The book could not have been completed without her efforts. And Judith Gomel Yudof gave me the will to continue when so often I was tempted to give up the game.

Preface

This book arose from my concern that legal scholars and courts have failed to grapple with the realities of communication in the twentieth century. With few exceptions, they are taken with the dying metaphor of the marketplace of ideas; they concern themselves with government attempts to regulate private speech and ignore the massive role of governments in communications networks. Their reality is an eighteenth-century reality, one which ignores the fact that the "state shapes society almost as much as society shapes the state."[1] Communications processes in a modern welfare state are complex; and simplistic, static models of the impact of the expression of the governed on the governors fall wide of the mark and doom legal analysis of democratic precepts to irrelevance. Tyranny does not lie simply in government censorship. As Albert Camus saw well, "Tyrants indulge in monologues over millions of solitudes."[2] And solitude may be less a function of government-imposed silence than of government-imposed consensus. The burden of this enterprise is to identify the scope of government expression in modern America, to isolate its dangers, and to determine what, if anything, needs to be done. In this task, the work goes substantially beyond judicially imposed constitutional solutions, looking to the nature of communications processes and to the structure of, and relationships in, the American system of governance.

The underlying assumption is that First Amendment principles go significantly beyond protecting the rights of individuals to express positions inconsistent with the prevailing wisdom or policies of government. Informing such democratic aspirations as majority rule and representative government are notions of informed consent of the governed and of a continuous process of consultation with the people. If government dominates the flow of ideas and information, the ideal of the self-controlled citizen, making informed choices about his government, is destroyed. This, in turn, means that the people may be more responsive to the wishes and agenda of their leaders than the leaders are to the

1. Laurence H. Tribe, "The Puzzling Persistence of Process-Based Constitutional Theories," 89 *Yale Law Journal* 1063, 1078 (1980).
2. Albert Camus, *Resistance, Rebellion, and Death* 104 (New York: Knopf, 1961).

preferences of those whose welfare they oversee. The First Amendment then should be perceived as protecting the processes of consent—as seeking to prevent the mutilation of the independent judgment of the citizenry. Conversely, even democratic governments must lead, inform, teach, and seek to expand the knowledge of people. Liberty does not consist of the denial to government of its ability to accomplish public policy and to expand private choices through communications processes. In a well-ordered democracy, communications flow both ways— between the governors and the governed, each mutually affecting the judgments, perceptions, and communications of the other. This book seeks to address the issue of government participation in communications networks.

From yet another vantage, I attempt to move courts and scholars toward a partial reformulation of the questions that are asked about freedom of expression. Wrong questions generate wrong answers. For example, there has been much discussion of whether government defamation of an individual interferes with a liberty interest that the individual is guaranteed under the due process clause of the Fourteenth Amendment. The notion is that such defamation may stigmatize the individual and hence injure his reputation and make it difficult for him to obtain gainful employment. But are these the right questions to ask? Suppose we posit instead that all of us have an enormous interest in allowing governments to speak freely—to teach, to report research results, to provide useful information, and to give leadership. A private individual then seeks to require government to hold a due process hearing before it speaks in order to insure that information disseminated about him is accurate. Why should we tolerate such interference with the government's ability to speak? We do not require private individuals who may defame others to hold a hearing before publishing their remarks.

Is the analogy an apt one? Does a hearing requirement intrude too deeply into normal governing processes? Is a hearing requirement rational, given the nature of the alleged wrong? Would forbidding the dissemination of government information be more sensible? Would a recovery of damages after the fact be more efficacious? And who is to decide these issues? Are they best addressed to courts acting in a constitutional role? To legislative bodies? To the executive agency disseminating the information? In short, the traditional framework for deciding a stigma case may cloud analysis of the real interests at stake.

My hope is that this book will spark scholarly debate of long-neglected issues—even if it is the wrongheadedness of the analysis that provokes others to write. In any event, this book suggests the direction of my own future research, and perhaps others more insightful than I may perceive the wisdom of investigating government speech in the context of the system of freedom of expression.

Part I

*Government Expression
in a Democracy*

Introduction

Part I develops some general theories of government expression, defining the nature and extent of government participation in communications networks. Chapter 1 focuses attention on the "nerves of government"—the communication processes and channels that enable governments to interact with one another and with institutions and actors in the larger political framework. The potential danger to the whole represented by government origination of messages is described: (1) sins of commission—deliberate distortion or misrepresentation of facts to strengthen government's position; and (2) sins of omission—withholding of information that might undermine perceptions of the success of government programs or of the competence of government leaders. Technology, I argue, exacerbates these dangers by increasing governments' information-gathering and communications abilities and increasing the contacts between governments and their constituents in ways that make the constituencies more dependent on government. The chapter concludes with a discussion of the dilemma created when a world in which people respond to governments confronts a theory of democracy that posits that governments respond to the people. The general failure of legal scholars to deal with, or even to recognize, the problem of government speech is attributed to (1) the text of the First Amendment; (2) empirically unsound notions of the communications process in a democracy; (3) preoccupation with constitutional interpretation and enforcement as matters exclusively for the courts; and (4) the predictable lag of social institutions and research behind social change.

Chapter 2 is devoted to one of these reasons for the failure of law to accommodate life—the empirically unsound political theories too often relied on in legal scholarship. A critique of both authoritarian ideal types (change mandated from the top down) and democratic ideal types (change mandated from the bottom up) concludes that both are inherently unstable. Stability requires a "mutually affective" relationship between government and the governed. Governments influence citizens' perceptions and opinions, just as citizens influence government policies. The cybernetic concept of "feedback" is developed to describe one of the ways structures, institutions, and actors change through time as a result of communications interactions. Mutual causation requires that analysis of communications networks address not only problems of structure, but the elements of time and complexity—the interaction of many parts over time to produce change in the system as a whole. Time and complexity, however, are not elements in traditional legal analysis, and hence the discussion draws heavily on analyses of these concepts in such fields as physics, art, and political science.

From a general treatment of time and complexity, the discussion then turns to two ramifications in communications and democratic theory. First, the plethora of messages generated in an advanced welfare state produces a communications overload. I argue that the danger of this overload—that government will decide who and what is to be heard—can be avoided by relying on "self-controlled" citizens, who select intelligently from the menu of messages. Second, the creation of the self-controlled citizen requires that government influence over the channels of communication be constrained. Government may advance or retard the creation of self-controlled citizens, a condition for political legitimacy.

Chapter 3 turns from social science to legal theory, beginning by distinguishing the legitimacy of government communication in general from the legitimacy of particular types of government messages. I argue that practice and policy combine to moot questions about the legitimacy of government speech generally, but that there are good reasons to believe that democracy and liberal values will *not* survive unless proper distinctions are made as to the legitimacy of particular kinds of communication. The chapter then turns to a discussion of whether the necessity of government expression generally should be accommodated by recognizing a constitutional right of government to speak. I conclude that such an approach would be unwise.

Chapter 4 elaborates more fully on the need to distinguish "good" speech from "bad," with three examples of the dangers that can arise when the distinction is not made. I first discuss public education and the danger of necessary socialization to democratic norms becoming indoctrination, then describe the immense volume and range of messages emanating from the federal executive branch, and conclude with an account of the merchandising of the First World War to Americans.

[1]

The Nerves of Government:
Government Communication,
the Welfare State, and Technology

Karl Deutsch observed more than a decade ago that political science was myopic in its development of theories and knowledge about power. He complained that political scientists "described the laws and institutions of states, much as anatomists describe the skeleton or organs of the body." But the "nerves of government," "the channels of communication and decision" by which government so often asserts its power, were overlooked.[1] Governments not only act, but communicate—through the manipulation of symbols and images, ceremonies, written words, laws, speeches, meetings, debates, and in a myriad of other ways. Even before Deutsch wrote, there was a reasonably well-developed social science literature on communication theory and practice,[2] and a more or less unsatisfactory literature on propaganda.[3] The latter often suffered from the zeal in wartime, both cold and hot, to distinguish the American system of government from that of the totalitarian enemy—whether Germany, Japan, or the Soviet Union. Since Deutsch's remarks, social

1. Karl Deutsch, *The Nerves of Government* xxvii (Glencoe, Ill.: Free Press, 1966).
2. See, e.g., Winston Brembeck and William Howell, *Persuasion: A Means of Social Control* (Englewood Cliffs, N.J.: Prentice-Hall, 1952); Leon Festinger, *A Theory of Cognitive Dissonance* (Stanford, Calif.: Stanford University Press, 1957); Carl Hovland, Irving Janis, and Harold Kelley, *Communication and Persuasion* (New Haven, Conn.: Yale University Press, 1953); Joseph Klapper, *The Effects of Mass Communications* (Glencoe, Ill.: Free Press, 1960); Wilbur Schramm, *Mass Communications* (Urbana, Ill.: University of Illinois Press, 1960).
3. See, e.g., Harwood Childs, *Propaganda and Dictatorship* (New York: Arno Press, 1936); Leonard Doob, *Public Opinion and Propaganda* (Hamden, Conn.: Shoe String Press, 1966); Lindley Fraser, *Propaganda* (London: Oxford University Press, 1957); Harold Lasswell, *Propaganda Techniques in the World War* (New York: Garland Publishing, 1927); Talcott Parsons, "Propaganda and Social Control," 5 *Psychiatry* 551 (1942); Bruce Smith, Harold Lasswell, and Ralph Casey, *Propaganda, Communication, and Public Opinion* (Princeton, N.J.: Princeton University Press, 1946).

scientists have made significant progress in analyzing the processes of communication, persuasion, and socialization by government and others.[4] Social scientists have certainly perceived the problem, but legal scholars generally have not noted it, despite the increasing volume of government communications.

The expansion of government at all levels has increased its opportunity to communicate with the populace. The increase is in part simply a function of the widening role of government in the lives of its citizens. Technology has also contributed to the growth of government, creating more opportunities for government involvement and at the same time supplying the tools needed to govern on a larger scale. Among the most important tools are the mass media that provide direct access to the minds and attention of citizens. As government and its opportunity to communicate have expanded, so have its institutional interests as perceived by its functionaries. Inevitably, government, or those who are part of it, seeks to persuade citizens to act, or to allow it to act differently than they would have without the information supplied by government. The transfer of information thus becomes a policy tool. The obvious danger is that government persuaders will come to disrespect citizens and their role of ultimate decider, and manipulate them by communicating only what makes them accede to government's plans, policies, and goals. The opportunities for such abuse are numerous. Though a fuller discussion of the potential for manipulation is contained in chapter 4, some examples should serve to illustrate the very real dangers to democratic processes posed by government expression.

Sins of Commission

The power of government at all levels to communicate, and thus to shape public attitudes, has aroused increasing attention in recent years. The campaign by political and military leaders to overcome the arguments and influence of dissidents during the Vietnam War is a still controversial example.[5] The Arab oil embargo ushered in the energy crisis and a massive public-relations effort, from the president down, to convince Americans to conserve energy. Some accused the Carter administration of manipulating government data, information, and re-

4. See, e.g., Elliot Aronson, *The Social Animal* (New York: Viking Press, 1972); Ernest Bettinghaus, *Persuasive Communication* (New York: Holt, Rinehart, and Winston, 1968); Walter Davison and Frederick Yu, *Mass Communication Research: Major Issues and Future Directions* (New York: Praeger, 1974); Murray Edelman, *The Symbolic Uses of Politics* (Urbana, Ill.: University of Illinois Press, 1967).

5. See, e.g., J. W. Fulbright, *The Pentagon Propaganda Machine* (New York: Liveright, 1970); Edward Sherman, "The Military Courts and Servicemen's First Amendment Rights," 22 *Hastings Law Journal* 325, 348-349 (1971).

ports to generate support for its energy proposals.[6] Patrick H. Caddell advised President Carter to consider "going on television in a series of spot commercials in an effort to persuade voters to go to the polls."[7] The Department of Agriculture, through its extension service, reaches millions of people to educate them on such matters as nutrition, home economics, rural development, and agricultural production.[8] It has also hired Spiderman to do 30-second commercials describing the nutritional benefits of fresh fruit.[9] A recent study found that the federal government spends at least $500 million a year on hundreds of films, slide shows, TV programs, and radio broadcasts to communicate with the populace.[10] In 1975 the federal government was "one of the 10 biggest national advertisers" in America.[11] Government messages include warnings about smuggling drugs abroad, pleas to parents of handicapped children to write for information about special education programs, information on the metric system, investment advice on government bonds, and military recruitment. State governments regularly use ad campaigns to push such things as farm and industrial products (oranges, rice, potatoes, peaches), to attract out-of-state industries, or to promote tourism.[12] Some local and state communications activities have, however, been more controversial. The Alaska legislature voted to fund a $2.3 million advertising campaign to win support for pending federal legislation to allow development of Alaska's natural resources. The money was used primarily for newspaper advertisements "to match a 'massive war chest' by environmental groups."[13] Taxpayers in California sought to enjoin the Los Angeles Board of Education from expending money to inform voters of the

6. President Carter at one point proposed that Boy Scouts, Girl Scouts, and other young people be employed as door-to-door energy detectives. See "AASA Blasts Carter Idea to Use Youths as Energy Detectives," *Education Weekly* 4 (Sept. 9, 1977).

7. "Carter Ponders Voting Commercials," *Austin American-Statesman* A8, col. 3 (Nov. 2, 1978).

8. Wayne Rasmussen and Gladys Baker, *The Department of Agriculture* 84-86 (New York: Praeger, 1972).

9. "Can Spiderman Zap Junk-Food Pushers? Tune In to Find Out," *Wall Street Journal* 1 (Dec. 26, 1980).

10. "Government-II, Uncle Sam's Angels," *Time* 29 (May 8, 1978). Apparently, the federal government has been in the film business almost from the beginning of the industry. In 1937 the U.S. Information Service noted that the federal government had produced 456 movies, including such gems as "Helping Negroes to Become Better Farmers and Homemakers" (James McCamy, *Government Publicity* 85-86 [Chicago: University of Chicago Press, 1939]).

11. "Military Studies New Ad Plans as Budget Slash Appears Likely," *Advertising Age* 3 (Oct. 6, 1975).

12. See Council of State Governments, *Advertising by the States* (Chicago: The Council of State Governments, 1946).

13. "Alaskan Ads Seek 'New Independence,'" *Austin American-Statesman* D18, col. 5 (July 3, 1979).

fiscal impact of the Jarvis-Gann tax-limitation initiative (Proposition 13).[14] And the Equal Rights Amendment debate in the states has prompted charges and countercharges that federal and state funds finance lobbying and "propaganda" campaigns for or against ratification.[15]

Beyond these specific examples are more generalized concerns. One is the power of the president, executive agencies, and the military to control and manipulate the private mass media by leaking selected information, creating pseudo-events, and lying about matters not easily verified by those outside government.[16] The Watergate ordeal and the Vietnam War exacerbated these fears.

The tendency of executive-branch agencies to seek to influence legislative processes is another major concern. Congress in 1977 passed a law to limit efforts by the Departments of Agriculture and Interior to promote public support of or opposition to pending bills.[17] Congress itself, however, has not been free of communications excesses.[18] The power of Congress to expose and to communicate under the guise of investigation is a case in point.[19] Another example is the ability of incumbents to use franking privileges, government personnel,[20] and taxpayer funds for their own reelection. Congress has given House members an office allowance of approximately $400,000, and senators between $700,000 and $1.2 million. Congressional rules let a repre-

14. "Judge OKs School Board Comment on Prop. 13," *Los Angeles Times* § 1, at 21, col. 4 (Mar. 29, 1978).

15. See, e.g., *Mulqueeny v. National Commission*, No. 76-39 (S.D. Ill. 1976), vacated and remanded, 549 F.2d 115 (7th Cir. 1977); "Carter Orders Aids to Make Pleas for ERA," *Austin American-Statesman* § A, at 4 (July 26, 1978). Cf. *Stern v. Kramarsky*, 84 Misc. 2d 447, 375 N.Y.S.2d 235 (Sup. Ct. 1975).

16. See, e.g., Douglass Cater, *The Fourth Branch of Government* ch. 2 (Boston: Houghton Mifflin, 1959); Elmer Cornwell, *Presidential Leadership of Public Opinion* (Bloomington, Ind.: Indiana University Press, 1965); Dale Minor, *The Information War* (New York: Hawthorn Books, 1970); Benno Schmidt, *Freedom of the Press v. Public Access* (New York: Praeger, 1976); Thomas Curtis, "The Executive Dominates the News," in Robert Blanchard, ed., *Congress and the News Media* 100 (New York: Hastings House, 1974). The classic discussion of presidential dominancy over the Congress in terms of access to the media is Woodrow Wilson, *Constitutional Government in the United States* 67-69 (New York: Columbia University Press, 1908).

17. See Appropriations—Agriculture and Interior Departs., Title III, § 304, Pub. L. No. 95-74, 91 Stat. 307, 18 U.S.C. § 1913 (1977).

18. See, e.g., James MacGregor, *Congress on Trial* (New York: Harper & Row, 1949); Douglass Cater, *The Fourth Branch of Government* ch. 3 (Boston: Houghton Mifflin, 1959); Robert O. Blanchard, ed., *Congress and the News Media* (New York: Hastings House, 1974); Ernest Griffith, *Congress—Its Contemporary Role* ch. 17 (New York: NYU Press, 1961).

19. See, e.g., *Barenblatt v. United States*, 360 U.S. 109, 134 (1959) (Black, J., dissenting); *Uphaus v. Wyman*, 360 U.S. 82 (1959) (Brennan, J., dissenting); *Watkins v. United States*, 354 U.S. 178 (1957).

20. See "Congressional Aides Can Work on Campaigns, Court Says," *Austin American-Statesman* A5, col. 4 (Feb. 4, 1981).

sentative send newsletters to every "postal patron" in the district. Senators may send only individually addressed newsletters. In fiscal 1977 House and Senate members mailed nearly 300 million letters at the taxpayers' expense. Congress recently put minimal restrictions on the use of newsletters by incumbents, limiting mass mailings during political campaigns.[21] Giving rise to closely related problems are the activities of the Government Printing Office,[22] public television,[23] and federally financed election campaigns.[24] All give federal officials significant opportunities to advance their policies or personal interests by seeking to control the flow of information to the public.[25]

Potential abuse of government expression is a more subtle problem in the context of public institutions whose mission, in whole or in part, is to indoctrinate, educate, or care for a particular group. Government control varies from extensive to nearly total in such institutions as schools, prisons, hospitals, and military installations. All have a legitimate governmental purpose, but all present considerable opportunities for government to shape the attitudes and beliefs of those served. In varying degrees, the "inmates" of such institutions lack contact with the outside world and access to alternative sources of information and opinion. Further, the inmates may have a disability—immaturity or mental retardation, for example—that makes them susceptible to government persuasion. Policies, laws, and court decisions that allow outsiders access to such institutions, permit individual expression within the institutions, or limit modes of institutional socialization may be perceived as responses to government expression in closed settings.

Sins of Omission

What government does not say is frequently as important as what it does say. Governments have an almost unique capacity to acquire and

---

21. Richard Cohen, "Incumbents in Congress—Are the Cards Stacked in Their Favor?" 10 *National Journal* 1509, 1512-1513 (Sept. 23, 1978).

22. See, e.g., *Doe* v. *McMillan*, 412 U.S. 306 (1973). In general, the standards governing the public printer and superintendent of documents impose no realistic limits on what the federal government may print or distribute, e.g., "necessary to the public business," "necessary for the public service," "necessary in the transaction of the public business" (see 44 U.S.C. §§ 1101-1103, 1108 [1970]). Interestingly, the Office of Management and Budget must approve the use of appropriated funds for printing and binding, indicating a greater concern for the level of expenditures for printing than for the content of government publications (see 44 U.S.C. § 1108 [1970]).

23. See, e.g., *CBS* v. *D.N.C.*, 412 U.S. 94, 148 (1973) (Douglas, J., concurring); *Network Project* v. *Corp. for Public Broadcasting*, 561 F.2d 963 (D.C. Cir. 1977); William Canby, "Programming in Response to the Community: The Broadcast Consumer and the First Amendment," 55 *Texas Law Review* 67 (1976).

24. See, e.g., *Buckley* v. *Valeo*, 424 U.S. 1 (1976).

25. See, generally, Edward Ziegler, "Government Speech and the Constitution: The Limits of Official Partisanship," 21 *Boston College Law Review* 578 (1980).

disseminate information in the modern state. This stems in part simply from superior resources—government has the personnel, the computer banks, and the interest in the current state of affairs to accumulate and disseminate information. But this unique capacity also stems from the broad reach of the modern welfare state. Governments report frequently on activities that touch the lives of nearly every citizen. In the case of the federal government, we rely on public agencies to furnish us with information on the cost of a tax cut, the rate of inflation or unemployment, the safety of various drugs, the size of the federal budget deficit and the rate of change in the money supply, the progress made at the Strategic Arms Limitations Talks, and the state of affairs abroad that justifies foreign policy initiatives.

But informed debate is impossible if government operates in secrecy or reveals only selected facts and opinions.[26] It may be that only government knows what actually occurred in the Gulf of Tonkin, or why a regime fell in Chile or Czechoslovakia. Withholding the Pentagon papers may be as effective in distorting national policy debates as silencing antiwar advocates. Government reports can omit inconvenient facts and opinions, amplifying only what is favorable to the political leadership. Careers can be ruined by selective publication of facts about individuals. When government keeps its policy initiatives secret, or characterizes events in the absence of other sources of information, it undermines full discussion of public policy matters and, ultimately, the electoral process. Thus, government secrecy may itself be thought of as a powerful communications device. The need in this area is to compel government to speak. Freedom-of-information acts, open meetings and record laws, declassification of secret documents, and constitutional, statutory, and common-law rights of access to government proceedings, institutions, and documents are responses to government secrecy.

The Exacerbating Effects of Technology

As suggested earlier, technological advances have contributed to government's increased opportunity to communicate, thus exacerbating the threat government communication poses to the political process. In *The Collapse of Liberal Empire*, Paul Goldstene laments that after centuries of harmony, "liberalism and technological innovation are in conflict." They are now in a "struggle for power." Liberalism, stressing the individual and personal freedom and autonomy, is an "ideology out of phase with the realities of power in the modern world."[27] It is not

26. See, generally, David Wise, *The Politics of Lying* (New York: Random House, 1973); Freedom of Information Center Report No. 274, "Leaks: Manipulating Secrecy" (Dec. 1971).

27. Paul Goldstene, *The Collapse of Liberal Empire* 77 (New Haven, Conn.: Yale University Press, 1977).

just, as Durkheim would have it, that technology and the division of labor lead to alienation.[28] Nor is it just, as the romantic communitarians of the last two decades have reminded us, that technology can bring with it a loss of community and of identification with mediating institutions.[29] The tension between technology and liberalism is fundamentally political. Can advanced technology and individual freedoms coexist (or continue to coexist), and, if so, under what conditions may a balance be achieved?[30] What is the relationship among majority rule (however defined), liberalism, and technological innovation?

The political significance of technology lies in the enhanced capacity of government officials to preserve their positions of power, to gain support for themselves and their policies, and to dominate discussion of public issues. Technology is ethically neutral, but unethical leaders seize upon it to advance their interests. Human nature has not changed over the centuries in this respect. The new critical variable is the material power of those who govern to dominate the populace. This power competes with the immaterial, yet vigorous, ideologies of liberalism and democracy. Alfred North Whitehead put the matter well:

> If we attend to what actually happened in the past, and disregard romantic visions of democracies, aristocracies, kings, generals, armies, and merchants, material power has generally been wielded with blindness, obstinacy and selfishness, often with brutal malignancy....
>
> It is obvious that the gain in material power affords opportunity for social betterment.... But material power in itself is ethically neutral. It can equally well work in the wrong direction. The problem is not how to produce great men, but how to produce great societies. The great society will put up the men for the occasions.[31]

Throughout history, governments have utilized murder, torture, agents provocateurs, dossiers, propaganda, and intrigue to achieve their objectives. But such techniques are crude and often make it difficult to reach large numbers of people quickly. The modern state is far more efficient in the light of technological advances in weaponry, communication, and detection. Indeed, the crude measures of the past have in part given way to more subtle, pervasive, and effective means of controlling large populations. Computers and modern data-retrieval

28. See Emile Durkheim, *Division of Labor in Society* (Glencoe, Ill.: Free Press, 1933).

29. See, e.g., Paul Goodman, *Growing Up Absurd* (New York: Random House, 1960); Theodore Roszak, *The Making of a Counter Culture* (Garden City, N.Y.: Anchor Books, 1969).

30. Goldstene, *Collapse of Liberal Empire.*

31. Alfred North Whitehead, *Science and the Modern World* 182-183 (New York: Free Press, 1967).

techniques have facilitated the accumulation of information about individuals and provided ready access to that data. The need to pass on a greatly enlarged exogenetic heritage from generation to generation and a concern for equality of opportunity have been at least partially responsible for the establishment of specialized learning institutions to socialize the young to the new technology. These institutions represent an opportunity, almost invariably taken, for the state to control the education of future citizens. Technology, at least in industrially advanced nations, has also led to the centralization of economic production, with a concomitant rise of urbanization. Population density enables government to reach the masses far more easily than it could when the population was dispersed in rural areas. And modernization and industrialization frequently occasion rising popular expectations about living standards and about rights against the state to have economic, health, and social needs met by government. The responses to such demands dramatically increase the number of contacts between governments and individuals and groups. So, too, as Weber observed, technology facilitates the creation of bureaucracies, which, whatever their other shortcomings, provide a more structured, uniform, and sometimes efficient system for implementing government policies.

Majority Will in the Twentieth Century

The technological revolution has not slipped by unnoticed in twentieth-century jurisprudence. Dramatic shifts in legal doctrine have occurred as the legal system adapted itself to the changing technological and industrial climate.[32] The nineteenth-century shift from theories of strict liability (damages allowed even though the defendant was not careless) to negligence (requiring proof of defendant's carelessness or fault) in tort cases, for example, may be perceived as a response to the industrial revolution and the need to subsidize industrial development. Later, mass marketing and its accompanying technology contributed to the rise of modern products-liability doctrines. Contract law has undergone similar developments. But noneconomic matters—the libertarian implications of advanced technology—have also drawn attention. Consider the concern expressed by judges and legal scholars about biological manipulation of genetic material, use of mind-changing drugs to rehabilitate criminals, wiretapping by our own and other governments, accumulation and dissemination of intimate facts about individuals from computer banks, and use of human subjects in medical and social science experiments. As technology progresses, libertarian values such as privacy and autonomy have been perceived as endangered. Govern-

32. See, generally, Laurence Tribe, *Channelling Technology Through Law* (Chicago: Bracton Press, 1973).

ment is implicated in many of these activities, either by its own efforts or in its subsidization of the private sector.

This book examines only one aspect of the tension between the values of democracy and liberalism and the onslaught of technology: the dilemmas posed by government's increasing influence on and involvement in communications networks.[33] Though *government* is used in the singular, such a task obviously is complicated greatly by the vast numbers of governments in America—by the balkanization of the governing process.[34] Government speech here will include organized (local, state, and federal) governments' efforts to communicate symbols, ideas, information, perceptions, and values to the citizenry. Overlapping this public rhetoric, and difficult to disentangle from it, are the private utterances of government officials. Also troubling is the problem of distinguishing propaganda or indoctrination from information or education. The modes and types of government discourse include time-honored methods as well as those provided by modern technology: direct access to the broadcast media, mass distribution of documents, speeches and other activities of political leaders reported in the private media, the gathering and dissemination of statistics and research results, advertising, preparation and dissemination of official reports, activities of government public-relations offices, dissemination of official records of government proceedings, press conferences, public schooling, military training, and so on. The list might well include government conduct (e.g., passing energy conservation legislation or making child abuse a criminal offense) that symbolically communicates values. The pervasiveness and potential power of these communication devices and the opportunity for centralized direction they present justify this inquiry.

C. Wright Mills has described these phenomena and their implications in these terms:

> The rise of the mass media, especially radio and motion pictures, had already been accompanied by an immense enlargement of the scale of economic and political institutions, and by the apparent relegation of primary face-to-face relationships to secondary place. Institutions become centralized and authoritarian. . . . In brief, there is a movement from widely scattered little powers and laissez-faire, to concentrated powers and attempts at monopoly control from powerful centers.[35]

33. Some observers perceive no such conflict. See, e.g., McCamy, *Government Publicity* 260-261.

34. See, generally, Morton Grodzins, *The American System* (Chicago: Rand McNally, 1966).

35. C. Wright Mills, *Power, Politics and People* 581 (New York: Ballantine Books, 1953).

The relationship between technology and government power to communicate raises a number of vital issues. Increasingly, government communication is an element of public policy. Government does not simply run the public household, providing goods and services, or order private affairs by direct regulation, subjecting people to imprisonment, fines, taxes, physical coercion, and civil liability in order to accomplish public objectives. Government also seeks to gain compliance with rules and policies by persuading people of their rightness, of the advantages of voluntary compliance, and of the risks of alternative modes of action. It seeks to arouse peer pressure against individuals who deviate. It seeks to educate and to rehabilitate. The greater government's ability to reach mass audiences and to communicate successfully with those audiences, the greater the potential for effective implementation of government policy.

To put the matter in perspective, there are a variety of ways government may attempt to influence behavior in accordance with its legitimate authority. For example, government may rely upon values that have been widely internalized by individual members of the society, use rewards and punishments, or try to alter people's perceptions of rewards and punishments. It may also rely upon market systems.[36] But the trend today is toward government control mechanisms that rely as much, or more, on the word than the gun. Charles Lindblom designates such a system of social control a "preceptoral system," one "based on massive unilateral persuasion."[37] He believes that the "preceptoral system" is a hallmark of the Communist state, especially China. A number of characteristics typify this system:

1. The government's communications are addressed to an entire population, and not simply to certain identified elites. Thus, it reinforces movement "toward centrally desired aspirations, not a system for widespread participation in the establishment of social goals."[38]
2. Unlike fascist regimes, the appeal is to the rational side of men and women, and the hope is that they will be transformed, personality by personality, into "new" men and women who will ordinarily not need to be subjected to external direction by government in order to achieve behavioral objectives.[39]
3. The aspiration is to use other forms of control only when persuasion is unsuccessful. Since this is often the case, the preceptoral system remains largely aspirational.[40]
4. The most significant aspect of the preceptoral system is its reliance "on individual energy and resourcefulness rather than on social coordination."[41]

36. Charles Lindblom, *Politics and Markets* 12-13 (New York: Basic Books, 1977).
37. *Id.* at 13, 52.   38. *Id.* at 55-56.   39. *Id.* at 56, 59.
40. *Id.* at 56.   41. *Id.* at 60.

Thus, the preceptor state is a response to technology and to the perceived needs for centralized planning and control of individual behavior while, paradoxically, seeking to achieve these objectives by appealing to rational man and by promising a democratic future.

Substantial dangers lurk, even in democratic countries, in government's sweeping power to communicate and in the accompanying preceptoral attributes. There is the danger that government communications will be employed to falsify consent. In a democratic polity, it is one thing to employ mass communications to *implement* decisions that in some loose sense represent the majority will. It is quite another thing to attempt to *fashion* a majority will through uncontrolled indoctrination activities. The line is a blurred one. At issue is the basic notion that those who govern do so with the consent of the majority—or, at a minimum, through processes that afford opportunity for the governed to influence those who govern. This is the philosophical basis of the obligation of citizens to obey government.[42] Yet the preceptoral mode of social control also has its roots in democratic theory—individual responsibility, the need for an informed electorate, personal autonomy, and a preference for avoiding coercion as a means of gaining compliance with governmentally imposed norms. Thus, government expression remains a paradox in both democratic theory and practice. It calls into question the conflicting values of government leadership of the people and government responsiveness to the people. Put somewhat differently, government has an affirmative obligation to promote individual choice and autonomy by expanding the individual's knowledge, and yet, in a negative sense, it should be constrained from programming the citizen to make preconceived choices. Preconceived choices can be defined as choices *compelled* by indoctrinated value systems rather than the product of considered judgments arrived at by a process of evaluation of the efficacy of both the particular choice and the value systems which generate various decisions.

Social Change and the Rigidity of Law

Compared to social science scholarship, legal scholarship has failed to confront the realities of the modern nation state and its vast ability to communicate with the masses. With the exception of some brief comments by the great First Amendment theorists Chafee and Emerson and

42. See generally, John Plamenatz, *Consent, Freedom and Political Obligation* (London: Oxford University Press, 1968); John Rawls, *A Theory of Justice* (Cambridge, Mass.: Belknap Press, 1971); Joseph Tussman, *Obligation and the Body Politic* (New York: Oxford University Press, 1968); Michael Walzer, *Obligations: Essays on Disobedience, War, and Citizenship* (Cambridge, Mass.: Harvard University Press, 1970); Robert Paul Wolff, *In Defense of Anarchism* (New York: Harper & Row, 1970).

a recent book by Joseph Tussman,[43] one looks in vain for any sustained and coherent treatment of the impact of government communication on the theory and practice of free expression in America.[44] Students of the Constitution endlessly debate whether small groups of Nazis may march. But the march of government, a communicator immensely more powerful than a small group of malcontents, is ignored. Few legal theories or concepts of speech in a liberal democracy reach beyond government regulation of private speech to consider the government's own involvement in communication enterprises.

Legal scholars of the mass media and mass communications assume that only television networks, radio stations, and the multitude of newspapers, magazines, and other publications communicate. The government is omnipresent, but only in its role as regulator of the communications of private institutions, associations, and individuals. An occasional word comes forth on the easy access political incumbents have to the broadcast media, or some sniping at a president or presidential candidate who appears too image-conscious,[45] or a complaint that the government is staging pseudo-events to influence media reporting.[46] But law and lawyers essentially look at government in terms of its institutions, its power to coerce behavior and compliance with law, and its organization. This is an almost classical, positivist view of law defined in terms of rules and sanctions emanating from formally recognized legal institutions. In this myopic view, only individuals and institutions in the private sector both act and communicate. This perspective is bizarre in the light of the actual operations of government:

> The tendency, when we think of government, to think simply of coercion, of commands and sanctions of law-maker, judge and police, is simply a failure of understanding and imagination. Consider, for example, the public school. It is a governmental insti-

43. Zechariah Chafee, 2 *Government and Mass Communications* 732-734 (Chicago: University of Chicago Press, 1947); Thomas Emerson, *The System of Freedom of Expression* 712-716 (New York: Random House, 1970); Joseph Tussman, *Government and the Mind* (New York: Oxford University Press, 1977). The scope of Tussman's work is considerably broader than an analysis of government communication in the framework of the system of freedom of expression.

44. But see the recent contributions of Laurence Tribe, *American Constitutional Law* § 12-4 (Mineola, N.Y.: Foundation Press, 1978); Steven Shiffrin, "Government Speech," 27 *University of California-Los Angeles Law Review* 565 (1980); Edward Ziegler, "Government Speech and the Constitution: The Limits of Official Partisanship," 21 *Boston College Law Review* 578 (1980); Robert Kamenshine, "The First Amendment's Implied Political Establishment Clause," 67 *California Law Review* 1104 (1979); William Van Alstyne, "The First Amendment and the Suppression of Warmongering Propaganda in the United States: Comments and Footnotes," 31 *Law and Contemporary Problems* 530 (1966).

45. See, e.g., Joe McGinnis, *The Selling of the President* (New York: Trident Press, 1968); David Wise, "The President and the Press," *Atlantic Monthly*, 55 (April 1973).

46. See, e.g., Dale Minor, *The Information War* 174-178 (New York: Hawthorn Books, 1970).

tution as clearly as is the fire department, the board of health, the municipal court. . . .

The schoolteacher works for the government as unmistakably as does the deliverer of the daily mail. In fact, if we consider the question afresh, we may well conclude that the public school teacher in America is the most appropriate symbol of government in action, the paradigmatic government agent. Government acts in a variety of modes and it is not precluded, simply by virtue of a narrow misconception of government as essentially coercive, from acting deliberately and appropriately on the mind.[47]

Why such inattention to so pervasive a phenomenon? Perhaps it is because the text of the First Amendment, addressing itself to congressional abridgement of "freedom of speech," rivets attention to government interference with speech in the private sector. This is reinforced by the reference to the rights of the people "to petition the Government for a redress of grievances."[48] Whatever the framers of the First Amendment had in mind, they do not appear to have contemplated the possibility that government might speak so loudly that it would drown out their voices.[49] No clause in the Constitution prohibits Congress from "establishing" communications centers or promulgating secular "truths."[50] And it is natural to think of an "abridgement" of speech in terms of laws silencing private speakers, not in terms of government

47. Tussman, *Government and the Mind* 8.

48. U.S. Const. amend. I: "Congress shall make no law respecting an establishment of religion, or prohibiting the free exercise thereof, or abridging the freedom of speech, or of the press; or the right of the people peaceably to assemble, and to petition the Government for a redress of grievances."

49. See *Doe* v. *McMillan*, 412 U.S. 306, 344 (1973) (Rehnquist, J., concurring in part and dissenting in part).

50. As Laurence Tribe notes,

Government cannot compel an individual to display on his person or property a message fostering public adherence to an ideological view the individual finds unacceptable, and it may not force a newspaper to print a story it does not want to print [citing *Wooley* v. *Maynard*, 430 U.S. 705 (1977); *Miami Herald Publishing Co.* v. *Tornillo*, 418 U.S. 241 (1974)]. . . .

But none of this means that government cannot add its own voice to the many that it must tolerate, provided it does not drown out private communication. The first amendment does not, for example, prevent government from promoting respect for the flag by proclaiming Flag Day or by using public property to display the flag. Those who disdain the national symbol may express that view but may not silence government's affirmation of national values, nor may they insist that government give equal circulation to their viewpoint. . . . And if government expends public funds to subsidize flag production, the fact that some people object to this expenditure of their tax money to propagate the state's patriotic message is likely to be deemed irrelevant, either in a challenge to the expenditure itself or in a challenge to the payment of the full amount of the tax (*American Constitutional Law* 589, 590)

But see Kamenshine, "The First Amendment's Implied Political Establishment Clause."

efforts to persuade them not to speak or to submerge their messages in a plethora of government voices.[51] This is hardly surprising, given the primitive state of mass communications in the second half of the eighteenth century. Government censorship of individual expression, particularly by the newly formed federal government, was the central speech problem of that age.[52]

Building upon text and history, the law has created the metaphor of the marketplace of ideas,[53] so forcefully pursued as the ideal behind the First Amendment over the last fifty years. The metaphor itself conveys the notion of private expressions competing with each other. An essentially laissez faire notion, it excludes government participation either by assumption or by the normative demand that the government refrain from entering the fray, lest it alter the socially desirable results of competition. In turn, the marketplace metaphor, at least in this century, rests in part on empirically unsound notions as to the communications process in a modern democracy. Messages are sent to Washington, as Governor Wallace reminded us, or to Montgomery, Sacramento, or Austin. The people communicate with those who govern them so that the government will be responsive to their needs and wishes. Rarely is it recognized that government communications can shape those needs and wishes, that government provides information and increases public awareness of policy questions, and that the people may be as responsive to leadership as the leadership is to the people. Government secrecy and withholding of information are often not perceived as being inextricably tied to the health of the "marketplace" of ideas and information. In its naiveté about how the governing process works, the law is reminiscent of the king of the planet in Saint-Exupéry's *Little Prince*, whose vast ermine robe covered much of his domain. The planet was so cramped that the little prince could find no place to sit, and "since he was tired, he yawned":

51. Cf. *Standard Scale Co.* v. *Farrell*, 249 U.S. 571, 575 (1919): "But the opinions and advice, even of those in authority, are not a law or regulation such as comes within the scope of the several provisions of the Federal Constitution designed to secure the rights of citizens as against action by the States."

52. See, generally, Leonard Levy, *Legacy of Suppression* (Cambridge, Mass.: Belknap Press, 1960), particularly p. 221.

53. See, e.g., *Abrams* v. *United States*, 250 U.S. 616, 630 (Holmes, J., dissenting). See, generally, John Stuart Mill, *On Liberty* (1859); John Milton, *Areopagitica—A Speech for the Liberty of Unlicensed Printing* (1644); Martin Shapiro, *Freedom of Speech: The Supreme Court and Judicial Review* 52-56 (Englewood Cliffs, N.J.: Prentice-Hall, 1966). But see Jacques Ellul, *Propaganda* (New York: Knopf, 1965); Mills, "Mass Society and Liberal Education," in *Power, Politics and People* 353; Jerome Barron, "Access to the Press—A New First Amendment Right," 80 *Harvard Law Review* 1641, 1647-1648 (1967); Andrew Hacker, "Liberal Democracy and Social Control," 51 *American Political Science Review* 1009 (1957); Herbert Marcuse, "Repressive Tolerance," in Robert Paul Wolff et al., *A Critique of Pure Tolerance* 95 (Boston: Beacon Press, 1965).

"It is contrary to etiquette to yawn in the presence of a king," the monarch said to him. "I forbid you to do so."

"I can't help it. I can't stop myself," replied the little prince.
... "I have come on a long journey, and I have had no sleep ..."

"Ah, then," the king said, "I order you to yawn. It is years since I have seen anyone yawning. Yawns, to me, are objects of curiosity. Come, now! Yawn again! It is an order."[54]

Lawyers are also all too accustomed to thinking of constitutional interpretation and enforcement as matters exclusively for the courts. If direct judicial regulation of government expression proves unwise or impractical, many would jump to the conclusion that government speech presents no cognizable constitutional questions. But legislative and executive officers also carry out their functions within constitutional limits. They too have an obligation, independent of judicial oversight, to determine the meaning of the Constitution as applied in the framework in which they operate. Thus, for example, Congress might conclude that certain communications activities of executive departments are fundamentally dangerous to First Amendment values and should not be funded, while a court might decline to interfere with such activities, once funded, on grounds of its incapacity to deal with such systemic issues in an adversary setting. A reformulation of First Amendment theory to account for government communication, then, does not necessarily imply a dramatic change in the case law of the First Amendment.

Finally, lawyers may be like losing generals, so preoccupied with learning the lessons of the last war that they fail to prepare for the innovation—the blitzkreig—which routs them. Legal theories are attempts to organize the past and to render it comprehensible. Our past experience with the First Amendment has consisted largely of government attempts to silence private speech and of judicial and other responses to those attempts. But the changes wrought by technology, the welfare state, and preceptoral strategies are relatively recent. One must live in the modern world of communications networks and government expression as a policy tool to appreciate the paradoxical nature of government communications activities. Law lags behind social change. Only in the 1980s and beyond, when we have collectively experienced the new reality, can lawyers be expected to reflect upon those experiences and to seek to bring intellectual order to events not readily explicable in terms of traditional legal theories.

54. Antoine de Saint-Exupéry, *The Little Prince* 41–42 (New York: Harcourt, Brace & World, 1971).

[2]

Government Communication and the "Self-Controlled Citizen"

Democratic and Authoritarian Ideals

Resistance to the notion that communication between government and the governed occurs may be rooted in ignorance and an inability to reflect upon recent experience. It may also have its genesis in the idealism of many conventional views of democratic and authoritarian processes. As Kenneth Boulding so elegantly described it, the authoritarian ideal naturally, and understandably, assumes a rigid hierarchy of political roles. Those in lower roles, subordinate to those in higher roles, are expected to obey orders without cavil. This expectation has implications for the communication process:

> Information is transmitted from lower roles to higher roles on request of the higher role. All decisions originate at the top and are transmitted downward, where they are supposed to be executed in acts. The information which ascends the role structure is supposed to be feedback from these acts. The form of the information, however, is governed from above not from below. It is not volunteered, it is requested.[1]

In the standard metaphor, the authoritarian government holds a communications pistol and shoots message-bullets into the inert body of the powerless masses.

By contrast, the democratic ideal embodies the notion that the voters or followers take aim at the political leadership. Authority emanates from below; government depends on the consent of the governed.[2] This mandate is the basis for the legitimate exercise of govern-

---

1. Kenneth Boulding, *The Image* 99 (Ann Arbor, Mich.: University of Michigan Press, 1963).
2. *Id.*

ment's power over individuals[3] and has implications for the communications process in the political arena:

> The higher roles are supposed to act on behalf of and to be responsible to the lower roles. What this means in practice is that the decisions of the higher roles have to be made by discussion. That is to say, hypothetical decisions are made and communicated to the lower roles. The lower roles react to these hypothetical decisions and as a result of these feedbacks the decisions are modified until substantial agreement is reached—the discussion proceeds until the higher roles announce the decision which receives the approval of the lower ones or at least of a majority of them.[4]

These ideal types foster belief in a sharp dichotomy between communication processes in authoritarian and democratic societies. But these ideal types do not correspond to the real world. If a tyrant controls the sources of information and response, "these sources become increasingly unreliable." His image of the world diverges from the images held by those he governs. Unless the governed accept the governing structure itself, dissatisfaction will build "until, finally, there is revolution and the tyrant is dethroned." Faced with this prospect, a tyrant may employ violence to bolster his position. But violence, while perhaps successful in the short run, will often further corrupt the communications system, and thereby heighten public dissatisfaction. The most attractive option for a tyrant is to permit some response from those below and to give some response, however limited, in turn.[5]

The ideal democratic type also has flaws. If democratic leaders decline to lead, to communicate, and to respond to the people, they are likely to be unable to maintain themselves and provide stability:

> If the feedback from the followers destroys the image of the leader instead of merely modifying it, the process is likely to be self-defeating. The leader will cease to be respected or accepted.[6]

3. See, e.g., Edmond Cahn, *The Predicament of Democratic Man* (New York: Macmillan Co., 1961); Henry Steele Commager, *Majority Rule and Minority Rights* 4 (London: Oxford University Press, 1943); Felix Frankfurter, *The Public and Its Government* 125 (New Haven, Conn.: Yale University Press, 1930); Sidney Hook, *The Paradoxes of Freedom* 64 (Berkeley and Los Angeles: University of California Press, 1962); Harold Laski, *Authority in the Modern State* 93 (New Haven, Conn.: Yale University Press, 1919); Alexander Meiklejohn, *Political Freedom* 9 (New York: Oxford University Press, 1965).

4. Boulding, *The Image* 99-100.

5. *Id.* at 100, 101.

6. *Id.* at 101-102. In *The End of Liberalism* (New York: Norton, 1969), Theodore Lowi argues that democratic pluralism has reduced the capacity of democratic governments to plan, govern, and implement laws. See also Charles Lindblom, *Politics and Markets* (New York: Basic Books, 1977).

Inevitably, then, a working democracy requires at least some of the leader-to-people communication generally identified with the authoritarian ideal type. Legal scholars have too quickly embraced an idealistic view of the communications process in a liberal democratic state, viewing government communication as inherently tyrannical. This has led them to ignore the obvious: in their ideal types, "both democratic and authoritarian forms are inherently unstable."[7] The preservation of democracy, then, requires a balance between communications from government and those addressed to it. In short, there is a need for a consciously fostered pluralism in communications networks that treats government neither as impotent observer nor as omnipotent participant.[8] Such pluralism rests on the mutually affecting relationship between private- and public-sector communications centers.[9]

The Mutually Affecting Relationship Between Government and Nongovernment Expression

Mutually Affecting Communications

Traditional First Amendment analysis, focusing only on communications from the people to the government, is reminiscent of the outmoded mechanical models of the sciences. These models characteristically overemphasize structure and minimize the importance of changes through time. Based upon steady-state dynamics, a mechanical model is essentially static: it is assumed that the system will return to a state of equilibrium following any disturbance. In the development of modern theories of cybernetics, the mechanical model has been attacked and largely abandoned because of its failure to explain social and physical phenomena:

> Equilibrium theories . . . are not well suited to deal with so-called *transients*; that is, they cannot predict the consequences of *sudden* changes within the system or in its environment, such as the sudden starting or stopping of a process. Altogether, in the world of equilibrium theory there is no growth, no evolution; there are no sudden changes; and there is no efficient prediction of the consequences of "friction" over time.[10]

Cybernetics takes a more dynamic and subtle approach to communications and control in organizations of all kinds, emphasizing communication and mutual feedback.

7. Boulding, *The Image* 102.
8. For a more detailed discussion of pluralism, see chapter 6 below.
9. I have borrowed the useful phrase "mutually affecting" from Philip Bobbitt, *Constitutional Fate* (New York: Oxford University Press, forthcoming).
10. Karl Deutsch, *The Nerves of Government* 89-90 (Glencoe, Ill.: Free Press, 1966).

Cybernetics begins with the understanding that, as Norbert Wiener has put it, "communication is the cement that makes *organizations.*" Communication is the device that "enables a group to think together, to see together, and to act together." Transmission of messages and reaction to them are the foundation of any organization, whether "organization of living cells in the human body . . . , organizations of pieces of machinery in an electronic calculator, . . . [or] organizations of thinking human beings in social groups."[11] An essential feature of such organizations is *feedback*, which is necessary to make them self-modifying.

> By feedback . . . is meant a communications network that produces action in response to an input of information, and *includes the results of its own action in the new information by which it modifies subsequent behavior.*[12]

Communications and actions are modified in response to information and reactions to previous communications and actions; the mutually affecting relationship between input and output in the organization is an ongoing process. Karl Deutsch gives the simple example of the gunner who reacts to the appearance of an airplane (target) by aiming his gun at it and shooting. If the gunner overshoots the mark, he reacts to this feedback by a process of continuation and reaction until he has accomplished his objective or, perhaps, abandons the enterprise entirely. The gunner's behavior is self-modifying. But more than this is occurring. The pilot of the airplane will engage in evasive action to avoid the bullets. There is a mutually affecting relationship between the gunner and the pilot as each acquires information about the impact of his actions on the other.

In this example, the explanation of behavior does not depend upon steady-state equilibrium analysis. Not only is the target moving, but the actions of the gunner and the pilot influence each other over time. There may be lag in the time it takes the gunner to respond to negative feedback ("I missed the target") and gain to the extent that the gunner is able to compensate for the lag. Cybernetics theorists claim that people and institutions in a community are a part of the same sort of dynamic processes of communication. Changes in "communication habits or communication experiences may be indicative of later changes in the social functions of existing political units."[13]

This communications-theory approach is useful in thinking about the mutually affecting relationship of government and nongovernment expression. When citizens speak, they may well influence government policies and the government's own messages. In turn, the government's

---

11. Wiener, *Communication*, quoted in Deutsch, *Nerves of Government* 77.
12. *Id*. at 88.   13. *Id*. at 178.

responses to citizens' utterances may influence the behavior and messages of the people. Hence there is an endless chain of interaction between government and nongovernment expression. In addition, communications from one branch or level of government may influence the behavior and communications of other branches and levels of government,[14] just as communications from one private institution may have an impact on other private institutions and ultimately on the original organization itself, as it acquires secondary information about the responses of other institutions. This process of "feedback loops," interreactions, and interdependency more closely approximates the dynamic state of communications in a modern polity than the static, mechanistic approach taken by traditional First Amendment theorists.

Time and Complexity

The dynamic, mutually affecting relationship among communicators suggests that merely analyzing structure—distinguishing, for example, gunner, gun, pilot, and target, in Deutsch's example—cannot alone provide an understanding of modern communications networks. An accurate analysis of the parts of the system should not only account for the complexity of mutually affecting communications but also for the changes that occur in them over time. Traditional legal approaches to the First Amendment take insufficient account of these factors because, as Chayes has noted, traditional litigation is backward-looking: it seeks to determine what occurred in the past.[15] The episode is, so to speak, self-contained. The remedy focuses on the present and is designed to cure a present injustice—not to anticipate the future. A corollary is that some simple causal relation must be proven or assumed; for the necessity of decision making requires a "yes" or "no" answer to the question of whether one party's actions or words caused injury to the other party. While there is substantial departure from this model in many modern public and private litigations, the older model still pervades much of the law. Did Jones breach his contract with Smith, and, if so, what were Smith's losses in terms of his reliance or expectancy interest in the original contract? Did one party drive his automobile negligently, causing injury to the other party? In Tribe's metaphor, the law describes reality in terms of a snapshot rather than a motion picture.[16] Perhaps in many situations the necessity for decision making requires judges, lawyers, and legal scholars to distort reality—if only because the elements of complexity and time would result in paralysis

14. See, generally, James MacGregor Burns, *Leadership* (New York: Harper & Row, 1978); V.O. Key, *Public Opinion and American Democracy* (New York: Knopf, 1967).

15. Abram Chayes, "The Role of the Judge in Public Law Litigation," 89 *Harvard Law Review* 1281 (1976).

16. Laurence Tribe, "Childhood, Suspect Classifications, and Conclusive Presumptions: Three Linked Riddles," 39 *Law and Contemporary Problems* 8, 19 (1975).

when the decision maker attempted to fit them into a mechanistic model.

But consideration of time and complexity is necessary to an understanding of modern communications networks and to the fashioning of a responsive legal structure. Under prevailing legal theories, expression is perceived simplistically as the independent variable, and the resultant behavior or attitudinal changes as the dependent variable. Did the political dissident's speech incite the crowd to commit violence or other unlawful acts? Was there a "clear and present danger" (to use a phrasing much out of vogue) that the nation's war efforts would be impeded, that draftees would fail to report for duty? Were citizens brainwashed by reports emanating from the federal government on the nature of the Vietnam conflict? Did a person's defamatory statements inflict an injury on the reputation of the victim? To resolve these matters, the world stands still. The variables are largely reduced to two. Questions of changes over time, of communications that mutually affect each other, of reversals in cause and effect, and of the enormous complexity of communications activities are largely cast aside. We are left with only the snapshot—and, at that, a picture of a small, spartan corner of an enormous furnished room.

In modern legal systems it is extraordinarily difficult to stifle the drive to order an unsimple world.[17] This is as true of legal perceptions of communications activities as in any other area of law. But recognition of the problem may be the beginning of wisdom. And scholars in other disciplines have recognized the problem; for coping with time and complexity, far from being unique to law or communications, is pervasive in virtually every area of inquiry. Consider, for example, recent development in physics relating to nonequilibrium thermodynamics. Ilya Prigogine won a Nobel Prize in 1977 for his work in this area. In a lecture addressed to a lay audience at the University of Texas, he put his thinking this way:

> There exists in nature a class of structures which were [well] understood, . . . crystals, liquid crystals. These structures come from the fact that at low temperature the system tends to have . . . a regular order between the particles. . . . Then the question can arise, are all structures which we see in nature of this very type? And once you ask this question, the answer is obviously "no." If you take a town . . . you see that [its] structure depends on [its] interactions . . . with the outside world. The structure of the town can only be understood . . . [as] embedded in some economical and human society. And the same is true, of course, of

17. See, generally, Laurence Tribe, "Seven Pluralist Fallacies: In Defense of the Adversary Process—A Reply to Justice Rehnquist," 33 *University of Miami Law Review* 43, 50-51 (1978).

cells, of biological cells, which have membranes and surfaces, and interact through the surfaces with the outside world. While you can take a crystal, put it aside, and it will there remain, you cannot put aside a cell . . . or a town, isolated; it would decay. The basic question, then, is how to incorporate [dissipative] structures into the laws of physics and chemistry.[18]

For this inquiry into the nature of "dissipative structures," Prigogine finds classical physics severely lacking: physicists in this tradition took too little account of time and complexity and the interdependencies they reflect, preferring a simpler, static world to a world of change:

In classical physics we have a kind of statical world. Calculation of the future or thinking what was past are [viewed as] the same problems. In a sense, physics corresponds to an impoverishment of the idea of change as studied by the Greeks, notably by Aristotle. . . . Why? Because this idea could easily be, or more easily be, mathematized. . . . Change [in this view] is nothing but the denial of becoming; a time is only a parameter, unaffected by the transformation which it describes. Three characteristics are in this way firmly linked together in the [traditional] formulation of dynamics: the statical description of the world; the reversibility of the transformation, and the determinism of the transformations. Now, this image of a stable world, a world which escapes the process of becoming, has remained until now the very ideal of theoretical physics. . . . *In a sense, the idea was to go away from the changes, from the turmoil of human existence, and to go to an ideal world in which time could not exist.*[19]

Prigogine's great insight was to see the necessity to turn away from harmony, equilibrium, and order, and to recognize the "instabilities, mutation, and diversification" in the physical world. His interests lay not in the periodic orbits of the planets or the "planetary model for the atom"; rather he thought about pulsars, unstable particles, and thermodynamics.[20] And his "focus on irreversible processes"—on things that once done cannot be undone—required a consideration of time and complexity:

When you go further away from equilibrium in hydrodynamical situations, you may have creation of order; you may have transformation of disorder, chaos, into order. If you heat a liquid from below, . . . at some point, at a final distance from equilibrium, you have cells which are formed . . . by millions and millions of

18. Ilya Prigogine, "Order Out of Chaos?" 2-3 (unpublished public lecture, Nov. 18, 1977).
   19. *Id.* at 3 (emphasis added).   20. *Id.* at 3-4.

molecules moving up over macroscopic times. . . . The chaotic motion has been transformed into order.

And this is, of course, extremely interesting, because it shows that nonequilibrium [disorder] may be a source of order. . . . For example . . . we may have chemical clocks; we may have oscillations in space and time; we may have completely different types of behavior, in which millions of molecules cooperate to form a motion as a whole.[21]

Prigogine's cooperating molecules provide a model or metaphor for thinking about the complex interactions of institutions and individuals in the modern communications network. To illustrate the directions analysis can take in dealing with complex systems with intricate interdependence among the millions of parts, Prigogine uses an example from art history. It is one thing to be impressed with Italian Renaissance paintings and to analyze each painting separately. It is quite another to look at them in relation to one another and to inquire into the fundamental question of what sort of civilization would produce such paintings. As he puts the matter in the context of physics,

Complexity and time are, of course, closely related concepts. Things which are simple do not know time. . . . It is only in complexity that you can find the complex laws of change, that you can find a new science centered around time and complexity. And, therefore, instead of . . . looking [for] the basis of physics in . . . simplicity, you can now also go the other way, and try to find the laws of complexity.[22]

Prigogine does not deny that there is order in the physical world: he denies that such order can be ascertained without consideration of time and complexity.

Morse Peckham, in thinking about the arts, reaches a different conclusion about the "activity of artistic perception," while confronting problems quite similar to those of Prigogine. Peckham finds the "drive to order" the environment, so useful in many situations, to be counterproductive in other circumstances. His view is that individuals suppress much relevant data in meeting particular situations in the real world because their orientations deal only with certain classes or kinds of situations. That is, just as in law and physics, there is a tendency to oversimplify, to discard information that will not fit present operational patterns. Peckham fears, in contrast to cybernetic models, that people will stick with their orientations notwithstanding relevant con-

21. *Id.* at 4.
22. *Id.* at 5. See, generally, Herbert Simon, *The Sciences of the Artificial* (Cambridge, Mass.: MIT Press, 1979).

trary data.[23] The central thesis, then, is that there must be some human activity which weakens the drive to order, which breaks up static orientations, and that this activity is artistic behavior:

> Man desires above all a predictable and ordered world, a world to which he is oriented, and this is the motivation behind the role of the scientist. But because man desires such a world so passionately, he is very much inclined to ignore anything that intimates that he does not have it. . . .
>
> Art, as an adaptational mechanism, is reinforcement of the ability to be aware of the disparity between behavioral pattern and the demands consequent upon the interaction with the environment. . . . Art is the reinforcement of the capacity to endure disorientation so that a real and significant problem may emerge.[24]

In short, art for Morse Peckham is a device for addressing the complexities of the environment, for accounting for chaos, for dealing with data that flies in the face of our static orientations. The point is not whether Peckham is right—I suspect that he accounts only for some artistic behavior at some points in history—but that his concept of the problem is similar to that of Prigogine in physics. His departure is that he appears to despair of treating artistic behavior as a method of ordering chaos. For him, "art is not reality" or truth: it is a necessary "biological adaptation."[25]

Andrew S. McFarland has grappled with the complexities introduced by time and mutually affecting relationships in the field of political science. McFarland is concerned with the age-old problem of power in a social or political order, "power being conceived as a type of social causation."[26] His work has direct bearing on communications systems; for the ability to communicate, to persuade, and to reach various elites and audiences is an aspect of power. In rejecting static and simplistic models of power in modern states, McFarland paves the way for a rethinking of the ways in which communications networks should be understood, and hence for a reconceptualization of legal theory as it seeks to address the interrelationships between government and private expression.

Relying on the organizational theories of Herbert Simon and the theories of pluralism of Dahl, Lindblom, and others, McFarland begins his analysis of power relationships with an important distinction. "Asymmetrical relationships," which involve "dominance and one-way action," are contrasted with "symmetrical relationships," which

23. Peckham, *Man's Rage for Chaos* xi (Philadelphia: Chilton Books, 1967).

24. *Id.* at 313, 314.   25. *Id.* at 314.

26. McFarland, *Power and Leadership in Pluralist Systems* 21 (Stanford, Calif.: Stanford University Press, 1969).

"involve reciprocity and mutual interaction among components."[27] This asymmetrical model closely approximates legal approaches to expression under the Constitution:

> In an asymmetrical relationship, one component is the causal agent, and another component is the affected object; the first component is the *independent variable*, and the other is the *dependent variable*; the first dominates or controls the action of the second. Within the sphere of social causation, the first systemic component (individual, role, group, etc.) *influences* the second and possibly exercises power over the second.[28]

In modern America, however, many power relationships are symmetrical, and they are characterized by fluctuation over time and by reciprocity:[29]

> In a symmetrical, reciprocal relationship, however, both components may be causal agents at the same time over different activity areas (e.g. issue areas) of their relationship, and accordingly both may be affected objects at the same time. Or the direction of causation may change with time in one or more activity areas. Thus, we may say that both components influence one another, perhaps over different matters at the same time, or perhaps over the same matter at different times.[30]

Thus, just as in Prigogine's physics, there is a need in political science to move away from the simple linear descriptions of reality and toward descriptions that recognize the disharmonies, instabilities, and interdependencies of the real world.

McFarland amplifies these themes in the context of modern discussions of pluralism, which he identifies with complexity, reciprocal relationships, and variability in relationships over time. Systemic reciprocity means that "more components cause changes in the activities of other components more of the time." "The extent and incidence of relational interdependence" increases, and identifying simply causal links becomes more difficult. In short, complexity is a measure of the degree of "systemic reciprocity." Complexity is reflected in a political system by a pluralist power structure:

> The greater the extent of reciprocal power relationships, the greater the extent of systemic complexity, and hence the greater

27. *Id.* at 20.   28. *Id.*

29. *Id.* at 23-31. See also Nelson W. Polsby, *Community Power & Political Theory* (New Haven, Conn.: Yale University Press, 1980). But see Philip Green and Sanford Levinson, eds., *Power and Community: Dissenting Essays in Political Science* (New York: Vintage Books, 1970).

30. McFarland, *Power and Leadership in Pluralist Systems* 20.

the extent of systemic pluralism, the embodiment of complexity in political form. Conversely, systemic simplicity and elitism vary inversely with the extent of reciprocity in power relationships. For example, a very simple power structure is characterized by one-way relationships at any particular time: leaders change the behavior of followers in significant areas of activity, but followers do not change the behavior of leaders in such areas. Similarly, reciprocity does not develop over time in a very simple power structure: the power elite *always* determines the behavior of the other components in significant areas. . . . On the other hand, a complex power structure is characterized by reciprocal relationships at any particular time: A changes the behavior of B in respect to one activity, but B changes the behavior of A in respect to another, different activity. *Moreover, reciprocity increases through time in the complex power structure: A changes the behavior of B at an earlier time, but B changes the behavior of A at a later time.*[31]

Thus, McFarland, like Prigogine and Peckham, seeks to understand his discipline in a way that accounts for time and complexity. Note, too, the similarity to the analysis of Kenneth Boulding discussed earlier. The authoritarian model of communications closely conforms to asymmetrical relationships (dominance, one-way communication, simple cause and effect), while the democratic model of communications more closely conforms to the symmetrical, reciprocal relationship (mutually affecting communications, complexity, two-way communication, feedback).

What are the implications of this analysis for conceptualizing the First Amendment and the nature of modern communications networks? There are a number. The legal scholar should be aware of the fact that there are a handful of major problems in every age that cut across disciplines. The necessity of accounting for time and complexity is one that can be found in physics, chemistry, biology, art, political science, and perhaps nearly every other discipline. There is a unity in different types of knowledge:

> As emphasized by Whitehead, one of the main objects of science and philosophy was always to unify knowledge, to avoid what he called bifurcation of thought. As long as science . . . was dealing mainly with idealization, with museum pieces . . . , this was unavoidable. But, in a sense, this is no more true. The unification of culture . . . becomes again possible.[32]

31. *Id.* at 21-22.
32. Prigogine, "Order Out of Chaos" 8.

And this is as true for law and communications systems as for any other area of study.

Despite Peckham's pessimism, the task is not so much to recognize chaos, as it is to make sense out of chaos, to take account of what does not neatly fit into static models of the world. Consideration of time and complexity does not mean that order cannot be imposed, that decisional paralysis must result: it means only that we need to seek different rules to respond to what is observed. Without claiming to understand all of the complexities and mutually affecting relationships, it is clear that the law has tended to ignore government discourse in the system of freedom of expression. There is a need to recognize the existence of such discourse and its relationship to governance and private expression. The urge to ignore government communications activities, grounded in the need to simplify and to avoid messy complexities, should be suppressed. Rather, as Prigogine has expressed it, complexity and connectedness should lead to "recognition of unity in diversity."[33]

Communications "Overload," Selectivity, and Power Configurations in the Private Sector

The two-way flow in communications between government and the citizenry and the effects that each has on the other are complicated by two additional phenomena: the communications "overload" in advanced societies and changes in the power configuration of the private-sector communications network. The communications overload to which Americans are subjected has occasioned much discussion.

The "communications revolution" is perhaps the great achievement of the twentieth century. As Daniel Boorstin notes, "in one sense we could actually define the rise of civilization as the rise of communication."[34] But it is also our collective cross:

> Nowadays communication is an everywhere all-the-time thing. To escape messages we have to make a special effort—and we seldom succeed. . . . New forms of involuntary reception . . . remind us that there's always somebody out there trying to sell us something . . . and there is no escape.[35]

The intrusiveness of modern communications, from radio and television transmissions to the "witticisms of an airplane captain," loudspeakers in elevators, and billboards along the highway, does not simply

33. *Id.*
34. Boorstin, *Democracy and Its Discontents* 4 (New York: Random House, 1974).
35. *Id.* at 8. See also Charles Black, "He Cannot Choose But Hear: The Plight of the Captive Auditor," 53 *Columbia Law Review* 960 (1953).

annoy or divert, but raises profound problems of selectivity.[36] Consider
what would happen to the gunner in Deutsch's example if his target
were to overload his sensory apparatus with spurious information that
produced a multitude of "blips," any one of which could be the target.
The gunner's already difficult task would become almost impossible,
especially where rapid reactions are required. Indeed, modern weapons
(e.g., fake electronic missiles, MX missile systems) seek in part to create
such confusion. In the same way, individuals overloaded with a multitude of "blips" may be unable to respond rationally. In this situation,
the abstract right to choose is in practice little more than an invitation
to gamble. Both gunner and individual pick a "blip" as they would a
card out of a deck, and the odds favor the house. The implications for
representative government are obvious. As Boorstin observes, "democracy thrives on selective communication . . . and to keep the society democratic, the selection must be made not by some outside political agency, but by the self-controlled citizen."[37] Thus, since history
gives us no reason to believe that government will be passive, the
ultimate goal in perfecting the two-way communication process between government and the people is the production of an effective
selector—the "self-controlled citizen." This in turn requires a communications structure that will enable citizens to choose among messages, whatever their source. The danger is that government may
attempt to control the selection process with message overloads or
selective amplification.

The concept of the "self-controlled citizen" is critical to this analysis. The ideology of democratic government posits the existence of
autonomous citizens who make informed and intelligent judgments
about government policies, free of a state preceptorship that substantially impedes individual choice and consent by selective transmission
of information.[38] The essential problem, as Ronald Dworkin has noted,

36. Boorstin, *Democracy and Its Discontents* 8-10.
37. *Id.* at 10.
38. Boorstin's analysis is quite analogous to Meiklejohn's more limited notion of self-
governing speech:

> When men govern themselves, it is they—and no one else—who must pass
> judgment upon unwisdom and unfairness and danger. . . . The principle of the
> freedom of speech springs from the necessities of the program of self-government.
> It is not a Law of Nature or of Reason in the abstract. It is a deduction from the
> basic American agreement that public issues shall be decided by universal suffrage.
> (Alexander Meiklejohn, *Political Freedom* 27 [New York: Oxford University Press,
> 1965])

See also *Young* v. *American Mini Theatres, Inc.*, 427 U.S. 50, 60 (1976); Robert Bork, "Neutral
Principles and Some First Amendment Problems," 47 *Indiana Law Journal* 1 (1971); Kent
Greenawalt, "Speech and Crime," 1980 *American Bar Foundation Research Journal* 645, 673;
Alexander Meiklejohn, "The First Amendment Is an Absolute," 1961 *Supreme Court
Review* 245.

is that government may seek to expand the individual's horizons and imagination and thereby promote autonomy and choice, or it may act to confine choice and to deny autonomy.[39] How does one tell which the government is doing? Wht sort of formal line may be drawn? Can such a line be applied to distinguish between desirable and undesirable government communications activities? In a philosophical or social science framework, one may argue that citizens are never "self-controlled" in the sense of being uninfluenced by the events, environment, community, and communications networks in which they are enveloped. A physical scientist might argue that there is always choice, even if only between one's life and one's money. Intuition, however, suggests that there is a point at which expression becomes coercive rather than just persuasive in nature. But what does this mean and how does one tell? One possibility is that coercion never exists in mere communication, however manipulative, but only in actual interference with bodily integrity, e.g., psychosurgery, torture, or administration of mind-changing drugs. But functionally this means that citizens are presumed to be "self-controlled" or autonomous in the absence of assault on their physical integrity, and denies that government communications powers, standing alone, ever have a coercive impact.

An alternative conception of the self-controlled citizen may be derived from the notion that discontinuities that drastically and expeditiously assault the processes of personality development should be avoided. This is akin to Dewey's progressive education techniques, which build on the growth potential of each individual.[40] Individuals grow and mature gradually, and are able to look back on their lives and perceive a continuous chain of development over time. Where government seeks to interrupt this gradual process, a discontinuity results. The objection is not that such discontinuities are more coercive than incremental socialization, but rather that they are an assault on the dignity of the individual. Government seeks to stultify the normal processes of growth and ruthlessly alter the individual's personality at a single point in time. Putting aside physical coercion, there may be great difficulty in defining such discontinuities. Does even the most virulent form of propaganda qualify? A stronger objection to this analysis, however, is that the essence of the preceptoral state is the recognition that modest and graduated appeals to reason are the most efficacious manner of effecting attitudinal and behavioral changes. The discontinuity line may seem worth drawing in the abstract, but functionally most government expression in modern nation states may well fall on the acceptable side of that line. The conception of the self-

39. Bryan Magee, "Three Concepts of Liberalism: A Conversation with Ronald Dworkin," New Republic 41, 48 (April 14, 1979).

40. See John Dewey, Democracy and Education 100-123 (New York: Macmillan Co., 1966).

controlled citizen is thus reduced to terms very much like our original problem. It is gradual socialization to state dogma that traditional analysis does not address.

We may feel intuitively that the idea of the self-controlled citizen remains inconsistent with preceptoral government. This suggests that the true objection is neither coercion nor discontinuity *per se* but rather the disrespect for personal autonomy embodied in the concept of a preceptoral state. The relevant analysis may be once removed from the government messages themselves. Once the self-controlled citizen has received government's messages and reacted to them, how does he reflect back on the experience? Does he feel manipulated? Does he feel that he would have made the same decision anyway? Does he feel that he has been treated as a child whose dignity and personality count for nothing except as a basis for achieving the state's objectives? Or does he feel that his personality and dignity have been respected, that his self-esteem and happiness are the ends and not the instruments of government policy? The idea of the "self-controlled citizen" may be as firmly rooted in notions of an entitlement to equal respect from the state as it is in notions of voluntary choice making. The former depends upon difficult interpretive judgments; the latter upon the chaotic concept of voluntariness in a real world filled with constraints. This suggests that while a formal line cannot be drawn between government speech that denies citizens' autonomy and government speech that enhances it, the aspiration should be to fashion a communications structure consistent with the principle that government should treat its citizens with equal respect. This assumes, of course, that the citizen is worthy of government's respect—that he is, indeed, self-controlled and capable of conscious analysis of whether he has been manipulated or persuaded. Whether this assumption is true will depend to a large extent on the socialization process. Thus it is incumbent on government to seek actively to promote citizens' autonomy, to program the citizen to program himself.

One might anticipate an attentiveness to communication, given its ubiquitous role in determining the relationship between government and governed. But too often the law treats the communications process as if it were still what it used to be. Just as contract law, before its recent death,[41] seemed to revolve around a dickering between two farmers over the price of a cow (perhaps pregnant, perhaps barren), First Amendment analysis often proceeds on the assumption of face-to-face discussion (fighting words, incitement), pamphleteering, teaching,

41. See Grant Gilmore, *The Death of Contract* (Columbus, Ohio: Ohio State University Press, 1974) (liability imposed even though no bargained-for agreement). See, generally, Lawrence Friedman, *Contract Law in America* (Madison, Wis.: University of Wisconsin Press, 1965).

and door-to-door solicitation.[42] The recognition of mass form contracts dictated by powerful business entities is a relatively recent legal development,[43] a product of alterations of power configurations in the private sector. So, too, even in the private sector, we must learn not to think of communications entirely in terms of Eugene Debs's speeches[44] or Abrams's written heresies.[45] Modern communications networks involve sophisticated, complex, massive, and intrusive phenomena, subject to control by powerful forces. The most powerful of these forces are large economic enterprises,[46] the mass media,[47] and government.[48]

C. Wright Mills was among the earliest and most perceptive of those observing a fundamental change in the nature of the private communications network. Before the advent of the mass media, "the

42. See, e.g., *Cohen* v. *California*, 403 U.S. 15 (1971); *Brandenburg* v. *Ohio*, 395 U.S. 444 (1969); *Dennis* v. *United States*, 341 U.S. 494 (1951); *Feiner* v. *New York*, 340 U.S. 315 (1951); *Cantwell* v. *Connecticut*, 310 U.S. 296 (1940); *Whitney* v. *California*, 274 U.S. 357 (1927); *Gitlow* v. *New York*, 268 U.S. 652 (1925); *Abrams* v. *United States*, 250 U.S. 616 (1919); *Schenk* v. *United States*, 249 U.S. 47 (1919). Leading constitutional law casebooks frequently begin with such direct advocacy and confrontation cases when they introduce the speech and association areas—not with cases involving commercial speech, the broadcast media, and the press. See, e.g., Paul Freund, Arthur Sutherland, Mark Howe, and Ernest Brown, *Constitutional Law* 1130-1140 (Boston: Little, Brown, 1977); Gerald Gunther, *Constitutional Law* 1118-1153 (Mineola, N.Y.: Foundation Press, 1980); William Lockhart, Yale Kamisar, Jesse Choper, *Constitutional Law* 652-668 (St. Paul, Minn.: West Publishing, 1980).

43. See, e.g., Albert Ehrenzweig, "Adhesion Contracts in the Conflict of Laws," 53 *Columbia Law Review* 1072 (1953); Friedrich Kessler, "Contracts of Adhesion—Some Thoughts About Freedom of Contract," 43 *Columbia Law Review* 629 (1943); John Murray, "Unconscionability: Unconscionability," 31 *Pittsburgh Law Review* 1 (1970).

44. See *Debs* v. *United States*, 249 U.S. 211 (1919).

45. See *Abrams* v. *United States*, 250 U.S. 616 (1919).

46. See, e.g., *First National Bank* v. *Bellotti*, 435 U.S. 765 (1978); *Abood* v. *Detroit Bd. of Educ.*, 431 U.S. 209 (1977).

47. See, e.g., *First National Bank* v. *Bellotti*, 435 U.S. 765, 795 (1978) (Burger, C.J., concurring); *Columbia Broadcasting System* v. *D.N.C.*, 412 U.S. 94 (1973); *Red Lion Broadcasting Co.* v. *FCC*, 395 U.S. 367 (1969).

48. See, e.g., *Buckley* v. *Valeo*, 424 U.S. 1 (1976). In *West Virginia Bd. of Educ.* v. *Barnette*, 319 U.S. 624, 641 (1943), Mr. Justice Jackson noted that

> We set up government by consent of the governed, and the Bill of Rights denies those in power any legal opportunity to coerce that consent. Authority here is to be controlled by public opinion, not public opinion by authority.

See also *Stanson* v. *Mott*, 17 Cal.3d 206, 551 P.2d 1, 130 Cal. Rptr. 697 (1976); *Stern* v. *Kramarsky*, 84 Misc.2d 447, 375 N.Y.S.2d 235 (Sup.Ct. 1975); *Harrison* v. *Rainey*, 227 Ga. 240, 179 S.E.2d 923 (1971); *Porter* v. *Tiffany*, 11 Or.App. 542, 502 P.2d 1385 (1972); *Mulqueeny* v. *National Commission*, No. 76-39 (S.D. Ill., 1976), vacated and remanded 549 F.2d 1115 (6th Cir., 1977) (plaintiffs lack standing). All of these lower court decisions involve efforts to prohibit or enjoin various government entities from engaging in communications activities (usually by application of an *ultra vires* doctrine), as opposed to *Barnette*, in which government sought to speak through citizens (compulsory flag salute) irrespective of their personal beliefs (see chapter 15 and Conclusion, below).

public of public opinion" consisted of small groups and individuals talking and competing among themselves and electing spokesmen. The notion was that each person thought through policy problems and contributed ideas to the formation of the end product—public opinion. Obviously, some discussants had more influence and power than others. Many, among them blacks, were excluded from the policy-making processes. But the formation of public opinion largely involved face-to-face bargaining within voluntary discussion groups.[49] These relatively autonomous organs of public opinion operated within the institutional framework of the democratic polity, primarily the party system:

> The public, composed of innumerable discussion circles knit together by mobile people who carry opinions and struggle for powers of larger command, is organized into parties. Each party, representing a shifting viewpoint, which it pushes in discussion and expresses formally by vote, may in turn, with the circles composing it, acquire a place in parliament or congress, and there the discussion continues. It is a conception of authority by discussion. . . .[50]

So viewed, the "eighteenth-century idea of public opinion parallels the economic idea of the free market economy":

> The people are presented with problems. They discuss them. They decide on them. They formulate viewpoints. These viewpoints are organized, and they compete. One viewpoint "wins out." Then the people act out this view, or their representatives are instructed to act it out, and this they promptly do.[51]

What has occurred in modern America is a partial shift from relatively informal and autonomous discussion circles to a more centralized mass communications system. The public-private mass communications industry has increased the ratio of receivers to communicators and reduced face-to-face communications. These changes make answering back more difficult, and provide instituted authorities with the opportunity to "infiltrate the public," interfering with the autonomy of the "self-controlled citizen." C. Wright Mills describes this phenomenon by differentiating between a "community of publics" and a "mass society":

> The public and the mass may be most readily distinguished by their dominant modes of communications: in a community of publics, discussion is the ascendant mode of communication, and

49. Mills, *Power, Politics and People* 353, 356-357 (New York: Ballantine Books, 1953).
50. *Id.* at 577, 579.
51. *Id.* at 353, 356-357.

the mass media, if they exist, simply enlarge and animate discussion, linking one *primary public* with the discussions of another. In a mass society, the dominant type of communication is by the formal media and the publics become *media markets*, by which I mean all those exposed to the contents of given mass media.[52]

In Mills's view, modern America is characterized by both models of communication, with the relative importance of each depending on the type of opinion, the times, and their relationship to each other under particular circumstances.[53] The result is a synthesis: "both mass media and person-to-person discussion are important in changing public opinion":

> The American public is neither a sandheap of individuals each making up his own mind, nor a regimented mass manipulated by monopolized media of communication. The American public is a complex, informal network of persons and small groups interchanging, on all occupational and class levels, opinions and information, and variously exposed to the different types of mass media and their varying contents.[54]

The hybrid nature of the communications network in America is itself a form of balance between mass communication and less formal discussion circles. The opportunity for individual selectivity among messages must be protected if the role of individual citizens in the balance is to be maintained. Otherwise, the self-controlled citizen cannot survive. The concentration of communications power in the private sector, at least where such communicators are not allied with the government, increases the ability of the private sector to counter government rhetoric, despite a countervailing tendency to reduce the diversity of private-sector messages. But when the two are allied, the mass media are likely to magnify government's messages, thereby undermining the independence of the self-controlled citizen and increasing the tendency toward an authoritarian communications network.

52. *Id.* at 353-355; see also C. Edwin Baker, "Scope of the First Amendment Freedom of Speech," 25 *University of California-Los Angeles Law Review* 964, 965 (1978).
53. Mills, *Power, Politics and People* 577, 586. Scholars have long noted the two-step process in mass communications where government leaders relay messages through the mass media, which are, in turn, passed on by private opinion leaders, e.g., friends, bartenders, parents, ministers. See, e.g., Joseph Klapper, *The Effects of Mass Communications* (Glencoe, Ill.: Free Press, 1960); Paul Lazorsfeld, Bernard Bevelson, and Hazel Gaudet, *The People's Choice* (New York: Columbia University Press, 1948).
54. *Id.*

[3]

Communication and the Polity:
Legitimacy, Policy, and
Government "Rights" of Expression

The Legitimacy of Government Speech

The tendency to dichotomize authoritarian and democratic communication ideals and to ignore the complexities introduced by selectivity
and mass communications institutions may lead to a crisis of legitimacy. The objective observer cannot fail to perceive the massive level
of communication activities in the daily operations of government. But
as a normative matter there may be great discomfort with government's role; for traditional democratic theory does not take account of
government as a participant in communications networks. Given the
"tendency toward governmental intrusion, monopoly, and centralization abroad in the world,"[1] all government communication may be
identified with totalitarianism and hence viewed as a threat to the self-
controlled citizen. Alternatively, in a strange twist, no normative
power may be attached to the actual; what "ought" to be colors the
perception of what is. The conflict between ideals and reality is resolved by a form of cognitive dissonance in which observers blind
themselves to their experiences, an example of the sometimes dysfunc-
tional results Peckham ascribes to the "drive to order."

But it is critical for those who wish to confront the reality of the
mutually affecting communications relationship between government
and citizens to differentiate between the legitimacy of government
communication generally and the legitimacy of particular types of
government utterances. In a recent book, Joseph Tussman expends a
good deal of effort defending the legitimacy of government "acting
deliberately and appropriately on the mind."[2] In doing so, he over-

---

1. Joseph Tussman, *Government and the Mind* 14 (New York: Oxford University Press, 1977).
2. *Id.* at 8.

estimates the benefits of government's attempts to influence the mind, and underestimates the potential for conflict with democratic and liberal values. Though largely inattentive to questions of excess and to means of limitation, he does, however, make sound points about the legitimacy of government discourse generally.

Tussman contends that government efforts to influence the minds of the citizenry are not only legitimate but an essential responsibility and obligation. He begins by noting that the success and maintenance of any human enterprise requires an "appropriate condition of mind" among the participants.[3] If a polity is to survive, it must be able to recruit new members, to direct attention to its problems, to provide "a fruitful life of communication," and to "cultivate the knowledge and wisdom it needs."[4] This conception of community life within a polity carries with it a bundle of significant implications. The democratic character must be nurtured by government: men and women do not inevitably adopt democratic and liberal values when left to their own devices.[5] Anarchy is not synonymous with democracy.[6] In this respect, democracy does not differ from other forms of government in terms of the need for government communication: democratic and authoritarian polities differ over the content of the messages.[7] In democratic nations, governments should affirmatively promote liberty—the expansion of choices and possibilities through knowledge.[8] The self-controlled citizen is both a beneficiary and an instrument of this effort.

Tussman also elaborates on Boulding's leadership theme. Government should not manipulate public opinion, he says, but should enlighten, teach, and attempt to persuade the populace "to attend to the

3. *Id.* at 10-11. See also Emile Durkheim, *Selected Writings* ed. Anthony Giddens 203-205 (Cambridge: Cambridge University Press, 1972). Compare Charles Lindblom, *Politics and Markets* ch. 14 (New York: Basic Books, 1977).

4. Tussman, *Government and the Mind* 14.

5. *Id.* at 13-14. See also Charles Frankel, *The Democratic Prospect* (New York: Harper & Row, 1962). Malinowski puts the matter this way: "We shall see that human beings can either be trained to be free, or trained to be rulers, tyrants, or dictators, or else they can be trained to be slaves" (Bronislaw Malinowski, *Freedom and Civilization* 140 [Westport, Conn.: Greenwood Press, 1976]). Such views have a long philosophical tradition behind them. See, e.g., Montesquieu, letter 3 to the Chevalier DuBruant, 3 *The Works of M. De Secondat, Baron de Montesquieu* 356 (London: Vernon and Hood, 1798). But see, generally, Edward Purcell, *The Crisis of Democratic Theory* 204-210 (Lexington, Ky.: University Press of Kentucky, 1973) (description of "naturalist" theory of democracy).

6. See R. H. Tawney, *The Radical Tradition* 81, 83-84 (New York: Minerva Press, 1964).

7. Tussman, *Government and the Mind* 13-14. See also Malinowski, *Freedom and Civilization* 151; and *United States v. Butler,* 297 U.S. 1, 74 (1936) (dicta): "But an appropriation to an educational institution which by its terms is to become available only if the beneficiary enters into a contract to teach doctrines subversive of the Constitution is clearly bad."

8. See, generally, Isaiah Berlin, *Four Essays on Liberty* xxxvi-lii (London: Oxford University Press, 1969).

necessary agenda." Legislators, administrators, judges, and other officials should attempt to "reshape public awareness."[9] Government is also a major source of information, which it is sometimes uniquely fitted to acquire and disseminate.[10] The failure of government to disclose facts, particularly facts about its own operations, is destructive of informed, democratic processes. It may also be antithetical to other legitimate policy objectives. Government should make provision for science and research, and make known the results of those efforts. Government provides useful census data, floods the nation with reports and studies, and subsidizes the distribution of newspapers, magazines, and books.[11] Government calls our attention to domestic hazards—forest fires, drug abuse, alcoholism, and child abuse—and keeps us abreast of developments abroad that have consequences for the nation —revolutions, embargoes, military initiatives, etc. In all of its efforts, government may be said to be expanding choice and reinforcing personal autonomy.

More controversially, Tussman defends the teaching and public-forum functions (providing times, places, and means for private communication) of government. He views public schools and other public teaching institutions as essential government enterprises:

> The *teaching power* is the inherent constitutional authority of the state to establish and direct the teaching activity and institutions needed to ensure its continuity and its legitimate general and special purposes. . . . The teaching power is a peer to the legislative, the executive, and the judicial powers, if it is not, indeed, the first among them.[12]

Additionally, he asserts that government must share in setting up a "system of opportunities and protections" for ensuring the adequacy of public forums. In a compelling passage, markedly at odds with prevailing constitutional wisdom, he makes the following observation:

> The forum is not something we have before government takes a hand and which is "free" until government intrudes. It is a system in which government is a constitutive element. To say that government should, in the name of freedom of speech, leave the forum alone is like saying that government should, in the name of justice, have nothing to do with courts.[13]

9. Tussman, *Government and the Mind* 19, 20.

10. Cf. William Van Alstyne, "The First Amendment and the Suppression of Warmongering Propaganda in the United States: Comments and Footnotes," 31 *Law and Contemporary Problems* 530 (1966).

11. Tussman, *Government and the Mind* 110.

12. *Id.* at 54. Compare Berlin, *Four Essays on Liberty* liv.

13. Tussman, *Government and the Mind* 99.

Tussman's view of the legitimacy of government communication and attempts to influence are persuasive, but lead to no inevitable normative conclusion: it is easy to imagine socialization and awareness functions being carried out largely in the private sector, with or without government regulation. For example, government could finance private schools, without asserting power to control the curriculum or set standards for teachers. Establishment of a democratic community is hardly the exclusive province of government. But, as C. Wright Mills so often reminded us, mass society, economic and political institutions of unprecedented scale, and advanced technology appear to bring with them substantial centralization of communications functions.[14] Efficiency, productivity, and equity may require specialized institutions such as public schools to educate the masses of children. It would be immensely difficult, and impractical, to preclude government from these communication activities.

Beyond Legitimacy: Policy

It is absurd, then, in the modern contexts, to adopt the position that government speech, in its many manifestations and irrespective of its advantages, is an illegitimate enterprise in a liberal democratic state. To do so would strip government of a primary means of protecting and enhancing democratic values (e.g., the self-controlled citizen); of improving its leadership capacity; of enforcing its public policies; and, in the end, of securing its ability to survive. But to admit this is not to embrace the vast communication powers of modern government as an unmitigated good. Legitimacy, after all, is not the end-all of the discussion. While Tussman is right in maintaining that "there is nothing inherently totalitarian in a position which considers that the operation of a public educational system . . . and institutions of communication"[15] is legitimate, neither is there anything inherently democratic or liberal in it. It depends on how and when that power is exercised and restrained. And if "we are, among the countries . . . the most hospitable to the dogma that government has no business meddling with the mind," this does not mean that America has not had moments of excess, that no system of limitations is needed, or that the future will be untroubled by government intrusion "into the process by which we make up our minds."[16]

Tussman perceives that there is a threat to the communicative powers of government lurking in an assault on its legitimacy. I concede the

14. C. Wright Mills, *Power, Politics and People* 353, 361 (New York: Ballantine Books, 1953).
15. Tussman, *Government and the Mind* 14.
16. *Id.* at 115, 128.

legitimacy, but worry about questions of linedrawing, policy, and balance. When should governments be required to speak, to disclose information, to give reasons and justifications? When is government speech too threatening to democratic and liberal values? When does it threaten the processes by which majority sentiment is verified? When is it too likely to create artificial majorities, creatures of government policy? Who should play the policeman? What should the policeman do about inappropriate government speech? Who watches over the police and their efforts to inform and persuade and educate?

While admitting that totalitarian tendencies are abroad in the world, Tussman appears to tolerate nearly anything short of a full-fledged government monopoly of communications institutions. Even here, no more than a few paragraphs are devoted to methods of limiting the government's power over the mind. In a question-begging paragraph, he simply remarks:

> I do not encourage or support [the genuine totalitarian tendency]. My own inclinations are strongly pluralistic. My general thesis leaves questions of the desirable degrees of centralization or decentralization, of modes of governmental or private control quite open, as important questions of policy.[17]

But it is precisely those "open" questions of policy that should be the central concern. And there is good reason to believe that democracy and liberal values will *not* survive unless those policy judgments are made wisely.

A Government Right of Expression?

The paradoxical nature of government speech makes it difficult to decide which way constitutional protection should cut. Expression by government is critical to democratic processes, but the power of governments to communicate is also the power to destroy the underpinnings of government by consent. The power to teach, inform, and lead is also the power to indoctrinate, distort judgment, and perpetuate the current regime. Persuasion, like coercion, can be employed for many different purposes, some more acceptable than others. Emphasizing the affirmative side of government communications, one might argue that they are entitled to the same protection as the expression of private persons and organizations. The omnipresent fact of government expression and the consequent dangers may make it seem artificial to ask at this juncture whether government has a constitutional right to speak. But the First Amendment decisions in *Buckley* v. *Valeo*,[18] which held that expenditures on protected speech are also constitutionally

17. *Id.* at 14.   18. 424 U.S. 1 (1976) (per curiam).

protected, and in *First National Bank* v. *Bellotti*,[19] which held that corporations also have rights to speak, have been used by one commentator
"to support a constitutional argument that the first amendment protects
municipal speech":

> By suggesting that the first amendment protects political speech
> from any source, Bellotti's reasoning directs courts examining
> legislative or judicial bans on municipal electoral expenditures to
> determine initially whether those bans restrict political speech.
> Buckley's reasoning implies that a city's political speech includes
> its expenditures to express views on political issues.[20]

While communications emanating from such institutions do not
vindicate individual self-expression and dignity, they do serve a functional purpose within the system of freedom of expression: they provide
information and other prerequisites for the exercise of the citizen's
judgment about political issues and candidates; they may increase the
citizen's "ability . . . to make informed choices."[21] Indeed, such an argument has been advanced in the Supreme Court, with no less a constitutional scholar than Laurence Tribe representing the municipality.[22]
The argument for government First Amendment rights is buttressed
by a number of additional considerations. Government speech can
amplify the voices of the local populace that seek to participate in
debates dominated by mass institutions—the press, corporations, state
government, organized single-issue or multiple-issue interest groups,
and so on. The parallel would be Supreme Court decisions involving
the right of association for the purpose of conducting protected First
Amendment activities.[23] Further, after *Bellotti*, it might be argued that
government speech is a necessary check on the now enhanced powers
of corporations, with their tremendous resources, to dominate communications networks.[24] Finally, if it is constitutionally protected by

19. *First National Bank* v. *Bellotti*, 435 U.S. 765 (1978); see also *Consolidated Edison
Company* v. *Public Service Commission*, 447 U.S. 530 (1980); *Central Hudson Gas* v. *Public
Service Commission of New York*, 447 U.S. 557 (1980).

20. Note, "The Constitutionality of Municipal Advocacy in Statewide Referendum
Campaigns," 93 *Harvard Law Review* 535, 541 (1980).

21. *Buckley* v. *Valeo*, 424 U.S. 1, 14 (1976) (per curiam).

22. Tribe was representing the City of Boston, its mayor and several elected officials
in an appeal of a judgment of the Supreme Judicial Court of Massachusetts that enjoined
the applicants from expending city funds in support of a referendum on the ballot of an
upcoming general election. The Supreme Court dismissed the appeal for want of a
substantial federal question. See *City of Boston* v. *Anderson*, 439 U.S. 1060 (1979), dismissing
appeal from 380 N.E.2d 628 (1978).

23. See *NAACP* v. *Alabama*, 357 U.S. 449 (1958); *Thomas* v. *Collins*, 323 U.S. 516 (1945);
De Jonge v. *Oregon*, 299 U.S. 353 (1937).

24. *City of Boston* v. *Anderson*, 439 U.S. 1389 (1978) (Brennan, sitting as circuit judge,
Oct. 20, 1978) (order granting application for stay of mandate of the Massachusetts
Supreme Judicial Court). See generally Lindblom, *Politics and Markets* chs. 13 and 14. But

the First Amendment, presumably limits on government expression would be infrequent, and the burden would be on those who would curtail it to demonstrate overwhelming necessity.[25] Such a model would comport not only with the notion that government communication is legitimate and serves important democratic functions, but also with notions, developed in detail in the concluding section of chapter 9, that "excessive" government speech is hard to identify and even harder to remedy.

The beguiling symmetry inherent in the notion of treating municipal corporations and states (not to speak of the federal government) as the constitutional equivalents of private corporations has been rejected, albeit ambiguously, by the Supreme Court.[26] The First Amendment has been viewed historically as involving limitations on government, not as a source of government rights.[27] Constitutional rights like those embodied in the Bill of Rights have not been extended to government bodies, but only to individuals and groups within the private sector.[28]

see Charles Anderson, "The Political Economy of Charles E. Lindblom," 72 *American Political Science Review* 1012 (1978).

25. This situation is the reverse of that normally found in First Amendment cases. Usually it is the government that must justify under strict constitutional standards the restraint it wishes to impose on speech. In cases where government speech is the issue, this burden of justification is placed on the other party.

26. *Williams* v. *Mayor*, 289 U.S. 36 (1933).

27. See, generally, Van Alstyne, "The First Amendment and the Suppression of Warmongering Propaganda," 531-537. Van Alstyne quotes from John Whitton and Arthur Larson, *Propaganda: Toward Disarmament in the War of Words* 233-240 (Dobbs Ferry, N.Y.: Oceana Publications, 1964): "The problem of freedom of speech in the constitutional sense simply does not arise when the government itself is doing the speaking."

28. "A municipal corporation created by a state for the better ordering of government, has no privileges or immunities under the federal constitution which it may invoke in opposition to the will of its creator" (*Williams* v. *Mayor*, 289 U.S. 36, 40 [1933]). See *Trenton* v. *New Jersey*, 262 U.S. 182 (1923); *New Orleans* v. *New Orleans Water Works Company*, 142 U.S. 79 (1891) (a city cannot assert rights under the contract clause against its creator, the state); *City of Boston* v. *Anderson*, 439 U.S. 951 (1978) (Stevens, dissenting) (order denying motion to vacate Mr. Justice Brennan's order to stay mandate).

Nor can a municipality assert constitutional rights against the federal government. *South Carolina* v. *Katzenbach*, 383 U.S. 300 (1965) held that a state could not raise a due process claim against the federal government. Since a city is but an arm of the state, it would follow that a municipality cannot raise this type of claim either. But see *Aguyo* v. *Richardson*, 473 F.2d 1090 (2nd Cir. 1973) (in dicta claiming that *Katzenbach* left open the question of whether cities may for some purposes be "persons" entitled to protection under the Fifth Amendment).

Municipalities have, however, been allowed to assert equal-protection, due process and privacy rights in some very restricted circumstances, such as when the city is acting in a proprietary capacity (*Proprietors of Mount Hope Cemetery* v. *City of Boston*, 158 Mass. 509, 33 N.E. 695 [Sup. Ct. 1893]); when the city is asserting the rights of its citizens rather than its own constitutional rights (*Town of Huntington* v. *New York State Drug Abuse Control Commission*, 84 Misc.2d 138, 373 N.Y.S.2d 728 [Sup. Ct. 1975]); or when the city is raising the constitutional claim against another state (*Township of River Vale* v. *Town of Orangetown*, 403 F.2d 684 [2nd Cir. 1968]).

Governments, at least when pressing their own interests, have not been thought to have due process or similar rights, albeit they may invoke constitutional provisions specifically designed to protect them, e.g. the Tenth and Eleventh Amendments.[29] It would be standing the world on its head to think that the extension of First Amendment rights to private sector organizations requires a constitutionalization of government expression in order to counter the distortions brought about by such private institutions. Governments, particularly the federal government, are not fledgling communicators, needing protection from the community's excesses; they may pose more of a threat than do corporations.[30] The emasculation by state or federal courts of the government's power to communicate, or self-emasculation of these powers by other branches of government, is unlikely. Policy reasons may warrant protection of government speech for the good of all. But it is inconceivable that governments should assert First Amendment rights antagonistic to the interests of the larger community.

A rights approach to government utterances also raises serious questions as to what we view as an abridgement of speech. If a congressional committee and its staff write a report and vote to publish it, and the entire membership of the House of Representatives votes not to make the report public, is this a "prior restraint" giving rise to a First Amendment claim? Suppose the president orders a cabinet member not to appear on a television show or not to release a documentary film? The difficulty is that all government decisions involve hierarchies of authority, and it seems inconceivable that the commands of those at the top— at least with respect to official government communications—should be countermanded by the courts on First Amendment grounds.[31] A stronger case perhaps occurs when one branch of government, e.g., Congress, forbids another branch, e.g., the executive, from engaging in some types of communication activities. Or if the federal government were to forbid *states* or *local governments* from engaging in certain sorts of expression activities in relation to federal programs or policy debates. But these stronger cases are amenable to a separation of powers or federalism approach, making it unnecessary to distort the First Amendment.[32]

Constitutional protection for government utterances might be prem-

---

29. See, e.g., *National League of Cities* v. *Usery*, 426 U.S. 833 (1976); *Edelman* v. *Jordan*, 415 U.S. 651 (1974); *Ex Parte Young*, 209 U.S. 123 (1908); *Hans* v. *Louisiana*, 134 U.S. 1 (1890).

30. See ch. 2, above. But cf. Lindblom, *Politics and Markets* 202-213.

31. Cf. *Central Hudson Gas* v. *Public Service Commission of New York*, 447 U.S. 557 (1980) (Rehnquist, J., dissenting).

32. Cf. *National League of Cities* v. *Usery*, 426 U.S. 833 (1976) (the federal government's attempt to include state employees within the Fair Labor Standards Act is in conflict with the Tenth Amendment and principles of federalism).

ised not on its rights as speaker, but on the rights of the audience to receive information, to be informed, "to know" in modern jargon.[33] In the *Bellotti* case, the Court opined that "the inherent worth of the speech in terms of its capacity for informing the public does not depend upon the identity of its source, whether corporation, association, union, or individual."[34] In a few Supreme Court precedents, the rights of nonprisoners to receive uncensored mail and the rights of consumers to be informed through advertising are thought to be paramount to the First Amendment rights of the speakers.[35] The "right to know" in these cases, however, seems little more than artistic camouflage to protect the interests of the willing speaker. It seems unlikely that a citizen could require a private individual to acquire and disseminate specific types of information or to allow access to his home or private records.[36] In any event, the analogy would be that governments must be permitted and should exercise far-reaching communications powers if the rights of citizens to be informed are to be preserved. This is akin to Dworkin's metaphor about government expanding the imagination of the people. The argument is strengthened by the fact that government is sometimes uniquely situated to gather and disseminate particular types of information. And in some cases governments may be virtually the only entities with resources willing to present a particular side of a public issue. The majority, as represented by its elected officials, has a right to speak.

As a matter of policy, this view is compelling. The Court noted the importance of public expenditures to "facilitate and enlarge public discussion" in *Buckley* v. *Valeo*.[37] In terms of construing the First Amend-

33. See, generally, *Kleindienst* v. *Mandel*, 408 U.S. 753, 762-765 (1972); *Lamount* v. *Postmaster General*, 381 U.S. 301, 305, 307 (1965); *Red Lion Broadcasting Co.* v. *F.C.C.*, 395 U.S. 367, 386-390 (1964); Thomas Emerson, "The First Amendment and the Right to Know," 1976 *Washington University Law Quarterly* 1; Walter Gelhorn, "The Right to Know: First Amendment Overbreadth?" 1976 *Washington University Law Quarterly* 25; James Goodale, "Legal Pitfalls in the Right to Know," 1976 *Washington University Law Quarterly* 29; Frank Horton, "The Public's Right to Know," 3 *North Carolina Central Law Journal* 123 (1972); Wallace Parks, "The Open Government Principle: Applying the Right to Know under the Constitution," 26 *George Washington Law Review* 1 (1957). Note, "Access to Government Information and the Classification Process—Is There a Right to Know?" 17 *New York University Law Forum* 814 (1971); Note, "The Rights of the Public and the Press to Gather Information," 57 *Harvard Law Review* 1505 (1974).

34. 420 U.S. 984 (1975). See also *Consolidated Edison Company* v. *Public Service Commission*, 447 U.S. 530 (1980); *Central Hudson Gas* v. *Public Service Commission of New York*, 447 U.S. 557 (1980).

35. *Bates* v. *State Bar of Arizona*, 433 U.S. 350 (1977); *Virginia Pharmacy Board* v. *Virginia Consumer Council*, 425 U.S. 748 (1976); *Procunier* v. *Martinez*, 416 U.S. 396 (1974).

36. See, e.g., *Kleindienst* v. *Mandel*, 408 U.S. 753 (1972). See generally Note, "The First Amendment Right to Gather State-Held Information," 89 *Yale Law Journal* 923 (1980).

37. 424 U.S. 1, 92 (1976).

ment as embodying limits on government speech, this policy concern may be a critical factor in a judicial decision refusing to interfere with such speech. Where government declines to reveal already acquired information vital to the making of informed judgments by citizens about policies and leaders, the "right to know," as a constitutional right or as embodied in statutes such as the federal Freedom of Information Act, may be decisive in the absence of compelling reasons to withhold the information. Perhaps the puzzling "right to know" gains meaning in the case of the unwilling government speaker. So, too, public officials in a democratic polity might do well to recognize the importance of their expression in informing the public as to their conduct in office and the wisdom or folly of their policies or the policies of other private or public entities. But this is a far cry from bootstrapping from the "right to know" to what is tantamount to a recognition of a constitutional right on the part of governments to engage in extensive communications activities. The "right to know" formulation simply obfuscates the problem of how and why governments should have rights against the community under a First Amendment designed to limit government powers. Further, it appears to place no boundaries on information that a citizen could require a government to disseminate.

The greatest threat of government domination and distortion of majoritarian processes emanates from executive bodies and officers. The greatest hope of restraining that power lies with the legislative branches of government.[38] If a legislative body determines that particular government expression threatens democratic processes, the courts should not second-guess that decision.[39] To pick some hyperbolic examples, is Congress's ban on the dissemination within the United States of government-produced propaganda for foreign audiences[40] unconstitutional?[41] Is there a constitutional problem with congressionally imposed limits on the "Pentagon Propaganda Machine" or the public-relations activities of the Departments of Interior and Agriculture?[42] Suppose Congress refuses to fund agencies such as the

38. See ch. 10, below.

39. See Conclusion, below. Obviously, this may require that the courts determine whether a particular entity is a part of the government or a part of the private sector. For example, the Supreme Court has held, in the First Amendment context, that a publicly regulated utility is not a public entity even though government sets its rates and gives it monopoly powers. See *Consolidated Edison Company* v. *Public Service Commission*, 447 U.S. 530 (1980); *Central Hudson Gas* v. *Public Service Commission of New York*, 447 U.S. 557 (1980).

40. 22 U.S.C. 1461 (1977).

41. See Van Alstyne, "The First Amendment and the Suppression of Warmongering Propaganda" 536–540.

42. See ch. 1, above.

Office of War Information.[43] Are these actions to be judged by the typical "compelling state interest" doctrine? Should the government (Congress) lose if it cannot demonstrate specific harmful effects of the banned communications activities, such as the complete domination of one channel of communication?

Perhaps a stronger case can be made for local governments. Local governments, indisputably, are generally much less menacing communicators than the vast federal agencies in Washington. Their voices would be only a few among many, and the probability of their drowning out other centers of communication slight. Almost invariably, they raise a large proportion of their revenues from local taxes, and they often have wide-ranging powers under home-rule charters and similar statutory devices.[44] The argument would be that they have strong independent stakes in legislative decisions and voter approval or disapproval of state constitutional amendments, bond issues, and referenda.[45] In such circumstances, it is natural for local governments to seek to influence such decisions, including resorting to legislative lobbying or to public advertising to persuade or inform their own constituents—and perhaps those in other areas of the state—of the most advantageous outcome of the political processes for the local government and its citizens. Indeed, many states specifically allow lobbying activities by local governments.[46] The most common type of judicially imposed ban, however, relates to government-sponsored speech during an election or referendum,[47] albeit California expressly permits some government-sponsored communications on sample ballots.[48] But the constitutional question is whether a state law, as interpreted by the judiciary of that state, is unconstitutional if it forbids municipalities from devoting local or state resources to some or all public relations and advertising activities. The Supreme Court has held that such a claim raises no substantial federal question.[49]

43. See Allan Winkler, *The Politics of Propaganda: The Office of War Information* (New Haven, Conn.: Yale University Press, 1978).

44. See 1 Charles Antieau, *Municipal Corporation Law* § 3.00-3.40 (Albany, N.Y.: Matthew Bender, 1978), especially § 3.13.

45. Jurisdictional Statement of Appellant at 17, *City of Boston* v. *Anderson*, 439 U.S. 1060 (1978).

46. Mass. Gen. Laws Ann. ch. 40 § 5 (15) (West 1958); Mass. Gen. Laws Ann. ch. 3 § 50 (Supp. 1977); N.Y. Mun. Home Rule Law § 40 (McKinney 1969); N.Y. Legis. Law §§ 56, 66 (McKinney Supp. 1977).

47. See Conclusion, below; *City of Boston* v. *Anderson*, 439 U.S. 1060 (1978).

48. Cal. Elec. Code §§ 3525-3567, 3578, 3714, 4015, 4015.5., 4018, 5012-5016, 5157, 5157.5 (1977, Supp. 1978). See, generally, Steven Shiffrin, "Government Speech," 27 *University of California-Los Angeles Law Review* 565, 639-640 (1980); Comment, "The Direct Initiative Process: Have Unconstitutional Methods of Presenting the Issues Prejudiced Its Future," 27 *University of California-Los Angeles Law Review* 433 (1979).

49. *City of Boston* v. *Anderson*, 439 U.S. 1060 (1979). See, generally, Mark Yudof, "When Governments Speak: Toward a Theory of Government Expression and the First Amendment," 57 *Texas Law Review* 863 (1979).

But even constitutional protection of local government expression under the guise of the listeners' "right to know" has difficulties. One is the slippery distinctions that would be called for. Government speech that did not monopolize a segment of the communications network or did not distort the political processes would be constitutionally protected. Such lines are difficult to draw, as we will see in chapter 9. If the expression of local governments is protected, federal and state expression, or local utterances of a more dangerous nature, may also be protected. Further, given justifiable fears of at least some aspects of government expression and the power of governments in the welfare state, why should courts invalidate self-imposed limitations on government communications activities? While there may be differences in degree, local governments are creatures of the state every bit as much as federal administrative agencies are creatures of the Congress.[50] They should be subject to the same hierarchical controls.

Finally, as argued in chapter 8, there is no assurance that governments truly represent majorities in the absence of a process of informed consent to governmental policies. A ban on local government advertising and public-relations activities is a reasonable prophylactic measure to insure that consent processes are not distorted. This is particularly true where the question is the constitutionality of the ban, and not the alleged unconstitutionality of the expression. The fact is that in any given case municipal governments may be expressing the views of public officials who are attempting to *create* a majority, and not *representing* a majority in the pending policy debates. Perhaps this is also true when local government leaders present their facts and opinions to the legislature. But why must legislatures ban all communications rather than only those they deem most harmful? Perhaps legislatures consider elections and referenda to be more at the heart of the democratic process than legislative lobbying. Perhaps they think they are better able to resist the wiles of local government officials than the public is.

Legislators may also view lobbying by municipal officials and employees as falling closer to the private rights of officials to express themselves than to official government communication. And this may be the strongest argument against constitutionalizing a right of government expression, even at the local level. Public officials remain free to express themselves; their views carry considerable weight in the political processes. Generally, they will have access to the mass media simply

50. "A municipality is merely a department of the State, and the State may withhold, grant or withdraw powers and privileges as it sees fit" (*Trenton v. New Jersey*, 262 U.S. 182, 187 [1923]). See also *United States v. Wheeler*, 435 U.S. 313, 321 (1978); *Hunter v. Pittsburg*, 207 U.S. 161, 178 (1907); *Williams v. Eggleston*, 170 U.S. 304, 310 (1898); Antieau, *Municipal Corporation Law.* Cf. *Consolidated Edison Company v. Public Service Commission*, 447 U.S. 530 (1980); *Central Hudson Gas v. Public Service Commission of New York*, 447 U.S. 557 (1980).

because their opinions are news. So long as the First Amendment rights of such officials are preserved, the point of view of those who perceive a particular political outcome as most desirable for the municipality will be expressed, and the people will be informed about the policies under consideration by the electorate. It is simply not necessary to accept the dangerous and unprincipled position that local governments are constitutionally entitled, despite contrary state laws, to allocate large sums of public money to advertising campaigns in order to vindicate the interests of citizens in receiving information and in being informed.

[4]

The Opportunity for Abuse
of Government Communication

It is a truism that totalitarian states treat their citizens as children, not trusting them to reach informed judgments based upon uncensored information. They do not respect the autonomy of their citizens. These states often seek to destroy or dominate mediating institutions such as churches, unions, clubs, and families that are able to counter the word of the government. This is the essence of the preceptor state. And, far from dying out, governmental concern with the communications process is on the rise in many nations. Democracies are rare in the world.[1] Among developing nations, dictatorship is the rule rather than the exception. The very first step toward dictatorship is usually the take-over of the press and the public broadcasting stations; the remolding of public education in order to reinforce the views of those in power soon follows.[2] These measures are not always successful; revolutions do take place. It is difficult to disentangle the effects of propaganda *qua* propaganda, from those of propaganda strengthened by harsh police measures against dissidents.[3]

Experience in the United States, fortunately, does not reflect such catastrophic occurrences. The dangers posed by government participation in communications activities can, however, be seen in many government programs. Government expression is essential to achieve policy objectives and to promote democratic and liberal values—to expand citizens' choices—but too much expression is fatal to those

1. See Charles Lindblom, *Politics and Markets* (New York: Basic Books, 1977).
2. See, generally, Hannah Arendt, *The Origins of Totalitarianism* ch. 11 (New York: Harcourt, Brace & World, 1951, new ed. 1966); Lucian Pye, ed., *Communications and Political Development* (Princeton, N.J.: Princeton University Press, 1963).
3. See Arendt, *Origins of Totalitarianism* ch. 11; Eric Hoffer, *The True Believer* 97-99 (New York: Harper & Row, 1966).

same values and destroys the ideal and reality of the self-controlled citizen.

Public Education and Indoctrination

The central issue in the socialization of children is the degree of autonomy they should be afforded.[4] How can public education successfully prepare children for adult life without simultaneously sacrificing their ability to reflect upon the ends for which they are being prepared—without indoctrinating them to the status quo or to the rightness of maintaining government and its leaders in power? As we have seen, the question is one of balance, not of whether the government should be running educational institutions at all.[5] The utility of what is done to prepare the child for adult life must be balanced against the potential adverse impact of such preparation on the child's personal liberties and ability to deal flexibly and successfully with the environment as an adult. Basic attitudes, skills, and knowledge must be communicated while attempting, as best we can, to give the young "ample opportunity of making the decisions upon which these principles are based, and by which they are modified, improved, adapted to changed circumstances or even abandoned if they become entirely unsuited to the new environment."[6] To speak in absolutes of children's "liberation" or of complete discipline and obeisance to cultural and political authority demonstrates an insensitivity to the complexities of the problem.[7]

4. The discussion of socialization of the young in the text is largely taken from Mark Yudof, "The Dilemma of Children's Autonomy," 2 *Policy Analysis* 387 (1976). See, generally, Robert Weissberg, *Political Learning, Political Choice, & Democratic Citizenship* (Englewood Cliffs, N.J.: Prentice-Hall, 1974).

5. But see John Stuart Mill, *On Liberty* 104-105 ed. Elizabeth Rapaport (Indianapolis: Hackett Publishing, 1978): "A general state education is a mere contrivance for molding people to be exactly like one another"; Milton Friedman, *Capitalism and Freedom* ch. 6 (Chicago: University of Chicago Press, 1962). See, generally, John Coons and Stephen Sugarman, *Education by Choice: The Case for Family Control* (Berkeley and Los Angeles: University of California Press, 1978); Stephen Sugarman and David Kirp, "Rethinking Collective Responsibility for Education," 39 *Law and Contemporary Problems* 144 (1975).

6. Richard Hare, "Decisions of Principle," in Israel Scheffler, ed., *Philosophy and Education* 72, 85 (Boston: Allyn, Bacon, 1958). See also Richard Hare, *Applications of Moral Philosophy* 48-66 (Berkeley and Los Angeles: University of California Press, 1972). Alfred North Whitehead beautifully states this principle in *Science and the Modern World* 179, 319-320 (New York: Free Press, 1967):

There are two principles inherent in the very nature of the things . . . —the spirit of change, and the spirit of conservation. There can be nothing real without both. Mere change without conservation is a passage from nothing to nothing. . . . Mere conservation without change cannot conserve. For after all, there is a flux of circumstances, and the freshness of being evaporates under mere repetition.

7. See, generally, Gabriel Almond and Sidney Verba, *The Civic Culture* (Princeton, N.J.: Princeton University Press, 1963); Ruth Benedict, *Patterns of Culture* (Boston: Hough-

This socialization process is inevitable; the only questions are who will do the socializing and what values and information will be transmitted. It is not possible for educators to convey only information; for information itself, and the manner of its selection and presentation, will lead to socialization to widely accepted values. Elliot Arnson has remarked that one man's propaganda is another's truth.[8] Bertrand Russell gave an ideal example:

It is not altogether true that persuasion is one thing and force is another. . . . Consider what we do to our children. We do not say to them: "Some people think the earth is round and others think it is flat; when you grow up, you can, if you like, examine the evidence and form your own conclusion." Instead of this we say: "The earth is round." By the time our children are old enough to examine the evidence, our propaganda has closed their minds, and the most persuasive arguments of the Flat Earth Society make no impression.[9]

But to say that socialization is inevitable or even that socialization by government-operated institutions is legitimate is not to say that all forms of socialization are desirable or wise. The failure of the adult generation, through the polity, to bring the young into the larger political and economic culture would have disastrous consequences.[10] We have no reason to think that children are inherently good or democratic or tolerant or peaceful, much less to believe that they are capable of inventing gasoline engines, theories of relativity, and neurosurgical techniques on their own, without the benefit of the community's experiences. Public education is an affirmative effort on the part of the state to expand the mind and the imagination.[11] Conversely, as Ruth Benedict remarks, "no civilization has in it any element which in the last analysis is not the contribution of an individual."[12] The problem is one of degree. The child who is taught nothing of his

ton Mifflin, 1961); George Counts, *The American Road to Culture* (New York: John Day Co., 1930); Robert Nisbet, *The Quest for Community* (New York: Oxford University Press, 1953); Weissberg, *Political Learning*; David Easton, "The Function of Formal Education in a Political System," *The School Review* 304 (Autumn 1957).

8. Aronson, *The Social Animal* 55 (San Francisco: W. H. Freeman, 1972).

9. Russell, *Power: A New Social Analysis* 368-369 (London: Allen & Unwin, 1938).

10. It is important to note in this regard how significant the exogenetic heritage is to the growth and development of human intelligence. For a popular account of both the genetic and exogenetic factors bearing on human intelligence, see Carl Sagan, *The Dragons of Eden* (New York: Random House, 1977).

11. See, generally, Isaiah Berlin, *Four Essays on Liberty* liv (London: Oxford University Press, 1969).

12. Benedict, *Patterns of Culture* 219. See also Margaret Mead, *Growing Up in New Guinea* 136 (New York: New American Library, 1961); William McNeill, *The Shape of European History* 30-43 (New York: Oxford University Press, 1974).

country's cultural, political, and intellectual heritage must be pitied as much as the child who is compelled to conform in all respects to the dominant cultural mores. Individuality does not exist in a vacuum: it is defined by the background of community.[13] And community, if it is to survive, must allow for individual growth and nonconformity.[14] Thus, liberty may also be defined negatively,[15] as the absence of restraints on the individual's capacity to choose to reject the prevailing wisdom. This, too, is an object of education.

The perceived need to accommodate both change and stability, and knowledge and criticism, suggests particular values to which the young should be socialized. John Dewey noted more than sixty years ago that the social ideal of American public education should be the inculcation of democratic values consistent with the tensions of order and disorder and with notions of the desirable society.[16] While doubtless there is no consensus on their ordering, their precise meaning, and how they should be applied in particular instances, the democratic ideal presumably embodies such values as tolerance, civility, liberty, equality, respect for individual dignity, participation in political decisions, freedom of expression, freedom to own and dispose of property, and respect for minority interests. Dewey put the matter this way:

> The two points selected by which to measure the worth of a form of social life are the extent in which the interests of a group are shared by all its members, and the fullness and freedom with which it interacts with other groups. An undesirable society, in other words, is one which internally and externally sets up barriers to free intercourse and communication of experience. A society which makes provision for participation in its good life of all its members on equal terms and which secures flexible readjustment of its institutions through interaction of the different forms of associated life is insofar democratic. Such a society must have a type of education which gives individuals a personal interest in social relationships and control, and the habits of mind which secure social changes without introducing disorder.[17]

Perhaps these values seem clichés, truisms without much substantive content in the day-to-day working of educational institutions. But this criticism is wide of the mark. If they seem clichés, it is only because these values have been internalized. Democratic forms of education

13. See, generally, Bronislaw Malinowski, *Freedom and Civilization* 319-320 (Westport, Conn.: Greenwood Press, 1976); Roberto Unger, *Knowledge and Politics* (New York: Free Press, 1975).

14. See, generally, Weissberg, *Political Learning*.

15. See Berlin, *On Liberty* xxxvii-liii, 121-131.

16. Dewey, *Democracy and Education* (New York: Free Press, 1966).

17. *Id.* at 99.

should be contrasted with their alternatives: education carried on in the interests of the state; education for social discipline and political subordination; education that ignores the development and worth of the individual.[18] Our social ideal is a democratic education, one that both prepares our young to choose for themselves and teaches them that their freedom to do so hinges on their respect and tolerance of the freedom of others to choose differently. This kind of education involves a process of growth over time:

> The idea of education ... is ... [one of the] continuous reconstruction of experience, an idea which is marked off from education as preparation for a remote future, as unfolding, as external formation, and as recapitulation of the past.[19]

Federal Executive Department Speech

A second example of the need for wise policy choices to maintain the proper balance in communications can be found in the obligation of government officials to lead and to make the public aware of threats to the survival and stability of the polity. The president's power to utilize the mass media is perhaps the most startling example of this phenomenon, and has occasioned detailed analysis by the academic community.[20] As Elmer Cornwell has noted,

> The leverage the President has acquired in the lawmaking process has been indirect, based on the use of the arts of persuasion, and ultimately grounded in the popular support he can claim or mobilize. Hence his link with the public is his key relationship.
>
> The President, in the nature of things, must deal with the citizenry largely through the media of communication.[21]

Press conferences, daily news coverage, radio and television broadcasts, and the like, give the president and the executive branch the ability to reach the citizenry "with an ease and rapidity unknown in the last century." The president's power has increased enormously as

18. *Id.* at 81-123.

19. *Id.* at 80.

20. See, e.g., Douglass Cater, *The Fourth Branch of Government* ch. 2 (Boston: Houghton Mifflin, 1959); Elmer Cornwell, *Presidential Leadership of Public Opinion* (Bloomington, Ind.: Indiana University Press, 1965); Sidney Hyman, *The American President* (New York: Harper & Row, 1954); Walter Johnson, *The American President and the Art of Communication* (Oxford: Clarendon Press, 1958); V.O. Key, *Public Opinion and American Democracy* 414-416 (New York: Knopf, 1967); Dale Minor, *The Information War* (New York: Hawthorn Books, 1970); Richard Neustadt, *Presidential Power* (New York: Wiley, 1976); James Wiggins, "Government and the Press," in David Clark and Earl Hutchison, eds., *Mass Media and the Law* 86 (New York: Wiley-Interscience, 1970).

21. Cornwell, *Presidential Leadership* 4.

he has become an "omnipresence in the general flow of news."[22] Max Lerner has opined that the president is expected to be a "Communicator-In-Chief."[23]

Is this power illegitimate? Hardly. Can it be abused? Of course. Once again, the question is one of the proper balance. Is the president manipulating public opinion or is he informing the people? Is he acting in a dictatorial manner or is he courageously exercising leadership?[24] Does he respect citizens' autonomy and choice or does he seek to circumvent them? The questions are clearly worthy of detailed analysis.

Federal utilization of the broadcast media to reach mass audiences is neither new nor limited to the president. The long history of such activity dates at least to World War I. In the New Deal days of the 1930s, Henry Wallace's Department of Agriculture pioneered government use of radio broadcasts to persuade audiences of the rightness of the department's policies. The federal government now relies most on ten-, thirty-, and sixty-second television spots.[25] The Department of Defense, promoting the volunteer army, is the biggest advertiser, followed by such government organs as the United States Information Agency, Environmental Protection Agency, Veterans Administration, and the Departments of Agriculture, Transportation, Treasury, Interior, and Health, Education, and Welfare. Most federal agencies have a division or office responsible for such activities. Some even produce spot advertising in-house. Other government agencies rely in whole or in part on contracts with private advertising firms. The J. Walter Thompson Agency, for example, developed a toy safety campaign for the Food and Drug Administration and a recruitment campaign for the Marine Corps. Grey Advertising and the Department of Transportation developed a campaign to reduce drunken driving that included the famous "Janie" spots, in which a young mother is killed by a drunken driver.

Most government agencies do not pay for broadcast time, though the army spent about $3.5 million between March and June 1971 to gain access to space in prime time that was unavailable to it without pay-

22. *Id.* See also Ernest Griffith, *Congress—Its Contemporary Role* 41-42 (New York: New York University Press, 1961); Hyman, *The American President*; Thomas Curtis, "The Executive Dominates the News," in Robert Blanchard, ed., *Congress and the News Media* 100 (New York: Hastings House, 1974).

23. Newton Minow, John Martin, and Lee Mitchell, *Presidential Television* 159 (New York: Basic Books, 1973), citing Lerner, "Television: The Fourth Branch of Government," *TV Guide* 6-7 (Nov. 28, 1970).

24. See, generally, Bernard Rubin, *Public Relations and the Empire State* 3-10 (New Brunswick, N.J.: Rutgers University Press, 1958); J. T. Romans, "Moral Suasion as an Instrument of Economic Policy," 56 *American Economic Review* 1220 (1966); David Wise, *The Politics of Lying* (New York: Random House, 1973).

25. The following discussion of government advertising is taken almost entirely from David Paletz, Roberta Pearson, and Donald Willis, *Politics in Public Service Advertising on Television* (New York: Praeger, 1977).

ment. Paid advertising was discontinued in the light of congressional criticism, but later reinstituted by the armed services on what appears to be a permanent basis.[26] Other government agencies, lacking the financial ability to pay for advertising, have embraced elaborate distribution schemes for their public service ads, and tried to insure a high degree of technical quality so that broadcasters won't turn to superior spots produced by nongovernment entities. In this process, government agencies emphasize their public status. HEW enclosed personal letters from the secretary to station managers requesting air time for spots. Sometimes the ads are delivered personally to regional and local broadcasting offices by a government official. Fear of antagonizing the broadcast media appears to deter government agencies from trying to pressure broadcasters into showing their spots. But the evidence indicates that broadcasters are more willing to air government spots free than they are to run public service announcements originating with other organizations (with the possible exception of the Advertising Council). Perhaps this in part reflects the power of the FCC over licensing of stations and the requirement that licensees serve the public interest.

The time of day when free government spots are shown is the biggest source of tension between government and the broadcast media. Station operators prefer to run them in blocks of time in low demand by advertisers who pay for the opportunity to reach mass audiences. It is not uncommon for the government's spots to be attached to reruns, the 2 A.M. movie, or to the station's sign-off for the day. Insomniacs may be the government's biggest audience. This has led to criticism and appeals by government agencies to the networks and local stations. Perhaps the most famous was an appeal by Secretary of the Army Froehlke after the temporary abandonment of paid advertising, emphasizing that "radio and television stations which are licensed by the United States government should provide effective public service time to support essential national programs."[27] The networks rejected the request.

The dangers posed by government advertisements may lie less in their explicit message than in the background messages. The agency involved and its officials are invariably portrayed as helpful and understanding, competent, and fully in control of a government apparatus that is successfully solving pressing societal problems. "Thus, while PSAs [Public Service Ads] may explicitly instruct viewers on how to deal with a specific problem, they appear implicitly to suggest that the government is beneficent and working to their advantage."[28] The White

26. *Id.* at 28-29. See "Ayer Named to $40 Million Army Account," *Advertising Age* 1, col. 1 (March 21, 1975).

27. Paletz, Pearson, and Willis, *Public Service Advertising* 29.   28. *Id.* at 27.

House does not appear to be orchestrating the advertising of executive agencies, perhaps because of the sheer volume of government communication and the difficulty of monitoring the countless bureaucracies nominally subject to presidential direction. Nonetheless, White House clearance is occasionally sought in "sensitive areas." For example, scripts of public service announcements for the Internal Revenue Service have been sent to the White House for review prior to production. Less justifiably, in 1973 President Nixon's inauguration committee (directed by Jeb Magruder) used public service advertising to promote the sale of inaugural parade tickets, commemorative license plates, and bronze and silver inaugural medals. But, notwithstanding some exceptions, direct government advertising appears to be highly fragmented, with duplications of effort by different agencies and no sustained executive attempt to gain greater influence over public service advertising.

More serious concerns are raised by the relationship of the federal government to the Advertising Council, the nominally private organization which controls roughly 40 percent of all the public service advertising shown in the country (television and radio, billboards, magazines, newspapers, transit signs). The Advertising Council was established in 1942 as the War Advertising Council, and originally handled only government campaigns in cooperation with the Office of War Information. After World War II, it dropped the "war" from its title, established itself as "a private non-profit corporation supported entirely by American business and the advertising and communications industries," cut its ties with the War Information Office, and began to undertake nongovernment campaigns. Since its inception, the Advertising Council has utilized more than $8 billion in donated air time, space, and campaign materials. Each year it undertakes about twenty-five major campaigns. In 1975, its television spots were shown over 5,000 times by the networks and over one million times by individual local stations. The council's cooperation is widely sought, because its support guarantees a larger audience for a major campaign. Many groups, however, are excluded by the council's requirement that a fee of $75,000 to $150,000 be paid. Others are excluded, knowledgeable observers say, because their ideas "either threaten business interests or provoke controversy in the society." Organizations such as Freedom from Hunger, various consumer groups, and Planned Parenthood either have been denied council cooperation or compelled to modify their messages to make them more acceptable to the council. Further, the most significant aspect of public service advertising by government and those acting in concert with government may be that it takes up such a large proportion of the available free air time that dissenting voices are rarely heard. The preemption of such air time may well be as effective as specific laws and policies limiting access to the mass media by groups which seek to promulgate messages that the government and the business community do not approve of.

The Advertising Council is overseen by a board of directors consisting of executives from the mass media and advertising firms, and corporate advertising and public relations directors. An "industries advisory committee" consisting of prominent business leaders and a public policy committee representing a more diverse constituency in labor, agriculture, medicine, religion, social work, journalism, education, and so on, also provide direction. The most important point to note about the Advertising Council is that a significant number of its twenty-five major campaigns each year are developed in cooperation with the federal government. Funding comes from the government, with substantial supplementation by private business contributions. In 1972-73, there were ten such joint campaigns: Forest Fire Prevention (Office of Education); Rehabilitation of Handicapped People (Department of Health, Education, and Welfare); Drug Abuse Information (Departments of Health, Education, and Welfare, and Defense); Productivity (National Commission on Productivity); ACTION (volunteer service programs); U.S. Savings Bonds (Department of the Treasury); Minority Business Enterprise (Department of Commerce); and Food, Nutrition, and Health (Departments of Agriculture and Health, Education, and Welfare). The council assigns each of these campaigns to an advertising agency, not infrequently to an agency that handles commercial accounts in the same field. Thus, for example, the Food, Nutrition, and Health campaign was run by the same advertising agency that conducted campaigns for General Foods. Critics charge that these cooperative efforts by the Advertising Council and the federal government are heavily biased toward business interests, citing the worker-productivity campaign as a prime example.

Unlike advertising produced by the government itself or by its contractors, cooperative ventures with the Advertising Council appear to receive substantial, centralized direction from the White House:

> White House clearance is the sine qua non for a governmental agency hopeful of becoming one of the major campaigns of the Council. As an executive of the Council put it, "If they [the White House] don't recommend it, we don't touch it." . . . The indications are that once the White House does approve an agency's proposal, the Council has very few reservations about accepting the campaign for major support. Obviously the Council is responsive to political influence; as Council President Keim stated, "A political atmosphere can color what you do." Thus, one might expect some Council campaigns to reflect social or

cultural interests and perhaps even aspects of the political stance of the current occupant of the White House.[29]

Since the Truman administration, the incumbent president has generally designated a member of his staff to coordinate activities with the Advertising Council. Campaigns advertising the Peace Corps (President Kennedy), the National Businessmen's JOBS program (President Johnson), the need to prevent drug abuse (President Nixon), and President Ford's Whip Inflation Now (WIN) program are all examples of presidential involvement in the Advertising Council's agenda. Perhaps the most notorious example of such involvement was President Nixon's overseeing of the "Don't Be Fuelish" campaign, which urged citizens to conserve energy by observing a 55 mph speed limit and setting thermostats no higher than 68°F.

> According to one informant, before the campaign was implemented it had to receive President Nixon's approval. This was granted at a full-scale cabinet meeting where the PSAs were screened to ensure that the administration was depicted favorably in advertising on this issue. The influence of such an administration-Advertising Council combination to achieve speedy access is suggested by the January 1973 announcement that 100 radio and 25 television stations in New York State would be broadcasting such PSAs hourly.[30]

While, doubtless, each of these campaigns was a serious effort to address important policy problems by seeking to arouse public support, it is equally clear that the administrations then in power saw in the campaigns an opportunity to gain a partisan political advantage or to inculcate values which they deemed fundamental. Moreover, the Advertising Council provided a mechanism for raising private dollars for the administration's purposes, allowed for the circumvention of FCC requirements of fairness, sidestepped the question of the independence of public broadcasting, and, in a fashion, coopted the mass media into aiding the government's advertising efforts.

The content of public service announcements is fascinating. The modal approach is a personal admonition to do or not to do something, with the stress laid on individual responsibility. The etiology of modern social and economic problems is traced to "individual carelessness, incapacity, bad luck, affliction, or fate."[31] "Society" and business are rarely blamed for the problems identified. One study could not find a single public service advertisement in which the government or a government official was blamed for the problem being addressed.[32]

---

29. *Id.* at 10.   30. *Id.* at 11.
31. *Id.* at 80.   32. *Id.* at 84–86.

The solution to forest fires is individual care, not more forest rangers. America is kept beautiful by individuals picking up their litter, not by industries controlling their air and water pollution. Energy conservation is a function of voluntary choices to reduce energy consumption, not of market or government incentives. Inflation is generated by the private sector, not by federal deficit spending. Productivity increases depend on the worker, not on efficient management or improved technology.

In any event, the spots tend to depoliticize issues by emphasizing individual, professional, or technical solutions to problems and deemphasizing political conflict. Consensus and not conflict is at the heart of these messages. One study found nearly two-thirds of the advertisements had no overt portrayal of political authority. Where reference was made to public or private authority, the depiction of such authority was predictable:

> PSAs . . . seem crafted, although not necessarily always consciously, to show public and private institutions and organizations, as well as the people occupying positions of authority in them, as both instrumentally effective and deserving of our approval and affection. We are told over and over again, for example, that the Department of Housing and Urban Development (HUD) helps people by providing flood insurance, that HUD is for America, "A Nation of Neighbors." The Veterans Administration tells us it can help (G.I. Bill). The President's Council on Physical Fitness and Sports wants us to live longer. The Agriculture Department warns us about salmonella. . . . And around Christmas time, the marines collect Toys for Tots by PSA.[33]

Even the Internal Revenue Service makes no reference to the sanctions it may employ against taxpayers who seek to cheat the government of its due: its PSA slogan is "We Want to Help." And the child-abuse prevention spots understandingly ask parents to seek out government aid if they are abusing their children, failing to mention the frequently employed sanction of termination of parental rights.

Government advertising, even when it is done in conjunction with the Advertising Council, is not, of course, unchecked. The actual effects of campaigns are difficult to ascertain. Frequently, the spots simply seek to channel values which are already widely held and which have been and are being transmitted by myriad public and private communicators. Further, if the objective is to persuade people to trust government, it may be beyond the abilities of even the most gifted or professional persuaders to sway a skeptical and

---

33. *Id.* at 83-84.

suspicious public. There are also some preliminary signs of the evolution of institutional constraints on government public service advertising. A number of members of Congress complained to the networks that the WIN campaign should give rise to the application of the fairness doctrine, requiring a fair presentation of both sides of the issue (although not necessarily a right of reply). The FCC has begun to move timidly in the direction of considering public service advertising within the framework of the fairness doctrine, albeit this may simply contribute to the bland and noncontroversial nature of most spots. As noted above, congressional pressure forced temporary abandonment of paid spots seeking to persuade young men and women to join the volunteer army. In 1975, members of Congress were so outraged by a Department of Commerce grant to the Advertising Council to mount "an effective campaign to improve public understanding of our American economic system," that a subcommittee of the House Committee on Government Operations held hearings on the matter. At a minimum, government public service advertising is no longer insulated from public debate over its propriety.

Propaganda in Wartime

Nearly every constitutional law course covers the espionage acts[34] enacted during World War I by the federal government to punish those who criticized or otherwise undermined the war effort. The "clear and present" danger test developed by Holmes and Brandeis,[35] and the

34. Act of June 15, 1917, ch. 30, § 30, 40 Stat. 217 et seq., incorporated as amended in 18 U.S.C. § 2388; the original espionage act was amended by the Act of May 16, 1918, ch. 75, 40 Stat. 553, repealed, Act of March 3, 1921, ch. 136, 41 Stat. 1360 (see Zechariah Chafee, Free Speech in the United States 42-46 [Cambridge, Mass.: Harvard University Press, 1941]). By World War I, and the period thereafter, many state governments also enacted criminal anarchy and criminal syndicalism laws (see Thomas Emerson, The System of Freedom of Expression 101-110 [New York: Random House, 1970]).

35. See, e.g., Whitney v. California, 274 U.S. 357, 374 (1927) (Brandeis, J., concurring); Abrams v. United States, 250 U.S. 616, 624 (1919) (Holmes, J., dissenting); Schenk v. United States, 249 U.S. 47, 52 (1919) (Holmes, J., writing for the Court). See, generally, Walter Berns, Freedom, Virtue and the First Amendment (Baton Rouge, La.: Louisiana State University Press, 1957); Emerson, Freedom of Expression 62-70; Laurence Tribe, American Constitutional Law § 12-9 (Mineola, N.Y.: Foundation Press, 1978); Zechariah Chafee, "Thirty-Five Years with Freedom of Speech," 1 Kansas Law Review 1 (1952); Gerald Gunther, "Learned Hand and the Origins of Modern First Amendment Doctrine: Some Fragments of History," 27 Stanford Law Review 719 (1975); Harry Kalven, "Ernst Freund and the First Amendment Tradition," 40 University of Chicago Law Review 235 (1973); Hans Linde, "'Clear and Present Danger' Reexamined: Dissonance in the Brandenburg Concerto," 22 Stanford Law Review 1163 (1970); Frank Strong, "Fifty Years of Clear and Present Danger: From Schenck to Brandenburg—and Beyond," 1969 Supreme Court Review 41. For a contemporary critique of the Holmes and Brandeis approach, see John Wigmore, "Abrams v. U.S.: Freedom of Speech and Freedom of Thuggery in War-Time and Peace-Time," 14 Illinois Law Review 539 (1920).

evolution of First Amendment protection of private speech from government interference came out of this era.[36] While students are taught about espionage-act prosecutions both during and after the war, as well as about prosecutions under state laws, few learn about the other side of the coin: the systematic efforts by the executive branch to create favorable attitudes to American military intervention.

In pursuit of favorable publicity about World War I, President Wilson formed the Committee on Public Information (known also as the Creel Committee for its head, George Creel).[37] In addition to a "voluntary" censorship program, the Creel Committee published an official bulletin for the "purpose of assuring full and authoritative publication of all official acts and proceedings."[38] It also subsidized the publication of books, produced films and slides, authored "canned" editorials, and even had a staff that drew political cartoons.[39] The idea grew out of Wilson's dissatisfaction with reporters and the press, and was an effort to reach the public directly.[40] The official bulletin and other materials were circulated to editors, government officials, private citizens, and publicity agencies, and printed matter was posted in post offices and all military installations. In short, the Creel Committee was a kind of "embryonic 'propaganda ministry' for the national Executive." The committee explicitly linked its appeals and information to President Wilson "as national leader and prime mover in the war effort."[41]

The Creel Committee quickly turned from the official bulletin to an array of communications devices to impress upon the people the need for national unity and the "despicable qualities of the enemy."[42] Brochures were sent twice a month to every school teacher in the country under the National School Service program. Teachers were expected to utilize them in class discussions.[43] A speakers' bureau was organized, and some 75,000 speakers enrolled as "Four-Minute Men" to relay the committee's messages in motion picture theatres. More than 75 million pamphlets were distributed. A substantial portion con-

36. See, generally, Emerson, *Freedom of Expression* chs. 4 and 5.

37. Cornwell, *Presidential Leadership* 44, 48-49; James Mock and Cedric Larson, *Words That Won the War* (New York: Russell and Russell, 1968).

38. Cornwell, *Presidential Leadership* 48, quoting George Creel, *How We Advertised America* (New York: Harper & Brothers, 1920).

39. See Mock and Larson, *Words That Won the War* chs. 4 and 6.

40. Cornwell, *Presidential Leadership* 48. Interestingly, this appears to be a complaint of most modern presidents, including Lyndon Johnson, Richard Nixon, and Jimmy Carter. See, generally, Wise, *Politics of Lying*. Cf. Allan Winkler, *The Politics of Propaganda: The Office of War Information* (New Haven, Conn.: Yale University Press, 1978).

41. *Id.* at 48-49.

42. *Id.* at 50.

43. Semi-monthly pamphlets were sent to about 600,000 public school teachers (*id.* at 54).

sisted of reprints of Wilson speeches and statements.[44] A handbook was prepared for the Boy Scouts which began:

> Every one of the 285,661 Scouts and 76,957 Scout Officials has been summoned by President Woodrow Wilson, Commander-in-Chief of the Army and Navy, to serve as a dispatch bearer from the Government at Washington to the American people all over the country.[45]

President Wilson was apparently well aware of the magnitude of the program, as he and Creel met about three times a month for the duration of the war.[46]

The Creel Committee's operations, although wider in scope and more blatant, are not different in kind from other publicity campaigns organized by the executive branch to combat real or imagined emergencies.[47] This is particularly true in the military sphere. The Office of War Information performed a similar, if less effective and offensive, role during World War II;[48] General MacArthur had 175 aides assigned

44. *Id.* at 50. See, generally, Mock and Larson, *Words That Won the War* ch. 5.

45. *Id.* at 51. See ch. 1, n. 6, above.

46. *Id.* at 55. Cornwell sympathetically notes that

> It seems clear that neither Creel nor Wilson himself saw the role of the committee as a vehicle for the President's political or personal aggrandizement. If Creel's decision to portray the war effort in Wilsonian terms did not stem from this, it probably was the unconscious product of something akin to hero worship. He once wrote the President: "I find it hard always to think of you as a person, for you stand for America so absolutely in my mind and heart and are so inseparably connected with the tremendous events of the time." (Cornwell, *Presidential Leadership* 55)

47. See, e.g., *id.* at 132-137 (discussion of President Franklin Roosevelt's Committee on Economic Security, which conducted a "public discussion and educational campaign" on behalf of the president's anti-Depression programs); *id.* at 225-226 (discussion of President Roosevelt's establishment of an Office of War Information during World War II); *id.* at 243 (discussion of President Kennedy's response to the steel price increases of April 1962). See also, e.g., Key, *Public Opinion and American Democracy* ch. 14; James McCamy, *Government Publicity* (Chicago: University of Chicago Press, 1939); Minow, Martin and Mitchell, *Presidential Television*; Winkler, *Politics of Propaganda*; David Wise, "The President and the Press," *Atlantic Monthly* 55, 56-60 (April 1973) (discussion of the mass media strategies of Presidents Nixon and Johnson).

48. See John Blum, *V Was for Victory* ch. 1 (New York: Harcourt Brace Jovanovich, 1976):

> The executive order of June 1942 establishing the Office of War Information denied a seemingly broad mandate: "to coordinate the dissemination of war information by all federal agencies and to formulate and carry out, by means of the press, radio and motion pictures, programs designed to facilitate an understanding of the war effort and of the policies, activities, and aims of the Government."

See ch. 7, below; Winkler, *Politics of Propaganda*; Robert Merton, *Mass Persuasion: The Social Psychology of a War Bond Drive* (New York: Harper & Brothers, 1946).

to publicize his Far East Command in 1948.[49] A mandatory troop indoctrination program was implemented to respond to statements by American prisoners of war held in Korea.[50] From the late 1950s on, the military services have each attempted to sell to the public and Congress their own strategic weapons systems[51] (for example, chemical weapons). In 1969 nearly $28 million was allocated officially for military public relations,[52] although the real figure was probably significantly higher.[53] Indeed, the Department of Defense operated an extensive speakers' bureau during the Vietnam War:

> Through speakers' bureaus which each Army post is encouraged to maintain, an estimated 1,000 audiences a month are provided with Army speakers. Young returned veterans from Vietnam are urged to address public gatherings; *Army Digest* noted proudly that, since returning from Vietnam, a Col. John G. Hughes had delivered 240 speeches. *The Washington Post* reported in December 1969 that an Army major was used by the Pentagon to provide public counterattacks to critics of the War. . . . In several of his appearances, the major . . . questioned the patriotism of Sen. George McGovern, and charged that the American liberal press was printing material which breaks the morale of the American prisoners.[54]

One commentator has gone so far as to state that "military propaganda aimed at civilians, even if deceptive, has generally been taken for granted in wartime."[55]

These examples of efforts to influence public opinion during wartime, or about the military, are not given as examples of typical propaganda campaigns foisted on an unsuspecting public. They are, at least in degree, quite atypical, barring the exigencies of war. Particularly in peacetime, Congress and the military have played a cat-and-mouse

49. See Edward Sherman, "The Military Courts and Servicemen's First Amendment Rights," 22 *Hastings Law Journal* 325, 348, n. 137 (1971).

50. *Id.*, citing *Hearings of the Special Preparedness Subcommittee of the Senate Armed Services Committee*, 87th Cong., 1st sess., pt. 1, at 72-73 (1961).

51. Key, *Public Opinion and American Democracy* 416-417 (1967). See, generally, J. W. Fulbright, *The Pentagon Propaganda Machine* (New York: Liveright, 1970).

52. Sherman, "Military Courts" 348, n. 137.

53. Fulbright, *Pentagon Propaganda Machine*. In 1967, the Associated Press estimated that $400 million was being spent annually for public information and public relations by the federal executive branch as a whole (*id.* at 17). See also *id.* at 27-28; Herbert Schiller, *Mass Communications and American Empire* 76-78 (Boston: Beacon Press, 1969). In 1975, the Army alone awarded a $40 million advertising account to N.W. Ayer (see "Ayer Renamed to $40 Million Army Account," *Advertising Age* 1, col. 1 [March 21, 1975]).

54. Derek Shearer, "The Brass Image," 210 *The Nation* 460 (1970); see also Minor, *Information War* 174-176.

55. Sherman, "Military Courts" 349.

game, with Congress frequently seeking to limit the public relations activities of the military.[56] Nor is the purpose here to label these communication campaigns as illegitimate, though this might be argued. Information, leadership, and national unity are all important values, particularly during wartime. But to say in general that such activities may be appropriate is not to suggest that they are in every instance, that governmental rhetoric is not used to stifle dissent, or that democratic politics may not be in some danger. Once again, the question is one of degree and balance, and there is ample reason to be wary. Hundreds of thousands of potential critics of American entry into World War I, for example, may not have been deterred from speaking out by the fear of prosecution; it may be, rather, that they were taken in and their judgment distorted by an omnipresent campaign of persuasion and information.

56. See Fulbright, *Pentagon Propaganda Machine* 26-27.

Part II

*Limits on
Government Expression*

Introduction

Part II turns from government participation in communications networks to factors that mitigate the dangers of such participation. Chapter 5 considers whether the massive government efforts to communicate described in chapter 4 in fact have any effect. The communications literature discloses that time and complexity have so far prevented formulating a satisfactory description of communications processes and their outcomes. Social scientists have been unable to tell us whether, when, or how government efforts to communicate succeed, or how to differentiate between messages that persuade and those that coerce behavior. Radical polemicists' claims that the communications system is a part of a greater system anesthetizing citizens to their subservience to an elite class are cause for concern but are ultimately unpersuasive. Given the lack of knowledge and the great potential for government abuse, however, I conclude that extrinsic limits on government speech are desirable.

Chapter 6 examines the pluralist faith as a limitation on government speech. Despite differences in power in the interplay between government and different elements in the private sector, each affects the other, and neither solely determines the outcome. This observation undercuts the notion that a powerful business elite controls government decision making. And, since pluralism involves a considerable degree of faith and consensus on first principles such as tolerance, diversity, individual freedom, civility, and majoritarian processes, democratic governments have in fact acted "unnaturally," that is, at a cost to their own power to persuade, in promoting pluralism.

Chapter 7 examines attitudinal and structural limits on government persuasion. The danger of government speech decreases as complexity, or the number of message originators, increases: "good" government speech—socialization to democratic norms—is perhaps the best protection against "bad" government speech, because it strengthens the role of self-controlled citizens. A similar check on government control of communication is found in the rigidity of citizens' minds, for inflexible minds select by discarding what they disbelieve and remembering that which confirms what they believe. The fragmentation of government and the private control of the mass media that transmit government messages are structural obstacles to government speech abuses. The gap between government goals and achievements characterized in implementation theory constitutes another structural obstacle to government abuse.

Two examples illustrate the intricate interplay of communications structures and public attitudes. First is an account of the complicated interactions that produced the demise of a federal World War II propaganda agency without recourse to constitutional resolution in the courts. Second is a discussion of the growing independence of public broadcasting. I conclude that we may have developed a public broadcasting structure in which decentralization of decision making allows us to accept the risks of using government funds not just to report events but also to promote choice and autonomy.

[5]

The Indeterminate Impact
of Mass Communications

That modern governments devote more and more resources to mass persuasion activities is not necessarily an indication that those governments are increasingly successful in influencing particular publics. The social science literature of the last ten years, especially in the aftermath of the war-on-poverty programs of the Johnson era, indicates that increased government expenditures and activity frequently cannot be correlated with measurable improvements in outcomes.[1] More dollars for public education or for rehabilitation programs in prisons do not necessarily mean that achievement levels will rise or recidivism will decline. The failure of many programs has led to a whole literature on implementation theory.[2] The realm of communications has an even

1. See, e.g., David Cohen and Janet Weiss, "Social Science and Social Policy: Schools and Race," in Ray Rist and Ronald Anson, eds., *Education, Social Science, and the Judicial Process* (New York: Teachers College Press, 1977); Gilbert Steiner, *The Children's Cause* (Washington, D.C.: Brookings Institution, 1976); Martha Derthick, *New Towns In-Town* (Washington, D.C.: Urban Institute, 1972); James Coleman *et al.*, *Equality of Educational Opportunity* (Washington, D.C.: U.S. Dept. of Health, Education, and Welfare, 1966); Christopher Jencks *et al.*, *Inequality* (New York: Basic Books, 1972). Much depends, of course, on how one defines the objectives of the policies and what constitutes compliance with those objectives. See, e.g., Milbrey McLaughlin, *Evaluation and Reform: The Elementary and Secondary Education Act of 1965, Title I* (Cambridge, Mass.: Harvard University Press, 1975); Aaron Wildavsky, "The Strategic Retreat on Objectives," 2 *Policy Analysis* 499 (1976); and Richard Elmore, "Organizational Models of Social Program Implementation," 26 *Public Policy* 185 (1978).

2. See, e.g., Elmore, "Organizational Models"; McLaughlin, *Evaluation and Reform*; Derthick, *New Towns*; Eugene Bardach, *The Implementation Game* (Cambridge, Mass.: MIT Press, 1977); Harrell Rogers and Charles Bullock, *Coercion to Compliance* (Lexington, Mass.: Lexington Books, 1976); Walter Williams and Richard Elmore, eds., *Social Program Implementation* (New York: Academic Press, 1976); Note, "Implementation Problems in Institutional Reform Litigation," 91 *Harvard Law Review* 428 (1977); Paul Berman, "The Study of Macro- and Micro-Implementation," 26 *Public Policy* 157 (1978); Herbert Kauf-

longer tradition of questioning whether specified communications activities have the intended impact on the opinions of particular persons or groups.[3] The question is critical in the present context, because it suggests that there may be limits on government's ability to persuade which, for better or worse, inhere in the very processes of communication.

Questions of the impact of mass communications and of the success of particular communicators are empirical. But the effects of mass communication are subtle and difficult to measure given the complexity of communications systems—the large number of variables, the mutually affecting relationship among variables, the absence of simple causal links, the uncertainties introduced by time, and the nonstatic nature of such systems.[4] Determining effectiveness is also difficult because of disagreement as to the desired or observed outcomes of the process and a tendency to focus on the individual and his psychology rather than on "the dyad, the clique, the network, or the system of individuals," i.e., on relationships.[5] The apparent ineffectiveness of some forms of mass communication may be more a function of a primitive social science than a realistic appraisal of persuasion processes.[6] No Prigogine has yet emerged in communications research to perceive order in the face of complexity and time. At the present stage of research, the effects of mass communications are largely unknown or indeterminate—at least insofar as one seeks to disaggregate complex variables and to fashion general theories. This is not to say that we know nothing about cause and effect in mass communications. We have reason to believe that some types of communications, in certain

man, *The Forest Ranger* (Baltimore: Johns Hopkins Press, 1967); Paul Berman *et al.*, *Federal Programs Supporting Educational Change* (Sant Monica, Calif.: RAND, 1974); Jerome Murphy, *State Education Agencies and Discretionary Funds* (Lexington, Mass.: Lexington Books, 1974); Jeffrey Pressman and Aaron Wildavsky, *Implementation* (Berkeley and Los Angeles: University of California Press, 1973).

3. See, e.g., Carl Hovland, Irving Janis, and Harold Kelley, *Communication and Persuasion* (New Haven, Conn.: Yale University Press, 1953); Joseph Klapper, *The Effects of Mass Communication* (Glencoe, Ill.: Free Press, 1960); Paul Lazarsfeld, Bernard Berelson, and Hazel Gaudet, *The People's Choice* (New York: Columbia University Press, 1948); Melvin Defleur and Otto Larsen, *The Flow of Information* (New York: Harper & Brothers, 1958); Elihu Katz and Paul Lazarsfeld, *Personal Influence: The Part Played by People in the Flow of Mass Communications* (Glencoe, Ill.: Free Press, 1960); Wilbur Schramm, *Mass Communications* (Urbana, Ill.: University of Illinois Press, 1960).

4. See Everett M. Rogers and Rehka Agarwala-Rogers, *Communication in Organizations* 18–26 (New York: Free Press, 1976).

5. *Id.* at 21.

6. Herbert Simon has noted that in complex systems characterized by a large number of interdependent variables, generalization is no mean task. See "The Architecture of Complexity," in Joseph Litterer, ed., *Organizations: Systems, Control, and Adaptation* (New York: Wiley, 1969).

circumstances, will significantly influence attitudes and behavior. Thus reinforcement of the intrinsic limits on persuasion processes alone may not be sufficient to control government speech abuses. Other limiting mechanisms should be identified and pursued. Certainly corporate and government leaders act on the assumption that communications alter attitudes and behavior, and perhaps they intuitively grasp what eludes scientific verification.

The efficacy problem is exacerbated by the fact that all speech has a persuasive character and that persuasive government rhetoric is often desirable. What is to be feared is a form of state coercion which undermines personal autonomy and dignity. Yves Simon has well described the problem of characterizing government speech as coercive or persuasive in a democracy:

> What distinguishes persuasion from coercion is not precisely the psychical nature of the former as opposed to the physical nature of the latter, but it is the essential part played in persuasion by the freedom of the subject on whom persuasion is exercised. When the means of influence operate determinately, there is necessitation from without, i.e., coercion, regardless of whether the means are physical or psychical. Great difficulties, however, result from the fact that psychical coercion often bears appearances which make it hardly distinguishable from persuasion.
>
> Of all processes of psychical coercion, the clearest and those which it is fitting to use as points of reference are hypnotic and post-hypnotic suggestions. It seems that contemporary research has disposed of popular beliefs concerning the extent of the power wielded by the operator. . . . More recently we have come to understand that propaganda, when carried beyond a certain point of intensity, becomes a process of psychical coercion. Significantly, *nobody can say where this point is found.* Moderate propaganda is a process of persuasion. It is the normal instrument used by various parties in order to obtain votes for their candidates or for the measures that they recommend. A few speeches, a few leaflets, a few newspaper articles, balanced by speeches, leaflets, and articles in the other direction of about the same intensity and in about the same number, leave the voter free to form an opinion and to govern his action according to his prudence. But if propaganda is intense and succeeds in gaining a monopoly in a community, it is likely soon to become a process of coercion that can be likened to hypnotic suggestion in more than one respect. . . .
>
> *Between moderate propaganda, which is a process of persuasion, and intensive propaganda, which is a process of psychical coercion, nobody can trace a clear line. . . . Of all conceivable forms of coercion, the only one which*

*certainly conflicts with the essence of democracy is precisely the one which
bears the greatest resemblance to the democratic process of persuasion.*[7]

While a preference for pluralism and limits on government communication is clearly based on political values, the characterization of
speech as coercive or persuasive is another empirical matter. At the
risk of incurring the wrath of social scientists for amateurishly oversimplifying the current state of communications theory, the literature
appears to be divisible into roughly three categories: (1) propaganda
studies; (2) experimental research in controlled environments; and (3)
polemical political critiques of mass communications processes. With
respect to the propaganda studies, there was a period between World
War I and the early 1950s in which the so-called "bullet theory" of
mass communications (a phrase coined by Wilbur Schramm) held sway.
There was much criticism of government propaganda, at least with
respect to totalitarian countries. It was assumed, without much evidence, that "communication was . . . a magic bullet that transferred
ideas or feeling or motivations almost automatically from one mind to
another," and that it operated against a relatively inert and hapless
populace: "The audience was typically thought of as a sitting target; if
a communicator could hit it, he would affect it." Propaganda was an
"insidious force" wielded by the mass media, and hence the very word
became hated. The critical assumptions were that people were defense-
less and passive against the power of mass media, and that "communication could *shoot something into them*, just as an electric circuit could
deliver electrons to a light bulb."[8] The ability to identify something
called "propaganda" was assumed, and its efficacy taken for granted.
Relief would come primarily from controlling the power of the mass
media to communicate. Many of these notions surely flowed from the
fear generated by World War I and, later, Communist and Nazi propaganda.

The trouble with the "bullet theory" was that it was not consistent
with the facts: sometimes mass communications failed in their purposes
or aroused unintended audience responses. From the mid-1950s to the
present, researchers have been a good deal more skeptical about the
impact of government and mass media communications.[9] Attempts to
measure the impact of particular communications on the behavior and

7. Yves Simon, *Philosophy of Democratic Government*, 125-127 (Chicago: University of
Chicago Press, 1951) (emphasis added).

8. Wilbur Schramm, "Nature of Communication Between Humans," in Wilbur
Schramm and Donald Roberts, eds., *The Process and Effects of Mass Communication* 7-9
(Urbana, Ill.: University of Illinois Press, 1971).

9. See, e.g., Hovland, Janis, and Kelley, *Communication and Persuasion*; Leon Festinger,
A Theory of Cognitive Dissonance (Evanston, Ill.: Row, Peterson, 1957); Klapper, *Effects of
Mass Communication*; Raymond Bauer, "The Obstinate Audience", in Schramm and
Roberts, *Mass Communication* 326; Schramm, "Nature of Communication."

attitudes of people—for example, to judge the effectiveness of political campaigns, presidential pronouncements, campaigns to sell war bonds, etc.—frequently found that correlations, much less causal connections, were difficult to pinpoint. Raymond Bauer goes so far as to state that "the chief discovery of field studies of the effects of mass communications is that it is exceedingly difficult to identify such effects."[10] Understandably, then, there was a shift toward psychological explanations and experimental research designs.[11] As Wilbur Schramm describes the change,

> By the middle 1950's the Bullet Theory, if you will pardon the expression, had been shot full of holes. If anything really passed from sender to receiver, it certainly appeared in very different form to different receivers. And the audience was far from a sitting target.[12]

In short, a myopic concern with the communicator was replaced by more subtle inquiries into the relationship among the communicator, the message, and the audience.[13] The loss was that the research focus moved away from consideration of government communication and toward consideration of private mass media and interpersonal communication.

The ineffectiveness of mass communications has not been demonstrated, but the process is demonstrably complex. Many relevant variables cannot be identified. Blithe assumptions about the efficaciousness and characteristics of propaganda are not warranted. "The intervening steps between communication stimulus and responses are less simple than they had generally been considered."[14] Research on audience characteristics gradually came to dominate research on communicator characteristics. Attentiveness, personality, attitudes, and intelligence of the audience have been isolated as variables greatly influencing acceptance of messages.[15] The simplistic nature of past propaganda studies is now recognized. For example, Hitler's alleged propaganda successes may have been less a function of propaganda creativity than of the fact that "many Germans were ready to support him and were eager to be nazified," and were, moreover, afraid of the penalties for noncompliance.[16] More attention is currently also paid to the social system in which communications take place. The role of intermediate opinion

10. Raymond Bauer, "Comments," 23 *Public Opinion Quarterly* 15 (1959).
11. Schramm, "Nature of Communication" 9-10.
12. *Id.* at 10.
13. See, e.g., Festinger, *Cognitive Dissonance*; Klapper, *Effects of Mass Communication*; Bauer, "Obstinate Audience."
14. Schramm, "Nature of Communication" 11.
15. *Id.* at 9-10.
16. See Eric Hoffer, *The True Believer*, 97-101 (New York: Harper & Row, 1951).

leaders and elites—those who reconvey messages on a more personal basis—in shaping public responses to government and mass media communications has become the object of greater scholarly attention.[17]

More recently, theoretical constructs, tested by controlled experiments, have yielded greater insight into communications processes and the conditions for effective government rhetoric. To questions about the efficacy of communications, distinguished social scientists such as Hovland, Festinger, Insko, Janis, Kelley, Lazarsfeld, Bauer, and Schramm have tended to reply with the cardinal rule of modern social science: it all depends. Without delving into intricate theories of reinforcement, assimilation contrast, congruence, cognitive dissonance, affective cognitive consistency, or inoculation, it is possible to identify a number of factors thought to influence the persuasiveness of communications, even if there is disagreement over the theory or set of theories that would explain why these elements are so influential.

Perhaps a preliminary caveat is in order. Much of modern communications research deals with interpersonal communications or communications between individuals and relatively small audiences. Mass communications, say between a congressional committee and a large television audience, appear to be more complex, and one should not make the facile assumption that what is true of interpersonal communications is necessarily true of mass communications. Most apparently, the mass media involve a larger audience, the ability to duplicate messages and to send them in greater numbers, a likelihood of greater heterogeneity of audience, and a weaker ability to provide feedback and to tailor responses to specific individuals.[18] Further, mass communications are likely to involve a "two-step flow" in which the mass media reach individuals through opinion leaders who transmit and interpret the original messages.[19] Nonetheless, the prevailing view appears to be that the similarities between interpersonal and mass communications are more striking than the dissimilarities:

> Mass communication faces the same defenses [as interpersonal communication]. It must jump the same hurdles: attention, acceptance, interpretation and disposition. It requires the same kinds of contact between sender and receiver for entertainment and instruction. It must depend on activating the same kinds of psychological dynamics if it is to persuade.

The fashion was for a number of years to worry about the great and awful power of mass communication, because of the

17. See, e.g., Lazarsfeld, Berelson, and Gaudet, *People's Choice*; Elihu Katz, "The Two-Step Flow of Communication," 21 *Public Opinion Quarterly* 61 (1957); Claus Mueller, *The Politics of Communication* 144-147 (New York: Oxford University Press, 1973).

18. Schramm, "Nature of Communication" 49-50.

19. Katz, "Two-Step Flow of Communication."

enormous numbers of hours people gave to media entertainment and the size of media audiences for political information. But the more scholars looked into the effect of the media, the more they found that the same resistances to change applied there as in person-to-person communication—in fact, more strongly. People come to the media, as to other messages, seeking what they want, not what the media intends them to have. Because there are so many media and media units, they still have considerable choice. They still have their defenses up; they still defend their strongly held positions.[20]

While this analysis may not be entirely persuasive, the discussion equates interpersonal communications with mass communications. In the present context, this is satisfactory. The apparent gaps in knowledge with respect to interpersonal communications reinforce the thesis that we know even less about the more complex mass communications processes.

The classic formulation of the basic question in communications theory is "who says what to whom with what effect."[21] This requires the analysis of four factors: (1) the characteristics of the communicator; (2) the characteristics or content of the message conveyed; (3) the characteristics and dispositions of the audience; and (4) the response of the audience to the communication. The first part of the formulation relies upon the intuitively appealing notion that the effectiveness of a communication will depend in part upon the source of the communication. A respected, trustworthy, or "expert" government agency, organization, or individual is more likely to gain acceptance of a message than an unrespected communicator.[22] This is particularly true where the speaker has specialized knowledge not generally at the disposal of the audience. In rare instances, the communicator may have a monopoly on persuasive communications, at least temporarily, and this total control of the communications environment may be most effective in gaining support for the message. In practice, only governments in closed societies and parents in relation to children ever achieve this, and those monopolies are often short-lived and reinforced by coercion.[23]

Someone with high credibility with the audience starts with an advantage, as does an articulate speaker, a striking personality, a speaker

20. Schramm, "Nature of Communication" 50-51.

21. Hovland, Janis, and Kelley, *Communication and Persuasion* 12; see Bruce Smith, Harold Lasswell and Ralph Casey, *Propaganda, Communication and Public Opinion* 3 (Princeton, N.J.: Princeton University Press, 1946).

22. Hovland, Janis, and Kelley, *Communication and Persuasion* ch. 2; Chester Insko, *Theories of Attitude Change* 43-49 (New York: Appleton, Century, Crofts, 1967); but see Brian Sternthal, Lawrence Phillips, and Roberta Dholakia, "The Persuasive Effect of Source Credibility," 42 *Public Opinion Quarterly* 285 (1978).

23. Robert Weissberg, *Political Learning, Political Choice and Democratic Citizenship* (Englewood Cliffs, N.J.: Prentice-Hall, Inc., 1974).

with a "good image," a member of a high status group, or a speaker wielding substantial power.[24] Simply stated, a critical variable is whether there is an expectation that the speaker will be truthful and right.

Even if a speaker is thought to be generally trustworthy and expert, the message may be rejected if the audience perceives that the speaker has some obvious self-interest in persuading it. Cues as to the speaker's intentions, expertness, and trustworthiness are thus critical.[25] The context and media of the appeal will influence the audience. For example, a front-page news story may be given more credence than a television message labeled as an advertisement. Timing is important. If the speaker can coordinate the message with events, he may be more successful. For example, a plea for increased military spending may be reinforced by aggression on the part of an adversary nation. Interestingly enough, however, there is not much difference in what is learned from more credible and less credible sources in terms of factual information; the differences lurk rather in the degree of willingness to accept the speaker's recommendations. Further, even with respect to acceptance of the message, differences in the credibility of the communicator virtually disappear with the passage of time in controlled experiments: immediate aftertests show the greatest differentials. If the object of the message is to produce something more than an immediate and short-lived opinion change, there is thus little evidence to sustain the proposition that communicator characteristics result in sustained effects on the audience.[26] Chester Insko concludes that social scientists really know very little about the widely observed source-credibility phenomenon:

> In view of the high degree of consistency in this source credibility literature we can safely generalize that a high credibility source will be more influential than a low credibility source. Being able to state this generalization, however, does not mean that we really understand source credibility. What is it that makes a source credible and how does source credibility operate? These are questions for which research has provided no ready answers. . . . It [is] quite evident that we are really just beginning to study source credibility.[27]

The content of messages has been studied in relation to their persuasiveness, although in glancing through the literature it is often difficult to differentiate content from audience characteristics. It is quite appar-

24. Hovland, Janis, and Kelley, *Communication and Persuasion* 35-36; Insko, *Theories of Attitude Change* 43-44.

25. Hovland, Janis, and Kelley, *Communication and Persuasion* 21-25, 35.

26. *Id.* at 38-40, 47-48.

27. Insko, *Theories of Attitude Change* 48.

ent that they are interacting variables. For example, if the topic is uninteresting and unfamiliar to the audience, or if it is highly technical and complex, the audience may be both inattentive and incapable of understanding the message. In any event, research on the content of messages appears inconclusive. One technique, "canalization," appears to hold great promise, or at least communicators think it does. This refers "to the use of preexisting attitudes or behavioral patterns" as building blocks to secure compliance with specific messages.[28] It seeks to move the audience from accepted attitudes to other, closely related attitudes. Appeals to patriotism, anticommunism, and free enterprise may fall in this category.

Another question, where two opposing points of view are involved, is whether a communication is more effective if it is presented first or second. This is the primacy versus recency debate. The evidence on this tends to be conflicting, and the general conclusion appears to be "that there is no universal law either of primacy or recency."[29] In a variation of the "it all depends" approach, such factors as familiarity with the topic, degree of controversy, awareness of manipulative intent, and time between communications may be decisive. "We still appear to be a long way from a completely accurate conception of primacy-recency effects."[30] Similar results attend such questions as whether the speaker should explicitly draw conclusions or allow the audience to do so, omit counterarguments or discuss them, repeat the message, eliminate non-essential elements of the message, respond to questions, and so on.[31]

Another aspect of content relates to the nature of the appeal or message. What is the relative efficacy of appealing to emotions, threats, logic, accepted symbols, and ego ideals?[32] Most of the studies have tended to focus on "fear-arousing appeals," perhaps because such appeals are intuitively thought to present the greatest danger of the sort of "psychical coercion" discussed earlier. Obviously, if the communicator has the ability to carry out the threats and they would impose substantial penalties, the effectiveness of the communication is inextricably tied to physical coercion. Expressed most broadly, the manner in which a communication is received may depend on a person's wants and needs. The audience will anticipate rewards and punishments, and

28. See Carl Hovland and Irving Janis, *Personality and Persuasibility* (New Haven, Conn.: Yale University Press, 1959).

29. Insko, *Theories of Attitude Change* 60.

30. Insko, *Theories of Attitude Change* 61; see also Hovland, Janis, and Kelley, *Communication and Persuasion* 112-126.

31. Hovland, Janis, and Kelley, *Communication and Persuasion* 99-112; Carl Hovland, Arthur Lumsdaine, and Fred Sheffield, *The Effect of Presenting "One Side" Versus "Both Sides" in Changing Opinions on a Controversial Subject*, in Schramm and Roberts, *Mass Communication*.

32. Hovland, Janis, and Kelley, *Communication and Persuasion* 56-60.

if the speaker has control of these things, the difficulty of persuasion is eased.[33]

One would expect that strong fear-arousing communications would tend to stimulate the attention of the audience and motivate them to comply with the message. To some extent, research appears to support this conclusion. But, as one might suspect, the picture is a good deal more complex than this, and the anticipated corollary that increasing levels of fear-arousal will lead to increasing acceptance of the message is not generally supported by the evidence. What appears to occur is that additional threatening material induces greater acceptance up to some threshold point, but that increases in fear-arousing material after that threshold tend to result in decreased acceptance of the speaker's recommendations. That is, it may be that "fear is curvilinearly related to persuasion, with moderate fear being little more persuasive than either high or low fear."[34] This may be a result of "counteracting defensive reactions" on the part of the audience, as well as the nature of the threat, feelings of aggression against the communicator, and other factors. The conclusion is that "our knowledge about the relative persuasive effects of strong and weak fear-arousing communications is still fairly primitive." And what is needed? More research; for "we can hope that future work will make significant advances."[35]

The most pervasive element in modern communications theory and research is a fascination with the characteristics, traits, beliefs, personality, prejudices, selectivity processes, and maturity of the audiences to whom communications are addressed. The character of the audience is significant not only in predicting the impact of messages, but in the communicator's selection of opinion leaders to channel communications to a wider public.[36] The literature is immense and complex, but a useful starting point is to note the obvious: people are obstinate, difficult to persuade, and have a way of avoiding or distorting messages which are inconsistent with deeply held values and beliefs. Their attention span is limited, they may be capable of grappling with only one difficult message at a time, and they may wish to avoid "cognitive strain."[37] As Raymond Bauer notes in his discussion of the "obstinate audience," this is even more true in the world outside of the laboratory, with its experimental situations.[38] Unless the audience is captive, it selects what

33. See, e.g., Hovland, Janis, and Kelley, *Communication and Persuasion* ch. 3; see also Insko, *Theories of Attitude Change* 41-43.

34. Insko, *Theories of Attitude Change* 41.

35. *Id.* at 41-43; see also Hovland, Janis, and Kelley, *Communication and Persuasion* 84-89.

36. Katz, "Two-Step Flow of Communication."

37. Bauer, "Obstinate Audience."

38. *Id.* at 331. See also Carl Hovland, "Reconciling Conflicting Results Derived from Experimental and Survey Studies of Attitude Change," in Schramm and Roberts, *Mass Communication* 495.

it will attend to. If people listen to, read, and watch things that already command their interest, these topics are usually those as to which they already have much information and strongly held beliefs. These people may prefer communications that support their views, or they may not.[39] The people most likely to be persuaded by the communicator, the open-minded, may never tune in. Those who tune in may be inattentive. This may explain the widely observed fact that "actual [communications] campaigns have often produced no measurable results, while quite marked effects could be produced in a laboratory."[40]

The list of audience variables that influence acceptance of communications has been greatly extended by the research of the last twenty-five years. The individual's attitudes and beliefs "are in part a product of his interaction in ... groups, both informal and formal."[41] Social status, class, gender, race and other individual and group characteristics may be important.[42] People who are highly motivated to maintain membership in a particular group tend to be more susceptible to influence by other members of the group.[43] It is erroneous to think that messages "strike the isolated and atomistic individual; if they strike, if they reach their target at all, they strike an individual living in a network of personal relationships that affect his outlook toward ... the mass media."[44] Mental ability may have an impact on the persuasiveness of the communication. But mental ability cuts both ways. Persons of greater intellectual ability may be better able to understand and learn what is being transmitted, but they are also more likely to be critical of the asserted arguments and conclusions. Hovland, Janis, and Kelley hypothesize that persons with low self-esteem are predisposed to be persuaded, while persons with "acute psychoneurotic symptoms" are predisposed to resist efforts at persuasion. So-called "authoritarian personalities" appear more resistant to persuasion.[45]

Motivation to accept or reject a communication is extremely important. The degree of discrepancy between the position advocated by the speaker and the audience's own attitudes or opinions is highly significant.[46] If the discrepancy is too great, the individual may perceive the communication as more extreme than it is and may evaluate it unfavorably. If the discrepancy is not so great, the individual may view the communication as espousing a less extreme position and evaluate it

39. Hovland, "Reconciling Conflicting Results" 497-498; see also Bauer, "Obstinate Audience."

40. Bauer, "Obstinate Audience" 331.

41. V.O. Key, *Public Opinion and American Democracy* 366 (New York: Knopf, 1967).

42. See Gary Cronkhite, *Persuasion* (Indianapolis, Ind.: Bobbs-Merrill, 1969).

43. Hovland, Janis, and Kelley, *Communication and Persuasion* 139-144.

44. Key, *Public Opinion and American Democracy* 366-367.

45. Hovland, Janis, and Kelley, *Communication and Persuasion* 181-192, 196-199.

46. Insko, *Theories of Attitude Change* chs. 6-10; Bauer, "Obstinate Audience" 337.

favorably. The individual may accept the information, but still retain opinions seemingly inconsistent with it. Or, under the "principle of congruity," when an existing attitude conflicts with a message, there may be a tendency to alter one's evaluations toward a point of equilibrium or conformity that accommodates both attitudes.[47] This is one of a number of homeostatic models in which a person acts in response to a message or in evaluating his response to a message so as to achieve or restore "equilibrium in his system of belief."[48] Festinger posits, for example, that if new information contradicts established cognitions, a form of "cognitive dissonance" will result. People will then act in such a way as to reduce this dissonance. "The dissonance resulting from involuntary exposure to new information may be reduced through defensive misperception of information, avoidance of or escape from the information, or opinion change," Chester Insko observes.[49]

The recent attention to audience predispositions and motivations and the development of cognitive theories of communication have added much to our knowledge. These few brief pages do not exhaust a subject to which many learned volumes have been devoted. But the nature and complexities of these theories and of the human animal they attempt to explain should make us wary of generalizations about the effectiveness of communications, particularly government mass communications. We know that certain things appear to matter: the maturity and malleability of the audience; its intelligence; the ability to be selective about what communications are received (the captive audience problem); and the consistency of established opinions against the positions being advocated by the communicator. We also know that access to other sources of information (the avoidance of monopoly), canalization, supplementary face-to-face contact, selection of opinion leaders, the credibility of the communicator, and his or her alleged expertise and perceived motive appear to count. The nature of the message, the degree of fear-arousal, the ability to individualize feedback, the manner of presentation, and the order of argument also determine the persuasiveness of the message in varying degrees. And the relationship of the rejection or acceptance of messages to anticipated or present rewards and punishments is difficult to deny.

The variables are, however, so numerous and difficult to weigh against one another, the determinants of effectiveness are so individualized, and the empirical findings are so inconclusive (even in the laboratory) that modern communications theory and research simply

47. Insko, *Theories of Attitude Change* ch. 6.

48. Bauer, "Obstinate Audience" 337; see also Nathan Maccoby and Eleanor Maccoby, "Homeostatic Theory in Attitude Change," 25 *Public Opinion Quarterly* 535 (1961).

49. Insko, *Theories of Attitude Change* 203. See, generally, Festinger, *Theory of Cognitive Dissonance*.

do not provide straightforward answers. It is extraordinarily difficult to predict the impact of mass communications emanating from the government. Joseph Klapper gently intimates this when he concludes that "mass communication *ordinarily* does not serve as a necessary and sufficient cause of audience effects, but rather functions among and through a nexus of mediating factors and influences."[50]

The problem of predicting effects is compounded by the fact that there is no agreement on what "effectiveness" means. A communication may be effective in the sense that it leads to immediate and sustained changes in opinion. It may be deemed effective if it brings about short-term changes in opinions, whatever the long-term prospects for adherence to the message. And then there is the problem of what we mean by imprecise terms like *attitude, belief*, and *opinion*. Do responses to a given testing device really evidence fundamental changes in attitudes? Perhaps in other circumstances we would obtain different answers. The attitudes of some people, particularly the young, are so unstable that test instruments tell us virtually nothing.[51] Or is it that the central focus should be on communications altering specific types of behavior? From this vantage, all that a test instrument can tell us is that a person will mark a piece of paper in a particular way after being subjected to specified communications.[52]

Why should we assume that attitudes and beliefs will closely correspond with behavior, even if the two can be conceptually distinguished? If a person opines that good dental hygiene is essential to good health, does this necessarily mean the person will brush his teeth three times a day? Does the fact that an individual believes smoking is bad for one's health mean that behavior will reflect belief and he will not smoke? Two commentators have concluded that "at best, the individual difference variable of attitude accounts for 10–12 per cent of the variance in predicting behavior."[53] This is hardly surprising. Equilibrium theories such as those of Festinger, if they tell us anything, indicate that people have a variety of techniques for reducing dissonance between actual behavior and accepted cognitive beliefs.[54]

The difficulties in establishing causal relationships and a base line for measuring the effectiveness of communications combine to lead us to even higher plateaus of uncertainty. In Wilbur Schramm's words, we have become increasingly aware of "mutual causation" factors

50. Klapper, *Effects of Mass Communication* 8.

51. Pauline Vaillancoult, "Stability of Children's Survey Responses," 37 *Public Opinion Quarterly* 373 (1973).

52. Steven Gross and C. Michael Niman, "Attitude-Behavior Consistency: A Review," 39 *Public Opinion Quarterly* 358 (1975).

53. *Id.* at 362-363.

54. Festinger, *Theory of Cognitive Dissonance* 264-265; Insko, *Theories of Attitude Change* ch. 10.

that make it virtually impossible to link particular communications in the world outside of the laboratory with specific changes in opinion, attitudes, and behavior. Communications centers stand in a mutually affecting relationship. Consider the examples that Schramm gives:

> The mass media contribute to change in taste, and audience feedback contributes to changes in program policy; policies change public opinion and public opinion changes policies; persuasion changes attitudes, which can change behavior, which reinforces attitude change; economic development brings about increases in communication and communication facilities, which bring about increases in economic development; and so forth.[55]

The multiple causation phenomenon is particularly acute if attention is focused on the long-term effects of mass communication. The picture one has is of a multitude of communicators—family, friends, social groups, peers, church, government, private mass media, foundations, educators, and corporations—in which it is impossible to identify the contribution of any single communicator, much less the effect of isolated communications. At best, particular mass communications may help to rivet public attention to an issue. Perhaps this explains why so many studies seem to indicate the ineffectiveness of mass communications during election campaigns:

> The main effect of a political campaign is to mobilize, not to convert. It revives the lagging interest of the average voter, but as it does so, it also revives whatever latent convictions he already had. In other words, the arguments he reads in the mass media or hears from speakers on television serve on the one hand in part to persuade him, but serve on the other hand to revive his recollection of his lifelong convictions. The latter will often be on the side of the issue diametrically opposite to what is being presented to him.
>
> For these reasons the main effect of the mass media in an election is to draw the election and the issues in it to the public's attention. Once the people have become aroused, their decision in the short run is more highly influenced by personal stimuli than by the mass media.[56]

The communications literature thus suggests that messages are more likely to be persuasive if they reinforce existing attitudes, or if they build incrementally on those attitudes. If the messages are addressed to a mass audience, common sense suggests that an appeal to widely-shared cultural, social, and political values is the key to success. Virtually by definition, such consensual values are likely to be embraced

---

55. Schramm, "Nature of Communication" 11-12.
56. Key, *Public Opinion and American Democracy* 397.

by a large number of mass communicators. If this is the case, the efficacy of the entire system of communications may be quite high even though empiricists cannot connect particular communicators or messages with specific effects. Schramm describes this process quite well, eschewing social science for interpretive judgment and metaphor:

> Among the long-term effect [of mass media], the most potent may well turn out to be the less dramatic ones—not the gross anti-social effects, but the gradual building up of pictures of the world from what the mass media choose to report of it; the gradual homogenization of images and behaviors over large populations, as a result of the universality of the mass media; the granting of status to persons who have access to the media. I once described this effect as resembling the gradual building up of a stalagmite in a cave, from the constant drip-drip of calcareous water upon it, each drop leaving a residue so small as to be invisible until the dripping had continued for years. And not until hundreds of years later could visitors see that the stalagmite had grown and altered its shape. This kind of effect, rather than quick and dramatic change, may be the chief impact of the mass media on human society.[57]

V. O. Key argues that multiple causation suggests that the cumulative effect of the total communications system, including the mass media, may be that there is "a net resistance to those messages of the media calculated to alter attitudes and a net reinforcement of messages calculated to maintain the status quo."[58] He treats this as a matter of conjecture, however, and not as established fact. Yet, in toto, he perceives a unity of themes in mass communication that closely approximates "a situation of monopoly propaganda":

> Propaganda has its greatest effect when it is unchallenged, when only a single theme is disseminated. To a remarkable degree the American mass media propagate the same broad political line. . . . Whatever the explanation, the unity of policy themes in the media doubtless enlarges their reinforcing effects.
> Even that substantial proportion of the content of the mass media that is not directly political—entertainment—needs also to reinforce values of the system and to maintain an indifference to questions that might touch upon controversial matters.[59]

Such observations are in part consistent with the polemical literature on mass communications and persuasion. These writings are essentially rooted in ideology—Marxist, feminist, religious, etc.—and treat the

57. Schramm, "Nature of Communication" 52-53.
58. Key, *Public Opinion and American Democracy* 347.
59. *Id.* at 396.

network of communications in a culture or society as reinforcing the dominant ideology to the point of disabling people from perceiving the ways in which the system "oppresses" them.

In writings by Jacques Ellul, Herbert Marcuse, and others,[60] the emphasis is on a false consciousness which allows individuals to be repressed without their being aware of it. Totalitarian aims are achieved not through coercion, but by working on the minds of the populace— on the ways in which they define their needs and satisfactions.[61] This is the preceptoral strategy. For example, sexism may be perceived as less a matter of overt discrimination by government or the private sector than it is a question of the values men and women have internalized.[62] Women may not be denied access to jobs, participation in politics, or equality in the home by the explicit discriminatory acts of men; rather women do not seek to fill "men's roles" because they have been socialized to believe that it is not women's place to assume them. Men fill these roles because they have been socialized to do so.

Marcuse argues that advanced capitalist society tends to reduce consciousness of oppression, reinforce the status quo, and avoid revolutionary change by instituting "new, more effective, and more pleasant forms of social control and social cohesion":

> In this society, the productive apparatus tends to become totalitarian to the extent which it undermines not only the socially needed occupations, skills, and attitudes, but also individual needs and aspirations. It thus obliterates the opposition between the private and public existence, between individual and social needs. . . .
>
> In the medium of technology, culture, politics, and the economy merge into an omnipresent system which swallows up or repulses all alternatives. . . .
>
> One-dimensional thought is systematically promoted by the makers of politics and their purveyors of mass information. Their universe of discourse is populated by self-validating hypotheses which, incessantly and monopolistically repeated, become hypnotic definitions or dictations. . . .[63]

In short, according to Marcuse, the communications efforts of the government and the private sector, the productive systems and the culture, acting in harmony, combine to impose ideological blinders

60. Jacques Ellul, *The Technological Society* (New York: Knopf, 1964); Jacques Ellul, *Propaganda* (New York: Knopf, 1965); Herbert Marcuse, *One-Dimensional Man* (Boston: Beacon Press, 1964); C. Wright Mills, *Power, Politics and People* (New York: Ballantine Books, 1953).

61. See, e.g., Marcuse, *One-Dimensional Man* ch. 1.

62. Marcuse, *One-Dimensional Man* 12.

63. *Id.* at xv, xvi, 14.

through a process of repression that closes the individual's political universe and stifles intellectual and political freedom.

In some ways, the arguments of the polemicists are reminiscent of the old propaganda theories, at least insofar as they assume the efficacy of government communications and the mass media in terms of shaping individual thought and behavior. In this regard, they ignore the complexities in communications networks and espouse simple, static, causal (one-way) relationships that do not comport with modern realities. On the other hand, they build on the intuitively appealing proposition that values, attitudes, and behavior do not come out of the air, and if social science cannot disentangle the various influences on the individual, perhaps this is because the processes of influence are too complex and the variables too numerous for current social science methodologies. If values and attitudes are widely shared, if the various powerful communicators are in agreement on fundamentals, if persuasion is a gradual process over an extended period of time, communication may be quite powerful, even if scientific proof is likely to be lacking in the near or distant future. In this sense, the polemicists' view may not be inconsistent with modern communications theory, particularly as articulated by such sensitive social scientists as Wilbur Schramm.[64]

The polemical approach to persuasive or coercive communications has both interesting and amusing features. It is most often advanced by those with a well-developed ideological framework for viewing and interpreting the world (one suspects that this is a group not very susceptible to persuasion by the forces they decry). The rejection of their ideology by the polity and most citizens, however, leads to a pervasive hostility to the polity and to the status quo. Little thought is given to the fact that any culture, community, or system of economic and political arrangements has its own set of fundamental principles, which are taken for granted and daily reinforced. These multiple variables may shape elite attitudes, behavior, and communications every bit as much as the elite influences others. Furthermore, if the need for social cohesion is recognized at all, the polemicists seek to achieve it through the recognition of their own fundamental principles, principles they deem superior to those currently and widely accepted. They tend to be highly paternalistic: they know what is right for the rest of us. If we choose *their* principles, we are acting freely. If we opt for principles inconsistent with their views, we are repressed, our true natures and preferences overwhelmed by the pervasive patterns of indoctrination. As Robert Wolff puts it,

The radical impulse feeds on a faith in the natural goodness of the people. If the state is permitted to act wickedly, it must be

64. Compare Schramm, "Nature of Communication," with Marcuse, *One-Dimensional Man.*

because the people are in chains. If there are no visible chains, then there must be invisible chains of ignorance or a habit of servitude. If the people are not tyrannized, it must be that they have been brainwashed.[65]

At bottom, the real weakness in the polemicists' ideological view of government communication, culture, politics, economics, and the mass media (apart from the absence of empirical support for their supposi- tions about the communications powers of government and business leaders) is that in erecting a structure to explain public and elite ac- quiescence to things as they are, they have largely destroyed the hope for change. Why is it that the beer-drinking blue-collar worker, glued to televised sporting events, does not feel the need for radical change or revolution to overthrow modern industrial capitalism? How is it that he dares to be happy or to remain confident about the American system of government and the opportunities that it affords? Answer: He has been hopelessly brainwashed to think that he is happy and that things are right. He cannot recognize oppression when he sees it. But if this is true, what is to be the source of change? What will enable the individual to overcome his own mind-set—to stand apart from his own psyche, as it were? In the absence of a cataclysmic national crisis of war or depression, why should people who think they are free, who think that they are making choices, and who think that fundamental American values are sound, reject their political, social, and economic arrangements?

If the problem is thought to be one of education, who will do the educating (persuasion)? How will the culture produce the cadre of teachers who, having a clear vision of the New Jerusalem, will spread the word? Why should we expect the public, or groups within the larger public, to be receptive? Recall the discussion of modern communications research, and the conclusion that people are obstinate and difficult to persuade where messages contradict well-established and deeply held opinions and attitudes. If education is a public enterprise, as it is to a considerable extent, are such institutions likely to propagate values so antithetical to widely accepted norms and fundamentals? Government surely is not the answer; for presumably, from Marcuse's perspective, it has the greatest interest in maintaining the status quo and contributing to the objectionable socialization and communications processes.

The question of whether federal or state government agencies can or should place limits on the communications activities of other govern- ment agencies is virtually unintelligible for the ideological polemicists. Governments are but a part of a totality that is the source of the repression that, assertedly, should be overcome. Thus, in the end, the

65. Robert Paul Wolff, *The Rule of Law* 23 (New York: Simon & Schuster, 1971).

polemicists' explanation of the status quo and the assumptions about psychic coercion in the society give rise to hopelessness. The enemy is not the military, the capitalists, the employers, the unions, the mass media, or even government officials in any immediate sense: the enemy is ourselves; for those entities have manipulated our minds to accept their wisdom. But in facing ourselves, defeat is inevitable.

The polemicists' view of the world of indoctrination and communication is overdrawn and too catastrophic. As their own writings attest, not everyone is drawn to the dominant cultural, political, and economic values. Pluralism is a matter of degree. Changes do take place in modern industrial states, some of them peaceful and some of them violent. Scholars such as Ruth Benedict and Roberto Unger are closer to the truth when they perceive the individual as defining himself and his goals within the broader traditions of the community, while change and progress are inevitably the result of some tension between the individual and the group.[66] There is an accretion process by which individuals are socialized and the rules of the game laid down, but this does not necessarily imply that such individuals are so victimized by psychic coercion that they may not be viewed as engaging in choice.

On the other hand, there is intuitive appeal in the notion that governments and some private institutions often attempt to manipulate the processes of consent, and that such efforts may not be wholly unavailing. Present knowledge is insufficient to unravel the mysteries of the communications process, the etiology of belief structures, and the line between persuasion and coercion. But, given the risks of government expression for the ideal of the self-controlled citizen, wisdom dictates attentiveness to all sources of limitation of government communications powers, both intrinsic and extrinsic to communications processes. The aspiration, again, should be the creation of a structure for government and nongovernment communication that enhances autonomy, choice, and respect for the person. The next chapter argues that a deliberately fostered pluralism contributes to such a structure. A stable of power centers that speak independently of government provides the self-controlled citizen with a choice of harmonies to which he can add his own voice. When sufficient numbers of individual voices join in chorus, governments may hear and respond.

66. Ruth Benedict, *Patterns of Culture* (Boston: Houghton Mifflin, 1959); Roberto Unger, *Knowledge and Politics* (New York: Free Press, 1975).

[6]

Government Expression and the Pluralist Faith

Introduction

Classic First Amendment theory generally fails to deal with questions of government falsification of majorities through leadership, education, persuasion, secrecy, and information dissemination. The assumption that communication is a static, one-way process—from the people to their leaders—tends to focus attention on the private sector and to assume that democratic government is functionally dependent on diversity among private communicators as citizens strive to acquire knowledge to evaluate the performance of government. Recall Madison's often quoted remark about the relationship between "popular information" and "popular government."

> A popular government, without popular information or the means of acquiring it, is but a prologue to a farce or a tragedy; or perhaps both. Knowledge will forever govern ignorance. And a people who mean to be their own governors, must arm themselves with the power knowledge gives.[1]

Note the difficulties in applying this formulation to a twentieth-century democracy. It is by no means clear that there is some inevitability about knowledge governing ignorance, particularly given the evidence as to how badly informed the masses of people are. The information of which Madison speaks seems infinitely manageable, bearing little relationship to the barrage of messages and information that modern men and women must somehow order. No concern is expressed that only government may be able to accumulate and disseminate certain types

1. Gaillard Hunt, ed., 9 *The Writings of James Madison* 103 (New York: G. P. Putnam and Sons, 1910).

of information (for example, in foreign affairs or nuclear policy), and yet it is precisely that information citizens are to employ to arm themselves against their governors. No provision is made for the use of governmental communications as a method of carrying out government policy. There is no suggestion that government and nongovernment expression mutually affect each other, changing the behavior, goals, and messages of each participant in a continuous mutual feedback process. There is no intimation that the government may address the populace in ways likely to distort their judgment. No fear is expressed that democratic consent may be "manufactured by official press agents."[2] In short, Madison was simply not confronted with the complexity of modern communication and the massive participation of governments in communications networks.

In groping for solutions to the dilemma of government speech, one promising approach is to extend the American tradition (or perhaps aspiration) of pluralism to it. In an era of mass communications organizations, pluralism may be perceived as responsive to the institutional basis of modern communications networks: "In pluralist democracy . . . the guiding principle is not 'one man-one vote' but rather, 'every group its share.'"[3] Structuring institutional interactions, then, is as important as tolerance of individual expression. In Madisonian fashion, powerful communicators should be played off against one another, preventing any one group or elite from gaining ideological dominance. Governments should be pitted against one another in the wars of words and symbols, and government communications generally should be subject to the counterforce of communications emanating from a healthy, diverse, and pluralistic private sector. This is consistent with a reaffirmation of traditional expression and associational activities. Disequilibrium, flux, tolerance, and change are to be cherished—only the recognition of government participation need be added to the formula. Such recognition may require acquiescence in the accumula-

2. C. Wright Mills, *Power, Politics and People* 573 (New York: Ballantine Books, 1953).

3. Robert Paul Wolff, *The Poverty of Liberalism* 131 (Boston: Beacon Press, 1968). See, generally, Henry Kariel, *The Decline of American Pluralism* (Stanford, Calif.: Stanford University Press, 1961); Theodore Lowi, *The End of Liberalism* (New York: Norton, 1969); Andrew McFarland, *Power and Leadership in Pluralist Systems* (Stanford, Calif.: Stanford University Press, 1969); Nelson W. Polsby, *Community Power & Political Theory* (New Haven, Conn.: Yale University Press, 1980); Robert Dahl, *Who Governs?* (New Haven, Conn.: Yale University Press, 1961); Raymond E. Wolfinger, *The Politics of Progress* (Englewood Cliffs, N.J.: Prentice-Hall, 1974); Charles Lindblom, *The Intelligence of Democracy* (New York: Free Press, 1965); Robert Dahl and Charles Lindblom, *Politics, Economics and Welfare* (New York: Harper & Row, 1963); Grant McConnell, *Private Power and American Democracy* (New York: Knopf, 1966); C. Wright Mills, *The Power Elite* (New York: Oxford University Press, 1956); Phillip Green and Sanford Levinson, eds., *Power and Community: Dissenting Essays in Political Science* (New York: Pantheon Books, 1970); Robert Dahl, *Pluralist Democracy in the United States* (Chicago: Rand McNally, 1967).

tion of communications powers in the private sector (television networks, news services, multinational corporations) which would be intolerable in the private sector alone, but are quite desirable when juxtaposed with the power of governments, particularly the federal government. And it would dictate a presumption against government secrecy, since secrecy is a powerful weapon in the communications process. Except in the most compelling circumstances, government should be denied the power to deliberate in secret, close its institutions to public scrutiny, and withhold information vital to evaluating its performance.

Critiques of Pluralism

Market Failure and Government Intervention

But the efficacy of pluralism in combatting the excesses of the powerful in a world in which power is not randomly or equally distributed has been severely criticized in recent decades. The whole notion of a marketplace appears to many to be an illusion of the liberal state, dependent upon a blind faith in equality and a hazy ontology obfuscating the real world processes of persuasion and domination. There is, to be sure, a mysterious and paradoxical quality to the pluralist faith. Consider the tendency in many markets—of goods, facts, or ideas—for oligopoly to develop. Why, then, should it not develop in the communications market? The concentration of power in the print and broadcast media and in corporations generally may be evidence of oligopoly. And what of the market power of the affluent, who can afford to disperse their messages more widely, have the knowledge about the available channels of communication, and know how to secure free coverage from other powerful communicators? Market failure is the basic contention behind Robert Wolff's observation that "pluralism always favors the groups in existence against those in the process of formulation." While pluralism is not premised on a philosophy of inequality, its "*concrete application* supports inequality by ignoring the existence of certain legitimate social groups."[4]

If pluralism falters, it is natural to look to government to provide the opportunities and resources to those who find it difficult to be heard. This is the "referee" theory of pluralism:

> The . . . "referee" theory . . . asserts that the role of the central government is to lay down ground rules for conflict and competition among private associations and to employ its power to

---

4. Wolff, *Poverty of Liberalism* 152, 154. See, generally, Charles Lindblom, *Politics and Markets* (New York: Basic Books, 1977).

make sure that no major interest in the nation abuses its influence
or gains an unchecked mastery over some sector of social life.[5]

But government may be a poor referee. If those who control private-
sector communications also control government communications and
members of the same elites shuffle back and forth between government and private employment, government is likely to reinforce only a
particular set of compatible values in the name of pluralism. There
would be pluralism only in the sense of a multitude of speakers, not in
the sense of a multitude of points of view. Think of the familiar
scenario in which government regulatory agencies are captured by the
industries they are ostensibly charged with regulating. Do we associate
government regulation of markets designed to approximate the outcomes of the marketplace (by curing market failures) with competition? This is essentially the criticism of pluralism propounded by Henry
Kariel, whose analysis argues for great caution in entrusting pluralism
in communications networks to government.[6] Indeed, Ronald Coase,
arguing from a related set of premises, urges that the free "marketplace of ideas" should be emulated in markets for goods and services.[7]

The curiosity of government promotion of pluralism is compounded
further once government's massive participation in communications
activities is taken into account. It is as if the federal government were to
seek to promote competition among automobile manufacturers, while
itself the nation's largest producer of automobiles. The problem is not so
much capture by those regulated, as promotion of the government's
product at the expense of competitors. Can the "referee" be fair-
minded when it has such an interest in the outcome of the process? Is it
not paradoxical to ask government to promote competition among
information sources and ideas when it is among the dominating forces,
seeking to diminish the persuasive power of other points of view by
advocating its own views? Government success in promoting pluralism
may diminish its capacity to govern and promote particular policy
choices. Can government, then, be trusted to decide how well the
communications market is operating? Do not public officials consistently complain that the private media distort their positions? In short,
is it plausible to expect democratic governments and officeholders to
act in unselfish, self-limiting ways? C. S. Lewis probed the core of this
issue when he asked "whether 'democratic behavior' means the behavior that democracies like or the behavior that will preserve a
democracy."[8]

5. *Id.* at 128.   6. Kariel, *Decline of American Pluralism.*
7. Ronald Coase, "Adam Smith's View of Man," 19 *Journal of Law and Economics* 529
(1976).
8. C. S. Lewis, *The Screwtape Letters* 161 (New York: Macmillan, 1962).

Government participation intrudes in still another way. There may be times when there can be no effective response to a particular government message—even where pluralism is thought to exist. The message is so distorting of judgment, the government's access to information so unique, and the point of action or judgment so close in time that contrary messages will be of no avail. In a particular context, the government may have great credibility as a communicator, and the audience may be so caught off guard that reality testing is near impossible. There is the temptation, under such circumstances, to envision restraints on government rhetoric. But what standards will be utilized? Who will make the necessary determinations? Who will do the restraining? How? Paradoxically, the temptation is to rely on the government agency itself or some other level or branch of government (federal judiciary, Congress) to perform the task in the name of the whole body politic. But this appears as idealistic as government regulation of the private sector to further the cause of those unequally situated in communications markets. Each branch or agency of government may seek an advantage over other public institutions—for example, by withholding information or supplying misleading or deceptive information.[9]

These criticisms of pluralism are largely empirical and descriptive questions as to whether pluralism, in fact, has been achieved. That individuals are not members of groups with powerful voices, that many go unrepresented in the pluralist process, or that established groups and the status quo are favored by existing pluralism is not necessarily an indication that the pluralist aspiration is bankrupt. The calls for "countervailing power" and the formation of various consumer and political interest groups (for example, Common Cause and Ralph Nader's consumer organizations) may be treated as responses to the crisis in the "concrete application" of pluralist principles. A suitable

9. Lest this be thought a "worst-case" example beyond the realm of possibility, consider the discussion of *Holtzman* v. *Schlesinger*, 484 F.2d 1307 (2d Cir. 1973), *rev'g* 361 F.Supp. 553 (E.D.N.Y.), in Edward Sherman, "Legal Inadequacies and Doctrinal Restraints in Controlling the Military," 49 *Indiana Law Journal* 539, 552-553. The court of appeals held that the legality of bombing and other military activities in Cambodia presented a political and not a justiciable question. Judge Oakes in dissent argued that the executive had exceeded his power in ordering military activities, because Congress had not consented. While recognizing that Congress's power to declare war could be implied from "authorization of appropriations with knowledge of our 'presence' in Cambodia," Oakes said, "for authorization . . . by way of an appropriation to be effective, the congressional action must be based on a knowledge of the facts" (484 F.2d at 1316). "Incredibly enough, it appears that neither the American people nor the Congress . . . were given the facts. . . . Air Force B-52 bombers were secretly attacking Cambodia in 1969, 1970 and even later while the United States was publicly proclaiming respect for Cambodian neutrality" (484 F.2d at 316-317). See, generally, Arthur Schlesinger, *The Imperial Presidency* ch. 10 (Boston: Houghton Mifflin, 1973).

response, in other words, may be to repair or reorder the system, even admitting the dangers of putting government in charge of such an enterprise. This may be done by public or, less dangerously, private initiative. But the answer to these criticisms is not less pluralism, but more. The need is not for simpler systems, but for more parts and greater complexity.

Market Failure and Democratic Theory:
Is Corporate Capitalism Incompatible with Democracy?

Suppose not only that market failure in the quest for pluralism has occurred, but that democracies are inherently incapable of creating the conditions to take corrective action while adhering to democratic principles. This is essentially the thesis of Charles E. Lindblom in his recent provocative and influential work, *Politics and Markets: The World's Political-Economic Systems*.[10] Lindblom's analysis is sophisticated and subtle, and is not dependent on the vulgar Marxist credo that capitalists are evil and run the government for their own good. As Wildavsky summarizes Lindblom's thesis, "business is uniquely and disproportionately privileged" in market-oriented democracies. The reason for this is that business performs essential economic functions. "In short, the business of government is the economy, and the economy is run by business."[11] If the economy is to be viable in a democratic private-enterprise system, business must largely get what it wants from the government, which is inconsistent with democratic accountability and pluralism. If business does not get what it wants, democracy will flourish at the expense of recession or stagnation.[12]

Lindblom spells out these ideas in great detail, in an interlocking set of arguments. He starts with the premise that corporate executives in all private-enterprise systems make highly significant decisions about "a nation's industrial technology, the pattern of work organization, location of industry, market structure, resource allocation," and other matters. Despite some government regulation, they get to determine what is to be produced and in what quantities, and ultimately this gives them enormous influence over prices, jobs, economic growth rates, standards of living, and economic security. Thus a businessman is a "kind of public official," exercising a broad array of public functions. And government, far from controlling corporations, must induce them to carry out those functions in order to make sure that they are

10. Lindblom, *Politics and Markets*.
11. Aaron Wildavsky, "Book Review: Lindblom, *Politics and Markets*" 88 *Yale Law Journal* 217, 223 (1979).
12. Lindblom, *Politics and Markets* 177-187, 202-213. See also Wildavsky, "Book Review" 225.

satisfactorily performed.[13] Given this power configuration, businessmen and their corporations are not simply another interest group competing with labor unions, churches, foundations, and other elements of
the private sector:

> In the eyes of government officials, therefore, businessmen do
> not appear simply as representatives of a special interest. . . . They
> appear as functionaries performing functions that government
> officials regard as indispensable. When a government official
> asks himself whether business needs a tax reduction, he knows he
> is asking a question about the welfare of the whole society and
> not simply about a favor to a segment of the population.[14]

Government leaders need not be bribed to grant corporations privileges; rather they need only recognize the need for collaboration to
make the system work. And collaboration often requires deference not
afforded to other groups in an avowedly pluralistic, market-oriented
system.[15]

The result is that government and corporations do not debate the
fundamentals of their "symbiotic relationship"—questions concerning
the normative value of private enterprise and the need for business
autonomy and private property are taken off the agenda of policy
making and discussion and are not subjected to pluralistic controls
(competing ideas and centers of power). The government-business relationship is reflected in ease of access to government leaders, political
contributions, disproportionate influence in interest group and party
politics, and participation in legislative deliberations. This in itself
circumvents normal electoral processes; for "the particular demands
that businessmen make on government are communicated to government officials in ways other than through the electoral process and are
largely independent of and often in conflict with the demands that the
electorate makes."[16] But, according to Lindblom, the influence of corporations penetrates deeper by successfully indoctrinating citizens so
that they will not express positions, in the voting booth or elsewhere,
contrary to the prevailing free-enterprise norms:

> Consider the possibility that businessmen achieve an indoctrina-
> tion of citizens so that citizens' volitions serve not their own
> interests but the interests of businessmen. Citizens then become
> allies of businessmen. *The privileged position of business comes to be*

13. *Id.* at 171-175. See Wildavsky, "Book Review" 223; Charles Anderson, "The
Political Economy of Charles E. Lindblom," 72 *American Political Science Review* 1012, 1014
(1978).
14. Lindblom, *Politics and Markets.*
15. *Id.*
16. *Id.* at 172, 179-180, 190-202, 205. But cf. Polsby, *Community Power.*

widely accepted. In electoral politics, no great struggle need [sic] to be fought. Circularity of this kind is a particular, a specific, possibility in polyarchy.[17]

Pluralism then becomes a farce, as corporations dominate opinion and thereby "remove grand issues from politics." Corporations need not seek affirmation of their values, but only "political silence on them." But the farce is not a result of a failure of will on the part of citizens and government: it is endemic to market-oriented democracies, in which businessmen must be privileged.

Business coopts and indoctrinates citizens and government through the "torrent of corporate communications addressed to the citizen on grand issues and not effectively challenged by any comparable contending communication."[18] Lindblom rejects, virtually out of hand, the notion that citizens may fail to succumb to this indoctrination due to the inefficacy of mass communications. There is, he asserts, not "a shred of evidence" to support this benign view:

> Corporations employ all possible methods, overt and covert. The source of their communications is usually obscure. The message usually reaches the citizens indirectly in a news story or broadcast, a magazine article, a film, an editorial, a political speech, or a conversation. Only a small part of it comes explicitly from a business source.
>
> The skeptic may believe, however, that most of the corporate message on the grand issues is transmitted through the mass media, which, he will claim, is relatively ineffective in changing volitions. *Some research evidence refutes him.* . . . A presidential campaign lasting five months, in which conflicting propaganda from the two parties cross-pressured the voters, was measured as achieving a switch of parties for 5 percent of those studied. If that is so, the cumulative effect of propaganda can be great indeed if it is only infrequently challenged by counter-propaganda and persists not for five months but for the lifetime of the citizen. *Nothing in the research literature on the mass media establishes any ground for doubting its effectiveness.*[19]

But, as discussed earlier, the research evidence does cast doubt on the efficacy of particular messages emanating from particular centers of power. As if to anticipate this, Lindblom argues that the task of businessmen in achieving indoctrination is rendered easier because they confirm existing volitions and do not require the citizen to "stir himself."

17. *Id.* at 202 (emphasis added).   18. *Id.* at 204-206.
19. *Id.* at 206 (emphasis added).

> [The corporations usually ask] . . . no more than that the citizen
> continue to believe what he has already since childhood been
> taught to believe. Early, persuasive, unconscious conditioning
> . . . to believe in the fundamental politico-economic institutions
> of one's society is ubiquitous in every society. These institutions
> come to be taken for granted. . . . When that happens, as is
> common, processes of critical judgment are short circuited. . . .
> In their attempts to influence the volitions of the citizenry, busi-
> nessmen often need do little more than evoke deeply embedded
> sentiments.[20]

Thus business privilege exists, is inevitable, and is supported by a
thoroughgoing indoctrination which appeals to already "embedded
sentiments." The interests of business are inextricably meshed with the
fundamental beliefs of American society, and to deny the success of
corporate indoctrination is virtually to deny the existence of *any* fundamental beliefs in the populace.[21]

Where to begin in this assault on the character of pluralism in
market-oriented democracies? Lindblom's argument is neat, logical,
self-contained—and probably wrong. This does not necessarily deny
that businessmen may be powerful—perhaps too powerful—in exert-
ing influence. Lindblom has simply overstated the nature and inevitability of their privileges. To begin with a lower order of criticism, it is
far from clear that corporations are as privileged as Lindblom asserts.
Charles Anderson rightly notes that Lindblom's portrayal of corporate
power "would not advance the argument in the eyes of an observer as
yet uncommitted to one of the standard orthodoxies. The case is overdrawn."[22] What of the fact that there is increasing public distrust of
business leadership? The business community often sees itself on the
defensive, resorting to public advertising where lobbying behind closed
doors used to suffice. What of the array of environmental, consumer,
and populist groups opposing business policies?[23] What of the fact "that
the prerogatives of corporations are being whittled down as they are
compelled to provide a variety of social services opposed to their
profit-making purposes?"[24] Lindblom's case for inordinate corporate
power is debatable, and the notion that corporate power is unique in
market-oriented democracies is also questionable:

> [Lindblom's] claim is that corporate power is distinctive and its
> public role unique. The labor union does not perform a public
> role like the corporation but rather has a purely private, or
> "factional" function. This is certainly an arguable proposition.

20. *Id.* at 207 (emphasis added).   21. See *id.* at 211-212.
22. Anderson, "Political Economy" 1015.   23. *Id.* at 1014-1015.
24. Wildavsky, "Book Review" 225.

The capacity of organized labor to sustain or to thwart macro-economic policy is a staple of contemporary political economic commentary. The idea that the trade union does not play a crucial role in public planning and policy making would certainly seem surprising to a Scandinavian or a Briton.

It is interesting to note that earlier in his career Lindblom made a case quite similar to the present one for the distinctive power of another political economic institution, and on that occasion, it was precisely the trade union that was the cause of his concern. In 1949, Lindblom saw a shift of power in the direction of big labor, on the grounds of its unique political advantages. Union leaders would be pushed by their followers to interfere with the market, creating rigidities and inflation.[25]

The Lindblom analysis, then, is vulnerable on empirical grounds. He generally seeks to prove only by assertion. To be sure, corporations in the United States are powerful. But his argument that their power is different in kind from other sources of power, and hence unique, is not compelling. For example, my impression, consistent with Anderson's, is that the business community is more on the defensive than ever.[26] It has resorted to advertisements about its search for energy, its gentleness with the environment, the impossibility of life without chemicals, the need to continue or discontinue government regulation, and the nonbusiness sources of inflation precisely because it is perceived as acting irresponsibly—the old interest-group politics is not working as well. Furthermore, the case for unique power can be, and has been, made for other groups, such as government, the mass media, labor unions, foundations, professionals, and single-issue interest groups.

Lindblom also places little stock in disputes within the business community (in large part because of the nature of the grand issues) and between government and corporations.[27] For him, these are superficial cracks, not negating his basic thesis. But how does one know that all or most corporations usually get their way with government? It is a mistake to equate the power of corporations to exercise a veto in one instance with sweeping claims for their overall power to veto in most instances.

The question of who controls the economy might first be approached by asking whether concrete manifestations of corporate power are actually to be found. One place Lindblom located them is in the alleged corporate veto over major matters of collective action. Do such vetoes exist? They do and they must.

25. Anderson, "Political Economy" 1015.
26. *Id.* at 1014-1015.
27. Lindblom, *Politics and Markets* 178-179.

Unless corporations are to lose on every try, they must stop some things that they do not like; since they are often divided on subjects such as free trade and oil prices, some corporations must veto, and some fail to veto, some of the time. *Actually, there are an enormous number of vetoes in our political system, creating a mirage of obstruction when there is really momentous movement. . . . In the past decade, because of the popularity of social policies, this pattern—many more policies accompanied by an even greater number of vetoes [over proposed policies]— has accompanied the growth of the welfare state.*[28]

The evidence of corporate privilege as a unique privilege in democracies is weak, since so many groups exercise vetoes over so many policy reforms. Short of evidence of corporate suicides, it is difficult to determine just how powerful corporations are.

Uncharacteristically, Lindblom also blunders in oversimplifying complex relationships. He presses for the efficacy of indoctrination efforts and finds that corporations continuously and successfully indoctrinate the citizenry and that government is at least sympathetic to these efforts. The fact is that not only is the efficacy of mass communications to be doubted, but in the real world of complex communications systems it is doubtful that there is a simple, one-way causal link between corporate indoctrination efforts and citizen attitudes. "If indoctrination is so successful, one wonders why business has to fight or how it ever loses."[29] Moreover, Lindblom is blind to the influence that government may have over corporations, including their perceptions of reality and values. As Wildavsky wisely remarks,

The argument to which Lindblom devotes the bulk of his book is unexceptional: the operation of government, and the actions of those who seek to influence it, depend critically "on the role of the market in political-economic life." The blind spot in this book . . . is the converse proposition: the operation of markets (and therefore corporations) depends critically on the role of government in economic life. What corporations do to government, to reverse the flow of causality, may be dependent on what government does to (or for) them.[30]

Business indoctrination is not the only variable, isolated from all others, which makes the world turn. The citizen will find in the world around him contrasting evidence. He builds a house on a site near Love Canal or perhaps near Three Mile Island. He drives cars with dangerous design defects, and is laid off when big cars stop selling and small foreign imports take over the market. Lindblom has ignored the exis-

28. Wildavsky, "Book Review" 226. See also Polsby, *Community Power.*
29. Wildavsky, "Book Review."
30. *Id.* at 221.

tence of mutually affecting relationships over time. Irate citizens spark government and corporate responses. Government, through its communications and other powers, helps to shape corporate responses, which in turn shape government messages and policies. In areas such as energy, taxation, automobile safety, environmental protection, and social services, I suspect that the corporate message has changed over the years in response to the behavior and communications of other powerful institutions, such as government and the mass media, and in response to citizen buyers' responses to those communications. Lindblom ignores these interdependencies to bolster his world view of democratic theory and behavior. And, in doing so, he has fled from complexity and change to a steady-state world: equilibrium is the inevitable triumph of corporate indoctrination; the parts of the system do not change or change other parts. Returning to Prigogine's metaphor, Lindblom is still puzzling over the Renaissance painting, ignoring the processes and conditions by which a culture produces such paintings.

The pièce de résistance of Lindblom's theory of the systemic failure of pluralism in market-oriented democracies is his equation of business indoctrination with all deeply held values in such societies. That most citizens believe in free enterprise or private property does not necessarily mean that this is a result of corporate indoctrination. There may be all sorts of socializing influences; these beliefs may simply be a by-product of other socializing forces. This is a chicken-and-egg problem, to which Lindblom gives no satisfactory answer:

> Can we expect, however, any society to debate its own fundamentals? Has there even been one that did? Can we not dismiss the evidence of constrained volitions on grand issues by acknowledging that all societies are marked by a core of common belief? They are indeed. . . .
>
> But our purpose is not to show that volitions on grand issues are constrained in the polyarchies and not in other systems. It is to show that they are constrained to a significant degree even in the polyarchies. . . . They therefore introduce, for good or bad, a significant circularity into popular control through polyarchy.[31]

This response gives away the game. If the etiology of indoctrination to the "grand issues" is unclear, how significant is it to say that volitions are constrained even in polyarchies? Who among us denies that volitions are constrained in democratic nations? That there is not strong indoctrination to the status quo? The world is not perfect, and there are underlying values even in the most pluralistic societies that are difficult to get people to reexamine and debate: "That indoctrination

---

31. Lindblom, *Politics and Markets* 211.

exists, no one can deny. None of us can jump out of our skins, free of influence from surrounding social forces."[32]

Lindblom is a victim of the same circularity that he observes in democratic pluralism. The existence of ingrained values and the accompanying constraints on volition somehow become evidence of corporate power and successful indoctrination. He fails to separate the part from the whole: to accept the existence of *any* indoctrination is to accept his thesis about corporate indoctrination. In the last analysis, what disturbs him is that constrained volitions are inconsistent with his view of pluralism:

> Constrained volitions are of special importance in polyarchal systems because of their aspirations to popular control. But what is critical, then, is not existence of core beliefs, but how the constraint is achieved—by whom or what, around what issues and why. . . . We should take note that at least hypothetically it is possible for a society to converge on a set of unifying volitions on grand issues that does not have its origins in a privileged position of any of that society's groups. To repeat, then, the significance of constrained volitions in the market-oriented polyarchies is that they are constrained in a particular way. The constraints are not consistent with the democratic theory or ideology often invoked to justify these systems. In the polyarchies, core beliefs are the product of a rigged, lopsided competition of ideas.[33]

The point is that one *can* deny, even hypothetically, that a society can converge on core beliefs without any "privileged" groups playing a role in this. Perhaps it all depends on what one means by privileged. But if privilege means influence, then in every pluralistic society one would expect some groups to be more privileged and powerful than others. Why should one assume that every group should contribute equally in acculturation processes? Are not parents and churches and peer groups privileged in this sense? Lindblom is too wrapped up in the idea of completely unconstrained volitions (as if that were possible) in democratic societies making claims to popular rule. If this is the case, the problem may lie more in a static theory than in fluid reality.[34]

Indeed, Lindblom implicitly recognizes this flaw in his attempt to mesh fact and theory:

> Constrained volitions are not an important phenomenon when set beside the control of public opinion in authoritarian systems.

32. Wildavsky, "Book Review" 230.
33. Lindblom, *Politics and Markets* 211-212.
34. See Anderson, "Political Economy" 1015-1016.

They become so only when examined in the light of democratic aspiration. In human history, the design of large national governments practicing a nonviolent competition for authority in such a way that men can be free, as liberals define freedom, is as great an accomplishment as man has ever achieved. It is difficult for citizens who enjoy that freedom to remind themselves of how unequal the competition of ideas is and of how far governments still fall short of achieving a larger liberation of man's minds to accomplish the degree of popular control that only then might be possible.[35]

The achievement Lindblom acknowledges implies change, the accomplishment of something new and different under the sun. Relationships and power configurations ebb and flow. New and different demands produce new and different responses. That corporate interests have sometimes triumphed does not mean that every triumph was a blow to other interests, or that corporate interests must always triumph. There is no predetermined outcome, no equilibrium to which the system returns. Reality is a process under creation, one shaped by many forces, only one of which is corporate America.

Beyond Market Failure: Is Pluralism Normatively Bankrupt?

Lindblom accepts the ideal of a pluralistic or polyarchical society, while profoundly doubting the capacity of democratic, market-oriented nations to achieve it. Robert Wolff goes further and challenges the normative implications of pluralism itself. For Wolff, pluralism is an anachronism of the liberal state that alienates individuals by denying them a sense of community and prevents problem solving by the whole society:

> [In liberal philosophy] society continues to be viewed as a system of independent centers of consciousness, each pursuing its own gratification and confronting the others as beings standing-over-against the self. . . . The condition of the individual in such a state of affairs is what a different tradition of social philosophy would call "alienation."
>
> To deal with such problems, there must be some way of constituting the whole society as a genuine group with a group purpose and a conception of the common good. Pluralism rules this out in theory by portraying society as an aggregate of human communities rather than as itself a human community; and it equally rules out a concern for the general good in practice by encouraging a politics of interest-group pressures in which there

---

35. Lindblom, *Politics and Markets* 213.

is no mechanism for the discovery and expression of the common good.[36]

Wolff's analysis attends to the values underlying the normative commitment to pluralism. In so doing, he explores a fundamental weakness in the positions of many of the defenders of pluralism. These defenders frequently eschew reliance on values, and urge that the rightness of pluralism may be derived from objective science or an agnosticism as to ultimate values. And frequently they confuse their normative faith in pluralism with the question of the degree of pluralism in the United States. John Dewey, for example, sought to show that "the relativist theory of democracy" was premised on its relationship to science and scientific method. He reasoned that scientific analysis indicated that social consequences were the criterion people used for choosing among values, and hence that democracy was defensible because "the greatest number of people" deemed it to be so.[37] Which people and at what time is unclear: the argument has the ring of contractarian concepts without their modern subtlety. Nor is it clear by what scientific method one might determine whether an overwhelming majority supports democracy and has a reasonably uniform concept of its meaning. Science cannot validate democracy in any empirical sense. (Would a scientist rather than a philosopher have the gall to even assert the contrary?) A more powerful argument by Dewey was, perhaps, that the scientific method and democratic governing processes share essential pluralistic attributes that increase the likelihood of human progress. Edward Purcell sums up Dewey's view this way:

> Since science was clearly the most reliable method of developing human knowledge, the social organization which most closely approximated the scientific method in its governing process was the most rational and desirable form of government.
>
> "Freedom of inquiry, toleration of diverse views, freedom of communication, the distribution of what is found out to every individual as the ultimate intellectual consumer," Dewey declared, "are involved in the democratic as in the scientific method." The two were in fact analogous, and it followed that if the scientific method was the best method of intellectual advance then the democratic process was the best approach to social advance.[38]

36. Wolff, *Poverty of Liberalism* 142, 159.
37. Edward Purcell, *The Crisis of Democratic Theory* 206-207 (Lexington, Ky.: University of Kentucky Press, 1973).
38. *Id.* at 206.

Without arguing the relationship between scientific progress and pluralism, a matter hardly beyond dispute given the concept of paradigms in scientific revolutions,[39] the implicit assumption in the science-democracy analogy is that in both cases pluralism reduces the risk of factual error and therefore moves us toward factual truth. But does "social advance" depend on facts? Inherent in the concepts of advance and progress is the notion that there are progressive values. Otherwise, how are we to know whether the New Jerusalem is in sight? But to make this judgment there must be a preliminary judgment as to how to derive values, or to choose among competing values, and values are not facts. If values may be derived through rational discourse in a pluralistic environment, Dewey has unwittingly adopted a theory of natural law. This is so because it implies a belief in the inevitability of the advance of "truth." The values one holds, like the political, social, and economic "truths" themselves, are thus products of evolutionary processes. This is not only contrary to his expressed assumptions about how to derive values, but, as Dewey would admit, it may place value-derivation questions in the hands of an elite rather than in the hands of the "greatest number of people." The argument becomes circular. Democratic pluralism breeds progress and therefore progressive values, but progress itself must be measured against pluralism unless there is some independent method of deriving its value—a proposition that Dewey rejects. And even if this problem is somehow resolved, there is still the historical vision, loosely linked to science, that pluralism leads to progressively higher stages of human development.[40]

If Dewey perceived an inevitable link between progress and democracy, other pluralists have not been so deceived. With Justice Oliver Wendell Holmes as their inspiration, modern advocates of pluralism have "doubted [their] ... way to democracy."[41] The same fear that sparks hostility toward the government's communication powers, the fear of absolutism and authoritarianism, fires enthusiasm for a relativist theory of democracy. Pluralism rests on doubts about the derivation of values and the ability to know existential truths, and on the assumption that adherence to moral absolutes often corrupts authority. Intellectual relativism and moral skepticism are, in short, the foundations of democratic pluralism. For Holmes, there was no room for Dewey's naive optimism, with its underpinnings in natural law:

> From his early conviction that all absolutes and all certainties were merely delusions, Holmes was directly led to a broad social

39. See Thomas Kuhn, *The Structure of Scientific Revolutions* (Chicago: University of Chicago Press, 1970).
40. Purcell, *Crisis of Democratic Theory* 207, 211-212.
41. *Id.* at 208-209.

toleration. Since nothing was certain and since men always disagreed, [Thomas Vernor] Smith explained, Holmes concluded
that the only humanly wise and intellectually justifiable course
was to allow men as much freedom as possible while at the same
time preserving a necessary minimum of social order. Unlike the
Nazis and the neo-Thomists who sought to escape from doubt,
Holmes embraced it and made it the basis for a theory of the
open society.[42]

Indeed, Holmes's logic was carried by his followers to the point of
postulating that democracy does not allow for agreement on fundamentals.

There is much wisdom in the relativist defense of democratic pluralism. It is easily connected with the view, expressed most recently by
Robert Bork, that the majority defines truth, but that liberal political
values must be protected to enable the majority to change its mind.[43]
And, emphasizing the element of skepticism, it is consistent with the
notion that the concept of a "popular majority" is an empty one—that,
at best, majority rule signifies a process of consultation and opportunity
for consultation between the government and the citizenry. But as an
epistemology of values, the relativist justifications for democratic pluralism succeed no better than Dewey's scientism, or than end-state
theories of community and natural law. The reason is that the pluralist
faith, far from being agnostic about values and outcomes, contains
within it several assumptions about the nature of the ideal or desirable
political community.

First, the very structure of pluralism suggests, as Wolff has noted,
an emphasis on conflict rather than on community. Carefully channeled
conflict is desirable, for it defines aims. Communitarian values, aspiring to a subjective reason in which means and ends mesh, are implicitly
rejected. The emphasis may also be on tolerance of groups and not
individuals: "If it is good for each individual to conform to some social
group and good as well that a diversity of social groups be welcomed in
the community at large, then one can consistently urge group tolerance
and individual intolerance."[44]

Second, it is clear that competition and conflict must be limited and
channeled in the pluralistic model. Otherwise, civil war and political
and social disintegration are likely. In other words, there are rules of
the game that constrain competition among interests, and these rules
must be abided by if democracy is to survive. This suggests, at a

42. *Id.* at 209. See Wolff, *Poverty of Liberalism.*
43. Bork, "Neutral Principles and Some First Amendment Problems," 47 *Indiana Law
Journal* 1 (1971).
44. Wolff, *Poverty of Liberalism* 149.

minimum, a diluted sense of community in which the various groups share such values as the need to abide by election results, the need to resolve disputes peacefully, the need to limit forms of influence on legislators (e.g., bribery), and so on. Groups that decline to abide by these premises will be treated as illegitimate and outside the scope of pluralism. And these shared values need to be passed on and nurtured in new generations if the society is to regenerate itself. The relativist view, if taken seriously, would lead to anarchy, and not to pluralism—unless one has an inherent faith that children are born with democratic instincts and common understandings.

Third, treatment of the government as a mere referee in pluralist society may rest not only on the assumption that government intervention may diminish competition, but also on the assumption that government initiatives may create conflict where none previously existed. Such governmentally inspired conflict might undercut the rules of the game that make pluralism an acceptable method for resolving policy issues.

Finally, pluralism may rest on the assumption that there are limits of scale on groups that can create a sense of community in individuals and prevent alienation. In the modern welfare state, with its huge bureaucracies and distant governments, it is unrealistic—except in the most diluted sense of the notion of community—to speak of constituting a community of the whole society. As Robert Nisbet and others have urged, the importance of mediating institutions—families, churches, corporations, unions, clubs, etc.—increases with the increasing scale of government institutions.[45] And such mediating institutions not only serve the purposes of pluralism and work to eliminate alienation, they may also act as a buffer against the excesses of overreaching government. At the very least, they provide zones of privacy and solitude that may enhance human development and achievement. This strength of pluralism effectively rebuts the normative criticism of Robert Wolff, who failed to recognize it. The effort to constitute a community of the whole[46] may result in the very forms of alienation that he identifies with the liberal state and pluralism. Further, there may already exist a diluted sense of community—enough to allow us to reinforce democratic values and to respond to crises that threaten the entire polity—sufficient to address broad policy issues without undergoing the trauma of aspiring to the community of the whole. With Holmes, one may worry about the implications of a stronger sense of community for democratic values.

45. See, e.g., Robert Nisbet, *The Quest for Community* (New York: Oxford University Press, 1953).
46. Wolff, *Poverty of Liberalism* ch. 5.

There are, then, values implicit in democratic pluralism. Tolerance is preferable to intolerance, community in small groups is preferable to alienation in the society at large, diversity is preferable to lockstep unity, individual freedom is preferable to subservience, civility is preferable to violence, majoritarian processes are preferable to dictatorship. Pluralism embodies a statement about the nature of the good life and a just society, and a formula for achieving those ends. It offers no metaphysical or even consensual or contractarian proof of its validity: it is an appeal to ethics and a commentary on history. And in its spaciousness, it does not preordain how conflicting values are to be adjusted: it provides only guideposts. Pluralism then involves a considerable degree of faith and consensus on first principles, and we are unlikely to penetrate its mysteries beyond explicit recognition of those principles:

> "Impenetrability! That's what I say!"
> "Would you tell me, please," said Alice, "what that means?"
> ". . . I meant by 'impenetrability' that we've had enough of that subject, and it would be just as well if you'd mention what you mean to do next."[47]

Living with Pluralism

Apart from epistemological questions, care must be exercised with respect to other aspects of the theory of democratic pluralism. There is the danger that existing social structures, empirically described, may be equated with the normative reach of the theory. Democracy may be "defined as the way American government . . . [works] in practice."[48] This would deny the necessity of reexamining those structures or ever altering the status quo. A concomitant danger, which is probably more likely, is that there is the temptation to assume that democratic pluralism has been achieved. The language of democratic pluralism—the analysis of its justifications and the ideology of fundamental rights—may blind us to the need to assess coldly and candidly whether the polity is tolerant of diverse points of view, whether there is an overarching orthodoxy that escapes attention, and whether political and economic power are sufficiently fragmented. Edward Purcell makes the point well:

> The major problem with the theory was not its prescriptive logic but its identification of America with the democratic ideal. Though some form of pluralism might theoretically provide a

---

47. Lewis Carroll, *Through the Looking-Glass* (New York: Macmillan, 1963).
48. Purcell, *Crisis of Democratic Theory* 256.

strong basis for democracy, that did not mean that the United States was actually pluralistic in the same theoretical sense.[49]

What this means is that we should attend less to the ideal of pluralism and more to the gap between the ideal and the reality. Success should be measured through pervasive evaluation of the strengths and weaknesses of the existing system, and not by a redefinition of the ideal. But what if the ideal is too demanding?[50] If this is the case, perhaps pluralism should be recognized as an appealing and desirable myth until something better comes along to replace it. Guido Calabresi once remarked that the law has many useful myths. For example, we may entertain the ideal that a man should never be tortured to elicit information.[51] Yet, had an accused person hidden an atomic bomb somewhere in downtown Manhattan, would we really wish to disable the police from torturing him to reveal its location? Of course not. But cases involving atomic bombs are rare. Do we then prefer policemen, prosecutors, and judges who refuse to embrace the ideal, or those who passionately do so, knowing full well that a nuclear threat might occur and that the ideal would need to be temporarily abandoned? Similarly, whom would you trust: leaders who profess loyalty to the ideal of democratic pluralism, knowing that some deviation is inevitable, or those willing to abandon it at every difficult turn in the road? And if we were to abandon pluralism, what critical theory should be adopted in its stead?[52]

The truly remarkable thing about democratic governments is the fact that they so frequently promote pluralism—sometimes through tolerance and at others by providing forums and other assistance to speakers. The protection afforded freedom of speech and association in the United States over the last fifty years is evidence of this, whatever the specific institutional arrangements for bringing about this result. The highest aspirations of pluralism may not have been met, but why do governments act in such an "unnatural" fashion, undermining their own ability to persuade? Will they continue to do so? Answers to these queries do not come easily. Fundamentally, if the communications

---

49. *Id*. at 269.

50. Anderson, "Political Economy" 1014-1015.

51. In an informal conversation, Calabresi attributed this example to Charles Black of the Yale Law School. See also Guido Calabresi, "The Problem of Malpractice: Trying to Round Out the Circle," 27 *University of Toronto Law Journal* 131, 140 (1977).

52. But see, e.g., Laurence H. Tribe, "The Puzzling Persistence of Process-Based Constitutional Theories," 89 *Yale Law Journal* 1063 (1980); Mark Tushnet, "Truth, Justice, and the American Way: An Interpretation of Public Law Scholarship in the Seventies," 57 *Texas Law Review* 1307 (1979).

powers of governments are not abused under circumstances of great temptation, this is probably a function of self-imposed limits, reflecting a democratic character or mind-set on the part of government officials, powerful elites, and perhaps the populace at large. But the culture of tolerance is fragile and of unclear etiology. The modern world is filled with counterexamples. Written constitutions do not guarantee democratic constitutions of the mind. Thus the inevitable paradox: survival of democracy in an age of vast increase in the material and communications powers of government is contingent on the willingness of leaders and institutions themselves to act in democratic ways, to encourage self-restraint and tolerate dissenting voices.

The next chapter turns from the clash of interest groups to a look inside the government machine itself, finding that internal attitudes and structures explain the tendency of government as a whole to grasp for itself less power in communications networks than is potentially within its reach.

[7]

Nonjudicial Restraints
on Government Expression

Attitudes

Perhaps the most important limits on government communication are
not functions of laws or court decisions; instead they flow from ingrained attitudes and mores, from ignorance about how to communicate
effectively to a mass audience, from political structures, and from
overlapping responsibilities of governance. Leaders in the United States
have far more opportunities to organize for propaganda purposes than
they have historically been willing to take advantage of. Despite my
earlier litany of examples, excesses have been more the exception than
the rule. With one notable exception, for example, political leaders
generally have remained aloof from the programming and editorial
policies of government-supported public broadcasting.[1] This is not true
in many democracies—France being particularly vulnerable in this
regard.[2] Despite massive federal subsidies to public schools, there is no
national program, coordinated at the top, requiring a certain form of
indoctrination in all schools and school districts. And, unlike the Soviet
Union, our government has not mobilized psychiatric institutions to
deal with dissenters.

Socialization to democratic norms and to the democratic rules of the
game may be the greatest safeguard in preserving a democratic polity.
Such attitudes and mores may be manifested in the government official's concept of what is right and wrong and perception of what will
be tolerated by the people. The absence of American counterparts to
the Nazi youth movement or Communist Chinese loudspeakers blaring

1. See, generally, 47 U.S.C. § 398 (1977), and discussion in this chapter.
2. See, generally, Ruth Thomas, *Broadcasting and Democracy in France* (London: Crosby
Lockwood Staples, 1976).

progovernment messages is probably less a function of formal legal constraints than of ingrained attitudes about the appropriate role of government. Presumably, individuals learn such norms from families, schools, and social and political organizations. The mass media, government, and other message promulgators reinforce this learning. The process by which such attitudes are formed is, however, mysterious; it is not clear how different socializing agencies contribute.[3] And the etiology of such democratic norms and their relation to culture is even more clouded. In any event, the importance of established mores and beliefs in limiting government expression can be described, even if dynamic explanatory models have not been identified.

The notion that socialization to democratic norms is a restraint on government indoctrination may strike the reader as paradoxical, especially since governments, particularly public schools, are a socializing force. Indeed the line between socialization and indoctrination is a product of what could be characterized either as socialization or indoctrination.[4] I concede that paradox. But democratic governments, as noted earlier, cannot decline to teach or lead or persuade; they are democratic to the extent to which they convey democratic values. To put the matter differently, government advertising, government publications, and government programs that consciously seek to reinforce notions of tolerance, electoral participation, government by consent, and the like need not be feared. They contribute to the establishment of a framework in which government indoctrination to "objectionable" values—there is no better way to describe them—is rendered more difficult. Thus, what seems at first blush a paradox or antinomy—a clash of conflicting truths—may really be a question of balance. The self-controlled citizen is the foundation of representative democracy, but a product of socialization. Government socialization designed to produce a self-controlled citizen able to resist the manipulation of externally imposed indoctrination lessens the danger of an engineered consent. When the aim of government is the enhancement of the self-controlled citizen, synergistic forces are brought into play. Increases in citizens' autonomy strengthen representative government, which then furthers citizens' autonomy. The two are mutually affecting and mutually enhancing.

In a circular fashion, attitudes and beliefs about the appropriate limits of government may influence leaders to communicate those attitudes and values, which may in turn be strengthened by this. Alter-

3. See, e.g., Robert Weissberg, *Political Learning, Political Choice, and Democratic Citizenship* (Englewood Cliffs, N.J.: Prentice-Hall, 1974); M. Kent Jennings and Richard Niemi, *The Political Character of Adolescence* (Princeton, N.J.: Princeton University Press, 1974).

4. Allan Winkler, *The Politics of Propaganda: The Office of War Information: 1942-45* 47 (New Haven, Conn.: Yale University Press, 1978).

natively, whatever the efficacy of such communications, they may be so consistent with what individuals already believe about political norms that their incremental effects on people are slight. Government socialization thus serves as a check on government falsification. At the same time and in the same circular fashion, the cultivation of liberal democratic values diminishes, over time, the danger of an overreaching majority.

Consistency with already established norms, even outside of the realm of democratic values, is another key to understanding the inherent limits on effective government indoctrination. Most, but by no means all, government communications seek to strengthen and channel values that are widely held and noncontroversial. Indeed, communications theory supports the idea that messages are most likely to be effective if the listener is already sympathetic to them. Thus few are likely to be outraged or much influenced by government advertising to increase the reporting of child abuse, to prevent forest fires, to acquaint unemployed youngsters with opportunities for job training, to invest in savings bonds,[5] or to provide information about social security entitlements. Further, such messages are usually consistent with policies duly enacted by legislative bodies, and are devices for making those policies work. The lines are often unclear; many people are fundamentally opposed, for example, to government training programs or to enlarging the national debt. Policy implementation cannot always be neatly disentangled from the process of creating supportive constituencies for those policies. Certainly there are other types of government messages—such as military recruitment advertisements—that may occasion greater controversy.[6] (A Government Printing Office pamphlet published months before the senate vote on ratification of the Panama Canal treaties, for example, purported to outline their "benefits for the U.S.") But in many instances the efficacy of much of what governments communicate may be undermined by the tendency to say what most already believe.

The true libertarian may be unimpressed with these inherent checks on the communications powers of government. Perhaps so-called consensus values are the very values most in need of critical public discussion. Even widely held beliefs can be utilized subtly to promote the interests of government officials. It is one thing to promote the social

5. But see "Bad News Bonds," *Time* 46 (Aug. 25, 1980). In 1979 a senior citizens lobby complained to the Federal Trade Commission that government advertisements for bonds, yielding 7 percent interest, misled investors into believing that government bond investments kept abreast of double-digit inflation. In August 1980, the Department of the Treasury agreed to change its bond advertising policies, emphasizing bonds as a good method of forced savings through payroll deductions rather than as a good investment.

6. See *Green* v. *FCC*, 447 F.2d 323 (D.C. Cir. 1971). See, generally, Peter Barnes, *Pawns: The Plight of the Citizen-Soldier* ch. 2 (New York: Knopf, 1971).

security system or the prevention of child abuse, and quite another for officialdom to congratulate itself publicly for the terrific job it is doing in these areas. Recall the Advertising Council spot broadcasts that tend to depict government agencies and officials as beneficent, caring, and competent.[7] But there are still other factors to be taken into account. People are attentive to the source of the message; for better or worse, I fear that governments face a skeptical audience. Convincing the American people that the Internal Revenue Service is more of a helping than a hurting arm of government may be a task beyond even the most accomplished propagandist. Furthermore, people may treat utterances labeled as advertisements as just that: self-promoting messages not to be accepted at face value. If anything, there appears to be a mounting distrust of government leaders and their motives,[8] a distrust nurtured by mass media that seem increasingly less deferential to political authority. And people tend to forget, to reinterpret messages as it suits them, to avoid disagreeable messages, and perhaps to ignore messages that do not contain implicit or explicit threats of sanctions for nonconformity with the norms they embody. In short, as the communications literature demonstrates, mass audiences are far from hapless victims of government expression. Persuasion techniques that appear to work well under exotic laboratory conditions are frequently of no avail in the real world of mass communications.[9]

Structural Limits

Formidable structural restraints within the political and economic system also limit effective government speech. The government does not directly control corporations or labor unions, and there are relatively few nationalized industries. While private enterprises and associations are, no doubt, subjected to a plethora of regulations, the survival of private economic entities is consistent with pluralism operating as a constraint on government communications.[10] This is one basis of interest-group politics. Equally important, the history of the mass media in this country is largely one of private ownership. While radio and television stations are subject to licensing laws and some controls, they are essentially privately owned. Public broadcasting did not develop until relatively recently, and then in a most modest fashion in comparison with the commercial networks and stations.[11] *Stars and Stripes* is not typically viewed as Washington's answer to the *New York Times* and the

7. See ch. 4.
8. See Daniel Moynihan, "Imperial Government," 65 *Commentary* 25 (1978).
9. But cf. Charles Lindblom, *Politics and Markets* 206 (New York: Basic Books, 1977).
10. Cf. *Consolidated Edison Company* v. *Public Service Commission*, 477 U.S. 530 (1980); *Central Hudson Gas* v. *Public Service Commission of New York*, 447 U.S. 557 (1980).
11. Cf. Roland Homet, "Communications Policy Making in Western Europe," 29 *Journal of Communication* 31 (1979).

Washington Post. Most of government's messages must be transmitted through the private mass media. The process of transmission inevitably alters the message—whether it appears on the front page or the editorial page.

Another structural element of the system is the balkanization of the nation (perhaps itself a misnomer in this context) into local, state, and federal governments. There are many governments, frequently divided into executive, legislative, and judicial branches, and this fragments the governing process. Fragmentation is inconsistent with the sort of single voice that appears to make government communications most effective. And it is not just a matter of numbers and geographical balkanization; for these governments increasingly have overlapping functions. Morton Grodzins noted in the mid-1960s that there were then 18,000 general-purpose municipalities, 3,000 counties, and some 92,000 tax-levying governments (including special districts of varying kinds).[12] His point, however, was not simply to emphasize the numbers, but to demonstrate that there was a substantial overlap in functions:

> The multitude of governments does not mask any simplicity of activity. There is no neat division of functions among them. If one looks closely, it appears that virtually all governments are involved in virtually all functions. More precisely, there is hardly an activity that does not involve the federal, state, and some local government in important responsibilities. Functions of the American governments are shared functions.[13]

In an arresting metaphor, Grodzins rejects the "three-layer cake" view of federalism in favor of a "marble cake" perspective:

> In fact, the American system of government as it operates is not a layer cake at all. It is not three layers of government, separated by a sticky substance or anything else. Operationally, it is a marble cake. . . . No important activity of government in the United States is the exclusive province of one of the levels, not even what may be regarded as the most national of national functions, such as foreign relations; not even the most local of local functions, such as police protection and park maintenance.[14]

The increasing complexity of intergovernmental structure and function itself constitutes a check on abuse of communications powers by any single government. There is a lack of congruence between area,

---

12. Morton Grodzins, *The American System* 3 (Chicago: Rand McNally, 1966).

13. *Id.* at 4.

14. *Id.* at 8. This is an excellent example of facing complexity and seeking order out of observations that do not fit conventional thinking patterns (see discussion of the work of Prigogine in ch. 2, above). See, generally, Todd LaPorte, *Organized Social Complexity* (Princeton, N.J.: Princeton University Press, 1975).

problem, constituency, and function. Police or transportation services in a large city, for example, may involve hundreds of government entities. Despite Grodzins's later allusion to "one government serving people for a common end,"[15] substantial coordination problems among governments with different goals and constituencies are apparent. Leadership functions and party roles are splintered in the process,[16] and policy becomes a mutually affecting relationship among many governments—each dependent on the others for the achievements of its objectives. Superimposed on all this are interest-group and electoral politics, coalition building, and the like. This jungle of governments makes speaking with one voice or even communicating successfully from the top down a much more difficult enterprise.[17] Consider, for example, the steps needed to move from a nationally articulated indoctrination program to successful indoctrination in each of the millions of classrooms in America.

Implementation

While I have found virtually no sustained treatment of the relationship between persuasive government communication and organizational theory and practice,[18] one should not be sanguine about the prospects of large-scale public and private institutions reacting favorably to messages promulgated by government agencies—either in altering behavior or transmitting the message to others unchanged by bureaucratic hands. Too frequently, we make the facile assumption that there is no distinction between altering institutional and individual behavior.[19] Often this is not the case. Policies and communications may have marginal or unintended consequences in an organizational setting. In this sense, they may operate serendipitously. Indeed, much modern implementation research is premised on the belief that laws and policies rarely have the effects intended by their promulgators (even assuming that intentions can be discerned, and that they are consistent, static,

15. Grodzins, *American System* 10.

16. See, generally, James MacGregor Burns, *Leadership* (New York: Harper & Row, 1978).

17. See, e.g., Jerome Murphy, "Title I of ESEA: The Politics of Implementing Federal Reform," 41 *Harvard Education Review* 35 (1971); Herbert Kaufman, *The Forest Ranger* (Baltimore: Johns Hopkins Press, 1967); Richard Elmore, "Organizational Models of Social Program Implementation," 26 *Public Policy* 185 (1978); Eugene Bardach, *The Implementation Game* (Cambridge, Mass.: MIT Press, 1977).

18. One exception is Everett Rogers and Rehka Agarwala-Rogers, *Communication in Organizations* (New York: Free Press, 1976).

19. But cf. Kenneth Boulding, *The Image* ch. 7 (Ann Arbor, Mich.: University of Michigan Press, 1961); Mancur Olson, *The Logic of Collective Action* (Cambridge, Mass.: Harvard University Press, 1965); Christopher Stone, *Where the Law Ends: The Social Control of Corporate Behavior* (New York: Harper & Row, 1975).

and unaffected by the choice of means).[20] Such laws and policies must, moreover, be communicated, and this introduces additional possibilities for distortion.

Consider an example with which I am familiar.[21] Rationalizing and predicting organizational behavior and choice, a pervasive problem in organizational theory,[22] is for several reasons particularly difficult for educational organizations.[23] In the first place, educational institutions are social institutions in the public sector with vague, contradictory, and often highly abstract objectives. One's view of good faith, compliance, efficacy, and other matters is likely to be a function of social values and ideology.[24] In turn, vague goals will be operationalized through a refinement process involving extensive internal and interorganizational communication, thereby enhancing the risk of distortion.

Education is also labor intensive. This mean both that implementation may depend upon the cooperation of a large number of individuals and that the technology "is a technology of learning, development, and change in people."[25] Such technologies are frequently so elusive that it is difficult to tie particular means to ends. They also call for extensive formal and informal communications networks and flows. But complex organizations, like schools and school systems, almost invariably suffer from communications overloads. An important function of the organizational structure is to restrict and manage the flow of communication.[26] This means that individuals and components of the insti-

20. See Paul Berman, "The Study of Macro- and Micro-Implementation," 26 *Public Policy* 157 (1978).

21. The following discussion is based on Mark Yudof, "Legalization of Dispute Resolution, Distrust of Authority, and Organizational Theory: Implementing Due Process for Students in the Public Schools," *Wisconsin Law Review* (forthcoming).

22. See, e.g., James March, "Bounded Rationality, Ambiguity, and the Engineering of Choice," 9 *Bell Journal of Economics* 587 (1978), and literature discussed therein. See also Jeffrey Pressman and Aaron Wildavsky, *Implementation* (Berkeley and Los Angeles: University of California Press, 1973).

23. See, generally, James March, "American Public School Administration: A Short Analysis," 86 *School Review* 217 (1978); Seymour Sarason, *The Culture of the School and the Problem of Change* (Boston: Allyn and Bacon, 1971); Karl Weick, "Educational Organizations as Loosely Coupled Systems," 21 *Administrative Science Quarterly* 1 (1974); Milbrey McLaughlin, *Evaluation and Reform* (Santa Monica, Calif.: RAND, 1975); Mary H. Metz, *Classrooms and Corridors: The Crisis of Authority in Desegregated Public Schools* (Berkeley and Los Angeles: University of California Press, 1978). Distinctions among types of organizations are critical: "Theories that assume schools are like business or industrial organizations encourage studies that ask the wrong questions or that provide invalid interpretations of results" (Terrence E. Deal, "Where Do We Go From Here? Interpretations and Applications," in National Institute of Education, *High School '77: A Survey of Public Secondary School Principals* 57, 58).

24. See March, "American Public School Administration" 223.

25. *Id.*

26. Rogers and Agarwala-Rogers, *Communication in Organizations* 91.

tution must condense information, filter it, and play a gatekeeping function if decision makers are not to be overwhelmed with paper work. Inevitably, many messages will be distorted or omitted; accurate reproduction is hence far from a certainty.[27]

There is also a tremendous amount of movement of personnel in and out of education bureaucracies. "Most educational administrators attain the best job they will ever have at an early age and leave it considerably before normal retirement age; and most educational administrators will spend most of their working lives doing something else," notes James March.[28] This may pose severe problems of continuity of leadership and institutional memory of prior communications. Furthermore, since there are no profits to be privately appropriated, administrators may seek to maximize "profit in kind," e.g., prestige, autonomy, and budgets.[29] This has a number of ramifications for communication efforts. Individuals within the institution may distort messages if they think this is necessary to obtain institutional rewards and promotion.[30] Subordinates will hide their mistakes, and tell superiors what they wish to hear. Institutional actors may distort messages from an external source if they are deemed inconsistent with professional autonomy.

"Educational administration is only loosely coupled to educational activities in the classroom."[31] Far from being a rigid hierarchy or typical bureaucracy, activities and components are only loosely coordinated and related to the formal structure of the school system. There are few rules regarding instructional practices, formal evaluations are infrequent or unused, and decision making tends to be decentralized.[32] While this picture is oversimplified, and not all organizational theorists would accept it,[33] the "loose-coupling" view would appear to make monitoring and implementation within school organizations more

27. *Id.* at 91-93.

28. March, "American Public School Administration" 227.

29. See Jacob Michaelson, "Revision, Bureaucracy, and School Reform," 85 *School Review* 229, 239 (1977).

30. Rogers and Agarwala-Rogers, *Communication in Organizations* 94-97.

31. March, "American Public School Administration" 224. See also John Meyer and Brian Rowan, "Institutionalized Organizations: Formal Structure as Myth and Ceremony," 83 *American Journal of Sociology* 340 (1977); Weick, "Educational Organizations"; Michael Cohen, James March, and Johan Olsen, "A Garbage Can Model of Organizational Choice," 17 *Administrative Science Quarterly* 1 (1972); James March and Johan Olsen, *Ambiguity and Choice in Organizations* (Bergen: Universitets Forlaget, 1976). Cf. James Anderson, *Bureaucracy in Education* (Baltimore: Johns Hopkins Press, 1968).

32. See National Institute of Education, *High School '77* 42-43.

33. "To describe American public school administration is to describe it badly. There is considerable variety in the organizations, the jobs, and the people. The distributions have variances as well as means, and the variances are often quite large. Moreover, time has provided changes and probably will produce more" (March, "American Public School Administration" 222). See also National Institute of Education, *High School '77*.

difficult—particularly if the objective were to alter classroom regularities. A formal organizational chart might tell us little about the informal communications networks so vital to the transmission of messages.[34] Thus March has come to think of educational organizations as "organized anarchies":

> The term [organized anarchies] is used to describe organizations in which technologies are unclear, goals ambiguous, and participation fluid. . . . Educational technology is poorly understood; assured educational objectives tend to be vague, contradictory, or not widely shared; participants in educational organizations include individuals and groups who move in and out of activity in the organization sporadically.[35]

"Organized anarchies" would not appear to be promising vehicles for transmitting the messages of government or altering behavior in response to those messages.

Educational organizations do share many characteristics with other institutions, and perhaps one of the similarities is a sensitivity to rule-sources: rules that are imposed on the organization by external agencies are less likely to be obeyed. Alvin Gouldner described this as the "mock" pattern of bureaucracy.[36] The idea is that external rules, having no internal constituency, are not likely to be viewed as important or legitimate by those responsible for running the institution. Communication theorists have long drawn a distinction between communication "across the boundary" (with the external environment) and communication within an organization.[37] Adherence to a rule requires some normative commitment on the part of those charged with implementing and obeying it. The classic example is a no-smoking rule imposed by a fire insurance company in a plant where no flammable materials are used or produced.[38] Management has little interest in enforcing a rule which does not promote efficiency, productivity, or harmonious relations with the workers. The workers on their part understand that management has little interest in compliance (unless an inspector is on the premises) and will not assimilate the no-smoking rule to other rules for plant safety that appear to be more directly and vitally related to their interests. The reception given a government message may thus be a function of perceptions of the

34. See, generally, Rogers and Agarwala-Rogers, *Communication in Organizations* 81.

35. March, "American Public School Administration" 223.

36. Alvin Gouldner, *Patterns of Industrial Bureaucracy* 182-183, 187 (New York: Free Press, 1964).

37. See, generally, Rogers and Agarwala-Rogers, *Communication in Organizations* 50-52; and Daniel Katz and Robert Kahn, *The Social Psychology of Organizations* (New York: Wiley, 1966).

38. Gouldner, *Industrial Bureaucracy* 182-183.

source and of the self-interest and normative commitments of those concerned. If this is the case, rules and messages promulgated by external institutions seeking formal compliance—in contrast to those manifested through collective bargaining, administrative prerogative, discussion, technical assistance, or other less formal means—will often go unheeded.[39] At best, they may give rise to intergovernmental "bargaining, persuasion, and maneuvering under conditions of uncertainty."[40] This heightens the prospect of communications distortion.

One should also take into account the routines, "regularities," and patterns by which such institutions are normally operated and governed.[41] One may preach to individuals with limited prospects of inspiring the new religion, but can one preach to an institution? The problem is also that hortatory communications tend to ignore status and roles within institutions in favor of dealing with individuals in the organization as if they were not subject to institutional constraints.[42] Change comes about only when institutional mechanisms that make the change a part of the routine of the institution come into play. For example, if a new policy disfavoring school suspensions is to be implemented, it will do little good simply to berate educators for continuing to suspend students. New means of dealing with miscreants must be found, and this requires identification of institutional alternatives to suspension. Whether this involves corporal punishment, "in-school suspensions" (a form of isolation), a lowered mandatory attendance age, or whatever, it is only the existence of such "enabling" alternatives that makes possible the success of the policy.[43]

Finally, account should be taken of what Eugene Bardach describes as "social entropy."[44] By this he refers to inept and incompetent bureaucrats, ignorance, lack of coordination, and similar factors that may impede adherence to rules in any organizational framework. Perhaps poor communications skills should be added to the list. Demands on public institutions such as schools may well have outstripped the competencies of those charged with operating them. If this is the case, and public schools are in no way special in this regard, then

39. See Paul Berman et al., *Federal Programs Supporting Educational Change* (Santa Monica, Calif.: RAND, 1974).

40. See Bardach, *Implementation Game* 56. See, generally, Martha Derthick, *New Towns In-Town* (Washington, D.C.: Urban Institute, 1972); Pressman and Wildavsky, *Implementation*; Elmore, "Social Program Implementation" 185.

41. See, generally, Peter Blau and W. Richard Scot, *Formal Organizations* (London: Routledge and Kegan Paul, 1963); Sarason, *Culture of the School*.

42. See Stone, *Where the Law Ends* 46-67. See, generally, Richard Mandel, "Judicial Decisions and Organizational Change in Public Schools," 82 *School Review* 327 (1974); Gouldner, *Industrial Bureaucracy*; Rogers and Agarwala-Rogers, *Communication in Organizations* 39.

43. See Sarason, *Culture of the School* 86-87; and Bardach, *Implementation Game* 112-115.

44. Bardach, *Implementation Game* 124-127.

change may be difficult to implement because of institutional or individual inability to comply rather than because of deliberate attempts to undermine new rules and policies. Perhaps this is simply another way of stating the previous point. Adherence to rules and implementation of changes requires the institutionalization of structures to accomplish those ends: reliance on individual initiatives may pose significant barriers to policy implementation. This is also true of effective message transmission.

This brief description, in the educational context, of the nature of organizations and bureaucracies tends to reinforce the notion that a government speaker cannot rely upon public and private organizations to convey messages or to comply with them. Organizations, like people, may reshape messages. Sheer inefficiency and lethargy, or "social entropy," may dampen an indoctrination campaign. While such factors may hinder the implementation of policy, however, they also may undermine the ability of any government to engineer consent and create fictional majorities.

The Office of War Information

A good example of the operation of political, structural, and attitudinal constraints on government expression is the somewhat haphazard operation of the Office of War Information during World War II. The legacy of the Creel Committee of World War I, as Allan Winkler has noted, was not a happy one. It left many Americans, including President Roosevelt, with a healthy suspicion of government propaganda activities:

> A member of Wilson's administration in World War I, Roosevelt remembered the hate and hysteria generated by Creel's Committee on Public Information. He was wary from the start of any similar program. Sensitive to public opinion, persuasive in his own way, he had no intention of allowing a formal government bureau the same latitude the CPI had enjoyed. His reservations and those of the people behind him had important effects on all further American efforts to use propaganda in the national interest.[45]

The ambiguity of Roosevelt's war aims, his trust in his own persuasive powers, the nation's relative unity on the new war effort (certainly as compared with World War I), and the bad example set by Joseph Goebbels's propaganda machinery in Nazi Germany made Roosevelt reluctant to create a powerful and centralized government propaganda ministry. He tended to act by creating overlapping mandates and by

---

45. Winkler, *The Politics of Propaganda* 5.

playing off government agencies and subordinates against one another. The Departments of War and State were, moreover, notably unwilling to cooperate with the new Office of War Information.[46]

The leaders of the OWI were hardly prototypical propagandists. Its head was Elmer Davis, a journalist and radio commentator who apparently "had come to Washington to 'see that the American people are truthfully informed,' for he felt that in a democratic society the people were entitled to full knowledge if they were expected to fight well."[47] He spent a good deal of his time haggling with the military about accurate reporting of casualties and losses, and he nearly resigned when the Navy was reticent about the sinking of the aircraft carrier *Hornet* by the Japanese.[48] His relations with the military improved only when the facts improved and the fortunes of war turned in favor of the United States.

Poet Archibald MacLeish, assistant director for policy, was the former head of the Office of Facts and Figures, the OWI's predecessor, which was popularly known by the press as the "Office of Fun and Frolic."[49] Playwright Robert Sherwood headed the overseas branch. Both men adhered to the view that their primary function was to inform and to provide the people with a basis for judgment, not to mislead, distort, or report inaccurate information.

The primary point of contention within the OWI appears to have been whether it should attempt to limit itself to its information function or seek to provoke public discussion of war aims. The agency never lived up to its institutional mission to ferret out the war news and provide a coherent story to the media. Newsmen treated it as "unnecessary or unhelpful or both." Some saw it as the "president's publicity bureau"; others as an inept government information agency.

The OWI's Bureau of Publications and Graphics turned out a series of pamphlets such as *Divide and Conquer* and *The Unconquered People*. Samuel Lubell wrote a short book entitled *Battle Stations for All*, dealing with different approaches to controlling inflation at home, including some controversial measures such as rationing and increased taxation. The Bureau of Motion Pictures produced such memorable films as *Fuel Conservation*, *Food for Fighters*, and *Troop Train*. The Bureau for Domestic Radio recorded one-minute spots supporting the war effort, which were distributed to radio stations. Material was also provided for such adventure series as "The Lone Ranger" and "Terry and the Pirates." The Bureau of Campaigns worked on promoting war bonds, energy

46. *Id.* at 31, 44-45. It is noteworthy that there were virtually no prosecutions under the espionage acts during World War II (see Thomas Emerson, *The System of Freedom of Expression* 66 [New York: Random House, 1970]).
47. *The Politics of Propaganda* 47.
48. *Id.* at 50.   49. *Id.* at 23.

conservation, salvage collection, and similar projects. Overall, most of the emphasis of the OWI's programs appears to have been on how to win the war—a remarkable shift from the Creel Committee's focus on persuading the people that the war ought to be fought. The people were already persuaded, probably for reasons having little to do with the OWI's activities.[50]

Later in the OWI's short life, political pressures on the agency mounted. Government departments wanted only the most favorable picture of their activities to be presented to the public.[51] Leadership changes took place in response to such pressures, and a number of OWI writers, including Arthur M. Schlesinger, Jr., resigned, releasing a statement to the press outlining their grievances:

> There is only one issue—the deep and fundamental one of the honest presentation of war information.... We are leaving because of our conviction that it is impossible for us, under those who now control our output, to tell the full truth. No one denies that promotional techniques have a proper and powerful function in telling the story of the war. But as we see it, the activities of OWI on the home front are now dominated by high-pressure promoters who prefer slick salesmanship to honest information.[52]

The departure of these writers contributed to the discrediting of the agency in the eyes of a Congress already somewhat unfriendly. Republicans and Southern Democrats in Congress began to see the OWI as one more target for their efforts to dismantle the liberal programs of the Roosevelt Administration. In February 1943, Senator Holman of Oregon attacked the OWI for its pamphlet on *Roosevelt of America— President, Champion of Liberty, United States Leader in the War to Win Lasting and Worldwide Peace. Battle Stations for All* came under congressional attack since it dealt with policy questions still pending in Congress. A publication called *Negroes and the War* was assaulted because "it gave undue attention to the achievements of the New Deal" and "favored racial equality." One member of the House of Representatives opined that the publication "'smacks of an attempt to use the war to force upon the South a philosophy that is alien to us.'"[53]

Roosevelt refused to become involved in defending the OWI. Southern Democrats and Republicans in the House of Representatives combined to abolish the agency's domestic branch by a vote of 218 to 114. A compromise in conference was reached with the Senate, allowing the domestic branch to continue, but with minimal funding. The OWI had to close its regional offices and abolish its Office of Publications and Motion Pictures Bureau. The domestic branch basically had nothing to

50. *Id*. at 41, 53-62.   51. *Id*. at 64.
52. *Id*. at 64-65.   53. *Id*. at 65-68.

do; it was even prohibited from distributing propaganda produced by the OWI for foreign consumption in the United States. Propagandizing abroad became the primary concern of the OWI. Domestically, it limited itself to noncontroversial themes, seeking "to generate an appreciation for the American way of life"—ballet, baseball, planting gardens, fighting boll weevils, electoral participation, and state legislative bodies.[54] Rather than seeking to influence public opinion, the agency came to reflect it:

> OWI . . . had finally hit on a vision of America that was not only noncontroversial but which reflected the ways that others represented the war as well. . . . [It was] a struggle for the American way of life and stressed the components—both spiritual and material—that to them made America great. And perhaps most important of all, the general image seemed consonant with the way ordinary Americans viewed the war. Both Bill Mauldin and Ernie Pyle noted the lack of interest among soldiers in the large causes of politics of war. Soldiers were interested in other things —home above all. . . . They hungered for the simple things they remembered and longed to see once more.[55]

The OWI was finally abolished by executive order of President Truman on August 31, 1945,[56] less than three weeks after the Japanese surrender.

The national experience with the OWI is a good example of the impact of political structures and attitudes on government communications activities. Members of Congress resented the notion of the executive branch "propagandizing" to put pressure on Congress with respect to pending legislative matters. Opposition Republicans and Democratic conservatives reacted strongly to efforts they perceived as attempts to enhance the image of the New Deal and President Roosevelt at government expense. As the war emergency began to subside, tolerance of propaganda declined. For whatever reasons, the president was not willing to go to the mat to defend the OWI. In a sense, the system worked the problem out for itself, without relying on a constitutional resolution in the courts.

Public Broadcasting

In most nations, government owns and operates public television and radio stations, with little, if any, room for commercial, privately operated broadcast stations or networks. Experience with public

54. *Id*. at 70-148.
55. *Id*. at 156-157.
56. *Id*. at 149.

ownership, even in democratic countries like France and Germany, has not been entirely encouraging.[57] In France, for example, the state broadcasting monopoly, formerly Radiodiffusion-Télévision Française (RTF), later the Office de Radiodiffusion-Télévision Française (ORTF), was long tightly controlled by various central government officials, particularly the ministers of information and finance.[58] Charges of government propaganda and bias in favor of the government in power had been persistent since 1936.[59] Various committees were appointed to recommend changes over the years and some were adopted, but the essential problem of government domination did not visibly diminish. In 1974, ORTF was abolished, and no new central government agency was created to replace it. An Audiovisual Institute was established, with an administrative council for each of four "national companies." One of these was designated an independent production company, although the government retained a majority interest. Lines to the central government were made more attenuated.[60] Whether these reforms will diminish government control of the broadcast monopoly in France is a question not easily answered, given the brief period of time that has elapsed since the reforms were adopted.

The American experience has been far different.[61] Federal funding of noncommercial programming has led to few charges that public television is a propaganda arm of the executive or legislative branches. If anything, controversy has centered on the possibility that an overly independent public television network would become dominated by biased elites, unfettered by congressional scrutiny of the expenditure of tax dollars. The reasons for government's inability or unwillingness to employ public broadcasting for partisan purposes are complex, and they will be explored briefly in this section.

Historically, broadcasting in America has been dominated by private entrepreneurs. Publicly financed broadcasting was a relatively late historical development, and was created against the backdrop of an already viable private broadcasting industry. Far from being a monopoly, public broadcasting has a relatively small share of the total market and is frequently perceived as being primarily in the business of airing educational and cultural programs—not entertainment, news, or editorials. Government thus has more incentive to seek to influence com-

57. This section relies heavily on research conducted by my former student Scott Martin Bowles.

58. Thomas, *Broadcasting and Democracy* 11, 22-24. Homet, "Communications Policy Making" 31, 37.

59. Walter Emery, *National and International Systems of Broadcasting* 241-242 (East Lansing, Mich.: Michigan State University Press, 1969).

60. Thomas, *Broadcasting and Democracy* 64-68.

61. See, generally, Robert Blakely, *To Serve the Public Interest* (Syracuse, N.Y.: Syracuse University Press, 1979).

mercial broadcasting than it does to control the fledgling noncommercial system.

In France and most other nations, public ownership came first, and
independent, private stations and networks were tagged onto the already operative state monopoly. The differing origins of American and
Western European broadcasting systems have produced, or are perhaps
a product of, differing perceptions of the dangers of abuse. Western
Europeans "are unwilling to cede control over a principal means of
communication to forces driven by the profit motive. This fear of
commercial distortion is every bit as strong and pervasive as is, in the
United States, the fear of government intervention."[62] For largely
ingrained attitudinal reasons, central governments in the United States
have been reticent about involving themselves in the programming of
public television and radio stations. This mind-set explains not only the
hesitance that until recently prevented large-scale federal funding of
public broadcasting, but also the many legal strictures on government
interference with programming.

Power over the public broadcast media has not been centralized in a
government office; rather it has been delegated to various agencies,
which despite their quasi-public nature operate more as private fraternities or foundations than as government bodies. In turn, power has
been further decentralized by giving individual noncommercial licensees effective control over their programming. Furthermore, government only funds public broadcasting in America; it has not sought to
play an editorial role. There is no analogy with the Voice of America,
Stars and Stripes, or a university administration's campus newsletter.
This again reflects an attitude toward the role of government in relation
to powerful mass media enterprises. The federal government in any case
contributes only about one-fourth of the budgets of noncommercial
stations, and is statutorily prohibited from contributing more than 40
percent.[63] Stations have access to private funding sources, and are
never obligated to air government-financed programming. Attempts in
recent years to boost revenues with paid advertising have died in
Congress.

The first noncommercial broadcasting station in America is thought
to have been Radio Station 9XM, established by the University of
Wisconsin in 1919. Despite the Federal Radio Act of 1927 and the
Federal Communications Act of 1934, it was not until 1939 that the
Federal Communications Commission (FCC) reserved space on the
airwaves for educational radio.[64] In 1952 the FCC reserved 242 channels

62. Homet, "Communications Policy Making" 34.

63. 47 U.S.C. § 396 (k) (3) (1975).

64. *Community-Service Broadcasting* v. *FCC,* 593 F.2d 1102, 1106 (D.C. Cir. 1978) (*en
banc*).

for "educational television,"[65] and by 1967 this number had expanded to 663 channels (the vast majority of which were UHF).[66] This decision was made at the insistence of FCC Commissioner Frieda B. Hennock,[67] but was not accompanied by any federal funding of educational programming. A major source of funding was the Ford Foundation, operating through the National Educational Television and Radio Center (NET).

According to Frederick Breitenfeld, noncommercial stations fall into four categories.[68] First, some stations are operated by institutions of higher learning, with a member of the journalism faculty as the station manager and with a staff consisting of university employees and/or student trainees. Second, there are community stations that are privately owned and operated by a nonprofit agency. Third, some stations are licensed to individual states and operated under the auspices of some special state-created agency. Finally, there are stations operated by local educational agencies, generally in large cities, which offer classroom television programming.

In 1957, Senator Warren G. Magnuson introduced a bill authorizing the appropriation of $1,000,000 to each state to promote the development of educational television. The bill passed the Senate, but died in the House of Representatives.[69] After another unsuccessful attempt, the Educational Television Broadcasting Facilities Act was passed in 1962.[70] By this time only sixty-two of the reserved channels for noncommercial broadcasting were operational, and the act made available $32,000,000 for public broadcasting over a five-year period.[71] The funds were distributed by the Department of Health, Education, and Welfare and were earmarked for the acquisition of transmission equipment, subject to a local matching requirement and a lid on funding per state. The federal funds could not be used for salaries, operating expenses, or program production.[72] By the mid-1960s, it became clear that the survival and growth of noncommercial broadcasting would require more substantial public financing.

The impetus for additional government funding came from the Ford and Carnegie Foundations. The Ford Foundation proposed a satellite

65. Douglas Ginsburg, *Regulation of Broadcasting* 20 (St. Paul, Minn.: West Publishing, 1979).

66. William Canby, "The First Amendment and the State as Editor: Implications for Public Broadcasting," 52 *Texas Law Review* 1123, 1149 n. 145 (1974).

67. George Gibson, *Public Broadcasting* 70-79 (New York: Praeger, 1977).

68. Frederick Breitenfeld, "Heart of the System: The Stations," in Douglass Cater and Michael Nyhan, eds., *The Future of Public Broadcasting* 39 (New York: Praeger, 1976).

69. Gibson, *Public Broadcasting* 98-99.

70. 47 U.S.C. §§ 390-395 (1970).

71. Gibson, *Public Broadcasting* 119.

72. *Community-Service Broadcasting* v. *FCC*, 593 F.2d 1102, 1107 (D.C. Cir. 1978) (*en banc*).

network to connect the noncommercial stations, and the Communications Satellite Corporation complied by including such stations in its satellite plans. A 1967 Carnegie Commission report, however, undertaken with the approval of President Johnson, became the basis of the landmark Public Broadcasting Act of 1967.[73] The Carnegie Report envisioned federal funding of "public television," indicating a shift from the narrow confines of educational or instructional television. Responding to the "special sensitivity" of government-financed public broadcasting, the report called for a chartered, nonprofit, nongovernmental corporation to finance and distribute programs and to insulate public television from political pressures.[74] The report recommended a corporation board consisting of twelve members, six appointed by the president and six appointed by the board itself.[75] Long-range funding, rather than year-to-year appropriations from Congress, was contemplated. This was to be accomplished by an excise tax on new television sets, with the expectation that eventually $100,000,000 would be generated for public television each year. The fear was that yearly appropriations would invite too much congressional scrutiny of "the day-to-day operations of the sensitive portions of the Public Television system."[76]

In general, the Carnegie Report received an enthusiastic reception. The Public Broadcasting Act created a Corporation for Public Broadcasting (including radio as well as television stations) with the powers "to disburse funds it receives to program production entities and noncommercial broadcast stations, to arrange for an interconnection system capable of distributing programs to noncommercial stations, to conduct research and demonstrations, and to encourage creation of new commercial stations."[77] Attached to this, however, were a number of safeguards designed to guarantee the independence of the corporation and the noncommercial stations from government control and interference, while somewhat inconsistently retaining some congressional and presidential oversight. As Judge Bazelon put it,

> Congress desired to establish a program funding agency free from governmental influence or control in its operations. Yet, the lawmakers feared that such complete autonomy might lead to biases and abuses of its own.[78]

73. Gibson, *Public Broadcasting* 121-123. See 47 U.S.C. § 396 *et seq.* (1970).

74. *Community-Service Broadcasting* v. *FCC*, 593 F.2d 1102, 1107 (D.C. Cir. 1978) (*en banc*).

75. Gibson, *Public Broadcasting* 125-127.

76. *Community-Service Broadcasting* v. *FCC*, 593 F.2d 1102, 1107 (D.C. Cir. 1978) (*en banc*). See, generally, Blakely, *To Serve the Public Interest* 196-199.

77. 593 F.2d at 1107.

78. *Accuracy in Media, Inc.* v. *FCC*, 521 F.2d 288, 291-292 (D.C. Cir. 1975).

Congress provided that all fifteen members of the governing board be appointed by the president, with no more than eight members coming from the same political party. As if to drive home the fear of partisanship, the corporation was prohibited from supporting any candidate for political office. Indeed, the act contained a prohibition on all editorializing in noncommercial programming, and the corporation was required to abide by a standard of "objectivity and balance in all programs . . . of a controversial nature."[79] A bias in favor of the traditional, "noncontroversial" educational broadcasting was also evident. The act provided that public broadcasting was essentially for educational and cultural purposes and not primarily for entertainment (an obligation that many would say has been too well satisfied).

Congressional oversight was built into the law by virtue of requiring annual reports from the corporation and annual audits conducted by the General Accounting Office. This was designed to bolster congressional supervision in the budgetary process. Funds were appropriated for only one year, thereby making intense periodic review more likely.[80] Nonetheless, government officers and Congress were expressly forbidden from controlling programming, the percentage of federal funding was limited, and the ultimate decision to broadcast a federally funded program was left in the hands of the local noncommercial stations (subject to the limitations on editorializing and endorsing political candidates).

It is important to recognize that the aspirations embodied in the Act have been largely achieved and the potential conflict between editorial independence and congressional oversight largely avoided without the intervention of the federal judiciary. Courts have held that private parties and the FCC may not judicially enforce the Broadcasting Act's provisions and that Congress, and not the judiciary, is the responsible public agency.[81] The courts have also largely managed to avoid the potentially difficult question of the extent to which Congress may constitutionally interfere with editorial judgments by local stations in order to achieve the objectives of its funding.[82] The law is unclear, but the facts are not. In operation, the real power lies with the local

79. Gibson, *Public Broadcasting* 141-142. But see *Accuracy in Media, Inc.* v. *FCC*, 521 F.2d 288 (D.C. Cir. 1975) (upholding FCC determination that it lacked jurisdiction to enforce the "objectivity and balance rule").

80. Gibson, *Public Broadcasting* 142.

81. See, e.g., *Community-Service Broadcasting* v. *FCC*, 593 F.2d 1102 (D.C. Cir. 1978); *Network Project* v. *Corporation for Public Broadcasting*, 561 F.2d 963 (D.C. Cir. 1977); *Accuracy in Media, Inc.* v. *FCC*, 521 F.2d 288 (D.C. Cir. 1975).

82. See, e.g., *Network Project* v. *Corporation for Public Broadcasting*, 561 F.2d 963, 975 (D.C. Cir. 1977); *Accuracy in Media, Inc.* v. *FCC*, 521 F.2d 288, 296-297 (D.C. Cir. 1975). But cf. *Community-Service Broadcasting* v. *FCC*, 593 F.2d 1102, 1135 (D.C. Cir. 1978) (Leventhal, J., dissenting).

stations, not the corporation, and this power has proved sufficient to overcome threats to the integrity and independence of public broadcasting. This power emanates from the influence of the local people that run local stations, the professional independence of the staffs, ingrained attitudes about station autonomy and government control, and the ability to utilize nongovernment funds for programming.

The primary mechanism for local station control is the Public Broadcasting Service (PBS), an unincorporated organization of noncommercial stations with responsibility for operating the interconnection service, i.e., allocating time for programs going out over the network, with grants from the corporation. PBS began operations in 1969, and originally it was thought that it would handle only the mechanics of network dissemination. It was not a program producing agency. In the words of William Canby, however, "Shortly after its creation . . . PBS, at the urging of member stations, began to assert some control over the content of programming to be transmitted as part of the regular network schedule."[83] PBS was largely controlled by the stations, since five places on its nine-person board of directors were allotted to them,[84] and its first president was general manager of public station WGBH in Boston.[85] The corporation was represented by only one member on the board.[86] Power was thus split between the corporation and PBS, and the history of public broadcasting since 1969 is in some measure a description of the jockeying for influence between the two agencies. It appears, however, that PBS has come out on top.

The evolution of public broadcasting proceeded in a hostile political environment.[87] According to recently released public documents, President Nixon believed that it had a "left-wing" bias and that funds should be cut off. Apparently Nixon was disturbed to learn that Robert MacNeil and Sander Vanocur would be cohosts of a weekly public affairs show. The Office of Telecommunications Policy (OTP), established in 1970 to oversee federal funding of public broadcasting, advised Nixon that cutting off funds would not be possible. Under the leadership of Clay Whitehead, however, OTP mounted a serious challenge to public broadcasting. As Scott Martin Bowles notes, Whitehead was "destined to become to public broadcasting what Spiro Agnew was to the commercial networks."[88] Whitehead attacked the central authority of the Corporation for Public Broadcasting, and the latter

83. Canby, "The First Amendment and the State as Editor" 1156.
84. *New York Times* 95, col. 4 (Nov. 5, 1969).
85. Gibson, *Public Broadcasting* 157, 161.
86. *New York Times* 95, col. 4 (Nov. 5, 1969).
87. See, generally, Blakely, *To Serve the Public Interest* ch. 8.
88. S. Bowles, *Public Broadcasting Systems in West Germany, France, Great Britain and the United States: Government Regulation and Public Feedback* 47, unpublished seminar paper (1979).

responded by dropping some controversial programming and plans for gavel-to-gavel coverage of the 1972 political party conventions. PBS responded by increasing the size of its board of directors from nine to nineteen, filling the additional places with six station managers and four public representatives.[89] Thus the interest of the OTP in diminishing the centralized power of the corporation fortuitously coincided with the stations' understandable impulse toward enhanced local power over programming.

In June 1972, despite these efforts at accommodation, President Nixon vetoed a two-year, $165,000,000 appropriation passed by the Congress, leaving the CPB with only $35,000,000 for fiscal 1973.[90] The president of CPB, the chairman of the board, and most of the top staff then resigned.[91] Nixon filled the vacancies with individuals thought to be more sympathetic to his point of view. In terms of programming, the consequences of the veto and changes in personnel were almost immediately felt. The dominant philosophy was that "public broadcasting and public muckraking do not go together." Cultural programming became dominant. The CPB dropped such "controversial" programs as William F. Buckley's "Firing Line," "Bill Moyer's Journal," "Washington Week in Review," and "America 1973." In lieu of such offerings, the CPB made available twenty-one hours of coverage of Apollo 17. By 1973 the corporation had clearly proved itself to be not much of a buffer between the government and the stations.[92]

Ironically, the very localism advocated by the Nixon administration became the vehicle by which government attempts to influence programming were blunted.[93] The courts, while invited by various plaintiff groups to intervene, ultimately declined to do so. Negotiations between PBS and CPB were initiated at a time when the Nixon administration had been weakened by the Watergate Affair and when the 1972 elections had reduced Republican representation in Congress. A tentative agreement was reached whereby the CPB would have substantial control over program selection, and PBS could transmit any programs it desired that were produced without federal funds. The CPB board tabled the measure, and the chairman of the board resigned, claiming that the administration was attempting to convert the corporation into a propaganda arm of the White House. The resignation of the administration's own appointed chairman proved to be embarrassing, and a Johnson appointee to the board was made chair-

89. Gibson, *Public Broadcasting* 176, 181.

90. Willard Rowland, "Public Involvement: The Anatomy of a Myth," in Cater and Nyhan, *Future of Public Broadcasting* 120.

91. Gibson, *Public Broadcasting* 186-187; Rowland, "Public Involvement" 120.

92. Gibson, *Public Broadcasting* 188-191.

93. *Id.* at 189, 196-198.

man, with the understanding that negotiations between PBS and the corporation would resume. At this point most of PBS's demands were met. The corporation would retain discretion only over what programs to fund with federal dollars, and would give money to PBS only for interconnection costs. PBS could distribute any programs it pleased, with the caveat that PBS and CPB would agree to a yearly schedule. A monitoring committee was set up to police the requirement of balance and objectivity, with each entity having three representatives. Four votes were necessary to drop a program. A task force was set up to study long-range financing, albeit President Nixon rejected their recommendations, "apparently stung by prime-time Senate Watergate hearings and the specter of televised impeachment proceedings."[94] Later, he relented, and a long-range funding scheme was enacted and signed into law by President Ford in 1975. President Nixon also signed an appropriations bill, allocating $50,000,000 for the remainder of fiscal 1974.[95]

The net result of the historic confrontation between public broadcasting and the chief executive was to weaken the Corporation for Public Broadcasting and to strengthen the local noncommercial stations. The Public Broadcasting System, far from performing only its network functions, is "a station-dominated membership organization, act[ing] largely as a trade association of public television licensees."[96] PBS now has two governing boards, a board of governors and a board of managers, and the membership of each is elected by public television licensees.[97] Further, the stations control the Station Program Cooperative (SPC), a device for funding programs constituting about 25 percent of the PBS schedule. The cooperative sponsors a series of "program selection," "elimination," and "purchase" rounds that determine which programs will be funded. Initially, stations indicate if they are willing to help produce particular programs and to split the costs proportionately with other interested stations. Obviously, the expense to each station and the likelihood of funding is dramatically affected by the number of stations willing to share the costs of production. If 80 percent or more of the stations bid on a program and the cost does not rise significantly, the program is declared purchased. If less than 30 percent of the stations bid on a program, the PBS staff determines if the remaining stations are willing to pay up to 80 percent of the production costs. If they are unwilling, the program is dropped. Stations may not air programs that they do not purchase.[98]

94. Bowles, *Public Broadcasting Systems* 52.
95. Gibson, *Public Broadcasting* 203, 206-218.
96. Bowles, *Public Broadcasting Systems* 53.
97. Gibson, *Public Broadcasting* 192.
98. Nathan Katzman and Ken Wirt, "Program Funding in Public Television and the SPC," in Cater and Nyhan, *Future of Public Broadcasting* 253-254, 256.

The picture of public broadcasting then is one of a substantial fragmentation of authority, and a significant degree of decentralization and station autonomy over programming—particularly with respect to programs produced from nonfederal funds. The system is complex, not simple. Local elites are powerful forces in this process. In some ways, it would be accurate to portray public broadcasting as a quasi-free enterprise system, operating with substantial amounts of private sector dollars. Especially in the light of the contretemps with the Nixon administration, there appears to be an overwhelming sense among the relevant participants that government should not dominate programming. While there is some inevitable carping from legislators about particular programs,[99] Congress has moved toward long-range funding and has declined to exercise extensive supervisory powers. The courts have largely stayed out of the fray. The Federal Communications Commission has largely declined to enforce Public Broadcasting Act provisions against individual, noncommercial stations.

This does not mean that there are not political pressures on public broadcasting (for example, the licenses of noncommercial stations must be renewed by the FCC), but, by and large, gross interference with programming decisions has been avoided. The real conflict appears to lie between the Corporation for Public Broadcasting, which would like to have a greater role in shaping an overall public television programming "package," and the Public Broadcasting System, which represents the diverse interests of local stations. Neither group appears to view itself as an auxiliary of the government, and both would prefer to work out their disputes free of congressional and executive branch interference.

Whatever else may be said about the content of noncommercial programming, the charge that public broadcasting is a propaganda arm of the federal government is simply ill-founded. The boards of directors of local stations tend to be drawn from prominent representatives of business, higher education, politics, "high culture," and mass entertainment. A more frequent charge is that public broadcasting is geared to "lofty, cultural programming" that largely keeps it out of politics. As FCC Commissioner Benjamin L. Hooks argued in a license renewal case involving WNET in New York City,

> WNET's sin, one of arrogance, is to have concentrated its efforts on one minority group, the cultured, white cosmopolites, and too often neglected the enlightenment of other less fortunate minorities which it has a fundamental duty to serve. . . .
> This is not to say that lofty, cultural programming is not properly within the province of public broadcasting. . . . [Minor-

99. See *Community-Service Broadcasting* v. *FCC*, 593 F.2d 1102, 1112-1114 (D.C. Cir. 1978) (*en banc*).

ity group representatives] agree that esoteric fare, spurned by the mass-targeted, privately-owned stations, belongs on public television because it is not mass-oriented. From its perpetually low ratings, it is evident that WNET's British drama, German music, French cuisine, and Russian ballet are of interest to a minimal portion of the television audience. . . .

By aspiring to titillate the sensibilities and sensitivities of the twentieth century Renaissance man, it has overlooked the intellectual needs and sensitivities [of Blacks, Chicanos, and other minority groups].[100]

While this charge is serious, perhaps Americans should be grateful that debate centers on these issues and not on issues of government dominance of the mass media through public broadcasting.

The allegation of cultural elitism has a number of dimensions. Local public broadcasting stations receive a good deal of political and financial backing from the relatively powerful groups that support ballet, drama, classical music, and other "upper-crust" cultural activities. If these groups are displaced in public broadcasting, the ability of local stations to resist political pressures from government may be reduced. Furthermore, the involvement of minorities and other less affluent groups could lead to a type of programming that might be perceived as more political or partisan, and hence more subject to government scrutiny. If the programs prove popular, this may increase government's stakes in controlling public broadcasting. This is not an argument for ignoring all but the "culturally elite," but it does indicate that there are some risks attached to dramatic shifts in public broadcasting programming and governance. Perhaps all one can hope for is a broad representation of interests and groups that leads to the sort of balanced programming that minimizes the risk of government interference.

The assumption of the Hooks argument is that the boards which oversee noncommercial stations actually control their programming and operating decisions. This may ignore the powerful influence of the professional staff. Frequently, the staff exercises the real power, with only occasional supervision by the busy part-time members of the governing board. The staff may have its own orientation, and certainly may be expected to be jealous of its prerogatives and creative impulses and resistant to board interference. By and large, career patterns for public and private broadcasting personnel are separate (so I am told), with the notable exception of some of the performers. The role of the staff may explain the movement over the last five years away from "highbrow" culture and dry documentaries. Consider, for example, the appearance of extensive children's programming, bilingual shows,

100. *PRMAEC* v. *Educational Broadcasting Corporation*, 51 F.C.C.2d 1178 (1975).

commercially produced movies, and the attention to popular country-and-western music. Indeed, one now hears charges that public television is becoming too much like commercial television.

Finally, perhaps Commissioner Hooks has implicitly hit upon a more profound flaw in the current operation of public broadcasting stations in the United States. In the general zeal to keep government out of public broadcasting, to satisfy the impulse for the balanced and non-partisan, and to focus on entertaining and/or culturally inspiring fare, perhaps the affirmative role of government in promoting the self-controlled citizen has been lost sight of. If the promotion of liberty is equated only with preventing government from dominating the mass media and from engineering consent, public broadcasting is an unmitigated success. But what of the obligation of government to expand the potential for choice by informing, teaching, and leading? From this perspective, Congress could sensibly require that its funds be utilized to cover political conventions, to broadcast legislative hearings, to investigate and air controversial political matters, and to produce documentaries and other shows on the economy, on the adequacy of service delivery by government, and on world crises.

In Western Europe, for example, "there is the institution of the party political broadcast both during elections and more regularly throughout the year; time is usually allotted in accordance with electoral strength."[101] Arguably, if the commercial networks and other mass media do not have sufficient market incentives to do these things, then the polity should act through publicly financed television and radio.[102] Inevitably, editorial judgments would be made; errors would occur; biases would slip in. But ultimately the processes of informed consent may be more aided by such concepts of affirmative government action than by a mindless policy of government abstention from communication activities. From this perspective, it is unclear whether public broadcasting has been a success. But perhaps we have developed a structure in which the fragmentation and decentralization of decision making makes acceptable the risks of affirmatively promoting choice and autonomy with government funds.

Delegation of Special Functions and the "Morality of Consent"

In reflecting upon the American experience, a significant check on government communications powers appears to lie in the delegation of authority by political branches of government to special institutions exercising quasi-public powers in areas of special expertise. Some may

101. Homet, "Communications Policy Making" 36.
102. But cf. *Community-Service Broadcasting* v. *FCC*, 593, F.2d 1102 (1978).

view such delegations as a charade. For example, what does it mean to characterize the Corporation for Public Broadcasting as a "private," "nongovernmental" corporation? It expends public funds, it is chartered by the government, its officers are appointed by the president. If the corporation were to engage in racial discrimination, a predictable judicial response would be that "state action" was involved in the unconstitutional conduct. But perhaps there is more to this notion of delegation than first meets the eye. There is great significance in the fact that the executive branch and Congress have largely chosen to give up their claim to day-to-day control of federally financed programming, and that the members of the corporation perceive themselves as relatively autonomous in the government structure. CPB is part of government, and yet, in a sense, it stands apart from government. Thus public broadcasting in the United States begins to resemble the British Broadcasting Corporation in Great Britain.

Consider institutions like public universities, which, surely, are subject to legislative control and are a part of the political system, but have their own governing boards and traditions of academic autonomy. Political intervention by elected officials is not unknown, but it is remarkable that politicians have yielded as much control as they have. And then there are the journals of schools within public universities. Why do legislatures and executives generally choose not to interfere in the editorial processes of publications almost entirely financed with tax dollars?

These traditions of delegation arise from a number of factors. One major factor is the specialization of functions. Running a university, editing a journal, teaching a class, or producing a television program all require skills going beyond those of the elected government official. While elected officials may set budgets and scrutinize performance, at some point the insights of professionals, honed by specialization, are deemed necessary to carry out the designated tasks. If specialization were not required as a matter of expertise, efficiency would demand it. As a matter of time and interest, for example, the governor of a state generally does not wish to be involved in deciding which articles on welfare economics or thermodynamics should be published at state expense in a university journal. There are not enough elected officials to monitor intensively the massive communications activities which the government sponsors. And, most importantly, traditions of autonomy, while sometimes not respected, make it unseemly for elected officials to attempt to bring their power to bear there. This is perceived as political interference with the neutrality of those institutions. Cumulatively, these factors do not mean that the representative branches of government do not have the power to control the communications activities they fund. Rather, the point is that most often they choose not to do so; the relative autonomy of the specialized institutions is perceived as legitimate.

These notions of autonomy and legitimacy are curious. The traditions and institutions themselves, abided and supported by generations of Americans, provide the basis for legitimacy—for a "morality of consent" in the words of the late Alexander Bickel. Taking Bickel's example of the university, it can hardly be contended that the university is "neutral," or that it is not a part of the political order:

> It may be admitted that the university is, by extension, politically involved. The university is committed to freedom of inquiry, to the method of reason, however fallible. It is agnostic, and it is neutral to a degree, and from certain vantage points, reason, agnosticism and neutrality can be seen as political. To the radical . . . intent on the attainment of immediate social ends which he conceives as moral imperatives, such neutrality appears as a commitment to the other side. Neutrality and agnosticism are, indeed, likely in practice to result in an attitude of gradualism and a rejection of absolute activism.
>
> All institutions which require substantial support from the society—even the universities—must realistically be viewed as resting on an assumption of generalized allegiance to that society. . . . Political involvement in these extended senses of the term is as defensible as it is ineluctable, and it is fully consistent with freedom of inquiry.[103]

There is a wisdom embodied in American traditions of delegation of authority to relatively autonomous institutions with substantial communications power. The university, the journal, the public broadcasting station are all integral parts of government, in the sense that they are parts of the broad political order. Nominally—and sometimes in reality—they are subject to hierarchical restraints imposed by the representative institutions of government. On the other hand, in a more specific sense, they are considered outside of the normal realm of electoral politics. Oddly, the appearance of isolation from politics further strengthens their claim to legitimacy in the performance of their specialized functions. The tension generated by simultaneously being a part of the political system and yet somehow apart from it, far from being a weakness, is a bastion of strength in guarding the polity from the potential dangers of government expression.

These concepts of delegation raise intriguing issues about the nature of government. As I have argued elsewhere, there may be some functions which government ought to be able to delegate to ostensibly

103. Alexander Bickel, *The Morality of Consent* 129–130 (New Haven, Conn.: Yale University Press, 1975).

nonpublic entities and some that it should refrain from delegating.[104] To the best of its ability, government ought to maintain a monopoly over the use of violence. Government should be able to delegate some lawmaking functions, but it should not be permitted to delegate all of its powers to enforce the law. It is one thing to give surrounding landowners the power to approve a zoning variance, and it is quite another to allow them to tear down a nonconforming use. In the American scheme of government, judicial institutions alone decide such matters.

Given the danger of falsified consent, prudence dictates that government voluntarily delegate as much of its power over communications activities as possible to autonomous agencies. These would include public and nonpublic entities with varying degrees of independence. In turn, this raises two sorts of legal issues. Are there times when government (in the specific sense) should be constitutionally bound to delegate its communications powers? If government is not so bound, are there times when government should not be permitted to revoke a delegation of authority over communications when it has voluntarily undertaken the delegation in the first instance? Discussion of these critical questions is postponed until chapter 13 in Part IV, to permit the development in Part III of a First Amendment framework which will accommodate government speech concerns.

104. Mark Yudof, "Reflections on Private Repossession, Public Policy and the Constitution," 122 *University of Pennsylvania Law Review* 954 (1974).

Part III

*Government Expression
and First Amendment Theory*

Introduction

Part III places government speech in a First Amendment framework. Chapter 8 argues that traditional First Amendment theory has created a false dichotomy between majoritarianism and the protection of individual rights, which in turn casts substantial doubt on the legitimacy of decisions by unelected judges. I argue that the social-contract route around this "countermajoritarian difficulty" affirms fundamental values while sidestepping difficult questions of legitimacy, utility, and consent. My approach, however, recognizes the mutually enhancing and protecting relationship between majoritarianism and individual liberties. It begins with two propositions: First, in a representative democracy officials should respond to citizens' preferences; second, the essence of democratic government is that autonomous, self-controlled citizens should make informed, independent decisions about government policies. The first refers to the problem of verifying majorities, i.e., majority rule. The second refers to the problem of government engineering, or falsification of majorities or consent.

These two propositions take account of complexities in political relationships. Majority rule should consist of a mutually affecting relationship between the people and their rulers in which government affirmatively promotes choice and respect for individual autonomy. Consent, not to be confused with consensus, consists of meaningful opportunity to influence and participate in the processes of decision. Government speech can enhance or endanger consent and majority rule. The First Amendment is valuable not only as a check on government censorship of private speech and association, but also as a constraint on the distortion of people's judgment. Access to nongovernmental sources of information and opinion lessens the probability of government domination of the thought processes of citizens. The symbiotic relationship between private rights and majority rule strengthens each, which may explain the survival and growth of civil liberties in the United States.

Chapter 9, following the methodology proposed by Charles Black, analyzes structures and relationships to argue that concerns about limits on government speech are clearly among the factors judges may legitimately consider in deciding hard cases. Recent First Amendment issues are reformulated to demonstrate that a concern for excessive government expression supports decisions on individual rights and helps to secure a balanced communications flow. The chapter concludes with some caveats about the efficacy of a constitutional right to curb government speech and the difficulty of distinguishing between "good" and "bad" speech.

Chapter 10 compares the tendencies toward excesses by the three branches of government and their relative competencies in constraining communications abuses. I argue that the executive branch presents the greatest threat and that legislators are less likely than the judiciary to verify the majorities that elected them, but more likely to be effective at restraining executive attempts to falsify consent. The legislature has more at stake, its processes are better suited to determine what speech is appropriate, and it is more capable of devising effective safeguards than the judiciary. On the whole, I conclude, history has shown that Congress's role in protecting democratic government from falsification of majorities has been credible, if imperfect. This augurs well for placing substantial responsibility on the Congress (and state legislatures) to guard against executive branch attacks on the self-controlled citizen.

Judicial competency to detect and protect against falsification requires an examination of four ways a court can act to limit abuses of government speech. It may:

1. Maintain traditions of pluralism when scrutinizing government activities and laws for violations of such fundamental First Amendment rights as freedom of expression and association;
2. Enforce laws that protect the polity, whether by design or effect, from overzealous government speech;
3. Impose direct constitutional limits on government speech;
4. Attempt to focus legislative attention on potentially dangerous speech.

The chapter concludes with an examination of judicial mastery of communications techniques that create respect for the *source* of messages, as distinguished from their content, and demonstrates that the Supreme Court of the United States, too, can falsify consent.

Chapter 11 elaborates on the two First Amendment modes for judicial handling of government speech discussed in the preceding chapter. I conclude that where individuals seek to vindicate speech or associational rights against the state in traditional First Amendment contexts, the implications of court decisions for limiting government expression should be among the factors judges consider. This approach bolsters liberty by strengthening the self-controlled citizen and by posing obstacles to government domination of communications networks. Each effect enhances the other. This approach also avoids the remedial quandaries engendered by imposing direct constitutional limits, which though generally less desirable, may be useful in egregious situations.

[8]

The Majoritarian Underpinnings of the First Amendment: Verifying and Falsifying Consent

The Countermajoritarian Difficulty

Traditional First Amendment theories of freedom of expression, of the press, and of association fail to take account of government participation in communications networks and of improved technologies of mass persuasion in the public and private sectors. Without exaggerating the influence of government expression, this failure seriously distorts the conceptual framework for analyzing the role of First Amendment values in a democracy. Government speech is hardly perceived as a problem; safeguards are designed to protect private communication from government censorship or interference. This may have been a forgivable oversight in the eighteenth or nineteenth century, but it is foolhardy in the light of twentieth-century government power and communications technology. A theory of freedom of expression that ignores the communicative powers of the public sector may fail to protect the liberal democratic values it is designed to serve. Government has the potential to engineer public consent by dominating communications networks and selectively disclosing or revealing information.

False or myopic assumptions about the nature of the communications process and the foundations of majority rule have created a false dichotomy between majoritarianism and the protection of individual civil liberties under the First Amendment. The First Amendment is sometimes conceptualized in terms of individually oriented end-state values[1]—human dignity or self-fulfillment, for example. More fre-

1. See, e.g., Thomas Emerson, *The System of Freedom of Expression* 6-7 (New York: Random House, 1970); Thomas Scanlon, "A Theory of Freedom of Expression," 1 *Philosophy and Public Affairs* 204 (1972). Emerson offers many other justifications, in communal and societal terms, for protecting freedom of expression. See Alexander Meikle-

quently, it is viewed in instrumental terms—the protection of minority interests thought to be poorly represented in the political processes.[2] Such minorities, loosely described, may have acquisitional, voluntary, or achieved status in ideological or other terms (e.g., communists, fascists, socialists, or Jehovah's Witnesses), or they may have largely involuntary, inherent, and ascribed characteristics (e.g., blacks). Both types of minorities are thought to be in need of protection from the majority's excesses, and this need is tied to judicial review, inasmuch as the Supreme Court and lower federal courts are defended as the institutions best suited to afford that protection.[3] Martin Shapiro, perhaps the ablest advocate of this point of view, has summed up the matter nicely:

> The Court's clientele are precisely those interests which find themselves unable to obtain representation from other agencies. . . .
>
> If the Court is to make its maximum contribution to the governing process, it should probably devote its major energies to those groups which have little access to government.[4]

From this perspective, it is far from accidental that landmark First Amendment cases often involve socialists, communists, Jehovah's Witnesses, pacifists, Ku Klux Klan members, and other who may be out of

---

john, *Free Speech* (New York: Harper & Row, 1949); Robert Dahl, *Polyarchy* (New Haven, Conn.: Yale University Press, 1971); Robert Bork, "Neutral Principles and Some First Amendment Principles," 47 *Indiana Law Journal* 1 (1971); Robert Dahl, "On Removing Certain Impediments to Democracy in the United States," 92 *Political Science Quarterly* 1 (1971); Paul Freund, "The Great Disorder of Speech," 44 *American Scholar* 541 (1975) (for Holmes, "freedom of expression was not instrumental in a quest; it created its own object, its Holy Grail" [*id.* at 543]); Harry Kalven, *The Negro and the First Amendment* 6 (Columbus, Ohio: Ohio State University Press, 1965); *idem*, "The Reasonable Man and the First Amendment: Hills, Butts, and Walker," 1967 *Supreme Court Review* 267; C. Edwin Baker, "Scope of the First Amendment Freedom of Speech," 25 *U.C.L.A. Law Review* 964, 966 (1978) (fosters individual self-realization and self-determination).

2. See, e.g., Learned Hand, *The Bill of Rights* (Cambridge, Mass.: Harvard University Press, 1958); Martin Shapiro, *Freedom of Speech: The Supreme Court and Judicial Review* (Englewood Cliffs, N.J.: Prentice-Hall, 1969); Walter Gelhorn, "The Right to Know: First Amendment Overbreadth," 1976 *Washington University Law Quarterly* 25. Compare Henry Steele Commager, *Majority Rule and Minority Rights* (New York: Oxford University Press, 1943) (there is an "assumption that majority will and minority rights are antithetical, that majority rule constantly threatens minority rights, and that the principal function of our constitutional system is to protect minority rights against infringement" [*id.* at 9]); Auerbach, "The Communist Control Act of 1954," 23 *University of Chicago Law Review* 173 (1956); Bork, "Neutral Principles and First Amendment Principles."

3. But see Terrance Sandalow, "Judicial Protection of Minorities," 75 *Michigan Law Review* 1162 (1977).

4. Shapiro, *Freedom of Speech*. But cf. Sidney Hook, *The Paradoxes of Freedom* 99 (Berkeley and Los Angeles: University of California Press, 1962).

step with the prevailing wisdom, or who feel aggrieved by prevailing policies. It is an uncontested truism that those who would deviate create the problems. Hence freedom of expression is often conceptualized as a contest between the conformists and the nonconformists, the defenders of government policies and their attackers, in which the interests of the majority, assimilated in government policy, are pitted or balanced against the interests of those resistant to the prevailing norms. In Vincent Blasi's words, judges and commentators "tended to view the speech, press, and assembly clauses of the First Amendment almost exclusively in terms of theories of fair play (really *noblesse oblige*) toward the ineffectual fringe elements of the society."[5] If the expression and associational activities of these fringe groups are not tolerated by the majority and are judicially insulated from majoritarian limitations, this may be perceived as diminishing the ability of the majority to govern and to implement its policies.[6] And it casts substantial doubt on the legitimacy of the decisions of the unelected judges who would cast aside the majority's preferences.

The "countermajoritarian difficulty"[7] was most articulately explained by the late Alexander Bickel. In his view, the reality is "that when the Supreme Court declares unconstitutional a legislative act or the action of an elected executive, it thwarts the will of representatives of the actual people of the here and now; it exercises control, not in behalf of the prevailing majority, but against it."[8] Given the lack of direct political accountability to the people (the very characteristic of the Supreme Court that strengthens the argument for judicial review in the eyes of Martin Shapiro), the charge can be made "that judicial review is a deviant institution in American democracy." While Bickel admits that there are "impurities and imperfections" in terms of the responsiveness of elected executives, bureaucracies, and legislative bodies, he rightly concludes that this is a specious argument "for total departure from the desired norm" by the judiciary:[9]

> But nothing can finally depreciate the central function that is assigned in democratic theory and practice to the electoral pro-

5. Vincent Blasi, "The Checking Value in First Amendment Theory," 1977 *American Bar Foundation Research Journal* 523.

6. See, generally, Commager, *Majority Rule and Minority Rights*. Cf. Robert Dahl, "Decision-Making in a Democracy: The Supreme Court as a National Policy-Maker," 6 *Journal of Public Law* 279 (1957): "The process is neither minority rule nor majority rule but what might be called minorities rule, where one aggregation of minorities achieves policies opposed by another aggregation."

7. Alexander Bickel, *The Least Dangerous Branch* 16 (Indianapolis, Ind.: Bobbs-Merrill, 1962).

8. *Id.* at 16-17. See also Jesse H. Choper, *Judicial Review and the National Political Process* (Chicago: University of Chicago Press. 1980).

9. Bickel, *Least Dangerous Branch* 18.

cess; nor can it be denied that the policy-making power of representative institutions, born of the electoral process, is the distinguishing characteristic of the system. Judicial review works counter to this characteristic.[10]

A *"morally supportable"* government governs on the basis of consent, and this requires public institutions "that reflect and represent us and that we can call to account."[11]

Bickel did not reject the concept of judicial review, despite his harsh criticisms. What he proposed was that "the good society not only will want to satisfy the immediate needs of the greatest number but also will strive to support and maintain enduring general values." And while he considered the case far from conclusive or overwhelming, he asserted that the judiciary may well be the sort of reflective, isolated, and principled institution to guard those enduring values. It is not my purpose to debate this proposition, or even to explore further the question of judicial review. What is important about this approach, in the present context, is its ramifications for the concept of majority rule and "enduring general values" of the type thought to be embodied in the First Amendment. A just society is one in which there is some accommodation between values, rooted in people's "better natures" and aspirations, and the ability of the majority to secure its immediate aims as expeditiously as possible. In this sense, there is conflict between the admittedly mystical will of the people and the preservation of end-state values that may thwart the majority and give consolation to a minority asserting them. Hence Bickel's conclusion about judicial review is rather an uneasy one, and he notes that the antimajoritarian charge is only blunted; for "full consistency with democratic theory has not been established."[12]

The approaches of Shapiro and Bickel are similar in that each sees the vindication of important values as being, in lesser or greater degree, inconsistent with majority rule. But each defends protection of such values by the judiciary from a different perspective. Shapiro's analysis is essentially functional and structural, focusing on the inability of popularly elected officials to represent the array of constituencies comprised in that ill-defined phrase, "the people." Bickel, on the other hand, confronts the problem from an ethical perspective: majority rule is not the sole aim of a just society and a reasonable accommodation of fundamental values, and the institutionalization of their protection, may require pragmatic if somewhat undemocratic solutions.

But Bickel alludes to a conception of values that may undercut the

10. *Id.* at 19.
11. *Id.* at 20 (emphasis in original).
12. *Id.* at 26-28. See also Alexander Bickel, *The Morality of Consent* (New Haven, Conn.: Yale University Press, 1975).

paradoxes of democratic theory. Far from resting on a philosophy of natural law, a difficult proposition for the relativists of our day,[13] those values may inhere in the people themselves and their ideals and aspirations. In a deeper sense, there is consent to such values, but the people may forget them in the press of the moment, or fail to articulate them intelligibly or apply them rationally. The Court, then, has the task of articulating, discovering, and amplifying consensual values. The principle assumes consent, and hence legitimacy, and relies on the notion that the people wish to be protected from their own excesses. At bottom, it embodies the philosophical tradition of social contract.

James Buchanan, an economist writing in the Lockean tradition, illustrates this contractarian theory for the enforcement of norms— seemingly contrary to notions of consent—in a purposefully over-simplified story of Robinson Crusoe in the role of "man as rule maker." His example is worth quoting at length.

> The individual recognizes, and acknowledges, that he is neither saint nor sinner, either in existing or in extrapolated society. Man adopts rules. The rule-maker explicitly and deliberately imposes constraints upon himself in order to channel his own expedient behavior toward rationally selected norms. No one could claim that Robinson Crusoe is not "free"; yet a rational Crusoe might build and set an alarm clock, a device designed deliberately to intervene in his behavioral adjustment to changing environment. . . .
>
> Crusoe imposes rules on his behavior because he recognizes his own imperfection in the face of possible temptation. This is not an acknowledgment of original sin but a simple recognition that behavioral responses are to some extent predictable by the person who chooses, and that some behavior patterns are better than others when a longterm planning horizon is taken. . . . Crusoe constructs his alarm clock, an impersonal and external device designed to impose constraints on his own choice behavior. . . . With the alarm clock, Crusoe disturbs his dozing in advance. He closes off one behavioral option that would continue to remain open under voluntaristic rule. . . .
>
> A somewhat different way of putting this is to say that Crusoe "makes contracts with himself" when he works out his planning program. He recognizes that the pleasant life requires work while the sun is young in the tropical morn, and agrees with himself during his contemplative moments that such work is a part of an optimal behavior pattern. But, knowing himself and his predispo-

---

13. See, generally, Bruce A. Ackerman, *Social Justice in the Liberal State* (New Haven, Conn.: Yale University Press, 1980).

sitions, he fears that he will not expediently and voluntarily live up to his own terms. The alarm clock becomes, for Crusoe, the enforcing agent, the "governor" whose sole task is that of insuring that the contracts once made are honored. For effective enforcement, the "governor" must be external to the person who recognizes his own weaknesses.[14]

Buchanan is careful not to move simplistically from Crusoe alone on his island and contracting with himself to the world where agreements are many and made among the many.[15] The point, however, is that a group may impose constraints on its members and grant the power to an independent enforcing agency to enforce those constraints as a check on its recognized proclivity to act out of the momentary impulse and contrary to its long-term interests. There is a difference between self-restraint and coercion. This is the "noble paradox" described by Charles Black: "The state itself must set up this limit on itself, and submit to the organ of its enforcement."[16] Laurence Tribe may also be right in saying that this is the very purpose of a written constitution, difficult to amend, and accompanied by various enforcement mechanisms, including judicial review.[17] This may well justify the protection of First Amendment values such as freedom of expression. The contractarian can argue that these values have received widespread assent, and that the conflict with majority rule is a spurious one. The real conflict is between the desires of the moment and long-range desires which have been incorporated in agreement.

Buchanan's amplification of what is inchoate in Bickel is a commendable effort to resolve the question of adherence to values, presumably including liberal values, in a democratic polity. There remains, however, the problem of disentangling the desires of the moment in a

14. James Buchanan, *The Limits of Liberty* 93–94 (Chicago: University of Chicago Press, 1975). See, generally, James Buchanan, "A Contractarian Perspective on Anarchy," in J. Roland Pennock and John Chapman, eds., *Nomos XIX: Anarchism* 29 (New York: New York University Press, 1978); Laurence Tribe, *American Constitutional Law* § 1-7 (Mineola, N.Y.: Foundation Press, 1978); and John Rawls, *A Theory of Justice* 17–22, 114–117 (Cambridge, Mass.: Belknap Press, 1971). But cf. Ackerman, *Social Justice in the Liberal State.*

15. Buchanan, *Limits of Liberty* 96–98.

16. Charles Black, *Structure and Relationship in Constitutional Law* 79 (Baton Rouge, La.: Louisiana State University Press, 1969).

17. Tribe, *American Constitutional Law* 10. Neither Tribe nor I intend to preclude constitutional interpretation and application by decision makers other than judges. See *id.* at § 1-9; Paul Brest, "The Conscientious Legislator's Guide to Constitutional Interpretation," 27 *Stanford Law Review* 585 (1975); Jesse Choper, "The Scope of National Power Vis-à-Vis the States: The Dispensability of Judicial Review," 86 *Yale Law Journal* 1552, 1573-1577 (1977); Archibald Cox, "The Role of Congress in Constitutional Determinations," 40 *University of Cincinnati Law Review* 199 (1971); Hans Linde, "Judges, Critics, and the Realist Tradition," 82 *Yale Law Journal* 227 (1972); Donald Morgan, *Congress and the Constitution* (Cambridge, Mass.: Belknap Press, 1966).

modern welfare state—those of the living—from the aspirations of the dead framers of a document "to start a governmental experiment for an agricultural, sectional, seaboard folk of some three millions."[18] And this suggests many of the traditional criticisms of social-contract theory. Why should the preferences of a present majority be subordinated to constraints to which it never explicitly assented?[19] Perhaps the simplest answer is that there is no normative imperative, but most people do, in fact, feel bound. They are, after all, the children of their parents and of the culture and milieu in which they were raised. [20] And they are most often educated by the state, which in a democratic society may have the responsibility of keeping those commitments alive until citizens "learn how to consent."[21] But the contractarian argument, in the light of the factors of time and history, is disturbingly mystical. Have all the members of any present society (or most of them) really entered into a contract about limitations on future conduct? Is a written constitution dispositive of the matter?[22] What were the terms of that agreement? How do we discern them? Do we not necessarily distort original understandings in the process of bringing them to bear on a changing world? Is the contract sufficiently specific to avoid delegating virtually unbridled discretion to those charged with enforcing it?[23]

Demurrer may be the best response to the contractarian approach to the countermajoritarian difficulty. But I cannot overcome the feeling not only that the contractarian position is empirically unverifiable, in both its past and present forms, but also that it is an artificial process construct designed to affirm fundamental values while sidestepping difficult questions of legitimacy, utility, and consent.[24] The contractarian must define the "chooser and choice set that structures the contractarian argument," and yet this exercise in "pseudohistory" inevitably involves characterization of the contract setting "in noncontractarian terms."[25] In its sheer faith and fantasy, the approach recalls the tale of the

18. Karl Llewellyn, "The Constitution as Institution," 34 *Columbia Law Review* 1, 3 (1934).

19. See, generally, Mark Kann, "The Dialectic of Consent Theory," 40 *Journal of Politics* 387 (1978).

20. See, generally, Alexander Sesonske, *Value and Obligation* (New York: Oxford University Press, 1964).

21. Kann, "Dialectic of Consent Theory" 395, citing Joseph Tussman, *Obligation and the Body Politic* (New York: Oxford University Press, 1960).

22. See, generally, Thomas Grey, "Do We Have an Unwritten Constitution?" 27 *Stanford Law Review* 703 (1975); Llewellyn, "Constitution as Institution."

23. Cf. Ronald Dworkin, *Taking Rights Seriously* ch. 4 (Cambridge, Mass.: Harvard University Press, 1977); H. L. A. Hart, "American Jurisprudence Through English Eyes: The Nightmare and the Noble Dream," 11 *Georgia Law Review* 969 (1977).

24. See Ackerman, *Social Justice in the Liberal State* 336-342; Kann, "Dialectic of Consent Theory" 387; Laurence H. Tribe, "The Puzzling Persistence of Process-Based Constitutional Theories," 89 *Yale Law Journal* 1063 (1980).

25. Ackerman, *Social Justice in the Liberal State* 338.

chemist, physicist, and economist marooned on a desert island. They had only one large can of beans for food and no can-opener. The chemist proposed mixing together certain substances found on the island to create an explosion and blow it open. The physicist recommended the use of levers and weights to smash the can open. The economist's response was more straightforward: "Let's pretend we have a can-opener!"

The Difficulty Reconsidered

Consideration of the role of government expression in the First Amendment should begin with two propositions. First, in a representative democracy public officials must by definition represent the preferences of the majority in some sense, or at least be responsive to citizen preferences in a procedural setting that is recognized as fair and legitimate. Second, the essence of democratic government is that autonomous, self-controlled citizens have the opportunity to make informed, intelligent judgments about government policies, free of a state preceptorship that substantially impedes individual choice and consent. The first proposition is the problem of verifying majorities: how do we know that legislative bodies, for example, represent the will of a majority of citizens at any particular time? The second proposition relates to the problem of government falsification of majorities: government may so seek to indoctrinate the public as to engineer false consent by producing citizens with a mind-set supportive of the leadership and its policies. This may be accomplished by bombarding the populace with information and opinions favorable to the leadership and its policies, or by withholding information that might lead to adoption of unsympathetic points of view. Consent and majority rule become circular as the state attempts to produce the conditions for its legitimacy, and legitimacy is lost precisely because of the nature of the state's interference with the processes of autonomous consent. As noted earlier, the quest for the self-controlled citizen may, at bottom, rest more on the principle that governments should respect the autonomy and dignity of each individual than on a clear distinction between coercion and persuasion.

In their crude form, these propositions are difficult to defend when measured against the reality of how democracies operate their institutions and against the frailties of individual citizens. The concepts of majority rule and consent need to be refined if we are to avoid the blind faith and mystical inventions of the contractarians. It is fatuous to think of majority rule as embodying a substantive concept of actual approval by the majority of the members of the polity at any specific point in time. Nor can consent mean the actual consent of all, or nearly

all, of the members of the polity to the exercise of powers by governments. Perhaps it means mere acquiescence to the system.[26] If so,
democratic governments are legitimate only in the sense that the majority does not feel put upon enough to object. But consider another alternative: majority rule and consent should refer to a process, a symbiotic, mutually affecting relationship between governors and governed
that aspires to—though it may never achieve—the democratic ideals of
majority rule and consent. Charles Frankel puts the matter well:

> "Government by consent" cannot be interpreted to mean that
> those who are governed necessarily agree with what their rulers
> decide to do. Nor can it mean that "the majority" agrees. For
> in a democracy the minority, too, is presumably governed by its
> consent.
>
> But to speak of majorities and minorities and the inevita-
> bility of disagreements is to suggest what "government by con-
> sent" expresses. *It expresses the hope for a society in which ordinary
> people can influence the actions their leaders take.* This means that they
> can exercise some control over who their leaders will be. *And it
> also means that they are required to obey only after having been actively
> consulted by those who issue the order.*[27]

Majority rule in a democratic society is not a simple *substantive*
concept; it is a complex *process* of consultation in which citizens are free
to make up their minds and express their opinions.[28] It is much more
sophisticated than the crude notion that there exists some unidimen-
sional thing called public opinion, the product of only one public; that
the masses of people are informed, "rational," or even care about some,
or most, policy issues;[29] that election of candidates with "bundles" of

26. See David Easton, *A Systems Analysis of Political Life* (New York: Wiley, 1965).

27. Charles Frankel, *The Democratic Prospect* 34 (New York: Harper & Row, 1962). See
also Hannah Arendt, *Crises of the Republic* 85 (New York: Harcourt Brace Jovanovich,
1972). Cf. Dan Nimmo, *Popular Images of Politics* (Englewood Cliffs, N.J.: Prentice-Hall,
1974).

28. See, generally, Dahl, *Polyarchy*; Frankel, *Democratic Prospect*. Kenneth Boulding puts
the matter this way: "The majority does not rule; a majority decision is simply a setting of
the terms under which the minority continues the discussion—a discussion which presumably goes on forever or at least for the lifetime of the organization" (*The Image* 103
[Ann Arbor, Mich.: University of Michigan Press, 1961]).

29. See, generally, Gabriel Almond, *American People and Foreign Policy* (New York:
Praeger, 1960); Winston Brembeck and William Howell, *Persuasion* 12-15 (New York:
Prentice-Hall, 1952); Edmond Cahn, *The Predicament of Democratic Man* 95 (New York:
Macmillan, 1961); Donald Devine, *The Attentive Public: Polyarchical Democracy* (Chicago:
Rand McNally, 1970); V.O. Key, *Public Opinion and American Democracy* (New York:
Knopf, 1967); Walter Lippmann, *Public Opinion* (New York: Macmillan, 1956); Nimmo,
Popular Images 83-88; Marbury Ogle, *Public Opinion and Political Dynamics* (Boston: Houghton
Mifflin, 1950); Stephen Monsma, "Potential Leaders and Democratic Values," 35 *Public
Opinion Quarterly* 350 (1971).

positions is decisive on any particular issue; or that the decisions of the people's representatives invariably reflect something called the preferences of the "majority."[30] It is the opportunity of citizens, groups, or organizations to influence those who govern and one another that is critical, and not whether on any particular issue they choose to do so, or whether 50 percent of the people plus one favor a policy. It consists of a mutually affecting relationship between the people and their rulers in which government affirmatively promotes choice and respect for the individual's autonomy. Consent should not be confused with consensus. It is the notion of meaningful opportunity which informs the otherwise untenable literal concept of actual consent.

Alexander Meiklejohn's classic theory of self-governing speech roughly corresponds to the felt need to verify the existence of majorities, the first of our two propositions. He holds, basically, that the people are their own governors in a democracy, and that in order to

30. The most interesting exploration of this question occurs in the social-choice literature, founded largely on Kenneth Arrow's "general impossibility theorem" (see Arrow, *Social Choice and Individual Values* [New York: Wiley, 1963]). As Michael Levine and Charles Plott have described this literature, it suggests

> that there probably is no single nondictatorial method of aggregating the preferences of an electorate that will reliably produce a choice which satisfies minimum consistency and rationality standards. Since reasonably plausible examples of paradoxical results can be developed for each commonly used system of preference aggregation, such as majority rule or preferential point voting, there is probably no single process that "best" reflects the "will" of the group. The social choice literature also tells us that the outcome of any given attempt to determine a group choice *theoretically* depends upon the particular method used. . . .
> What the Arrow Theorem and its progeny suggest . . . is that . . . if there is no way of uniquely defining a social preference, then it must be the case that two or more inconsistent outcomes are possible from any individual preference configuration. If *this* is the case, there must be associated with each inconsistent alternative a procedure by which it can be reached. ("Agenda Influence and Its Implications," 63 *Virginia Law Review* 561-562 and 561 n. 2 [1977])

See also Charles Plott, "Axiomatic Social Choice Theory: An Overview and Interpretation," 20 *American Journal of Political Science* 511, 514, (1976):

> This result is called a majority rule cycle or majority preference cycle. [This amounts] to throwing out the implied definition of social preference. "This cycle doesn't mean anything: the group will choose the best thing when they meet—just let them vote and things will be OK as long as they come to *some* agreement." The trouble is that the outcome depends only upon the voting sequence. The outcome is y, x, or z, depending only upon whether the agenda sequence A, B, or C, respectively is adopted. This is true in theory and in fact.

This does not, of course, mean that citizen preferences and official perceptions of citizen preferences are irrelevant to decision making by majoritarian institutions, for those preferences set the boundaries within which choices are made. It means only that described sets of preferences will lead to different choices among them depending on the agenda sequence.

perform this function they must be able to communicate with one another and with their agents, those who hold official government positions. This means that speech which relates to the governing process needs to be absolutely protected: questions of policy should be openly debated so that the people can freely and in an informed fashion choose who is to represent them and, once candidates have been elected, seek to influence their policy judgments:

> When men govern themselves, it is they—and no one else—who must pass judgment upon unwisdom and unfairness and danger. And that means that unwise ideas must have a hearing as well as wise ones, unfair as well as fair, dangerous as well as safe, un–American as well as American. *Just so far as, at any point, the citizens who are to decide an issue are denied acquaintance with information or opinion or doubt or disbelief or criticism which is relevant to that issue, just so far the result must be ill-considered, ill-balanced planning for the general good. It is that mutilation of the thinking process of the community against which the First Amendment of the Constitution is directed.* The principle of freedom of speech springs from the necessities of the program of self-government. It is not a Law of Nature or Reason in the abstract. It is a deduction from the basic American agreement that public issues shall be decided by universal suffrage.[31]

The Meiklejohn theory is essentially functional and instrumental, and it seeks to guarantee the *opportunity* for citizens to influence those who govern them. Meiklejohn is under no illusion that many or most citizens will grasp that opportunity, but a society is democratic and a people self-governing to the extent that such opportunities exist, are taken advantage of, and actually influence the governing elites. And "the point of ultimate interest is not the words of the speakers, but the minds of the hearers."[32]

Concern not with natural law but with the "minds of the hearers" and the implicit needs of a democratic society is imperative in the attempt to enhance the communications process. But Meiklejohn focuses exclusively on private speakers communicating with one another and with the government. This ignores the problem of government falsification of majorities. Government speech presents many hazards to the ability of autonomous citizens to make informed and intelligent policy judgments. There is the danger that a well-heeled government might so dominate the opportunities for mass communications (which are not infinite) that individual voices would be drowned out. As William Van Alstyne has so aptly explained:

31. Meiklejohn, *Free Speech* 26–27.
32. *Id.* at 25.

The government itself commands sufficient means to propagandize so much, so continuously, and so loudly in support of one
view that private voices feebly piping below the government's
noisier din are scarcely heard. A government need not directly
curtail the activities of private pamphleteers, for instance, if it
can effectively displace them by subsidizing the "friendly" press
or, better still, by establishing an inexhaustibly more powerful
press committed exclusively to its own view.[33]

There is the danger that the prestige and status of government will
give its utterances an advantage in competition with private-sector
communications. There is the danger that government will fail to
disclose vital information only it possesses. And, most importantly,
there is the danger that citizens will not perform their self-governing
functions because the government itself has indoctrinated them to its
point of view. When Meiklejohn puts the onus on government to
"attempt to so inform and cultivate the mind and will of a citizen that
he shall have the wisdom, the independence, and therefore, the dignity
of a governing citizen,"[34] he articulates the state's affirmative duty to
enhance individual choice and autonomy. But he is not mindful of the
dangers of a strong, affirmative communications role for government,
which may cultivate dependence and attempt to produce citizens who
will quietly acquiesce in its policies and decisions. The "thinking process of the community" may be mutilated as much by government
expression and nondisclosure as by government censorship.

The necessities of the present age present a new context in which to
apply the eighteenth-century idea of freedom of expression as a check on
despotism.[35] Vincent Blasi's idea of the First Amendment as a check on
abuse of power by government officials and agencies goes a long way
toward meeting the challenge of government expression:

Consider the most important ways in which the First Amendment
has made a difference in recent years. But for the peace marches
and other protests, the Johnson administration might very well
have escalated the war in Vietnam after the Tet offensive and the
Nixon administration might have attempted to sustain a wider
war after the Cambodian "incursion." But for the tradition of a
free press, the crimes and abuses of Watergate might never have
been uncovered. These incidents in our recent political experience
are so familiar that it is easy to underestimate their importance.

33. William Van Alstyne, "The First Amendment and the Suppression of Warmongering Propaganda in the United States: Comments and Footnotes," 31 *Law and Contemporary Problems* 530, 533 (1966).
34. Meiklejohn, *Free Speech* 25.
35. See Blasi, "Checking Value in First Amendment Theory".

In the last decade, the First Amendment has had at least as much impact on American life by facilitating a process by which countervailing forces check the misuse of official power as by protecting the dignity of the individual, maintaining a diverse society in the face of conformist pressures, promoting the quest for scientific and philosophic truth, or fostering a regime of "self-government" in which large numbers of ordinary citizens take an active part in political affairs.[36]

Blasi relies largely on the pervasive character of modern government and its near monopoly over coercive sanctions as justifications for the checking power. But his approach is still a step away from the more fundamental problem of government falsification of majorities. The First Amendment should not only function to ferret out abuses of power, it should also serve to prevent the distortion of the judgment of the people by government expression or secrecy. It should be a check on government indoctrination, not simply a check on government misconduct. To act against government misconduct, people must possess not only the relevant information, but the informed and independent standards with which to evaluate both information and conduct. Furthermore, government conduct, legitimated by false consent, is as inconsistent with democratic precepts as official attempts to limit private speech and association. This means that limitations on government expression itself are as important as the absence of limitations on private speech and association. The value of the First Amendment lies not only in checking isolated abuses of power, but in preserving the very processes of majority rule.

The symbiotic relationship between First Amendment rights and majority rule strengthens each and brings us closer to the ideal of the self-controlled citizen. This relationship may also help to explain the survival of civil liberties in the United States and the aspiration toward civil liberties in most nations. As Robert Ardrey has argued, liberal democratic values may enhance both group and individual survival, and thus they themselves survive precisely because they are functional.[37] For Ardrey, this is a sort of natural selection, linking social and political conventions to human "animalness." For others, it may be a straightforward utilitarianism. In any event, there are synergistic forces at work. The good accruing to society is greater than the sum of all instances of protecting individual expression and associational rights.

36. *Id.* at 527.
37. Robert Ardrey, *The Social Contract* (New York: Atheneum, 1970).

[9]

The First Amendment as a
Constraint on Government Expression:
Arguments from History and Structure

Constitutionalizing the Arguments

The idea that government expression can be inconsistent with democratic consent and majoritarian processes may be framed in constitutional terms. If government expression and secrecy can sometimes serve the same functions as direct government censorship, then, logically, sources of limitation of government communication abuses may be sought in the First Amendment, which has been construed as placing severe limits on government's power to silence nongovernment speakers. The nature of this constitutional argument is critically important. The interpretation is not premised on the text of the First Amendment, for the issue is not one of congressional abridgement of free speech in a literal sense. Nor is it premised on the extension of the First Amendment to the states under the due process clause of the Fourteenth Amendment. The interpretation is based on the relationship between the text and the structure of democractic government embodied in the Constitution and American institutions and in the pervasive assumptions and general purposes underlying the First Amendment. In this regard, I explicitly draw on the wisdom of Charles Black, the legal scholar who has most contributed to our understanding of the role of structure and relationship in constitutional interpretation.

With regard to the First Amendment and other constitutional guarantees expressly addressed to the federal government, Black asks an arresting question: What difference would it have made if the Fourteenth Amendment had never been adopted and its due process clause had not been textually construed as "incorporating" the Bill of Rights? His answer is that the protection of freedom of speech from state interference would have been constitutionally compelled anyway:

The nature of the federal government, and of the states' relation to it, compels the inference of some federal constitutional protection for free speech, and gives to a wide protection an inferential support quite as strong as the textual support [proffered in early First Amendment decisions].[1]

By way of example, Black notes that the First Amendment includes the right of the people to petition for redress of grievances, though the provision is not on its face applicable to the states. But what if a state makes criminal the gathering of signatures for a petition to Congress? Can this be constitutional? His answer is that the state criminal law would be unconstitutional, "because such a state law would constitute interference with a transaction which is part of the workings of the federal government." The law would interfere with the constitutionally established relationship between the federal legislative branch and the citizenry. And this conclusion follows for Black even though the text does not address the problem. He adds that it would be true "even if there were no First Amendment," because a contrary result would undermine the constitutional character of the Congress.[2]

Black's method of constitutional interpretation rests on both "textual and . . . relational and structural modes of reasoning." After all, constitutional structures and relationships are rooted in and controlled by the text. The critical question is this: "What relations and structures are soundly enough established to furnish a basis for this kind of legal thought?"[3] The basic contention here is that limitations on government expression are a natural inference to be drawn from the First Amendment and the concept of democratic government embodied in the Constitution. How meaningful are the rights to speak and to petition the government if the government dominates the minds of individuals, suppressing their ability to think critically about government leaders and policies? Does not the notion of electing a president and members of Congress embrace the assumption that voters are self-controlled citizens able to make reasonably unfettered decisions about candidates? If the general purposes of the First Amendment are to promote political discussion and to prevent government censorship, does all of this come to nothing if government adopts a preceptoral strategy for engineering consent? In the twentieth century, unlike the eighteenth, laws and practices that permit massive government communications activities may as effectively silence private speakers as direct censorship. What is left of religious freedom if government controls the mind, eschewing regulation of churches?

1. Charles Black, *Structure and Relationship in Constitutional Law* 39 (Baton Rouge, La.: Louisiana State University Press, 1969).
2. *Id.* at 40.
3. *Id.* at 23, 31.

More fundamentally, whatever the original intentions of the framers, the Constitution, and the institutional arrangements that have followed it over nearly two hundred years, have established the aspiration to, and to a large extent the reality of, a representative democracy.[4] People obey because in some sense they have consented to government's exercise of authority in return for the opportunity to influence those who govern them. Otherwise, government is not constitutionally legitimate. Freedom of expression and association are critical to the process of consent, which government speech may threaten by impairing independence of judgment—through indoctrination, withholding of vital information, and preventing the communication of political judgments among individuals. The structure of American constitutional government and the underlying historical assumptions about the relationship between the governed and the governors buttress the view that the First Amendment encompasses limits on government expression.[5] This is consistent with older notions that the Constitution embodies norms against government secrecy, that the First Amendment is a check on official abuse of power, and that it restrains and does not enhance government powers.[6]

The purpose of this argument is not necessarily to create some new "derivative" constitutional right of the sort so frequently scorned by scholars and courts. Nor is the purpose to draw some concise Dworkinian distinction between policies which should guide government decision making and rights which may be vindicated against the state.[7] All that is being argued, for the moment, is that in terms of the age-old jurisprudential debate about what judges may legitimately take into account in deciding "hard [constitutional] cases," concerns about limits on government expression clearly fall within the "gravitational field"[8] of constitutional text and structures, filling in the interstices of constitutional law. In this sense, the analysis is somewhat different from Black's and embodies Blasi's approach to structural and relational argument:

> The importance of the structural approach may lie precisely in its potential for broadening judicial perspectives. The textual approach is under some strain presently because it is striving to

4. But cf., e.g., Charles Lindblom, *Politics and Markets* (New York: Basic Books, 1977).
5. See William Van Alstyne, "The First Amendment and the Suppression of Warmongering Propaganda in the United States: Comments and Footnotes," 31 *Law and Contemporary Problems* 532-535 (1966); Laurence H. Tribe, "The Puzzling Persistence of Process-Based Constitutional Theories," 89 *Yale Law Journal* 1063, 1078 (1980).
6. See Vincent Blasi, "The Checking Value in First Amendment Theory," 1977 *American Bar Foundation Research Journal* 523.
7. See Ronald Dworkin, *Taking Rights Seriously* 111 (Cambridge, Mass.: Harvard University Press, 1977).
8. *Id.* at ch. 4.

cope with cosmic, systemic injustices, such as legislative mal-
functioning and political repression, with a set of rather modest,
narrowly conceived constitutional norms. Because the structural
approach recognizes a much broader, more comprehensive set of
constitutional norms, it may facilitate a judicial response to citizen
complaints that concern systemic shortcomings as well as those
that involve particularized grievances.[9]

Precisely so. The recognition of the constitutional ramifications of
government expression calls attention to broader norms of majority
rule, democracy, and consent, and does not bridle First Amendment
analysis with a myopic search for definitions of the words of the First
Amendment or for the specific intentions of the framers (even assuming
they could be ascertained).

Implications for First Amendment Analysis: Recent Controversies in Perspective

The defenders of free expression have handicapped themselves by ignoring majoritarian arguments rooted in the fabric and structure of
democratic government. The structural underpinning of these arguments makes them more likely to find general acceptance than antimajoritarian arguments. So, too, court decisions which appear difficult
and tortuously reasoned from the individual-rights perspective may be
more readily understandable and defensible from this structural perspective. At a minimum, even if judicial results do not change, an
alternative justification becomes apparent. More fundamentally, the
government-speech perspective allows us to frame many of the First
Amendment cases of the last decades in terms which are more intelligible than traditional theories; for the individualistic and antimajoritarian approaches of the past, whatever their merits, are not sufficiently
sensitive to the structures necessary to constrain modern government's
vast communication powers.

Given the expansive power of governments to communicate, the
central First Amendment issues of the age no longer exclusively concern
fringe groups expressing opinions contrary to those held by the majority. There is a need, rather, to bolster the communication powers of
institutions outside of government with the resources, energy, and
expertise to counter the government's messages. We have to rely on
organized constituencies like the press, corporations, public-interest
groups, labor unions, and so on. These tend not to be fringe institutions or groups, but "establishment" organizations with high claims to
legitimacy in the public mind. In a sense, they represent the mass of

9. Vincent Blasi, "Creativity and Legitimacy in Constitutional Law," 80 *Yale Law
Journal* 176, 186 (1970).

individuals who can rarely counter the government's power on their own. The primary restraints on such organized constituencies rarely involve direct censorship of opinions; rather, they are restrained by their lack of access to government institutions, proceedings, and documents and by their dependence on government for information.[10] The problem is frequently one of acquiring information, not one of publishing information already in hand or expressing opinions. And because government possesses such large quantities of data, over which it often has near exclusive control, it is in a position to amplify selected facts and to withhold other information.

Within this framework, one can begin to understand modern controversies over the access of the press to prison facilities, the rights of corporations to advertise on political matters, the asserted privilege of reporters to decline to disclose sources of information or notes, the press's right to report on criminal proceedings and to reveal the names of victims of particular crimes, and the lawfulness of searches of newspaper premises. In each case, government may have a substantial interest in limiting access to the facts it possesses, or in obtaining facts from others, even though this may hinder their information-gathering activities. The government may justify its actions as required to protect the integrity of the criminal-justice system, to maintain order in the prisons, to protect individual privacy, and so on. But the bottom line is that government has impaired the ability of private institutions, perhaps especially the mass media, to obtain information that might counter its influence and provide information to the people—those who stand in judgment over government officials and their policies. A rebuttable presumption of access, absent a strong justification by government for declining to reveal information, is the minimum required to maintain the balance. Statutory press shield laws, government-in-the-sunshine (open-meeting) laws, freedom-of-information acts, and the recent presidential executive order on national-security information (seeking to tighten controls over the misclassification of government documents as secret) are all indications of a movement in the direction of overcoming government secrecy and of giving the private sector the wherewithal to respond to government's selective publication of information.

While the Supreme Court frequently invokes the First Amendment to protect individuals and minorities from an overreaching majority, it has recently shown increased understanding of the structure of modern communications networks. In *First National Bank of Boston* v. *Bellotti*,[11] the Court addressed the question of whether the state of Massachusetts could constitutionally limit political advertising by corporations. Justice White, dissenting, emphasized the values of self-realization, self-ful-

10. Cf. *Richmond Newspapers, Inc.* v. *Virginia* 100 S.Ct. 2814 (1980).
11. 435 U.S. 765 (1978).

fillment, and individual freedom underlying the First Amendment, and declared his belief that these values were not advanced by protecting corporate speech. Indeed, he suggested that corporate speech could have deleterious effects:

> This Nation has for many years recognized the need for measures designed to prevent corporate domination of the political process. The Corrupt Practices Act, first enacted in 1907, has consistently barred corporate contributions in connection with federal elections. This Court has repeatedly recognized that one of the principal purposes of the prohibition is "to avoid the deleterious influences on federal elections resulting from the use of money by those who exercise control over large aggregations of capital.[12]

White not only takes an individualistic view of First Amendment values, he is apprehensive about corporate speech and its potential for dominating the marketplace of ideas.[13] This appears to ignore more functional views of the First Amendment and the fact that though large institutions with considerable resources may be involved in most communications, they also serve to check one another.

Justice Powell's opinion for the majority responded to White's analysis by emphasizing the organized nature of the modern communications network. He noted the role of the institutional press in informing and educating the public, and expressed the opinion that corporations in the business of communicating should not be distinguished from other corporations for First Amendment purposes.[14] His operating premise was that the First Amendment is not limited to advancing self-expression and self-fulfillment; other values are served as well:

> The Court's decisions involving corporations in the business of communication or entertainment are based not only on the role of the First Amendment in fostering individual self-expression but also on its role in affording the public access to discussion, debate, and the dissemination of information and ideas. . . . Even decisions seemingly based exclusively on the individual's right to express himself acknowledge that the expression may contribute to society's edification.
>
> The suggestion . . . that the First Amendment affords less protection to ideas that are not the product of "individual choice" would seem to apply to newspaper editorials and every other form of speech created under the auspices of a corporate body. No decision of this Court lends support to such a restrictive notion.[15]

12. *Id.* at 811-812.
13. *Id.* at 809-812. See, generally, Lindblom, *Politics and Markets*.
14. *Id.* at 781-784.
15. *Id.* at 783.

The free flow of information is thus advanced by institutional communications, and this is an important value in a democracy. To take the analysis beyond the Powell opinion, if information largely flows from individuals with relatively limited resources (as per Justice White), then perhaps there is much to be said for limiting the communications activities of corporate or other institutional actors in order to cure inequalities in the marketplace—albeit this may cut against the freedom of the institutional press and may call for a good deal of trust in the ability of legislatures and courts to draw such lines. Justice White appears not to worry about government's own participation and to have faith in the ability of government to correct market flaws. But if the fear is primarily one of the domination of large-scale government and private-sector institutions in the communications sphere, then it is incumbent upon the courts to cultivate the ability of all institutions to counter government and one another.[16] What is important about *Bellotti*, then, is its recognition of the institutional interplay and complexity in modern communications systems, even if the Court does not tie this theme to government's own communication capacities. This recognition takes First Amendment analysis beyond individual dignity and protection of minorities' values to the equally important values of preserving majoritarian processes and the self-controlled citizen.

Preliminary Caveats

Vindicating Structural Interests in the Courts

When governments dominate communications networks and withhold vital policy information, the injury is not generally to any specific individual or group asserting an interest contrary to the community's interest. The injury is to us all.[17] Democracy depends on an open and pluralistic structure of communications. Any individual or group seeking to curb government-induced distortions of the structure seeks to vindicate the interests of all. In specific instances, individuals may be uniquely injured as well—for example, where government communications defame named individuals, or where some are much more affected

16. Lindblom would not equate the communications powers of businessmen and their corporate enterprises with what he perceives as the lesser communications powers of non-business institutions (Lindblom, *Politics and Markets* 206-207).

17. In Dworkinian terms, the interest behind controlling government speech is a "policy" rather than a "principle," since it serves to benefit society as a whole by, among other things, protecting democratic goals. A "principle," on the other hand, protects individual rights as against other individuals, or society as a whole. Thus, when government speaks improperly, society as a whole is injured. Ronald Dworkin, "The Rights of Myron Farber," 25 *New York Review of Books* 34 (1978). This may be inconsistent with Dworkin's earlier views (See Dworkin, *Taking Rights Seriously*). Cf. David Lyons, "Human Rights and the General Welfare," 6 *Philosophy and Public Affairs* 113, 115 (1977).

than others (members of a captive audience), but I suspect that these cases are relatively rare.

The analogy that comes to mind is the establishment clause of the First Amendment.[18] All Americans have a vital stake in the continued separation of church and state—a sound principle. But those Americans with religious or other beliefs contrary to the "established" religion would probably be most hurt by failure to keep them separate. Some would perhaps base the rights of the latter on the free-exercise-of-religion clause and not on the constitutional doctrine of the establishment clause.[19] In any event, the generalized nature of the harm under non-establishment-clause precedents[20] cuts against the idea that individuals should have a right to a preferred communications structure, embodying limits on government speech. Federal courts are also reluctant to countenance claims that particular federal expenditures violate constitutional norms where one asserts the claim as a taxpayer and the violation of constitutional norms is an injury to all and not to a discrete set of individuals and groups.[21] Whether the courts (at least federal courts) would or should assimilate objections to government expression to the spending cases or to the establishment clause cases, is an open question.

Line-drawing

The constitutionalization of a right to limit government expression brings with it additional sets of analytical and institutional problems. The burden of justifying its communications would be on government if there is a constitutional right to curb excesses, subject to some very demanding test for the substantiality of the government's interest.[22] Plaintiffs would prevail in all cases, absent demonstration of a high degree of governmental necessity. Such a standard does not comport with the dual nature of government expression. If the falsification of consent and the domination of communications are perils, there are

18. See *Roemer* v. *Board of Public Works*, 426 U.S. 736 (1976); *Meek* v. *Pittinger*, 421 U.S. 349 (1975); *Hunt* v. *McNair*, 413 U.S. 734 (1973); *Levitt* v. *Committee for Public Education and Religious Freedom*, 413 U.S. 421 (1962); *Zorach* v. *Clausen*, 343 U.S. 306; *Everson* v. *Board of Education*, 330 U.S. 1 (1947).

19. See ch. 12, p. 215, below.

20. See *Simon* v. *Eastern Kentucky Welfare Rights Organization*, 426 U.S. 26 (1976); *Warth* v. *Seldin*, 422 U.S. 490 (1975); *Sierra Club* v. *Morton*, 405 U.S. 727 (1972). Generally the standing problems associated with direct challenges to government speech are very difficult. See, generally, Laurence Tribe, *American Constitutional Law* 590 (Mineola, N.Y.: Foundation Press, 1978).

21. See, e.g., *United States* v. *Richardson*, 418 U.S. 166 (1974); *Williams* v. *Riley*, 280 U.S. 78 (1929); *Frothingham* v. *Mellon*, 262 U.S. 447 (1923). See, generally, Tribe, *American Constitutional Law* 79-114.

22. See, generally, Tribe, *American Constitutional Law* ch. 12.

equal perils in cabining governments' power to educate, inform, sponsor and publish research, and lead.

And, as discussed in the following chapter, the agency primarily charged with making such decisions, the federal judiciary, is not particularly well-positioned among the branches of government to take responsibility for these judgments. It is a truism that of all the branches of government, the judiciary relies most on the power of words, symbols, and custom to persuade, and ultimately to enforce its decisions and legitimate its powers. Judicial power emanates more from its role of oracle than from the coercive tools at its command. The sword is not its strong suit. The implication of this is that courts are not disinterested observers and arbiters of government-speech conflicts; rather they are practitioners of the arts of persuasion, who may well fail to perceive the dangers in government participation in the system of freedom of expression. They may even use the Constitution as a mechanism to strengthen their own communications powers at the expense of other levels and branches of government. And, even if they act from the highest ideals and motives, there is the danger that constitutional decisions, difficult to overturn, will exaggerate errors of judgment about government speech and inhibit government from employing its communications powers for legitimate policy objectives.

Perhaps one way of managing the dilemmas posed by compelling governments to justify all of their communication activities when the matter is litigated is to focus only on certain types of government expression. This is most apparent in the case of government nonexpression or secrecy. Courts might construe the First Amendment to require government to give specific reasons and to justify withholding information from the public, as under the federal Freedom of Information Act.[23] This would serve the functional purpose of increasing the flow of information and reducing the ability of government to persuade by failing to present inconvenient information, while recognizing that sometimes it is better for government to be able to restrict access to information, e.g., national defense secrets. It might also apply to access to government institutions (prisons, military bases, hospitals, schools) and government proceedings (meetings of administrative agencies).[24]

Beyond this category of government communication are other lines that might be drawn, though only with exceeding difficulty. One possible way to proceed is to distinguish government propaganda and indoctrination activities from government information, research, education, and leadership activities. Many have attempted to make this distinction, but with little success. If the focus is on the content of the message, the distinction may boil down to an acceptance of one set of

23. 5 U.S.C. § 552 (1977).
24. See ch. 14, below.

values over another. Government speech encouraging racial hatred or communism would be seen as propaganda, while the same activities on behalf of racial equality or free enterprise are treated as informational. The distinction will turn largely on convention—the accepted truths at a given point in time within a particular culture.[25] The courts could be set up in the business of distinguishing democratic from nondemocratic values, treating only the latter as propaganda, and hence as unconstitutional. Propaganda about tolerance, majority rule, electoral participation, and respect for minorities would not be treated as propaganda at all.

Perhaps any advocacy by government of unconstitutional values (e.g., involuntary servitude, segregated schools, unreasonable searches) should be curbed.[26] What government does not have the power to do within the constitutional system, it should not have the power to say.[27] But the lines become fuzzy. Is it unconstitutional for a city government to recommend the abolition of the exclusionary rule in criminal prosecutions where evidence has been unlawfully obtained by the police? What if a state legislature passes a resolution critical of the Supreme Court's school-prayer decisions? What of government messages—say with regard to the interstate-commerce or equal-protection clauses—which fail to anticipate Supreme Court decisions? Do not constitutional decisions change? And what of the obligation of branches of the government other than the judiciary to interpret the Constitution and to publicly defend those interpretations?[28] May the Constitution not be amended? Perhaps skilled judges should and could apply such standards, and the justification would be that private individuals and groups may challenge constitutional and democratic dogma, but the government should not. One is hard pressed, however, to find many clear historical examples of governments in the United States explicitly voicing unconstitutional values. Some local and state governmental responses to efforts to eliminate racial discrimination are perhaps the best examples. This line of analysis may work in such circumstances, as suggested in

25. See, generally, Elliot Aronson, *The Social Animal* 55 (San Francisco: W. H. Freeman, 1972); and Bertrand Russell, *Power: A New Social Analysis* 368–369 (New York: W. W. Norton, 1938).

26. See ch. 15, below. But cf. *Joyner* v. *Whiting*, 477 F.2d 456 (4th Cir. 1973). In Nathaniel Nathanson and Egon Schwelb, *The United States and the United Nations Treaty on Racial Discrimination: A Report for the Panel on International Human Rights and Its Implementation* 7 (St. Paul, Minn.: West Publishing, 1975) the authors note that "The Treaty on Racial Discrimination prohibits States Parties from discriminating on the basis of race. In addition one section prohibits the State Parties and individuals from acting to disseminate 'ideas based on racial superiority or hatred, incitement or racial discrimination.'"

27. Nathanson and Schwelb, *The United States and the United Nations Treaty on Racial Discrimination.*

28. See Paul Brest, "The Conscientious Legislator's Guide to Constitutional Interpretation," 27 *Stanford Law Review* 585 (1975).

chapter 15, but generalizing from a few egregious cases may prove difficult.

A standard for unconstitutional government expression might focus on its tendency to distort the thinking processes of listeners. Propaganda consists of the "big lie," of outrageous efforts to create a pseudo-reality. An inept political leadership is characterized as courageous and wise. The opposition is disgraced by untruths about its wrongdoings. The economy is touted as booming, when it is in recession. Lost battles and wars are described as great victories. All of this comports with widely held notions about the essence of propaganda in totalitarian countries: it is self-serving; its purpose is not to illuminate or inform. Accuracy is not its hallmark. Such notions of improper government communications link up with the idea that the greatest danger of government expression lies in the possibility of undermining the self-controlled citizen—of interfering with his ability to think clearly about policy issues and leaders.

There are modest analogies in modern First Amendment law governing private expression. Commercial advertising may receive First Amendment protection, but governments may forbid false and misleading advertising and fraud.[29] Even innocent misrepresentations may sometimes occasion liability.[30] An employer may be forbidden from telling certain harsh truths to employees about the effects of unionization for fear of distorting the outcome of a union representation election.[31] The prosecutor may not wave the bloody knife before the jury in a murder trial because the emotional impact of that symbolic act may outweigh its evidentiary value.[32] Even classic incitement-to-violence cases—decided under the "clear-and-present-danger" test or some other First Amendment formula[33]—may be viewed as efforts to curb forms of expression likely to cause people to act in ways they would not upon calmer reflection.

The judgment-distortion test is quite appealing. It strikes at the heart of the most objectionable side of government speech. Yet there is

29. See *Virginia Pharmacy Bd.* v. *Virginia Consumer Council*, 425 U.S. 748, 775-781 (1977) (Justice Stewart, concurring).

30. See, e.g., John Murray, *Murray on Contracts* §§ 91-102 (Indianapolis, Ind.: Bobbs-Merrill, 1974); American Law Institute, *Restatement (Second) of Torts* § 552c (1976).

31. See *Yellow Cab Co.* v. *NLRB*, 229 NLRB No. 99 (1977); *Hanover House Industries Inc.* v. *NLRB*, 233 NLRB No. 36 (1977); Julius Getman, *Labor Relations* 67-68 (Mineola, N.Y.: Foundation Press, 1978); Robert Swift, "NLRB Overkill: Predictions of Plant Relocation and Closure of Employer Free Speech," 8 *Georgia Law Review* 77 (1973).

32. Relevant "evidence may be excluded if its probative value is substantially outweighed by danger of unfair prejudice, confusion of the issue, or misleading the jury" (Federal Rule of Evidence 403).

33. *Hess* v. *Indiana*, 414 U.S. 105, 108 (1973); *Brandenburg* v. *Ohio*, 395 U.S. 444 (1969); *Edwards* v. *South Carolina*, 372 U.S. 229 (1963); *Noto* v. *United States*, 367 U.S. 270, 297-298 (1961); *Feiner* v. *New York*, 340 U.S. 315 (1951); *Terminello* v. *Chicago*, 337 U.S. 1 (1949).

a natural reluctance to build on the obvious analogies. In the political sphere, the accepted First Amendment wisdom would not allow the state to forbid private expression that persuades people over time—perhaps through emotional appeals or lies—of some new political creed. It is here that the metaphor of self-correcting forces in the marketplace of ideas comes to the fore. The incitement cases under modern case law appear to be concerned with immediate unlawful consequences—incitement within a narrow time frame.[34] At least in democratic countries, however, government efforts at persuasion tend to be more subtle, untruths are harder to identify, self-aggrandizing characterizations of facts are common, and indoctrination is a cumulative process. It is exceedingly difficult to identify any single message or communications program as falling within the judgment-distortion category. Indeed, the conventional wisdom is that the modern preceptor state appeals to the rational side of its public.[35] So, too, it is one thing to show that Jones was misled to his detriment by Smith's deceptive advertising, and quite another to show that a skeptical public has been brainwashed by government. At some point, at gut level perhaps, we all know propaganda when we see and hear it, and perhaps judges, with equally sensitive stomachs, should respond to such propaganda by declaring it unconstitutional under the First Amendment. The inability to formulate reasonably precise and generalizable standards does not necessarily mean that judges should not act; but, as in the case of pornography, our collective inarticulateness should give us pause.

Perhaps a factor that should be taken into account in determining the likelihood of government distortion of the thinking processes of citizens is the degree to which the government has captured the audience.[36] While the empirical evidence is not entirely clear, it appears likely that government may be more persuasive when the audience, in a sense, has no choice but to listen to the message (or at least to appear to be doing so) and when alternative voices are muffled. Thus, the potential for government indoctrination may be greatest in the case of total institutions such as prisons, or semi-total institutions such as schools and military bases.[37] Of course, actual success may be dependent on

34. See, e.g., *Brandenburg v. Ohio*, 395 U.S. 444 (1969).

35. See Lindblom, *Politics and Markets* 59.

36. Thus far, all of the Supreme Court captive-audience cases have involved situations where private or public entities have "captured" an audience for *private* speech purposes. See, e.g., *Consolidated Edison Company v. Public Service Commission*, 447 U.S. 530 (1980); *F.C.C. v. Pacifica Foundation*, 438 U.S. 726 (1978); *Lehman v. Shaker Heights*, 418 U.S. 298, 306 (1974) (Douglas, J., concurring); *Rowan v. Post Office*, 397 U.S. 728 (1970); *Breard v. Alexandria*, 341 U.S. 622 (1951); *Kovacs v. Cooper*, 336 U.S. 77 (1949). See, generally, Charles Black, "He Cannot Choose But Hear: The Plight of the Captive Auditor," 53 *Columbia Law Review* 960 (1953).

37. The term "total institutions" is taken from Erving Goffman, *Asylums* 9 (Chicago: Aldine, 1961).

many factors; for it is axiomatic that some forms of indoctrination (for example, rehabilitation programs in prisons) are rarely effective. The maturity of the audience, the techniques of persuasion employed, the stubbornness of the listeners, and the openness or lack of openness of the institution and its captive audience to counter-messages may be critical factors in determining the constitutionality of government utterances. The greater the state's monopoly, the more apparent the dangers of government communications. The captive-audience phenomenon, however, standing alone, should not give rise to a finding of unconstitutional government expression, but it may be decisive in combination with other factors.[38]

A third sort of standard for distinguishing constitutional from unconstitutional government expression might seek to rely upon the partisan-nonpartisan distinction. The central idea would be that government officials should not use their offices, staffs, and public funds to promote their reelection or other personal political interests. As Thomas Emerson has said, "It is not the function of the government to get itself re-elected."[39] Perhaps more than the earlier arguments, this argument focuses not only on government domination of mass communications, but also on the wrong of requiring taxpayers to fund government rhetoric which they find objectionable. To some extent, this area is already covered by state and federal statutes dealing with abuse of public office; for it is generally unlawful to use public monies and personnel for reelection purposes.[40] Under these statutes, the question is largely one of tracking the flow of dollars and the activities of public employees and officers on government time. Sometimes this is relatively easy. For example, use of government funds and personnel for a mass mailing of pamphlets endorsing Democratic or Republican candidates would be unlawful in most jurisdictions (if not all) and might subject the wrongdoers to criminal liability.

Except in the most blatant cases of misuse of public funds or employees by government officials, the abuse-of-office statutes have been easily evaded and rarely enforced. Similar results are likely if the partisan-nonpartisan distinction is constitutionalized. This is particularly true if the emphasis is on government expression and not on misuse of tax dollars *per se*. Members of Congress do not send out "political" pamphlets at public expense; rather they send out news-

38. See ch. 12, below, and generally, Franklyn Haiman, "Speech v. Privacy: Is There a Right Not to be Spoken to?", 67 *Northwestern Law Review* 153 (1972); Van Alstyne, "The First Amendment and the Suppression of Warmongering" 534.

39. Thomas Emerson, *System of Freedom of Expression* 699 (New York: Random House, 1970).

40. See, e.g., Tex. Penal Code Ann. § 39.01 (1974); N.Y. Penal Law § 195.00 (McKinney 1975); 18 U.S.C. 203 (1977).

letters designed to "inform" the electorate of their own and Congress's activities. They are sternly warned in the United States Code that

> It is the intent of the Congress that a Member of or Member-elect to Congress may not mail as franked mail . . . mail matter which constitutes or includes any article, account, sketch, narration, or other text laudatory and complimentary of any Member of, or Member-elect to, Congress on a purely personal basis rather than on the basis of performance of official duties . . . [or] mail matter which constitutes or includes . . . mail matter which specifically solicits political support for the sender or any other person or any political party, or a vote or financial assistance for any candidate for any public office.[41]

The admonition amounts to saying that if you avoid being too blatant, you may use the franking privilege to endear yourself to the electorate; describe the "performance of official duties," but refrain from directly asking for votes or political contributions.

Except in rare cases,[42] it is virtually impossible to disentangle partisan from nonpartisan speech. The advancement of policy objectives through communications activities and the provision of information almost invariably advances the interests of those in power. For example, it is frequently difficult to ascertain when the president is speaking as national leader and when he is speaking on behalf of his party or of his own reelection. Unless he is a declared candidate for reelection, there are not even federal guidelines for allocating costs between the government and the political parties when the president goes on a speaking tour.

Perhaps the problem could be restated in terms of motivation. One might argue that if an official is motivated by partisan or political concerns, then the speech, if given at public expense and on public time, violates the First Amendment. But this argument is akin to saying that the government's motive was to propagandize and not to inform or lead. The fact is that the notion of institutional motive is a dubious one; we should not necessarily assume in animistic fashion that institutions have motives in the same sense as persons. Even if they do have such motivations, or if one can identify a single actor like the president with human motives, those motives are likely to be mixed. The president may speak because he believes it is in the nation's best interest, because he is looking forward to the next election, *and* because he wishes to unite his party behind him. If the question is whether the public official would have acted and spoken as he did but for partisan

41. 39 U.S.C. § 3210 (1973).
42. See ch. 4, above.

motivation, how do we tell? And, at least at the highest levels of executive and legislative policy making, it is not at all clear that there is a structural First Amendment interest in restraining partisan, political speech.

Perhaps the strongest argument for the partisan–nonpartisan distinction arises in the context of speech by government agencies and officials who are not elected officials and who are viewed as "employees" and not as policy makers involved in the political processes. For example, the mission of the therapist in a state mental hospital or of a commanding officer on a military base is generally not perceived as including indoctrination to a particular political viewpoint. Public school teachers may be charged with teaching about democratic processes and American history, but their duties are not thought to include the advocacy of the election of particular candidates for public office. Where such blatant abuses of public trust occur, perhaps federal courts would be justified in intervening. But, again, such cases will be rare. The commander of a military base can communicate ideas about appropriate military policy that subtly and by implication endorse the program of a particular political party. In describing the free-enterprise system, democratic institutions, the lives of famous American patriots, and the history of the Great Depression, a teacher can subtly convey values which are readily identifiable with the values of one political coalition rather than another.[43] In such circumstances, the difficulties of isolating unconstitutional partisan expression are extraordinary.

The ambiguousness of the partisan–nonpartisan distinction suggests yet another problem for a First Amendment theory of a right to be free of excessive government communications activities. Under the First Amendment, public officials and employees retain their personal rights to engage in freedom of speech and association. There is a danger that the right to restrain certain forms of government expression might violate such individual entitlements. An acceptable constitutional theory of limitation on government expression must thus be able to define a class of communication called government speech which can be disentangled from the private expression of public officials. It is one thing for a teacher to make a passing remark about the virtues of free enterprise or of socialism, and it is quite another thing for the school board to require each teacher to pound such points home on a daily basis. It is one thing for a mayor or members of a city council to advocate the passage or defeat of a statewide referendum, and quite another to mobilize city employees and organize an advertising cam-

43. For example, New York requires teachers to offer instruction in "principles of government proclaimed in the Declaration of Independence and established by the constitution" and permits instruction in "communism and its methods and its destructive effects." N.Y. Educ. Law §§ 3204(3a) (2), (3) (McKinney 1970). See, generally, *Ambach* v. *Norwick*, 441 U.S. 68 (1979).

paign, paid for from tax funds, for the same purposes.[44] The lines, once again, are not clear. Frequently government officials speak out on public issues while officially on the payroll, and we expect this.

The identification of unconstitutional government expression is a complex matter, and, as in the larger communications system, this complexity requires that we look at many interdependent factors, judging the cumulative impact of these factors on the expression. First, does the government body label the communication as a government message? A public official may fear to take responsibility for a statement and attempt to hide behind the anonymity of a government agency publication or news release. In such cases, it seems reasonable to attribute the communication to the agency itself. Second, to what extent have the resources of the agency in question been mobilized? If large numbers of employees work on the message, if there are a large number of speakers, and if an internal policy decision has been made to devote public funds to the communications activity, it seems reasonable to attribute the expression to the government. Isolated speeches or other presentations by top policy makers would not suffice to shift the characterization from private speech to government speech.[45] Third, is the content of the speech inappropriate to the agency's mission and yet frequently repeated? For example, required Bible readings in public schools, not tied to the immediate educational objectives of the schools and repeated daily, may aptly be characterized as a form of government speech. Fourth, to whom are the communications addressed? Is the audience captive? Does it have alternative sources of information and opinion? Are the audience characteristics (maturity, intelligence, etc.) such that judgment distortion appears likely?

In any given case, these factors may be difficult to weigh, and where the character of the speech is unclear, courts should err on the side of expansively protecting the individual First Amendment rights of government officials and employees.

44. See *City of Boston* v. *Anderson*, 439 U.S. 1389 (1978).

45. Compare *Bonner-Lyons* v. *School Committee of City of Boston*, 480 F.2d 442 (1973), with *Wickard* v. *Filburn*, 317 U.S. 111 (1942).

[10]

Verifying and Falsifying Majorities:
Legislative and Judicial Competence

Introduction

The tendency in constitutional writings is to turn every discussion of a constitutional question into a reexamination of judicial review. Determinations of constitutionality are not, however, the exclusive domain of the courts. Courts and legislatures have overlapping responsibilities. The First Amendment, by its own terms, is addressed to Congress (and to state legislative bodies in terms of the doctrine of incorporation under the Fourteenth Amendment); legislators and other government officials are required to take an oath to support the Constitution; deference is often afforded to the constitutional judgment (whether real or imagined) of legislative bodies; and legislative review of constitutional questions does not preclude later judicial review. Indeed, due to various mediating doctrines, prudential considerations, and case and controversy requirements under article III of the Constitution, some constitutional issues are never decided by the courts, even assuming they are litigated, and the legislative determination is final. Whether or not one accepts the proposition that the Supreme Court is "the ultimate interpreter of the Constitution," one can reasonably demand "that the lawmaking process take explicit account of constitutional values threatened by pending legislation."[1]

The need for a sharing of responsibility for making constitutional determinations between the judiciary and legislative bodies is particularly acute with respect to the proper scope of government speech and the methods for limiting abuses. The ability to manipulate or control the flow of information, and perhaps to "manage the news" for a

---

1. See Donald Morgan, *Congress and the Constitution* 361 (Cambridge, Mass.: Belknap Press, 1966).

variety of purposes,[2] which so enhances the power of modern governments, is generally exercised by members of the executive branch. This includes myriad administrative agencies, bureaus, boards, institutes, departments, and other bureaucratic structures. The federal executive is the strongest case in point. While the ability of Congress and the judiciary to falsify consent should not be underestimated, history demonstrates that it is centralized and bureaucratized executive authority which poses the greatest threat to a democratic polity. Under such circumstances, the combined authority of the Congress and judiciary is critical in restraining the awesome communications powers of the executive branch. Donald Morgan puts the matter well:

> The forces [that] have wiped out [many of the constraints on democratic governments] are concentrating political power at a pace hard to exaggerate. Science and technology are molding societies in unpredictable directions and [at] unparalleled speed. One result, however, is clear. Governments are demanding and exercising unprecedented powers. Into the hands of rulers, even in democratic countries, are drifting the means of regimenting the lives, the liberties, even the very thoughts of their citizens.

> Crisis urgency and demands for new policies and programs have intensified the concentration of power at the center, in the Executive and in specialized experts. That concentration of power calls for bold new thought about the preservation of human values, especially those safeguarded by constitutional principles.

> Yet at precisely this moment many would subordinate that task, postpone it, and consign it to an organ of government [the judiciary] distinct from those concerned with current policy, whose mode is ponderous, tied to precedent, and restricted in its reach.

> This denigration of constitutional principles and their consignment to a special guild [the legal profession] and forum [the courts] occurs precisely at the time of greatest peril to constitutional government.[3]

In this chapter, the focus will be on the parceling out of congressional and Supreme Court competence with regard to government speech. These bodies have diverse institutional characteristics with consequences for making judgments about relative competence. But, as always, institutional competence is only one factor in determining the legitimacy of institutional decision-making processes and the appropriate allocation of decision-making authority.

2. See Douglass Cater, *The Fourth Branch of Government* 31 (Boston: Houghton Mifflin, 1959).
3. Morgan, *Congress and the Constitution* viii-ix, 331.

Verifying Majorities

Congress and other legislative bodies are relatively disinterested in the question of verification of majority rule, while courts are more likely to be protective of such First Amendment related interests. This is most apparent in the historic reluctance of legislative bodies to reapportion themselves, to enact electoral reforms, and to forego the gerrymandering of districts for the gain of individual legislators and political parties. Though individual legislators may grouse about committee structures, the seniority system, lobbyists, filibusters, and other institutional arrangements likely to frustrate "majority" decisions in the legislative body itself, they have no reason to challenge the notion that legislative majorities in fact reflect popular majorities. Much of the legitimacy of legislative decision making is built on this assumed nexus.

The legitimate authority of each legislator rests in large part on the fact that he or she has been elected by a majority, or at least a plurality, of those voting in his or her district or state. Legislators claim to speak for their constituents. They often pride themselves on their openness to constituents and their responsiveness to the latter's wishes. While in their hearts legislators may know that they have tremendous discretion in making policy, emphasis on this would undercut the basis of their authority. If verification of majorities requires something more than the tabulation of votes in the legislative body, if it requires the maintenance of a process of opportunity for consultation and the preservation of freedom of expression and association to accomplish this end, one would not normally expect legislators to lead this effort.

This is not to say that a constitutional obligation to verify majorities should not be a consideration in the legislative process. The willingness and ability of legislative bodies consciously to consider the impact of legislation on civil liberties (particularly Congress) has, I believe, been grossly underestimated. Obviously, there have been lapses, e.g., the Communist Control Act of 1954.[4] But the liberal values of democratic government and ideology run deep in our culture. Legislators, no less than others, may be expected to share First Amendment values. This is particularly true given the moral force that the Supreme Court has added to such principles over the last fifty years and the deference accorded Supreme Court decisions concerning expression and association.

Consider also the distinction between electoral-participation values and First Amendment values. Affirmation of the former may almost invariably jeopardize the position of some legislators, while affirmation of the latter is less likely to entail discrete and identifiable risks to individual legislators. Thus, while the impetus for legislative review of

4. Communist Control Act of 1954, ch. 886, 68 Stat. 775 (codified in scattered sections of 50 U.S.C.); see Morgan, *Congress and the Constitution* ch. 12.

unconstitutionality under the First Amendment may be motivated by a concern for civil liberties as an end in itself, the effect may be to aid in the process of verifying majorities. The process of verification requires the affirmation of those same liberal values. Furthermore, as argued below, legislatures are likely to be peculiarly sensitive to the problem of falsifying majorities. To the extent that they act to prevent executive agencies from distorting the independent judgment of the citizenry—by enacting freedom-of-information laws, for example—they have indirectly bolstered the foundation of liberal values underlying the structure of majority rule.

Largely due to a sense of institutional role, courts are more responsive to the problem of verifying majorities. The common notion is that they are charged with protecting "fundamental" constitutional rights of individuals from the wrath of the majority. Civil liberties and majority rule are falsely perceived as inconsistent; not being politically accountable to the electorate, the judiciary is perceived, and perceives itself, as best positioned to prevent majoritarian excesses. The notion is misguided in a number of respects, as previously noted. But in keeping with this thinking, many strong arguments have been made that the federal courts, and the Supreme Court in particular, are better able to protect civil liberties because they are sufficiently isolated from popular pressures by virtue of life tenure and by their commitment to principle, and reasoned elaboration in decision making. Jesse Choper, for example, while emphatically denying the persuasiveness of the argument with respect to many types of cases currently within the scope of judicial review, has stated the conventional wisdom well:

> Due to the compartmentalized nature of the federal legislative process, issues of constitutionality often are explored only by a single committee in each chamber. If the committee fails to consider the point, the matter may lie submerged throughout the remaining legislative deliberations. In Congress, unlike in the courts, the constitutional validity of proposed legislation is only one of a multitude of factors to be considered; it takes its place alongside issues of policy and expediency that are frequently more pressing. Congressional reliance on negotiation and compromise to move the legislative machinery can inhibit the development of a "body of coherent and intelligible constitutional principle." Congressmen must make and fulfill commitments at different stages of the process without the opportunity to engage in the reflection necessary for enlightened constitutional decision-making.[5]

5. Choper, "The Scope of National Power Vis-à-Vis the States: The Dispensability of Judicial Review," 86 *Yale Law Journal* 1552, 1574 (1977).

To the extent that this description of competence and roles is accurate, the courts would appear to be better able than legislatures to assist in the process of verifying majority rule within the framework of protecting individual entitlements to expression and association.

With regard to the verification of majorities, unelected judges do not have the same axe to grind as their counterparts in the legislature, because they are relatively disinterested parties. They are not judging the legitimacy of their own institutional processes. The judicial process is not called into question if majority rule is conceived of in terms of a continuous process of consultation between legislators and self-controlled citizens who should be afforded the opportunity to receive information and make their own decisions about policy. Quite the contrary; if enforcement of First Amendment values is seen as resting on a majoritarian foundation, rather than on an antimajoritarian fundamental-rights foundation, the case for judicial review of such matters is considerably strengthened. What has been described as the preferred-interest model of constitutional adjudication[6] can then be shown to have its roots not only in end-state values, but also in the felt need for regularity in the majoritarian processes of political decision making. While this is not the place to explore the matter in detail, once the structural process linking majority rule and the First Amendment has been identified, that structure may impose limits on the process of defining constitutionally preferred interests.[7] Those interests necessary to maintain the representative character of the relationship between the governors and the governed are among the ones to be preferred. This structural and relational analysis need not displace individual-rights concepts rooted in constitutional text, but it may supplement them, assist in deciding hard cases, and ultimately strengthen the justifications for a particular result.[8] And by channeling judicial discretion, it increases the likelihood of principled decision making and strengthens the case for the legitimacy of judicial review.

Falsifying Majorities

The central concern of this book is not verification of majorities, though this concept sheds light on the majoritarian underpinnings of the First Amendment, but rather falsification of majorities—the potential for government communications to engineer consent to govern-

6. See Laurence Tribe, *American Constitutional Law* ch. 11 (Mineola, N.Y.: Foundation Press, 1978).

7. See, generally, Charles Black, *Structure and Relationship in Constitutional Law* (Baton Rouge, La.: Louisiana State University Press, 1969); and John Hart Ely, *Democracy and Distrust* (Cambridge, Mass.: Harvard University Press, 1980).

8. See Vincent Blasi, "Creativity and Legitimacy in Constitutional Law," 80 *Yale Law Journal* 170, 186 (1970); Ely, *Democracy and Distrust*.

mentally formulated programs and policies and support for those currently in power. The relative strengths and weaknesses of the legislative branch in policing the system for the constitutional infirmities considered above in connection with verification of majorities are, in some measure, reversed in the context of falsification of majorities. Legislative bodies have a greater stake in guarding against falsification of consent than courts; their processes are better suited to determine what is inappropriate government speech, and they are certainly more capable of devising ways to limit such utterances. This is not to deny the importance of judicial affirmation of individual civil liberties in creating a force countervailing to government communications. Nor does this deny that there are structural and normative constraints on the executive branch which may lead to self-imposed limitations on its communications.

The analysis that follows will be limited largely to a comparison of Congress and the Supreme Court, because the centralization of functions and resources of the federal government pose greater risks of communications excesses. But the analysis should apply equally well to state legislatures and courts. If there is a major difference, it lies in the greater willingness of state courts to face up to the problem of executive abuse of the communications power (at least at the local level). But, as will be discussed in the Conclusion, state courts have tended to frame "propaganda" questions in terms for ultimate resolution by legislatures. These decisions may be models for federal judicial decisions in this sensitive area.

The Congressional Power to Influence Public Opinion

There is little doubt that the communications powers of the presidency, the Congress, the executive bureaucracies, and the Supreme Court are immense. In a battle of words and symbols to gain public support for policies, most commentators would agree that the president has the upper hand. He can make news. His powers are centralized, his resources and access to information are excellent, and he is truly a national figure, constantly in the public eye.[9] Granting the executive's advantage, it is extremely difficult to compare Congress and the courts in terms of their ability to gain public acceptance of their policies—their potential for creating artificial majorities. This is particularly true if one focuses on the extraordinary occasions in the life of government institutions. Did the Supreme Court more profoundly influence attitudes about race relations in *Brown* v. *Board*[10] than Congress did by

---

9. Elmer Cornwell, *Presidential Leadership of Public Opinion* (Bloomington, Ind.: Indiana University Press, 1965); Ernest Griffith, *Congress—Its Contemporary Role* 41 (New York: NYU Press, 1961).

10. 347 U.S. 843 (1954).

passing the Civil Rights Acts of 1871 and 1964?[11] How does one compare, say, the Court's decisions on reapportionment and criminal procedure with widely publicized congressional hearings on communist infiltration of government, presidential misconduct, or organized criminal influence in labor unions? Are the day-to-day deliberations and legislation of Congress more effective in influencing the public than the Supreme Court's oral arguments and 100-150 published opinions each year?

These questions are highly speculative, affording little reason for optimism that some social science calculus will come along to provide answers. There are too many variables, too many contingencies, and too little knowledge about what makes for successful (i.e., persuasive) government communication. But complexity should not lead us to overlook these important matters. A plausible first premise is that the branch of government that either is in fact, or perceives itself to be, at a disadvantage in influencing the public with its communications will be more likely to stand up to perceived communications excesses by the other branches. This is particularly true if the appeal to the public is perceived as bypassing the institutional processes of the disadvantaged branch. A second plausible premise is that the branch of the government that relies most heavily on communication and persuasion will be most inclined to seek to limit the communications powers of the other branches, acting, in a sense, as a judge of its own case. This is especially true if it is conscious of the role of the communications techniques that are so much a part of its daily routines. Assigning responsibility for regulating government utterances to such an institution may have the effect of undoing a desirable equilibrium in propagandizing power among branches of government. Thus, an essential element of pluralism, playing off branches of government against one another, may be lost, and the prospects for attacking the falsification of consent diminished.

As Douglass Cater has noted, virtually all government agencies have demonstrated their capacity to manipulate the flow of information to public and media and to afflict themselves "with an acute public relations sense."[12] Congress, however, appears to be a mere giant among Olympians. Though Congress often engages in investigations and other enterprises primarily designed to influence public opinion, these communications activities are a minor part of its day-to-day concern with legislation and budgets. Congress has no large, permanent bureaucracy charged with persuasion activities. Put somewhat differently, Congress, unlike the judiciary, has substantial substantive powers which do not depend on its ability to mold a consensus. Members of Congress often

    11. Civil Rights Act of 1871, 42 U.S.C. §§ 1971 et seq., 1981 et seq. (1976); Civil Rights Act of 1964, Pub. L. No. 88-352, 78 Stat. 241 (codified in scattered sections of 42 U.S.C.).
    12. Cater, The Fourth Branch of Government 21.

perceive it to be their role to be responsive to an existing consensus, not to make one.

Congress finds it difficult to speak with one voice. Even what is considered strong leadership here falls far short of the party discipline found in many European parliaments. It is common for party leaders, who are likely to be professionals rather than ideologues, to brag about the broad range of political philosophies and points of view within the party. The Congress is, in some respects, a committee of 535, and such committees are unwieldy in terms of generating consistent and continuous messages to the media, elites, and public. To be sure, individual members, and particularly the leadership, have significant access to the press, to government publications, to the franking privilege, and to the public through speeches made on and off the legislative floor. But these contacts are unlikely to have a sustained impact. The messages often will be tailored to local issues and constituencies, and designed more to demonstrate fealty to an existing consensus than to generate enthusiasm for some new consensus. This reflects the fact that "members owe little or nothing to their party nationally for their election."[13]

Other factors impede the ability of Congress to manipulate majorities. Despite some healthy recent trends in the opposite direction, Congress and its members often have difficulty in obtaining information; in perceiving budgetary and other policies in the large, instead of in the bits and pieces of the legislative process; and in formulating alternatives to executive policies:

> The executive branch until relatively recently had a preponderance of access to facts, both because of experience in dealing with problems and because of its extensive research bureaus. Thus Congress had great difficulty in formulating an intelligent alternative policy on many issues, except in a few fields, such as taxation, in which it had a staff of its own. It was this superior command of information more than any other one factor that for many years gave the executive-legislative struggle the appearance of a losing battle for the latter. "It (Congress) can violently disturb, but it cannot often fathom, the waters of the sea in which the bigger fish of the civil service swim and feed." So wrote Woodrow Wilson in his *Congressional Government.*[14]

The result is that Congress is quite inhospitable to the efforts of executive agencies (unelected government bureaucracies) and the president to centralize communications activities, to "go over the heads" of elected representatives by appealing directly to the electorate, and to mount mass communications or lobbying campaigns. Any strengthening

13. Griffith, *Congress—Its Contemporary Role* 187-194.
14. *Id.* at 41-42.

of the communications power of government generally is likely to exact a cost in terms of the legislator's ability to exercise discretion, to compromise, and to be responsive to "real" majorities.

And, equally important, the gap in communications capabilities is likely to reinforce traditional legislative hostility toward large bureaucracies. The power of such bureaucracies to communicate makes them more formidable rivals "in the maturing of legislation—an area which Congress regards as its own under the Constitution."[15] They are able to stimulate popular support through dissemination of information and reports, press conferences, lobbying activities, etc., despite their lack of direct electoral accountability to the people.

At times Congress appears almost paranoid about the power of the Executive and executive agencies to spend public monies and to use public facilities and employees to influence the legislative process. Consider this hyperbolic statement by Representative Thomas Curtis in 1968, as he vented his outrage about executive efforts to "propagandize":

> The greatest lobby in Washington today has become the executive branch of the Federal Government. . . . Thinly disguised political blackmail and bribery backstopped by extensive campaigns to propagandize the people have subverted the study and deliberate process of the Congress in all too many instances.
>
> If the process is developed to its ultimate, the Congress will become no more than a sophisticated mechanism to record the effectiveness of the propaganda programs conducted by the Executive financed by tax moneys.[16]

Others have lamented that Congress has been reduced to a sort of ombudsman, attempting to intervene with bureaucracies to protect the interests of constituents.[17] The power to control the bureaucracies has been lost, at least in part, through the propaganda mill.

Needless to say, it is easy to underestimate the communications powers of Congress. Congressman Curtis, in the speech quoted above, self-righteously places Congress above the propaganda wars within government:

> The Executive, by definition, acts and so creates news. But not so the Congress which if fulfilling its proper function, essentially

15. *Id.* at 193-194.

16. Curtis, "The Executive Dominates the News," in Robert O. Blanchard, ed., *Congress and the News Media* 101 (New York: Hastings House, 1974).

17. James M. Burns, *Congress on Trial* (New York: Harper & Row, 1949). Cf. R. Douglas Arnold, *Congress and the Bureaucracy* (New Haven, Conn.: Yale University Press, 1979).

studies and deliberates. Its only easily reportable actions are the
final votes taken at the end of this long drawn-out process.[18]

These comments are wide of the mark. There is much that Congress
does, and does not do, which creates news. A committee's reaction to
the president's tax or energy packages, comments by members on a
State of the Union address, investigative hearings, and many other
facets of the legislative process may put Congress in the public eye.
More importantly, Curtis ascribes a purity of legislative purpose to
members of Congress which is belied by the record. This is particularly
true if one distinguishes between the legislative processes of the House
and the Senate.

In comparing the publicity powers of the Senate and House, Nelson
Polsby describes the Senate as a "publicity machine," while viewing
the House as primarily concerned with passing bills. Senators are fewer
in number than House members, are more socially prominent, represent
larger constituencies, and are more nationally oriented. Such factors
give them a superior ability to call media attention to their pronouncements. On the other hand, the House is not organized to encourage
wide reporting of its activities; for decentralization and specialization
are necessary for the House to carry out its assigned responsibilities.
Polsby puts the matter this way:

> The essence of the Senate is that it is a great forum, an echo
> chamber, a publicity machine. Thus "passing bills," which is
> central to the life of the House, is peripheral to the Senate. In the
> Senate the three central activities are (1) the cultivation of na-
> tional constituencies . . . by political leaders; (2) the formulation
> of questions for debate and discussion on a national scale (espe-
> cially in opposition to the President); and (3) the incubation of
> new policy proposals that may at some future time find their way
> into legislation.
>
> Where the House of Representatives is a large, impersonal, and
> highly specialized machine for processing bills and overseeing the
> executive branch, the Senate is, in a way, a theater where
> dramas . . . are staged to enhance the careers of its members and to
> influence public policy by means of debate and public investi-
> gation.[19]

Candor compels the admission that the "relative incapacity of Congress to influence public opinion" is more accurate of the House of
Representatives than of the Senate. Perhaps this is why a Representative

18. Curtis, "The Executive Dominates the News" 102.
19. Nelson Polsby, "Congress, Publicity and the Public," in Blanchard, *Congress and
the News Media* 132.

Curtis might feel more disadvantaged by executive "propaganda" than a Senator Curtis. In evaluating the Senate's publicity powers, however, it is important to note that it, too, is a committee, though one of 100 rather than of 435, and lacks strict party discipline. If nearly every senator aspires to be president, to be recognized as a national leader, and to influence policy, the publicity entrées of the Senate as a whole may suffer from too many chefs planning conflicting communications menus.

Substantial evidence indicates that legislative hearings and investigations are often designed primarily to influence public opinion—to be a sort of "broadcasting mechanism." It would be difficult to underestimate the impact on public opinion of the McCarthy hearings, the Watergate investigation, and the inquiries into the connections between labor unions and organized crime. By way of a brief explication of this theme, consider these points made by counsel to a House committee investigating the Federal Communications Commission in a confidential memorandum to committee members that was inadvertently made public:

1. Decide what you want the newspapers to hit hardest and then shape each hearing so that the main point becomes the vortex of the testimony. Once that vortex is reached, *adjourn.*

. . . .

3. Limit the number of people authorized to speak for the committee. . . . It plugs leaks and helps preserve the concentration of purpose.

. . . .

5. Do not space hearings more than 24 or 48 hours apart when on a controversial subject. This gives the opposition too much opportunity to make all kind [*sic*] of counter-charges and replies by issuing statements to the newspapers.

6. Don't ever be afraid to recess a hearing even for five minutes, so that you keep the proceedings completely in control so far as creating news is concerned.

7. *And this is most important:* don't let the hearings or the evidence ever descend to the plane of a personal fight between the Committee Chairman and the head of the agency being investigated. The high plane . . . should be maintained at all costs.[20]

This consciousness of the publicity aspects of congressional hearings reinforces the earlier point that Congress is not without significant communications capacity. But it does not follow from this admission that Congress's communications powers are as formidable as those of

20. Quoted in Douglass Cater, "The Congressional Hearing as Publicity Vehicle," in Blanchard, *Congress and the News Media* 347-348.

the other branches of government, that its communications are generally as sustained and coherent as messages from the other branches, or that its communication power is *generally* a more effective power than the power over budgets and laws. It is a mistake to generalize from the observation that the McCarthy hearings "remain a landmark of publicity gone riot"[21] to the conclusion that such communications effectiveness typifies the activities of the Congress. Rather one may observe that the publicity given floor debates, committee hearings, press releases of members, publication of committee and staff reports, and the like does not *usually* rival the coordinated communications efforts of other agencies of government.

If there is an "imperial" presidency[22] or an "imperial" judiciary,[23] such imperialism is in large measure a function of the communications powers of these branches of government. Given the fragmented structure of Congress, particularly the House of Representatives, and given the representative nature of the institution, an "imperial" Congress, relying extensively on its ability to influence public opinion through the mass media and its own communications network, is an unlikely development. The differences are ones of degree and likely to change from era to era and issue to issue; but the overall implication is that, in the long run, Congress will not win many battles with other branches of government, and certainly not the wars, by virtue of its capacity to influence public opinion. Congress is better able to block change than affirmatively to create the conditions for it.

This conclusion is reinforced by the fact that Congress has shown itself to be perfectly capable of venting its hostility toward executive communication by abolishing public-relations offices, enacting statutes against lobbying, repealing or amending the laws under which governmental agencies operate, influencing the selection of personnel, controlling appropriations, and retaining those informal, paternalistic contacts between committee members and bureaucrats that often, in effect, make executives out of legislators.[24]

The on-again/off-again war over the Pentagon propaganda machine aside, appropriations bills for the State Department, Justice Department, and judiciary regularly prohibit funds for "publicity and propaganda purposes." All federal employees are prohibited from using public funds to lobby or influence members of Congress with regard to appropriations or legislation, albeit "requests" through "proper official channels" are permitted. There are many other examples. Many of these, as one would expect, appear to be more concerned with the use

21. *Id.* at 350.
22. Arthur Schlesinger, *The Imperial Presidency* (Boston: Houghton Mifflin, 1973).
23. Nathan Glazer, "Towards an Imperial Judiciary," 41 *The Public Interest* 85 (1975).
24. See Burns, *Congress on Trial* 100–108; Griffith, *Congress—Its Contemporary Role* 42–43.

of public funds to support specific candidates and parties than with more generalized questions of government indoctrination about specific issues. But there can be little doubt about Congress's sensitivity to what it perceives as propagandizing.

Federally supported public television and radio stations are specifically forbidden from engaging "in editorializing or . . . [supporting] or [opposing] any candidate for political office."[25] The United States Information Agency is not authorized to show or broadcast domestically films and other matter produced for foreign audiences.[26] Similarly, the Hatch Act, the controversial statute limiting the political activities of federal employees (including parallel provisions for state employees working in federally financed programs), prohibits them from using their "official authority or influence for the purpose of interfering with or affecting the result of an election."[27] Civil Service Commission regulations go so far as to prohibit political activity with respect to questions "specifically identified with a political party."[28] Moreover, the regulations construe the Hatch Act as forbidding employee participation in public affairs that compromises the "neutrality" of the employee's agency.[29] (Interestingly enough, however, I have not found a single case in which the Civil Service Commission or the courts have enforced this provision.)

Congress's record with regard to falsification of consent issues is, however, hardly unblemished. As noted, Congress is often more concerned with ensuring that the bureaucracies and communications arms of government do not favor the party in office than with guarding against a governmentally imposed consensus. Perhaps the most interesting example of congressional disinterest in the potential for governmental falsification of consent is the failure to regulate the Government Printing Office (GPO). Congress has authorized the publication of reports and documents by a host of federal agencies, ranging from the Office of Hydrographic Surveys to the Patent Office. But the basic concern has been dollars and not fear of government indoctrination. Apart from very specific statutes on the number of copies of the *Congressional Record*, the types of binding, and the selling price of government publications, the laws governing the GPO and the superintendent of documents abound with such phrases as "necessary to the public business," "necessary in the transaction of the public business," and "necessary for the public service."[30] There are no limitations whatsoever on the power of the president to have addresses, reports, and

25. 47 U.S.C. § 399a (1976).
26. 22 U.S.C. § 1461 (1976).
27. 5 U.S.C. §§ 1502(a)1, 7324(a)1 (1976).
28. 5 C.F.R. § 733.111(a)11 (1980).
29. 5 C.F.R. § 733.111(a)13 (1980).
30. 44 U.S.C. §§ 1102(a), 1103, 1108 (1976).

other matters printed at public expense: "The Public Printer shall execute such printing and binding for the President as he may order and make requisition for."[31] As if to make explicit what is implicit in the congressional attitude toward publicly financed publications, ultimate authority to determine what shall be printed rests in most instances with the Office of Management and Budget:

> The head of an executive department, independent agency, or establishment of the Government, with the approval of the Director of the Bureau of the Budget [now the Office of Management and Budget] may use from the appropriations available for printing and binding such sums as are necessary for the printing of journals, magazines, periodicals, and similar publications he certifies in writing to be necessary in the transaction of the public business required by law of the department, office, or establishment.[32]

Presumably, this provision covers printing performed by the agencies themselves, or through private printers at public expense, as well as by the GPO, but the matter is far from clear.

Congress's reluctance to get involved in many aspects of government communication is quite understandable. The Government Printing Office, for example, does not appear to be guided by rigid ideological or political principles in its decisions, although some federal officials have informally told me that the same cannot always be said of the Office of Management and Budget. Many government publications are the result of government-sponsored research on the part of scholars inside and outside of government, and respect for freedom of expression may depoliticize government overseeing of the publication of the fruits of those efforts insofar as is possible. Furthermore, the sheer magnitude of government communications may make meaningful congressional control near impossible, and, on balance, this may be all to the good.

What Congress appears to have done, however inconsistently, is to isolate communication activities that have great potential for falsifying consent and are closely related to elective and legislative processes. The major failures probably lie in the inability to curtail or counter the president's dominance in the mass media and the widespread propagandizing in times of national emergency and hysteria. But effective measures in these spheres strike me as unlikely to emanate from elected legislative bodies—or, for that matter, from any branch of government. In short, Congress's role in protecting democratic government from the falsification of majorities through government communications has been credible, if far from perfect, and this augurs well for the

31. 44 U.S.C. § 1101 (1976).
32. 44 U.S.C. § 1108 (1976).

placing of substantial responsibility on Congress to guard against executive branch attacks on the self-controlled citizen.

The Supreme Court and Falsification of Majorities

The competency of the courts, particularly the United States Supreme Court, to detect and protect the nation from falsification of consent by government is far more complex. The Court may act in any of four ways.

First, an effective system for controlling the impact of governmental speech depends in large measure on maintaining traditions of pluralism in the communications network. By scrutinizing government activities and laws for violations of such fundamental rights as freedom of expression and association, the Court may strengthen the ability of myriad private communicators to counter government communications, whether this result is intentional or not.

Second, the Court may enforce statutes designed to protect, or having the effect of protecting, the polity from overzealousness in government speech. This may involve laws compelling government disclosure of information, holding government or its officers liable for defamation, or limiting communication activities. An example of the latter is the law creating the Women's International Year Commission. Funds appropriated by Congress for this purpose were subject to the statutory limitation that they not be employed for lobbying or propagandizing activities. Suit was commenced in federal court by private plaintiffs alleging that these limitations had been violated. The lower court ruled in favor of the plaintiffs. The court of appeals reversed on procedural grounds;[33] for such statutes raise substantial issues as to the standing of private plaintiffs to seek their enforcement.

Third, the Court may facilitate congressional action with regard to potentially dangerous government communications by attempting to focus legislative attention on such matters. The technique which should be employed is fairly straightforward and similar, but not identical, to that employed by the Court in ascertaining whether states have infringed on Congress's power over interstate commerce. The Court should examine the nature of the governmental communication and its potential for falsifying consent; if it may be so characterized, the Court should require explicit statutory authorization for the activity. This reflects the importance of vindicating First Amendment interests under such circumstances. In the absence of such explicit authorization, the Court should declare the activity to be *ultra vires*; the effect of which is not to declare the activity unconstitutional, but to remand the matter to the legislative branch for its determination. This reflects

---

33. *Mulqueeny* v. *National Commission on the Observance of International Women's Year*, No. 76-39 (S.D. Ill., August 16, 1976), *reversed*, 549 F.2d 1115 (7th Cir. 1977).

the view that ultimate responsibility for guarding against the falsification of majorities should lie with legislative bodies and not the courts.
But given the multitude of government communication activities and
the lack of a practical, institutionalized review process in Congress, the
Court may play a useful role in sounding the alarm and exercising a
kind of suspensive veto over questionable government communications
activities. If Congress authorizes the activity or class of activities, this
ends the matter. If Congress declines to act, failing to hear the alarm or
acquiescing in the judicial decision, then the judicial result would
stand.

The fourth way in which the Supreme Court may act is to impose
direct constitutional limits on government communications activities.
This may involve enjoining an activity, requiring balanced or fair
presentations, imposing procedural requirements before dissemination
of information or opinions, voiding mandatory fees or taxes for those
who object to the government communications, and other devices.
While in general such powers should be used sparingly, if at all, the
thrust of the present discussion is that Congress is better situated to
accomplish this complex task. There is a substantial risk that the Court
might significantly contribute to a breakdown in the balance of communications among branches of government if it became the final ar-
biter of government speech. The Court itself relies extensively on
communication and persuasion for its substantial powers in the governance structure, a point elaborated in the next section. Whether
consciously or not, limitations on the communications of other branches
of government may distort the Court's power by enhancing its ability
to falsify consent; for the Court may be more attentive to the communications abuses of other branches of government than to its own.
Alternatively, its own institutional characteristics may blind it to the
realities of government communication and persuasion.

The decision as to what constitutes unconstitutional "indoctrination"
by government is one the courts are not particularly well suited to
make. While majoritarian principles underlie, or should underlie, First
Amendment analysis, principled decision making is extremely difficult.
The lines between propaganda, education, persuasion, information,
and leadership are not easily discernible—some would say completely
elusive. There is little in the scholarly analysis of government propaganda to contradict this conclusion. And, given the developing tradition
of judicial protection of freedom of expression, courts may well feel ill
at ease with the role of national censor of government speech.

Decisions limiting the power of government agencies to engage in
communications activities need to take into account their real or potential impact on the capacity of government agencies and officials to
lead, educate, inform, and implement policies. This requires a broad

sensitivity to policy ramifications and an ability to analyze the total political context in which the government communications problem arises. The congressional process and the experience of legislators may better enable them to respond to government speech in these terms than the judicial process and the experience of judges do. This is all the more true if the Court is to render final constitutional judgment on government-communications activity; for this enlarges the consequences of erroneous judgments by making it difficult to reverse them without abandoning principled decision making. Given the indispensability of communication to policy and government stability, this risk should rarely be taken.

Finally, limitation of government speech without sacrificing its many benefits or infringing upon individual freedom of expression may require more refined remedies than simply cutting off the offending utterance. For example, government agencies may be required to disclose their sources of information, to allow a right of reply by affected individuals and groups, to refrain from some methods of communication and not others, or to attempt consciously to offer "balanced" messages. The practicalities of the situation are such that the judiciary is unlikely to be able to formulate such refined policies and enforce them on its own initiative. Congress, with its many powers over budgets, investigations, and legislation, is better suited—although perhaps still not well suited—to the task. And extensive regulation by the judiciary might well lead to an undesirable confrontation with other branches of government. Particularly in the case of executive agencies and the presidency itself, government officials are unlikely to acquiesce meekly in judicial decisions which they perceive as emasculating their ability to function effectively. Evasion may be the order of the day. Under such circumstances, the weight of congressional action may be necessary to the implementation of decisions cabining executive branch communications powers.

The Supreme Court as Communicator: The Schoolmaster Function and the Power to Falsify Consent

The power of the Supreme Court has traditionally been thought, as Hamilton expressed it in number 78 of the *Federalist* papers, to lie in "neither Force Nor Will But Merely Judgment."[34] Hamilton viewed the judiciary as the "least dangerous branch," for it was at the mercy of the executive arm for the enforcement of its decrees, and its only power was to cajole or persuade the executive to act. Judgment turned out, however, to be a strong force, inasmuch as government officers and the populace came to attribute a "unique legitimacy" to the Su-

34. Alexander Hamilton, James Madison, and John Jay, *The Federalist Papers* 465 (New York: New American Library, 1961).

preme Court's constitutional interpretations. The force of its judgment did not always prevail; decisions sometimes went unimplemented and strong executives resisted the Court's power. And, as Robert Dahl has noted, the Court tends to realign itself with existing majorities as presidents make new judicial appointments.[35] But, as Alexander Bickel observes, Hamilton's view of the power of the judiciary is not an accurate reflection of its present place in the political structure.[36]

Why has judgment been such a strong force? There are numerous reasons, few of which can be explored at any length here. Grant Gilmore notes the propitiousness of the moment when Marshall and his successors at the state and federal levels asserted their judicial competence to deal with all matters of public controversy:

> The early assumption by the Supreme Court of the United States of the power to declare acts of Congress, as well as the acts of state legislatures and the decisions of state courts, unconstitutional was only the tip of the iceberg. From the beginning our courts, both state and federal, seem to have been willing to answer any conceivable question which any conceivable litigant might choose to ask.
>
> I assume that this distinctively American development was the unplanned result of the several aspects of our pre-Civil War history. . . . We did cut ourselves loose from the English tradition. We did set out to create a rationally organized system of law. We did have to adjust that system—somehow—to the dizzying pace of social, economic, and technological change. *We did have to cope, in the real world, with the complicated problems which arose from the obscure metaphysical concept of an indissoluble union of indestructible states. The federal Congress did little; the state legislatures did less. The judges became our preferred problem-solvers.*[37]

Much of the power of the courts thus emanates from power assumed when there existed a need for leadership that the other branches of government were unwilling or unable to provide. Tradition does not necessarily justify the present-day exercise of judicial power. But it does help explain its existence.

Closely related to the tradition of a strong judiciary is the widespread feeling that courts operate differently from legislatures; that their decisions are more reasoned and principled; that they are more deliberate and thoughtful than legislatures in addressing constitutional questions; and that they identify and articulate fundamental values of

35. Robert Dahl, "Decisionmaking in a Democracy: The Supreme Court as National Policy Maker," 6 *Journal of Public Law* 279, 284-286 (1957).

36. Bickel, *The Least Dangerous Branch* (Indianapolis, Ind.: Bobbs-Merrill, 1962).

37. Gilmore, *The Ages of American Law* 35-36 (New Haven, Conn.: Yale University Press, 1977) (emphasis added).

the culture. Without assessing these virtues, the point is that Americans seem "to have acquiesced in, indeed to have enthusiastically welcomed, the arrogation of unlimited power by the judges."[38] This is all the more remarkable given the traditional distrust of lawyers, the historical and present-day debates over judicial review, and the unpopularity of many court decisions. Indeed, faith in the judiciary appears at times to be almost religious, with the Constitution as scripture and the Supreme Court Justices as the high priests.

While tradition and institutional characteristics are important to the Court's power, its continuing and significant influence in the governmental process is also a function of its ability to communicate. The Court has a superb ability to get its message across, and this, combined with the traditional deference afforded it, easily makes up for its lack of direct authority over bureaucracies, budgets, and law making. This aspect of the Court has not gone unnoted by scholars, but there has been a tendency to treat its communications and persuasion power as largely benign.

I once followed such distinguished commentators as Eugene Rostow and Paul Freund[39] in arguing that the glory of the Supreme Court lay in its power to persuade and educate through its pronouncements:

> The symbolic affirmation of values and the designation of certain activities as deviant help create the very consensus . . . critical to the enforcement of [judicial] . . . decisions. Many commentators have noted the role of the courts, particularly the Supreme Court, as educational bodies, or the "ultimate interpreter[s] of the American code" of social ideals and morality. As "symbols of an ancient sureness and comforting stability," the courts play a significant part in the formulation of public policy. A court decision often represents an appeal to the public conscience or to public idealism that may be accorded enormous weight in the legislative and political processes. The desegregation cases demonstrate that a judicial decision which is unenforceable at the outset may create the conditions necessary for its ultimate enforcement. As Paul Freund once stated, "The moral quality of law is itself a force toward compliance and the change of attitudes.[40]

Today, perhaps, I would be more concerned with the sources of the Court's moral expertise. The ability to communicate for purposes of

38. Glazer, "Towards an Imperial Judiciary".

39. Eugene Rostow, "The Democratic Character of Judicial Review," in Leonard Levy, ed., *Judicial Review and the Supreme Court* 74, 90 (New York: Harper & Row, 1967); Paul Freund, "Civil Rights and the Limits of Law," 14 *Buffalo Law Review* 199 (1964).

40. Mark Yudof, "Equal Educational Opportunity and the Courts," 51 *Texas Law Review* 411, 415 (1973). But cf. Donald Horowitz, *The Courts and Social Policy* (Washington, D.C.: The Brookings Institution, 1977).

uplifting the populace also involves the power to persuade to less worthy values, including the potential to contribute to the creation of a manipulated consensus based on the myth of the robe and not on any meaningful exercise of intelligence by the citizenry. For every decision like *Brown* v. *Board of Education*,[41] a counterexample can be found in cases like *Plessy* v. *Ferguson*[42] or *Dred Scott* v. *Sandford*.[43]

There can be no doubt that the Supreme Court's communications power is central to the Court's authority, legitimacy, and place in the political structure. In order to demonstrate this, a preliminary distinction should be drawn between the symbolic function of judicial decisions and their instrumental effects on the parties before the Court:

> We readily perceive that acts of officials, legislative enactments, and court decisions often affect behavior . . . through a direct influence on the actions of people. . . . The instrumental function of such laws lies in their enforcement; unenforced they have little effect.
>
> Symbolic aspects of law and government do not depend on enforcement for their effect. They are symbolic in a sense close to that used in literary analysis. The symbolic act "invites consideration rather than overt reaction."
>
> . . . Law can thus be seen as symbolizing the public affirmation of social ideals and norms as well as a means of direct social control.[44]

As this indicates, virtually all law and governmental activity may have both instrumental and symbolic implications. There is symbolism in laws and judicial precedents making a contract-breaker liable for damages to the injured party. There is a symbolic message in the provisions for senior citizens in the Social Security Act. And certainly there is a symbolism in laws making criminal the abuse of children or the paying of bribes to foreign officials. But what is different about the Supreme Court is that its power largely derives from the symbolism, from its ability to communicate, to persuade, and to appeal to the sensibilities of the populace and of those occupying positions of power in other branches and at other levels of government.

To be sure, the resolution of the specific controversy before the Court is often of great importance. In such cases, coercion and not persuasion may carry the day. But, as the Court moves from relatively simple bipolar litigation, to complex, multipolar public litigation re-

41. 347 U.S. 843 (1954).
42. 163 U.S. 537 (1896).
43. 60 U.S. (19 How.) 393 (1857).
44. Joseph Gusfield, "Moral Passage: The Symbolic Process in Public Designations of Deviance," in Lawrence Friedman and Stewart Macaulay, eds., *Law and the Behavioral Sciences* 308, 309 (Indianapolis, Ind.: Bobbs-Merrill, 1969). But cf. Murray Edelman, *The Symbolic Uses of Politics* (Urbana, Ill.: University of Illinois Press, 1964).

quiring ongoing judicial administration and alteration of remedies, its communications powers become more critical. Perhaps persuasion is not essential when the issue is whether a state has impaired the contractual rights of a small group of citizens. But where the Court orders structural changes in formerly segregated school systems, the implementation of its decree will be less a function of its coercive powers, which are relatively slight, than one of public and official acquiescence in the measures ordered. The decision "invites consideration" by the public and by those responsible for overseeing public schools. There may be fear of similar litigation in the future if the posited steps are not taken, but this fear must ultimately rest on the perception that what the Court has articulated, and may articulate again, is "right" or "ends the matter," and should or must be abided by. There may be elements in the process, as Phillip Kurland has suggested, of "Run the flag up the pole. See if anyone salutes."[45] But what is conspicuous about the process is how often the Court's flag is saluted.

Even in traditional bipolar litigation, the persuasive powers of the Supreme Court assume some importance. Whatever one's view of the wisdom of affording finality to judicial determinations of constitutionality, judicial decisions do far more than resolve a single controversy between government and a private party. Judicial review today is not perceived simply as an expression of the Court's view of what is constitutional in the case before it. Judicial decisions are not merely determinations of rights between the parties, leaving governments free to render their own constitutional interpretations in like cases. Rather the judgment of the Court in a particular constitutional case is treated as an authoritative statement of the law which binds all. And this power to make people feel bound is, in part, a function of the symbolism and belief structures enveloping judicial decisions. Thus, the power to communicate such judgments, for better or ill, is an immense power.

As Felix Frankfurter once wrote in a letter to President Franklin Roosevelt, there is a tendency to equate Supreme Court pronouncements with the Constitution itself, and not simply to treat constitutional decisions as the best efforts of the justices to interpret the Constitution:

> People have been taught to believe that when the Supreme Court speaks it is not they [the justices] who speak but the Constitution, whereas, of course, in so many vital cases, it is they who speak and not the Constitution. And I verily believe that this is what the country needs most to understand.[46]

45. Kurland, "Equal Educational Opportunity: The Limits of Constitutional Jurisprudence Defined," 35 *University of Chicago Law Review* 583, 598 (1968).
46. Max Freedman, ed., *Roosevelt and Frankfurter: Their Correspondence 1928-1945* 383 (Boston: Little, Brown, 1967).

Perhaps some academics understand, perhaps some judges understand, but clearly the bulk of people, including influential elites both inside and outside of government, often do not. Paul Brest suggests the enormity of the power to influence through judgment when he remarks that "it is not unduly naive to think . . . that officials have sometimes voluntarily abided by judicial declarations of constitutional doctrine simply because they believe that such declarations *are* the Constitution they are bound by oath to support."[47]

The Supreme Court is well situated to take advantage of the material advances in the technology of communication and the changes in the nature of the mass media. This makes it more powerful than in the past, and in part explains its potency in relation to state and federal legislatures and executives. While the presidency exceeds the centralized communications power of the Supreme Court, the president does not have the same legitimacy in the public mind in articulating constitutional principles. He also may lack the qualities of political detachment and principled decision making in the public mind, qualities thought to be necessary for constitutional interpretation. For better or worse, this is the lesson of the recent Watergate experience. The Court, and not the Congress, brought the president to heel.[48]

In order to appreciate the communications power of the Supreme Court, suppose that a supreme constitutional court had been established for the first time in 1980, and that it wished to exercise the sort of sweeping power we historically associate with the present Court. Realizing that its authority will ultimately turn on its ability to persuade and to create an atmosphere of deference, the court is unwilling to rely exclusively on its limited coercive powers, and contracts with a public-relations firm for advice as to how best to render and communicate its decisions. I suspect that the advice given would be something like this:

"To have the maximum impact on public opinion, you will need to be very careful about the way you operate. You want to focus attention on your decisions, but to do so in such a manner that there is broad governmental, elite, and public support for your pronouncements. This means that the press and broadcast media must be able to comprehend your decisions and interpret them sympathetically and expeditiously, and, it is to be hoped, make them widely known and respected.

"Your opinions should be spread out over the course of the year, say no more than an average of two or three a week. Preferably, each decision should be announced on a different day of the week. No

47. Brest, *Processes of Constitutional Decisionmaking* 72 n. 52 (Boston: Little, Brown, 1975).
48. See *United States* v. *Nixon*, 418 U.S. 683 (1974), and, generally, Paul Mishkin, "Great Cases and Soft Law: A Comment on *United States v. Nixon*," 22 *University of California-Los Angeles Law Review* 76 (1974).

matter how much your caseload increases, keep the number of cases decided by opinions down to this 100-150 range. Too many cases, decided too closely together, will diminish your effectiveness: The mass media, press, and politicians will feel bombarded with messages.

"Consider time and place factors. Render your decisions in the capital, the national center of political power, in some suitably impressive building—perhaps a Corinthian-style white marble structure resembling the Temple of Diana at Ephesus would give you the needed majesty. You are likely to get less media attention if you go gallivanting around the country deciding cases and issuing opinions.

"Be careful to write opinions only in cases of broad public significance. Don't waste your time correcting errors in lower court decisions that are important only to the parties involved and that would call for extended analysis of boring facts. Forget about the notion of ferreting out and resolving every conflict of law among the lower courts. Your job is to decide for the nation, not for the parties or for inferior courts. Control your docket! Use your power to communicate sparingly! Don't even agree to hear a case and write an opinion unless at least four of the nine of you think that it is absolutely necessary.

"Once you are committed to deciding a case and publicizing the grounds for your decisions, it is imperative that you work diligently to achieve unanimity, or at least a substantial majority. If the court is equally divided, simply affirm the lower court's decision without opinion. Try to keep down the number of concurring and dissenting opinions. Circulate opinions in advance, get comments from the other justices, bargain, and compromise your differences. Take advantage of the fact that you are a committee of nine, and not a committee of 535 or a vast bureaucracy. The public, politicians, and press will perceive close decisions, sharp dissents, and the like as signs of weakness, indecision, political motivation (liberals versus conservatives, 'judicial activists' versus 'strict constructionists'), and an admission that the decision is not grounded in some inexorable and inevitable constitutional logic. Remember the public-relations errors of the House of Lords in England, with its requirement that each lord hearing a case write a separate opinion. What a disaster!

"Perhaps a few of you will establish yourselves as the intellectual leaders of the court. The rest of you should follow their lead: too many prima donnas will result in more opinions. The chief justice can facilitate the process by assigning opinions to the right associate justice or to himself. Assign the opinion to the most undecided justice on the majority side, in the hopes of keeping his vote and of attracting additional votes to a moderate opinion. Be mindful of the relationship between a justice's background and public acceptance of an opinion. Assign 'activist' decisions to justices popularly perceived to be conservative. If an

opinion may trigger an adverse reaction among Southerners or Catholics, for example, assign it to a Catholic or Southern justice.

"Try to keep your opinions short. You must cater to professionals
and academics who may be critical of truncated, poorly elaborated
decisions, while still writing succinctly enough so that the journalists
do not get lost in a labyrinth of legalisms. We have a number of
suggestions in this regard. First, your opinions should be written in the
language of the Constitution and appeal to widely held values and
symbols: vague and abstract references are preferable to concrete statements that may evoke controversy. Second, go out and hire some
young and articulate lawyers (law clerks) to help you turn a good
phrase, to do the leg-work for your historical references and precedents,
and to insure some quality control over your use of language. Be
careful, however, to maintain the façade that you are entirely responsible for the opinions. Pretend 'that each and every justice passes on all
aspects of a case, at each of its stages.'

"Another approach is to persuade the American Bar Association or
the Association of American Law Schools or some other prestigious
legal group to write previews of the cases up for decision. These
synopses should be only a few pages long, and in lay terms should
explain the significance of the different ways in which the cases might
be decided. The previews should be available to the mass media considerably before decisions are announced.

"Do not simply distribute copies of the opinions in some isolated
room in the basement. Make a ceremony out of the occasion. Convene
the entire court. Perhaps the opinions should be read or commented
upon from the bench. Better yet, provide oral summaries or para-
phrases of the decisions: reporters do not like to read long documents,
and they want to be able to meet the deadline for the evening news and
afternoon newspaper editions.

"In order to increase public, professional, and political interest in
your decisions, provoke their curiosity. We suggest a preliminary 'media hype.' While you may be resistant to the idea, why not allow the
parties to present oral arguments to the court? These arguments may be
boring to you and rarely aid you in making your decisions, but they put
people on notice that something is in the offing. Keep the arguments
short, say thirty minutes to each side. Don't let the lawyers drone on
and read extended quotations. As the English experience demonstrates,
this puts people to sleep. Doubtless this will require you to read the
briefs and cases in advance (or at least your law clerk's summary of
them), but this is a small price to pay for good publicity. Liven up the
discussion with provocative questions, and keep the pressure on the
attorneys. But try not to reveal your position. Reinforce the elements
of mystery and surprise.

"Be sure that the hearing is public, but not too public. Keep the size of the audience down. You don't want a circus atmosphere. Around 300 seats would be ideal. Make special provision for the seating of influential elites, reserving as much as one-third of the seats for the press corps, members of Congress, outstanding lawyers, friends, and so on, but don't get carried away with giving valuable seats to family and friends just to impress them. And, as in the case of announcing the decisions themselves, do not allow for live television or radio coverage. Do not even permit the taking of photographs. This may be hard to swallow; for naturally you think that such modern communications technology will help spread your influence. Not so. Live coverage, with cameramen and announcers and the infernal racket they make with their devices, will spoil the ceremonial aspects of the proceedings. More important, you do not want this sort of constant close-up coverage. If you are on television frequently, the whole judicial process may become humdrum in the public eye. Perhaps charcoal sketches of the justices and counsel would be OK: they are likely to be more flattering and to impress upon the public your total devotion to justice. It is rather like the difference between a dignified oil painting of Washington or Lincoln and a newsclip of a president tripping or stuttering in public. Maintain a certain distance and aloofness, and allow influential media elites to get your message across. They are not as likely to pick up on, or at least publicize, an occasional mental lapse during the oral argument: they will have more perspective.

"After the oral arguments, you need to maintain the effort to arouse the public's curiosity—to leave them waiting anxiously for your decision. We would suggest the 'Greta Garbo' approach. This requires a high degree of secrecy and insularity. When the members of the court meet to discuss pending matters, no one else—not even the law clerks— should be permitted to be in the room. To preserve the qualities of mystery and ritual, try to meet on the same day of the week (say, Friday or Saturday) in the same conference room (which should never be photographed). Prior to their ceremonial disclosure, your deliberations and decisions should not be revealed. Law clerks should be sworn to secrecy, insofar as they inevitably gain knowledge of the court's proposed actions. Neither the justices nor any other person affiliated with the court should publicly comment on pending matters.

"The 'Greta Garbo' approach requires a good deal of self-restraint. A relatively low profile should be kept to solidify the image of deliberation and scholarship. Interviews with representatives of the mass media should be few. Justices should rarely, if ever, engage in public debate over their decisions. Being a bit spartan in the personal conveniences afforded the justices—secretaries, assistants, bathrooms, etc.—may reinforce the scholarly image. This does not mean that the justices must lock themselves in their chambers. An occasional visit to a law school, attendance at bar meetings, and the like are perfectly in order. Certainly attending big events—inaugurations, State-of-the-Union addresses, etc.—is fine if you are appropriately dignified and attired. But when speaking publicly, the justices should address themselves to arcane historical issues, speak in broad generalities (giving no insight into the decision-making process), or talk about how the courts are overburdened and understaffed, and the judges and their assistants underpaid. Perhaps a state-of-the-judiciary address by the chief justice would be appropriate. It would focus public attention on the court while not contributing to the demystification of its deliberative processes.

"If you follow this advice about a preliminary 'media hype,' keep the public guessing about what you are going to decide and when, and articulate your decisions in the preferred manner and atmosphere, you are well on your way to getting your message across. But the most important thing is to maintain the ritual and ceremonial aspects of your job and to reinforce the public's confidence in your omniscience and wisdom. This is the 'Delphic oracle' approach. Look like a justice. Wear black robes, sit behind an elevated bench (well above the lawyers and audience), allow your temples to gray, whatever your zeal for a youthful appearance, appear pensive, speak in as deep a voice as you can muster for the occasion. Your entrance into the courtroom should be highly ceremonial. Perhaps the chief justice should enter through parted drapes, with the associate justices following him in order of seniority. You are a group of wise men searching for truth, sensitive to history, the Constitution, and the highest aspirations of man, and you should act the part. Eschew the dress, speech, and manner of the man in the street, and model yourselves after the wise and religious oracles of the ages."[49]

This "advice" could go on *ad nauseum*. Perhaps it already has. The point is simply that the procedures of the Supreme Court, whatever their specific inspiration, are brilliantly devised for communicating messages effectively. This is not to say that those procedures are always effective from a public-relations perspective, or that each of the practices described cannot be justified on some other ground. Nor is it to say that Congress and the president do not make similar appeals by resorting to similar devices. Consider the secret memorandum to a congressional investigatory committee discussed earlier. The differences are ones of degree and not of kind. Rather the suggestion is that the immense ability of the Court to employ symbols, to persuade, and to appeal to higher principles makes it a risky guardian or umpire for governmental speech that may lead to the falsification of consent.

49. The "advice" is very loosely drawn from a current description of the operation of the Supreme Court (see Henry Abraham, *The Judicial Process* 27, 190-225 [New York: Oxford University Press, 1968]).

[11]

Government Expression, the First Amendment, and the Courts

Risky guardians they may be, but the courts nevertheless have a constitutional role to play in preventing the falsification of majorities and the demise of the self-controlled citizen in consequence of unregulated government expression. The First Amendment can be applied by the judiciary to government speech in two ways. First, concerns about government expression and the need to foster pluralism may be treated as additional factors to be considered when individuals seek to vindicate traditional First Amendment rights. The second approach involves direct judicial imposition of First Amendment limits on government expression. This chapter argues that the first approach is generally wiser, presenting fewer dangers of judicial overreaching and avoiding the remedial quandaries of the second approach. The discussion of both approaches is general and theoretical in this chapter. Specific applications will be explored in Part IV. Chapters 12 through 14 thus apply the indirect approach to a number of cases and bodies of case law, finding that explicit consideration of government expression in traditional private-rights contexts lends greater weight to some decisions, and that, occasionally, such consideration should lead courts to reach contrary results. Specific applications of the direct approach are examined in chapter 15 to illustrate the general conclusions reached here about the efficacy of such controls.

The Relationship Between Government Expression and the Vindication of Individual First Amendment Claims

The earlier analysis of the nature of modern communications and of the need to strengthen centers of communication which counter or check the persuasive powers of governments suggests a judicial approach to coping with the danger that government will engineer consent to its policies. Where individuals seek to vindicate speech or associational rights against the state in traditional First Amendment contexts, courts should consider the implications of their decisions for limiting government expression.

In the typical First Amendment calculus, the question is whether the state has abridged some protected speech or associational activity of a person or group, and, if so, whether (at least for most justices) some great necessity, compelling state interest, clear and present danger, or the like, justifies the abridgement. Courts, in these cases, entertain the idea that individuals and groups may have rights against the state that are inconsistent with the good of all, albeit there is no reason, *a priori*, to assume this to be the case. Courts frequently note that protection of those individual interests works to the advantage of the polity; for all of us have an interest in the free flow of information and opinions. Only a communications structure that permits this is conducive to democratic processes, the verification of consent, and the development of the self-controlled citizen. This benefit to the polity has been used to justify protecting the expression of private institutions such as unions and corporations that do not have the sorts of dignitary interests that real persons have. In the *Bellotti* case,[1] for example, Massachusetts was not permitted to silence corporate speech relating to a graduated state income tax on individuals, in part because of the impact the law's restraints would have on information flows to and among citizens. Equally plausible reasons justify consideration in traditional First Amendment cases of the need to limit government power to distort the citizen's judgment, falsify consent, and overwhelm other communications centers. Protection of private expression thus enhances liberty in two senses: it affirmatively promotes the autonomy of the self-controlled citizen, and it poses obstacles to government domination of communications networks.

The interests of society and discrete individuals in freedom of expression have long been integrated in First Amendment analysis. How should the fear of government communications excesses be factored into that analysis? At one level, the answer is simple. Any judicial decision protecting the right of *private* individuals, groups, or organizations to speak strengthens their ability to communicate and increases their potential to counter government messages. The *Bellotti* case, for example, was decided consistently with the view that the communications emanating from the welfare state pose a greater threat to democracy than those from a multitude of corporate, mass media, union, and other

---

1. *First National Bank of Boston* v. *Bellotti*, 435 U.S. 765 (1978); see also *Consolidated Edison Company* v. *Public Service Commission*, 447 U.S. 530 (1980); *Central Hudson Gas* v. *Public Service Commission of New York*, 447 U.S. 557 (1980).

voices.[2] All communicators are not equally powerful. Nor will corporate persuasion necessarily advance objectives inconsistent with those of government. But much more is at stake than the alignment of interests prevailing in the context of a particular case or the difference in communications ability of various private-sector communicators. The structural advantages of pluralism are best achieved by strengthening all elements of private-sector communication to offset the superior ability of the government to convey its message. Danger lurks in allowing government to pick and choose among private communicators, because it may opt for silencing the strong or critical voices. In this sense, First Amendment rights that protect individual entitlements are simply reinforced by concerns about government domination of public discussion. This fact should make courts more reluctant in traditional First Amendment cases to find countervailing state interests that justify censorship or other restraints on private expression.

Concerns about government expression may be particularly critical in First Amendment cases involving freedom of association, the right of the press to gather information for publication, the rights of individuals and organizations to obtain information, and the right to require the government to divulge information. Vindication of each of these rights takes us in the direction of limiting the power of governments to withhold vital information, to drown out private-sector voices, to conduct its business in secret, or to preserve a captive audience from outside, or contrary inside, influences. Each case involves a dispute over the flow of information. The power to control or curtail the transmission of information obviously increases the ability of government to channel decisions and makes engineered consent to government policies (including consent by other, poorly informed public agencies) more likely.[3] Communication activities are indeed, as Karl Deutsch observes, "the nerves of government."[4] This does not mean that plaintiffs should prevail in every such case; it simply means that the government-expression facet of the First Amendment provides additional reasons to protect the rights of individuals.

When government expression is part of the matrix in which traditional First Amendment claims are examined, the remedial quandaries of the right to be free of unconstitutional government speech are largely avoided. The individuals who bring the suit are discretely

2. See Aaron Wildavsky, review of Lindblom, *Politics and Markets,* 88 *Yale Law Journal* 217 (1978); but cf. Charles Lindblom, *Politics and Markets* (New York: Basic Books, 1977).

3. See, generally, Norman Dorsen and Stephen Gillers, eds., *It's None of Your Business: Government Secrecy in America* (New York: Viking Press, 1974); James Wiggins, *Freedom or Secrecy* (New York: Oxford University Press, 1964); Arthur Schlesinger, *The Imperial Presidency* ch. 10 (Boston: Houghton Mifflin, 1973).

4. Deutsch, *The Nerves of Government* xxvii (New York: Free Press, 1966).

injured. Governments or government officials can be ordered to abandon unconstitutional conduct or to compensate individuals who have suffered constitutional harms. Demonstrating that government caused the harm or proving the value of the loss may present grave difficulties, but at least the courts avoid having to determine such things for the entire polity. The traditional First Amendment case, then, becomes simply an occasion for considering the more general interest in cabining government speech. The remedy is directed to the individual or organization. But, indirectly, benefits flow to all. The approach is essentially epiphenomenal, in the best sense of that word, with limitation of government communications powers a convenient by-product of adjudicating traditional First Amendment claims against the state.[5]

Individuals and organizations have asserted in a variety of First Amendment cases that governments have unconstitutionally limited their rights of expression and association in contexts that raise concerns about the role of governments as participants in communications processes. Frequently, the courts, most importantly the Supreme Court, have failed to articulate these concerns.

Direct Controls on Government Expression

In a small number of federal court and a somewhat larger number of state court decisions, litigants have directly challenged government communication activities. One cannot speak with much assurance about such matters, for the information-management devices of the legal profession—digests, law reviews, indexes, etc.—simply do not classify cases according to their import for government expression. Such cases arise in incredibly diverse circumstances. And their legal characterizations run the gamut from substantive and procedural due process to the speech or debate clause (protecting members of Congress) and the commerce clause. The most common government speech cases involve taxpayer challenges in state court to local government advertising during the pendency of an election or referendum. A handful of cases involve suits by business entities seeking to quiet adverse publicity emanating from administrative agencies. Direct legal challenges to the massive federal communications programs described earlier have not occurred. Perhaps this tells us a great deal about the elusive nature of constitutional constraints in this area and about the tendency to rely upon nonjudicial approaches.

In this chapter, I make no bones about my agenda. I am deeply troubled by the constitutionalization of rights and remedies with respect to government expression. In Lon Fuller's wise counsel:

5. See Lindblom, *Politics and Markets* 257-258.

A sledge-hammer is a fine thing for driving stakes. It is a cumbersome device for cracking nuts, though it can be used for that purpose in a pinch. It is hopeless as a substitute for a can-opener. So it is with adjudication. Some social tasks confront it with an opportunity to display its fullest powers. For others it can be at best a *pis aller*. For still others it is completely useless. . . .

It is notable that the greatest failure in American administrative law has been with respect to those agencies that were assigned, or assumed for themselves, polycentric tasks which they attempted to discharge through adjudicative forms. . . . [Administrative agencies] have failed . . . because they were compelled, or thought they were compelled, to create and shape that [extra-legal] community through adjudicative procedures. . . .

Like many other precious human goals, the rule of law may best be achieved not by aiming at it directly.[6]

That the courts can or should directly attempt to reshape communications networks to limit the impact of government speech is a dubious proposition. The indirect approach, chipping away at the problem through the adjudication of more traditional First Amendment claims, is wiser. A purposeful reconstruction will fall wide of the mark and perhaps disable government from implementing policy objectives through communications processes. Yet there are egregious cases, and it is difficult to bring oneself to the point of closing the door to direct judicial intervention irrespective of the circumstances. I prefer instead to leave it open a crack, fearing that resort to the courts may yet prove necessary in a pinch.

The principal issue is how, and whether, to take account of the added dimension of government participation in communications networks in the sense of directly attacking government messages or communications programs under the First Amendment. A plaintiff alleges that a government utterance distorts the judgment of citizens, advocates undemocratic or unconstitutional values, violates the right of citizens not to be called upon to pay taxes to support expression they find objectionable, or drowns out opposing messages by virtue of the government's ability to capture the listening audience. All of these assertions portray government as undermining the aspirations of the self-controlled citizen. Most frequently, the litigant would not be uniquely injured by the government's communication, but would be attempting to vindicate the interest of all citizens in maintaining a pluralistic "marketplace of ideas," in insuring that government does not falsify

6. Fuller, "Adjudication and the Rule of Law," in Lawrence Friedman and Stewart Macaulay, eds., *Law and the Behavioral Sciences* 736, 743, 744 (Indianapolis, Ind.: Bobbs-Merrill, 1969); but cf. Abram Chayes, "The Role of the Judge in Public Law Litigation," 89 *Harvard Law Review* 1281 (1976).

consent by manipulating the public's judgment, in protecting the integrity of electoral processes, and in preventing government from spending money unconstitutionally. The litigant would draw on background constitutional provisions, precedents, statutes, democratic purposes underlying constitutional texts and government structures, and widely held moral views on the nature of majority rule and democratic participation.

This approach raises a fundamental question: What if the litigant wins (a result that should rarely occur), and a court rules a government communication unconstitutional under the First Amendment? A number of remedies are possible. The court might limit itself to a simple declaration of the unconstitutionality of the government expression, enjoin the speech, or order the offending agency or officials to pay damages for the harms inflicted (if they are not immune from damages under state or federal law). The court could instead require more balance in government presentations, or allow opposing speakers to reply through the same channels; it could order refunded to the taxpayer the pro rata share of taxes devoted to unconstitutional expression; or it could require governments to delegate authority over communications programs to "independent" decision makers. This catalogue of remedies should give pause to even the most avid proponents of constitutional limits on government expression.[7] The difficulties in fashioning remedies are so substantial that they corroborate the wisdom of courts in general in avoiding the attempt to delimit the boundaries of unconstitutional government expression.

Detailed discussion of most of these remedies is reserved for chapter 15. Their difficulties are best understood in the context of concrete cases in which they might be employed, but a few preliminary observations are in order. The notion that taxpayers who dissent from the messages promulgated by their governments have a constitutional right to recover back the few pennies or dollars of their personal taxes devoted to such enterprises is highly questionable. To my knowledge, federal courts have never granted such remedies. To do so would be inconsistent with the conventional wisdom that taxpayers may not challenge federal expenditures, even if they are alleged to be unconstitutional.[8] Perhaps there is a distinction between a flawed communication process, and hence an illegitimate decision-making process, and a single flawed decision or outcome. But given the legitimacy and necessity of government expression, the usefulness of the distinction is not

7. But see Robert Kamenshine, "The First Amendment's Implied Political Establishment Clause," 67 *California Law Review* 1104 (1979).

8. *Frothingham* v. *Mellon*, 262 U.S. 447 (1923); but see, e.g., *Lathrop* v. *Donohue*, 367 U.S. 820, 873 (1961) (Black, J., dissenting); *Consolidated Edison Company* v. *Public Service Commission*, 447 U.S. 530 (1980) (Blackmun, J., dissenting).

clear. Government might well come to a halt if each taxpayer could decide not to pay taxes for programs or communications activities to which he or she personally objected. Practice is not as finely tuned as theory. Even more to the point, if few taxpayers sued, it seems unlikely that the award of small sums of money to objecting taxpayers would deter governments from pursuing their communications objectives.

Declaratory relief might be available. Whether it would do more than produce ill-feeling among the branches of government is questionable, though it might serve a symbolic function. The most dangerous of the remedies by far is the injunction. It operates on government much the way that prior restraints operate on private expression. The principal problem is that the government never gets to communicate its message. Thus an error in judicial judgment, not unlikely in the government-communications area, is magnified. Given the importance of government speech to its policy functions, an inappropriate injunction may strip government of one of its most useful weapons in the pursuit of policy objectives. Other difficulties are with the scope of the injunction (it may sweep too broadly); with restraining the personal First Amendment rights of public officials; with monitoring the decrees; and with evasion by the recasting of the messages. Equally important, the injunctive power turns the courts into censors, ultimately responsible for overseeing every textbook adopted in public schools, every speech delivered by a public official, every governmental report, every news conference, and millions of other government communications each day. Injunctions may be appropriate in a few outrageous cases where a course of misconduct is likely to be repeated. But it would be unwise in the extreme to make the injunctive remedy widely available in government-communications cases.

Damages, except in cases of individualized and unique injuries, also strike me as unworkable, even assuming that some constitutional or statutory basis can be found for such suits against government entities or officials and that there is no sovereign immunity bar to such recoveries.[9] How can it be proved that a government propaganda campaign caused some harm? That a policy decision or election would have been decided differently but for the government's efforts at mass persuasion?[10] Even if causation can be shown, how are damages to be measured?[11] Are we satisfied with a remedy that may hold individual

9. See, generally, Laurence Tribe, "Intergovernmental Immunities in Litigation, Taxation, and Regulation: Separation of Power Issues in Controversies about Federalism," 89 *Harvard Law Review* 682-713 (1976); Mark Yudof, "Liability for Constitutional Torts and the Risk-Averse Public School Official," 49 *University of Southern California Law Review* 1322 (1976); Charles Wright, *Law of Federal Courts* §§ 46, 109 (St. Paul, Minn.: West Publishing, 1976).

10. Cf. *Mt. Healthy School District* v. *Doyle*, 429 U.S. 274 (1977).

11. See *Carey* v. *Piphus*, 435 U.S. 247 (1978).

government officials liable rather than the entity itself?[12] Even if the government entity pays the judgment, will this compensate the polity for its injury or deter future communications sins? The damage remedy makes sense only when individuals have been discretely harmed, as for example, when government defames particular individuals or invades their privacy. Recoveries would be based on common-law tort doctrines[13] and federal and state tort-claims acts (most of which would need to be amended to encompass such injuries).

12. See, generally, Yudof, "Liability for Constitutional Torts."
13. See, generally, Leon Green, "The Communicative Torts," 54 *Texas Law Review* 1, 21-41 (1975).

Part IV

*Limiting Government Expression
Through the First Amendment*

Introduction

Part IV applies the concepts and relationships thus far developed in several important contexts. The examples, reflecting my interests and experience, provide the perspective that comes from seeing a government speech analysis applied to different situations. Chapters 12-14 concern the indirect constitutional approach to judicial policing of government expression. Chapter 12 focuses on public schooling, perhaps the government's most pervasive and important exercise in communication. Some of the results reached are that the government-speech perspective provides an independent justification for the school prayer cases; a better rationale for the doctrine of academic freedom, particularly as extended to public elementary and secondary school teachers; support for a degree of autonomy for school newspapers; limits on state teacher-selection policies that may produce a homogeneous class of message transmitters; and increased support for student rights to communicate in the public school environment. My approach also justifies decisions that have the effect of prohibiting the state from eliminating private-sector schools that may serve to create heterogeneity and to counter the state's dominance over the education of the young.

Chapter 13 applies the government-speech perspective to several cases of government-subsidized speech, raising questions about government financing of election campaigns, and finding in the delegation doctrine a useful splintering of control over government communications. Chapter 14 focuses on the ways the judiciary can use traditional individual-rights litigation to strengthen communications centers which offset government speech. I conclude that the dangers of government rhetoric argue for a much more expansive view of the rights of individuals to demand and gather information from government. Similarly, I seek to justify the right of association, the right of individuals to form groups and to speak through them, in terms of increasing the ability of the private sector to communicate effectively. Perfection of the right of association may have the effect of facilitating the creation of organized centers of communication that may compete with the organized communications efforts of governments.

Chapter 15 turns to the efficacy of direct judicial controls on government expression in contexts including government incitement of unconstitutional or unlawful behavior; the due process clause (including government expression that stigmatizes individuals or organizations); the ambit of the protection afforded legislative speech by the speech or debate clause of article I of the Constitution; the limits of legislative and executive investigatory power; and the effect of misleading speech by an executive officer. I conclude with an exploration of issues raised by government speech and different kinds of "rights of reply" to that speech.

[12]

The First Amendment
and Public Schooling

Public schools present a kaleidoscopic panoply of First Amendment situations where policies promoting limits on government expression inform decisions on assertion of rights of association and expression. In some ways, public schools are a communications theorist's dream: the audience is captive and immature; the channel can't be changed (although students may only pretend to listen); the messages are labeled as educational (and not as advertising); the teacher can respond individually to the student (unlike the television set); adult communicators often have relatively high status in the eyes of the audience; and a system of rewards and punishments is available to reinforce the messages.[1] On the other hand, public schools hardly exemplify the worst tendencies of the preceptor state. Children are captive only a few hours a day, they have ready access to information outside of the school environment, and school messages tend to be consistent with what other important sources of socialization (family, church, clubs, etc.) are imparting. Furthermore, education affirmatively expands liberty by providing the knowledge for the making of informed choices. American public schools cannot be equated with the loudspeaker broadcasts which fill streets in Communist China. But some apects of communication in public schools, particularly the existence of a captive audience,[2] should make courts solicitous of individual First Amendment rights that reduce the power of government to persuade without seriously compromising its affirmative obligation to promote liberty.

1. See, generally, Carl Hovland, Irving Janis, and Harold Kelley, *Communication and Persuasion* (New Haven, Conn.: Yale University Press, 1963); Chester Insko, *Theories of Attitude Change* 12-63 (New York: Appleton-Century-Crofts, 1967); Paul Lazarsfeld and Robert Merton, "Mass Communication, Popular Taste and Organized Social Action," in Lyman Bryson, ed., *The Communication of Ideas* 95, 113-118 (New York: Harper, 1948).

2. See, generally, Charles Black, "He Cannot Choose But Hear: The Plight of the Captive Auditor," 53 *Columbia Law Review* 960 (1953); Franklyn Haiman, "Speech v. Privacy: Is There a Right Not to be Spoken to?" 67 *Northwestern Law Review* 153 (1972); R. Kenton Musgrave, "The Captive Audience and Majority Sentiment," 1 *Journal of Public Law* 507 (1952); Christopher Stone, "Fora Americana: Speech in Public Places," 1974 *Supreme Court Review* 233, 262-272.

One must be careful in all this; governments frequently capture audiences for limited periods of time for what are generally perceived as legitimate purposes (prisons, mental hospitals, military bases, schools, workers in public institutions, etc.). Thus, inevitably, First Amendment questions must be decided in highly situational terms.[3] Does the right asserted interfere too substantially with the mission of the public schools? Is the message consistent with permissible objectives of schooling or does it relate to other matters? What sorts of time, place, and manner restrictions make sense? How much have school authorities tilted in one direction or another in their messages?

The School Prayer Cases

The school prayer cases, while rooted in the constitutional ban on government establishment of religion, may be thought of as prohibiting the state from compelling a captive audience to listen to and participate in school prayers and Bible reading.[4] In a sense, establishment-clause cases, involving challenges to state support of religion or religious doctrine, are special: that clause is the only substantive constitutional restraint on what governments may say.[5]

But the government-expression perspective provides an additional, independent justification for excluding prayers from public schools. The sensitivity of the perspective to situational factors—the content of the message and the context of its communication—is noteworthy.

3. See, generally, Steven Shiffrin, "Government Speech," 27 *University of California-Los Angeles Law Review* 565 (1980); Ronald Cass, "First Amendment Access to Government Facilities," 65 *Virginia Law Review* 1287 (1979).

4. See *Abington School Dist.* v. *Schempp*, 374 U.S. 203 (1963); *Engel* v. *Vitale*, 370 U.S. 421 (1962).

5. Actually, the school prayer cases are more ambiguous than the text suggests. While declaring ritual prayers to be inconsistent with the First Amendment, the Court inserted this caveat:

> It might well be said that one's education is not complete without a study of comparative religion or the history of religion and its relationship to the advancement of civilization. It certainly may be said that the Bible is worthy of study for its literary and historic qualities. Nothing we have said here indicates that such study of the Bible or of religion, when presented objectively as part of a secular program of education, may not be effected consistently with the First Amendment. But the exercises here do not fall into those categories. They are religious exercises, required by the states in violation of the command of the First Amendment that the government maintain strict neutrality, neither aiding nor opposing religion. [*Abington School Dist.* v. *Schempp*, 374 U.S. 203, 225 (1963)]

Hence, it is not the entire subject of religion which is forbidden to government, but only ritualistic indoctrination to a religious point of view. Given the fuzzy line between subjective indoctrination and objective education, it is not difficult to imagine circumstances in which the application of the school prayer cases to particular school activities and communications will not be clear (see *Stone* v. *Graham*, 101 S.Ct. 192 [1980]).

The audience is captive and immature. Individuals who wish to withdraw from the activity are subject to severe peer pressure at a stage in life when the approval of friends is a powerful shaping force. The message goes beyond the educational mission of the schools; it does not teach communications or other skills, and, not infrequently, is inconsistent with such democratic values as tolerance and open-mindedness. The ritualistic nature of the message conditions impressionable minds to accept a model of the universe that depends in the end, like all such models, on faith. School prayer seems calculated to indoctrinate our young to beliefs best decided by the self-controlled citizen. Under these circumstances, it may be said that individuals have a right to prevent governments from speaking, and this would explain the Court's reliance on establishment-clause grounds. But even if there were no establishment clause, it would make sense to treat compulsory school prayers as interferences with the associational and free-exercise-of-religion rights of the listeners, with the indoctrination element supporting a limitation on school prayer activity.

The Academic Freedom Cases

A number of other constitutional cases in the field of public education appear sensitive to the First Amendment policy limiting government expression to captive audiences. Academic-freedom cases have always struck me as difficult to justify.[6] Only dicta in Supreme Court opinions indicate that such doctrine exists independent of other First Amendment expression doctrines.[7] Why should the fortuitous circumstances of speaking and teaching for a living invest an instructor with some special entitlement to autonomy that other government employees do not have? Why may a teacher deviate from the established curriculum while postal employees have no right to say what they please to superiors or customers?[8] If the editor of a private newspaper or broadcast station can

6. See, e.g., *Cary v. Board of Education*, 598 F.2d 535 (10th Cir. 1979); *Minarcini v. Strongville City School District*, 384 F. Supp. 698 (N.D. Ohio 1974), affirmed in part, vacated and remanded in part, 541 F.2d 577 (6th Cir. 1976); *Mailloux v. Kiley*, 436 F.2d 565 (1st Cir. 1971); *Parducci v. Rutland*, 316 F. Supp. 352 (M.D. Ala. 1970); *Keefe v. Geanakos*, 418 F.2d 359 (1st Cir. 1969). See, generally, Stephen Goldstein, "The Asserted Constitutional Right of Public School Teachers to Determine What They Teach," 124 *University of Pennsylvania Law Review* 1293 (1976), especially at 1293 n. 4.

7. See, e.g., *Keyishian v. Board of Regents*, 385 U.S. 589, 603 (1967); *Shelton v. Tucker*, 364 U.S. 479, 487 (1960); *Sweezy v. New Hampshire*, 354 U.S. 234, 250 (1957) (plurality opinion); *Wieman v. Updegraff*, 344 U.S. 183, 195-196 (1952) (Frankfurter, J., concurring); see also *Adler v. Board of Education*, 342 U.S. 485, 508 (1952) (Douglas, J., dissenting); and, generally, Thomas Emerson, *The System of Freedom of Expression* 593-626 (New York: Random House, 1970); Goldstein, "Asserted Constitutional Right of Teachers"; William Van Alstyne, "The Constitutional Rights of Teachers and Professors," 1970 *Duke Law Journal* 841.

8. See Goldstein, "Asserted Constitutional Right of Teachers."

dismiss an employee for failing to follow instructions in communicating with the audience, why should a government employee serving essentially the same function be any different?[9] When a government employee's poor communication skills provoke some punitive measure based upon the inadequacy of these skills, why isn't the First Amendment violated?

To make sense of all this, perhaps the focus should be not on the constitutional entitlements of the teacher *per se*, albeit that would presumably be the theory of any successful academic-freedom litigation, but on the place of the teacher in the system of government expression. Given the aspects of public schools described earlier that make them a communication theorist's dream, the greater the ability of the school system to control what goes on in classrooms, the greater the danger that publicly financed and operated schooling will promulgate a monolithic message to its captive listeners. Hence, just as the fragmentation of responsibility for education among governments reduces the potential danger of a thorough-going indoctrination, so, too, the autonomy of the classroom teacher contributes to a diminution of the power of government to work its communication will. If teachers were required to be automatons and to adhere rigidly to lesson plans and assignments of material promulgated by a central authority, the capacity to indoctrinate to a single ideological point of view would be increased. If they are free to interpose their own judgments, values, and comments that are not, cannot, or should not be closely monitored, we have introduced a sort of pluralism into the school environment. This is particularly important when student attendance is compulsory, and the audience, in practical terms, is not free to absent itself from the classroom.[10]

There is a paradox in this defense of academic freedom. The genesis of the doctrine is thought to lie in the nineteenth-century German concept of the university: academic freedom in the nineteenth and early twentieth centuries essentially "involved freedom of the faculty member as teacher and scholar within the university and as a citizen of the outside community."[11] The case for academic freedom has thus been thought stronger for university instructors than for public elementary and secondary school teachers; the former deal with more

---

9. See Stephen Goldstein, *Law and Public Education* 364-414 (Indianapolis, Ind.: Bobbs-Merrill, 1974); but see, e.g., *Joyner* v. *Whiting*, 477 F.2d 456 (4th Cir. 1973); *Dickey* v. *Alabama State Board of Education*, 273 F. Supp. 613 (M.D. Ala. 1967).

10. But see Mary-Michelle Hirschoff, "Parents and the Public School Curriculum: Is There a Right to Have One's Child Excused from Objectionable Instruction?" 50 *Southern California Law Review* 871 (1977).

11. Emerson, *System of Freedom of Expression* 593; see also Goldstein, "Asserted Constitutional Right of Teachers" 1299: "The modern development of the doctrine of academic freedom is derived largely from the nineteenth century German concepts of *lehrfreiheit* and *lernfreiheit*—freedom of teaching and learning."

mature students, are more likely to be engaged in research activities, and are traditionally afforded greater autonomy. From these premises, Stephen Goldstein argues that the elementary or secondary school teacher is engaged in a process of instilling values into a captive audience, and that concepts of academic freedom derived from the university setting have little application:

> The central fact in the distinction between higher and lower education is the role of value inculcation in the teaching process. The public schools in the United States traditionally have viewed instilling the young with societal values as a significant part of the schools' education mission. Such a mission is directly opposed to the vision of education that underlies the premises of academic freedom in higher education. If the purpose of teaching is to instill values, there would seem to be little reason for the teacher, rather than an elected school board or other governmental body ultimately responsible to the public, to be the one who chooses the values to be instilled.[12]

Without disputing Goldstein's observations about academic freedom in institutions of higher learning, one may argue that it is precisely because public school teachers are charged with instilling values into a captive audience that the protection of academic freedom should be extended to them. Goldstein has erred in equating the legitimacy of indoctrination in public elementary and secondary schools with the absence of any need to create entitlements or structures to place limits on that indoctrination process. Thus, for a distinctly different set of reasons, the case for academic freedom for public school teachers is at least as strong as that for university instructors.

This does not mean, however, that academic freedom should be defined so broadly as to allow teachers to make basic curricular choices independent of superiors and elected representatives. If the legitimacy of the state's education effort is accepted, academic freedom must be defined in situational terms. Justice Black presumably is right in arguing that teachers cannot substitute their notion of an appropriate course (e.g., geometry) for that of the school system or state government (e.g., algebra).[13] As Justice Stewart and William Van Alstyne[14] have noted, academic freedom should refer to a range of permissible presentational techniques and comments within the framework of legitimate state curricular choices.[15] The line-drawing will often be difficult, but

12. Goldstein, "Asserted Constitutional Right of Teachers" 1342-1343.
13. See *Epperson* v. *Arkansas*, 393 U.S. 97, 112, 114 (1968) (Black, J., concurring); see also *Cary* v. *Board of Education*, 598 F.2d 535 (10th Cir. 1979).
14. *Epperson* v. *Arkansas*, 393 U.S. 97, 115-116 (Stewart, J., concurring); Van Alstyne, "The Constitutional Rights of Teachers" 855.
15. See *Cary* v. *Board of Education*, 598 F.2d 535 (10th Cir. 1979).

it is a necessary exercise. The importance of freewheeling discussion and critical analysis in the special setting of an education institution should not be underestimated. But the relationship between academic freedom and limits on government expression should also be recognized. Courts need not necessarily decide actual cases along these structural lines, but they should consider the structure of government speech in defining individual entitlements in academic-freedom cases.

School Newspaper Cases

Closely related to the academic-freedom cases are those in which federal courts have held that school authorities may not expel, dismiss, or otherwise punish student editors of official school newspapers who publish articles contrary to the wishes of the school administration. Occasionally, courts have gone so far as to hold that such school newspapers are open public forums, at least where some controversial topics have been covered. Upon first blush, these decisions are difficult to justify. The newspapers are funded and set up by school authorities, with student editors delegated the task of editing them subject to official supervision. Under such circumstances, why can't a faculty advisor censor the newspaper? Why are student editors of a government-owned newspaper entitled to any more protection from interference by their publishers than the editors and reporters of a private newspaper?

School newspapers are a powerful instrument of communication and persuasion in the sense that they are addressed to a quasi-captive audience that is likely to read them to keep up with social events, athletics, policy changes in the school, etc. From the perspective of blunting government's communication powers, it is quite sensible to see student editors as having First Amendment rights that to some small extent reduce the capacity of school officials to control the information transmitted to student listeners.

An interesting school newspaper case at the higher educational level is *Joyner* v. *Whiting*.[16] In that case, Joyner, editor of the *Campus Echo* (offical newspaper of North Carolina Central University), published an article arguing that the university should retain its black character and not admit white students. The president of the university terminated the newspaper's financial support when Joyner refused to agree to a policy of "represent[ing] fairly the full spectrum of views on this campus." This was based on the view that the university should comply with applicable laws in not discriminating in admissions on the basis of race. The Fourth Circuit held that:

16. 477 F.2d 456 (4th Cir. 1973).

It may well be that a college need not establish a campus newspaper, or, if a paper has been established, the college may permanently discontinue publication for reasons wholly unrelated to the First Amendment. But if a college has a student newspaper, its publication cannot be suppressed because college officials dislike its editorial comment. . . .

Censorship of constitutionally protected expression cannot be imposed by suspending the editors, suppressing circulation, requiring imprimatur of controversial articles, excising repugnant material, withdrawing financial support, or asserting any other form of censorial oversight based on the institution's power of the purse.[17]

In the absence of substantial disruption, physical violence, incitement to harass whites, and the like, the newspaper's "message of racial devisiveness and antagonism," however distasteful to administrators, was constitutionally protected. Indeed, the court opined, even if the *Echo* were a state agency, "it would not be prohibited from expressing its hostility to racial integration":

The Fourteenth Amendment and the Civil Rights Act proscribe state action that denies the equal protection of the laws, not state advocacy. To be sure, the line between action and advocacy may sometimes be difficult to draw, but it is clear that nothing written in the *Echo* crossed it.[18]

This last part apparently was designed to quiet fears that the university would be subject to constitutional and statutory claims for the newspaper articles produced under its aegis.

As written, *Joyner* is difficult to defend. Perhaps advocacy of racial segregation by a public entity in a position to implement its advocacy is the rare case in which restraints on government speech are tolerable. But, in any event, this was a case where a superior within the entity dictated that its newspaper not publish remarks that, to say the least, might encourage unconstitutional segregation. *A priori*, this should be entitled to as much weight as when Congress limits the activities of the public-relations offices of the armed forces. The students do not own the newspaper; rather, they have been given a limited amount of authority to operate and edit it. They have not been denied the right to publish, but only the right to express themselves at public expense. One plausible rejoinder is that the First Amendment rights of editors are buttressed by a policy of limiting the impact of government speech. Editors, like teachers, ought not to be turned into unwilling conduits of

17. *Id.* at 460.
18. *Id.* at 461–462.

government indoctrination—even in so important an area as policy on racial discrimination.

Selection of Teachers

Another facet of the same problem is the procedure for selecting teachers and school newspaper editors. Focusing on teachers, it is important to deny school authorities power to hire or fire on the basis of personal ideology, political views, or membership in associations. The greater the diversity among those who carry the state's messages, the less capable the state is of finding willing communicators to express a monolithic message to a captive audience. In *Shelton* v. *Tucker*,[19] for example, the Court invalidated an Arkansas statute requiring public school teachers to file affidavits listing the organizations to which they belonged or contributed. So, too, the Supreme Court has had a skeptical attitude toward loyalty oaths for teachers.[20] This is not to say that school systems have no interest in protecting students from those with antidemocratic points of view or those who might be dangerous to the student body.[21] Rather, it is to say that in vindicating the First Amendment expression and associational rights of teachers, courts should be sensitive to the problem of allowing local and state authorities the power to recruit and retain a homogeneous class of employees who can be expected to transmit without deviation the favored messages of those making centralized curricular judgments.

The socialization questions implicit in teacher selection are graphically illustrated by a recent Supreme Court decision on the constitutionality of a New York state law denying certification to alien teachers in public schools who are eligible for United States citizenship but

19. 364 U.S. 479 (1960). See also, e.g., *Keyishian* v. *Board of Regents*, 385 U.S. 589 (1967). Cf. *Elrod* v. *Burns*, 427 U.S. 347 (1976) (plurality opinion). But see *Beilan* v. *Board of Public Education*, 357 U.S. 399 (1958); *Adler* v. *Board of Education*, 342 U.S. 485 (1952).

20. See, e.g., *Cole* v. *Richardson*, 405 U.S. 676 (1972); *Whitehill* v. *Elkins*, 389 U.S. 54 (1967); *Baggett* v. *Bullitt*, 377 U.S. 360 (1964); *Cramp* v. *Board of Public Instruction*, 368 U.S. 278 (1961). But see *Ohlson* v. *Phillips*, 397 U.S. 317 (1970), affirming *per curiam* 304 F. Supp. 1152 (D. Colo. 1969).

21. See *National Socialist White People's Party* v. *Ringers*, 473 F.2d 1010 (4th Cir. 1973); *Pickings* v. *Bruce*, 430 F.2d 595 (8th Cir. 1970); *Stacy* v. *Williams*, 306 F. Supp. 963 (N.D. Miss. 1969); affirmed, 446 F.2d 1366 (5th Cir. 1971). Cf. *Healy* v. *James*, 408 U.S. 169 (1972); *Zucker* v. *Panitz*, 299 F. Supp. 102 (S.D. N.Y. 1969) (public forum in school newspaper); *Brooks* v. *Auburn Univ.*, 296 F. Supp. 188 (M.D. Ala. 1969), affirmed, 412 F.2d 1171 (5th Cir. 1969). Compare *Dunkel* v. *Elkins*, 325 F. Supp. 1235 (D. Md. 1971). See, generally, Charles Alan Wright, "The Constitution on the Campus," 22 *Vanderbilt Law Review* 1027, 1050-1052 (1969); William Van Alstyne, "Political Speakers at State Universities: Some Constitutional Considerations," 111 *University of Pennsylvania Law Review* 328 (1963); Susan Garrison, "The Public School as Public Forum," 54 *Texas Law Review* 90 (1975).

who decline to seek naturalization. In *Ambach* v. *Norwick*,[22] a bare majority of the Court upheld the law. Justice Powell, writing for the majority, recognizes many of the systemic implications of the law before the Court. The question is not simply the alien's interest under the equal-protection clause in not being excluded from teaching in the public schools. Rather, resolution of the case turns in part on what governments seek to accomplish in public schools, and this distinguishes the case from those in which the Court has declared unconstitutional laws preventing aliens from serving as lawyers, engineers, or fishermen. As Justice Powell put it,

> Some state functions are so bound up with the operation of the State as a governmental entity as to permit the exclusion from those functions of all persons who have not become part of the process of self-government. . . . "Such power inheres in the State by virtue of its obligation . . . 'to preserve the basic conception of a political community.' . . ."
>
> The distinction between citizens and aliens, though ordinarily irrelevant to private activity, is fundamental to the definition and government of a State. . . . The assumption of . . . [citizen] status, whether by birth or naturalization, denotes an association with the polity which, in a democratic republic, exercises the powers of governance. . . . The form of this association is important: an oath of allegiance or similar ceremony cannot substitute for the unequivocal legal bond citizenship represents. It is because of this special significance of citizenship that governmental entities, when exercising the functions of government, have wider latitude in limiting the participation of noncitizens.[23]

Justice Powell views the government function of teaching in public schools almost exclusively in terms of the legitimacy and necessity of instilling democratic values and preparing the nation's youth for citizenship. Questions of assimilation, pluralism, homogeneity, and heterogenity are for the first time recognized as important issues in determining the constitutionality of selection procedures for public school teachers. For Powell, the interest of the state in promulgating particular types of messages in public schools outweighs any other interest. The conclusion is based on a syllogism: (1) Public schools perform an essential public function by inculcating values necessary to the survival of a democracy; (2) "teachers play a critical part in developing students' attitude toward government and understanding of the role of citizens in our society"; and (3) legislatures may therefore base eligi-

22. 441 U.S. 68 (1979).
23. *Id.* at 73–74, 75.

bility for teaching positions on the premise "that *generally* persons who
are citizens, or who have not declined the opportunity to seek United
States citizenship, are better qualified [to instill democratic citizenship
values] than those who have elected to remain aliens." In a passage
devoid of any concern for the possible dangers of government expression in public schools, the majority asserts that "a State properly may
regard all teachers as having an obligation to promote civic virtues and
understanding in their classes, regardless of the subject taught."[24]

The dissent, written by Justice Blackmun, largely goes off on the
question of whether it is rational to assume that all aliens eligible for
citizenship who fail to apply for naturalization may logically be presumed to be incapable of carrying out their important mission relating
to citizenship and assimilation. The dissenters make a strong case,
indeed a compelling case, that there are other means of determining
the ability of teachers to carry out socialization functions, e.g., loyalty oaths, courses for certification, and so on. But there is virtually
no discussion of the notion that perhaps the New York law goes too far
in allowing the state to recruit a homogeneous class of teachers intent
upon socializing youngsters to a particular set of norms. There is only
passing reference to diversity, and the dissent agrees with the majority's observations about the need for public schools to play an assimila-
tive role and to preserve the "values on which our society rests."[25] The
Court is divided over the question of efficiency and reasonable means
to instill democratic values, and not over the more fundamental question of the limits of government expression in public schools. Footnote
8 of the majority opinion goes unchallenged:

> The curricular requirements of New York's public school system
> reflect some of the ways a public school system promotes the
> development of the understanding that is prerequisite to intelli-
> gent participation in the democratic process. The schools are
> required to provide instruction "to promote a spirit of patriotic
> and civic service and obligation and to foster in the children of
> the state moral and intellectual qualities which are essential in
> preparing to meet the obligations of citizenship in peace or in
> war...." Flag and other patriotic exercises also are prescribed,
> as loyalty is a characteristic of citizenship essential to the preser-
> vation of a country.... In addition, required courses include
> civics, United States and New York history, and principles of
> American government....
>
> Although private schools also are bound by most of these re-
> quirements, the State has a stronger interest in ensuring that the

24. *Id.* at 80, 81 n. 14.
25. *Id.* at 85, 86 n. 6, 87-88 (Blackmun, J., dissenting).

schools it most directly controls, and for which it bears the cost, are as effective as possible in teaching these courses.[26]

Thus, while the justices recognize the relationship between government expression and selection of teachers, they are myopic in perceiving the former in terms only of affirmatively promoting liberty and not in terms of the perils of government infringing upon individual choice, autonomy, and creativity.

The appellees' (aliens') brief in the Supreme Court explicitly sought to ground the case on the need to limit the discretion of states to select teachers in order to achieve socialization objectives. The New York law sought "to suppress respect for diversity and to compel standardization of ideas."[27] Reliance was placed on the student-rights cases, loyalty-oath cases, academic-freedom cases, and communist-association cases for the proposition that the First Amendment does not tolerate "laws that cast a pall of orthodoxy over . . . [the] classroom."[28] If communists could not be excluded from teaching in public schools simply because of their affiliation, the appellees argued, aliens could not be excluded on grounds of interfering with socialization processes. Failure to initiate naturalization is not necessarily a sign of disloyalty to the nation, and aliens might well bring different perspectives to the classroom that would well serve the students.[29]

The Court simply did not understand, or chose to ignore, these points in the appellees' brief. Justice Powell's hyperbolic response to the academic-freedom argument largely misses the thrust of the appellees' contentions:

> We think the attempt to draw an analogy between choice of citizenship and political expression or freedom of association is wide of the mark, as the argument would bar any effort by the State to promote particular values and attitudes toward government. [The New York law] . . . does not inhibit appellees from expressing freely their political or social views or from communicating with whomever they please. . . . The only asserted liberty of appellees withheld by the New York statute is the opportunity to teach in the State's schools so long as they elect not to become citizens of this country. This is not a liberty that is accorded constitutional protection.[30]

It is simply untrue that any restriction on selection of teachers, or, implicitly, on the state's ability to shape a homogeneous people in public

26. *Id.* at 78 n. 8.
27. Brief for Appellees at 64, *id.*
28. *Keyishian* v. *Board of Regents*, 385 U.S. 589, 603 (1967).
29. Brief for Appellees at 69, *Ambach* v. *Norwick*, 441 U.S. 68 (1979).
30. *Ambach* v. *Norwick*, 441 U.S. 68, 79 n. 10 (1979).

schools, would "bar any effort" to inculcate values. There are many such restrictions, and the question should not be of the all-or-nothing variety. The question is rather whether, in the light of the interest of aliens in teaching in public schools, this particular selection process goes too far in allowing the state to recruit a homogeneous corps of teachers. The Court loses sight of the interest of the people as a whole in controlling government domination of educational processes. That aliens may associate and express themselves outside of the classroom is no answer at all when the total system of communication is taken into account. Diversity among teachers is a check on government indoctrination distinct from the ability of groups and individuals outside of the educational system to respond to the government's messages. The former dilutes the government's power to speak; the latter appeals to traditions of pluralism to create countervailing forces in the larger communications networks. In this light, the Court erred in upholding the New York law in *Amback* v. *Norwick*.

Students' Rights

The affirmation, subject to a substantial disruption test, of the rights of students to communicate in schools, to petition, to distribute privately printed "underground" newspapers, and to form clubs and associations is also consistent with countering government expression in public schools.[31] The case should not be overstated. Given the constraints of the school environment, individual students are not likely to be very powerful communicators of messages contrary to those of the established school authorities. Nor, perhaps, should they be, given the age of the students and the purpose for which they are in school. There is no right to speak at all times and in all places in schools, and the lecture method is hardly unconstitutional. On the other hand, Justice Fortas was exactly right in saying in the *Tinker* case that "in our system, state-operated schools may not be the enclaves of totalitarianism"; for students may not be regarded as "closed-circuit recipients of only that which the state chooses to communicate."[32] This is not a formula for the Court's preferred philosophy of instruction, as Goldstein would have it. Rather it is an embodiment of a constitutional policy in favor of limiting the state's power to communicate to a captive audience (public school students), and this is a policy which informs principles of First Amendment rights students carry with them into the school environment. *Tinker* and its progeny promote pluralism within an institu-

31. See *Tinker* v. *Des Moines Independent School District*, 393 U.S. 503 (1969), and, generally, Garrison, "The Public School as Public Forum."
32. 393 U.S. at 511; but cf. Stephen Goldstein, "Reflections on Developing Trends in the Law of Student Rights," 118 *University of Pennsylvania Law Review* 612 (1970).

tion with grave potential to dominate and distort thinking, whatever the legitimacy of its overall mission.

The Schools as Public Forums

There are public-forum school cases that contribute to staying government communications powers in much the same manner as the student-rights decisions. These cases stand for the proposition that once public school officials open their facilities to individuals and groups who express one point of view, they may not deny others access to the same facilities for the purposes of communicating contrary or different messages.[33] The most common examples are allowing only some forms of picketing adjacent to the schools; the allowance of some newspapers and magazines in the schools and not others; permitting speeches by individuals who express an approved point of view but not those of others; and recognizing clubs and other associations on the basis of administrative approval or disapproval of the objectives of the organization. This is the First Amendment equal-protection doctrine in action, and most courts are quick to point out that a ban on all such forms of expression would be constitutional. Most educational institutions, of course, would find a total ban inconsistent with their institutional mission; hence this equal-protection analysis tends to expand rather than to contract the scope of expression and association in public educational institutions. And to the extent that the public-forum doctrine opens the schools to outsiders, it is inconsistent with a government monopoly over messages to the students, and serves strong First Amendment policies against government domination of a channel of communication.

Laurence Tribe describes public schools as "quasi-public forums," indicating that while they differ from parks and streets, their mission and nature nonetheless allow for outsiders to use the schools as forums in particular circumstances where no substantial disruption is foreseeable.[34] But if the schools are "quasi-public forums," they are so in a most complex way. Someone who works (teachers) or studies (students) in public schools may have a limited right of expression on the institution's premises, even to the point of responding to the state's own message.[35] Nonparticipants generally have no such right. Furthermore, there is no general acceptance of the proposition that the state's

33. See, e.g., *Police Department of the City of Chicago* v. *Mosely*, 408 U.S. 92 (1972); *Pickings* v. *Bruce*, 430 F.2d 595 (8th Cir. 1970). See, generally, Kenneth Karst, "Equality as a Central Principle in the First Amendment," 43 *University of Chicago Law Review* 20 (1975); Shiffrin, "Government Speech."

34. Tribe, *American Constitutional Law* 690 (Mineola, N.Y.: Foundation Press, 1978).

35. *Tinker* v. *Des Moines School District*, 393 U.S. 503 (1975); but cf. *Parker* v. *Levy*, 417 U.S. 733 (1974).

own communications efforts may allow outsiders to successfully invoke the public-forum doctrine; rather, a right of access by outsiders is granted only when other outsiders have been afforded such rights.[36] There are opinions that say, in effect, that if the state's message is controversial enough, there is some possibility of a right of access or perhaps reply—but these cases are rare. Most courts have artfully skirted the issue. Yet a right of access subject to the *Tinker* caveats of substantial disruption and the like would appear vital in the implementation of a policy to prevent government from going to excess in the closed environment of the public schools.

At the moment, the case law is not at all promising in this regard. The sense one has is that institutions like schools are public forums only for those who "belong" there, or that there is some irrebuttable presumption that "outsiders" will disrupt the institution's activities.[37] Perhaps, notions of "private" public property or trespass are at work.[38] This would be consistent with judicial developments in the labor-law field, limiting the access of outside union organizers to employers' premises.[39] Why the average citizen-taxpayer "owns" the schools any less than those who work and learn there is not entirely clear. A better explanation may well be that students (not so much teachers) have few opportunities to speak to any audience outside of the school, inasmuch as they lack advertising resources, direct access to the mass media, and so on. The government's use of the institution to communicate or indoctrinate does not turn the institution into a public forum, but courts have simply recognized a right to speak on the part of students, who have difficulty being heard elsewhere. Questions of access by "outsiders" would then reduce themselves to evenhanded governmental treatment of different groups and individuals, and would have little to do with countering government expression.

The policy of limiting government expression should, however, form a basis for First Amendment entitlement of all individuals and groups to communicate in the public schools, subject to the context in which the right is asserted—the degree of foreseeable disruption, the content of the message (as it relates to the mission of the school), time and place problems, and the like. This is not to say that history classes should indiscriminately be opened to outsiders who wish to address young people reduced to a captive audience for them by the state. But analysis should start with the proposition that government communica-

36. See *Buckel* v. *Prentice*, 572 F.2d 141 (6th Cir. 1978). And indeed private use of the forum does not necessarily render it "public" (*Lehman* v. *Shaker Heights*, 418 U.S. 298 [1974]).

37. See Garrison, "The Public School as Public Forum" 122-123.

38. Cf. *Lloyd Corp* v. *Tanner*, 407 U.S. 551 (1972). But cf. *Pruneyard Shopping Center* v. *Robins*, 100 S.Ct. 2035 (1980).

39. See, generally, Robert Gorman, *Basic Text on Labor Law* 179-194 (St. Paul, Minn.: West Publishing, 1976).

tion in the schools itself activates a sort of public-forum doctrine, and that allowing access for purposes of expression is an important part of breaking down the state monopoly over communications in public schools. As Laurence Tribe has emphasized, a conscious fostering of diversity within the limits of the educational mission of schools is desirable.[40] It promotes tolerance and the exchange of information and ideas. Subject to the disruption standard, outsiders should be entitled to distribute pamphlets, give speeches in the school yard, participate in assemblies, and so forth, even if we all agree that they may not push the English teacher aside in order to teach social anthropology.

Recent judicial developments largely fail to articulate concern with government monopoly over captive audiences in access cases. In *Greer* v. *Spock*,[41] the Court refused to allow those who would distribute political pamphlets access to a military base. But there is no substantial reason why servicemen and women, entitled to vote, should not be the beneficiaries of such expression, or why the pamphleteers should be denied access to a possible constituency for their point of view. The military program of indoctrination may thus, but clear, political implications. Officers may thus decline to invite nonmilitary speakers with political messages, thereby avoiding the public-forum doctrine. The content of the message (e.g., advocating military insurrection) would be relevant, as would the maturity of the soldiers and their access to competing messages off the base. But I would create a presumption of access, just as in the case of the public schools.

Spock is a strong indication that the Court is not sympathetic to such access claims, and the justices may in due course extend that decision to public schools. *Spock* may also overrule *Brown* v. *Louisiana*,[42] decided ten years before *Spock*, in which the Court constitutionally protected a silent vigil in a public library as a civil-rights protest. Thus, despite Tribe's suggestion, one cannot be hopeful that libraries and schools will be differentiated for public-forum purposes from other public institutions because their purposes are "more closely linked to expression."[43]

Private Schooling

One way to counter the persuasive powers of governments in relation to captive audiences is to take steps to release all, or part, of the

40. See Tribe, *American Constitutional Law* 690.

41. 424 U.S. 828 (1976). Cf. *Houchins* v. *KQED*, 438 U.S. 1 (1978) (plurality opinion); *Lehman* v. *Shaker Heights*, 418 U.S. 298 (1974); *Adderley* v. *Florida*, 385 U.S. 39 (1966).

42. 383 U.S. 131 (1966). Perhaps *Brown* v. *Louisiana* is better understood as a race case rather than a First Amendment one.

43. See Tribe, *American Constitutional Law* 690. I rather think that in prisons, mental hospitals, and military installations the level of government communications activities is, and should be, quite high (see, e.g., Peter Barnes, *Pawns: The Plight of the Citizen-Soldier* [New York: Knopf, 1972]).

audience. A superb example in the context of education is *Pierce* v. *Society of Sisters.*[44] In that case, the Supreme Court held unconstitutional an Oregon statute requiring all students to satisfy compulsory attendance laws by attending *public* schools. The case appears to have been decided on now repudiated grounds of substantive due process in the economic sphere: the law would have put private-education entrepreneurs and teachers virtually out of business (except for classes held after public school), thereby infringing on their ability to make money and enter into contracts. Significantly, however, in the more than fifty years that have passed since the *Pierce* decision, the result of that litigation has not been repudiated by subsequent Supreme Court justices—not even by those noted for their hostility to economic substantive due process. Commentators and judges have referred to the free-exercise-of-religion claims inherent in the litigation (religious schools could not satisfy the Oregon law), the emanations from the First and Fourteenth Amendments as to the substantive due process rights of parents to raise their children, and other justifications for *Pierce.*[45] Suffice it to say that there appears to be widespread hostility to overruling *Pierce*, albeit some would expand and others would restrict its meaning as a precedent.[46]

Approached entirely in terms of individual entitlements, *Pierce* is highly problematic. Arguably, if the state wills it, private individuals should have no more right to run educational institutions than to organize a private army to defend the nation. The doctrine of academic freedom for teachers would appear to be twisted beyond all recognition if teachers had a constitutional right not only to make reasonable pedagogical decisions, but to make curricular choices and to force the state to tolerate institutions within which they might make those choices. Parents historically have been given considerable latitude in

44. 268 U.S. 510 (1925). See, generally, David Kirp and Mark Yudof, *Educational Policy and the Law* 1-10 (Berkeley, Calif.: McCutchan Publishing, 1974); Stephen Arons, "The Separation of School and State: Pierce Reconsidered," 46 *Harvard Education Review* 76 (1976); David Tyack, "The Perils of Pluralism: The Background of the Pierce Case," 74 *American Historical Review* 74 (1968).

45. See, e.g., *F.C.C.* v. *Pacifica Foundation*, 438 U.S. 726, 762 (1978) (Brennan, J., dissenting); *Carey* v. *Population Services International*, 413 U.S. 678, 684 (1977); *Cook* v. *Hudson*, 429 U.S. 166 (1977) (Burger, C.J., concurring); *Runyon* v. *McCrary*, 427 U.S. 160, 176-177 (1976); *Wisconsin* v. *Yoder*, 406 U.S. 205, 213 (1972) (Burger, C.J., for the Court); *Board of Education* v. *Allen*, 392 U.S. 236, 245 (1968); *Griswold* v. *Connecticut*, 381 U.S. 479, 481 (1965) (Douglas, J.); *Abington School District* v. *Schempp*, 374 U.S. 203, 248 (1968) (Brennan, J., concurring). Often, a reference to *Pierce* appears to be a throwaway line, whatever the actual result, indicating the Court's devotion to the preservation of family autonomy (see, e.g., *Smith* v. *Organization of Foster Families*, 431 U.S. 816, 842 [1977]).

46. See, e.g., *Zablocki* v. *Redhail*, 434 U.S. 374, 680 (1978), citing *Roe* v. *Wade*, 410 U.S. 113, 152-153 (1973); *Runyon* v. *McCrary*, 427 U.S. 160, 176-177 (1976); *Norwood* v. *Harrison*, 413 U.S. 455, 461 (1974); *Wisconsin* v. *Yoder*, 406 U.S. 205, 239 (1972) (White, J., concurring); Arons, "The Separation of School and State"; Judith Areen, "Education Vouchers," 6 *Harvard Civil Rights-Civil Liberties Law Review* 466, 501-502 (1971).

making decisions for their children, but, apart from the uncertain constitutional derivation of such entitlements, it is not clear why compulsory *public* schooling is an intolerable interference with parents' rights. The state frequently interferes with parental choice, and often more substantially. Compulsory-attendance laws themselves are a more significant interference with parental autonomy than the *Pierce* law; for the decision that children must attend *some* school for eight or more years of their lives appears more consequential than a decision that they must attend *public* school. Indeed, even in *Pierce*, the Court did not deny the state extensive authority to regulate what must be taught in private and public schools—presumably including courses in language, history, hygiene, and civics that some parents might find objectionable.[47]

And beyond compulsory education, there lurks such state regulation of intra-family affairs as the termination of parental rights (for child abuse, neglect, or abandonment); compulsory vaccinations and lifesaving medical procedures for children irrespective of parental choice; incest and fornication laws; prohibitions on the sale of pornography, tobacco, and alcoholic beverages to minors, even with parental consent; child-labor laws; and many other measures limiting the public and private rights of minors, whatever the parents' attitude toward such restrictions.[48]

The point is not that traditions of parental autonomy should be abandoned. Nor is it that minors are not entitled to at least some of the constitutional protection afforded to adults. The point, rather, is that *Pierce* becomes intelligible only against the background of a structure in which it is appropriate to limit the power of government to indoctrinate the young. *Pierce* may be construed (whatever the original motivations of the justices) as telling governments that they are free to establish their own public schools and to make education compulsory for certain age groups, but not free to eliminate competing, private-sector educational institutions that may serve to create heterogeneity and to counter the state's dominance over the education of the young. It is one thing to treat education as a legitimate enterprise for the state: it is quite another to treat private education as illegitimate. Similarly, it is

47. 268 U.S. at 534. See also *Farrington* v. *Tokushige*, 273 U.S. 284 (1927); *Bartles* v. *Iowa*, 262 U.S. 404 (1923); *Meyer* v. *Nebraska*, 262 U.S. 390 (1923); Stephen Sugarman and David Kirp, "Rethinking Collective Responsibility for Education," 39 *Law and Contemporary Problems* 144, 196 (1975).

48. See, generally, Robert Mnookin, *Child, Family and State* (Boston: Little, Brown, 1978); Andrew Kleinfeld, "The Balance of Power Among Infants, Their Parents, and the State" (pts. 1 and 2), 4 *Family Law Quarterly* 319, 409 (1970). There are, of course, some situations in which the child's interest has been deemed paramount to the state's interest—sometimes even in the absence of parental acquiescence. See, e.g., *Carey* v. *Population Services*, 431 U.S. 678 (1977); *Planned Parenthood* v. *Danforth*, 428 U.S. 52 (1976); *Wisconsin* v. *Yoder*, 406 U.S. 205, 241 (1972) (Douglas, J., dissenting).

one thing to require private schools to offer English courses, mathematics, or civics, and quite another for the state to forbid them to teach the German language, Bible study, or modern dance. Recall also *Ambach* v. *Norwich*, in which both the New York legislature and the Court were quite careful in noting that the exclusion of some aliens from teaching did not apply to nonpublic schools, despite the large number of curricular and other requirements applicable to such schools.[49]

A contrary decision in *Pierce* would have enabled the state to gain a monopoly over public education, and such a monopoly may pose significant dangers in terms of the state's ability to mold the young. To be sure, many of the values and attitudes conveyed in private schools may be identical to those conveyed in public schools. Virtually all schools tend to mirror consensual values and to promote the rules of the game. Further, five or six hours a day in school, for roughly half of each year, hardly preclude socialization in the family. And radio and television, films, peer-group norms and pressures, clubs, and other institutions and mechanisms for conveying messages and values may (and probably do) greatly reduce the danger of compulsory public schooling. But in the face of indeterminacy as to how the various participants and institutions contribute to socialization processes and interact with one another,[50] *Pierce* represents a reasonable, if imperfect,[51] accommodation of conflicting pressures. The state may promulgate its messages in the public school, while parents are free to choose private schools with different orientations. The state must tolerate private education, but need not fund it. The state may make some demands of private schools to satisfy compulsory schooling laws, but those demands may not be so excessive as to turn private schools into public schools managed and funded by the private sector. The integrity of the communications and socialization processes in private schools and families remains intact, while the state's interest in producing informed, educated, and productive citizens is not sacrificed. The desirable structure for limiting governments as communicators thus gives credence to the individual-rights arguments in *Pierce*, which may otherwise appear to be tenuous.

49. *Ambach* v. *Norwich*, 441 U.S. 68 (1979).

50. See, generally, Fred Greenstein, *Children and Politics* (New Haven, Conn.: Yale University Press, 1965); M. Kent Jennings and Richard Niemi, *The Political Character of Adolescence* (Princeton, N.J.: Princeton University Press, 1974); Richard Dawson and Kenneth Prewitt, eds., *Political Socialization* (Boston: Little, Brown, 1969); John Clausen, ed., *Socialization and Society* (Boston: Little, Brown, 1968).

51. See John Coons and Stephen Sugarman, *Education by Choice: The Case for Family Control* (Berkeley and Los Angeles: University of California Press, 1978), in which the authors outline and defend a plan for increasing family autonomy and choice in education. The historic criticism of *Pierce*, as it operates in fact, has been that only the religiously devout (by virtue of numbers) and the affluent (by virtue of being able to afford expensive private schools for their children) can take advantage of the rights afforded to parents in *Pierce*.

Releasing the Captive Audience

In two cases, *FCC* v. *Pacifica Foundation*[52] and *Rowan* v. *U.S. Post Office*,[53] the Supreme Court has upheld the right of government agencies to protect citizens from speech which they do not wish to hear. The former case involved the broadcasting of allegedly obscene words by a radio licensee at a time when children might hear them; the latter involved the right of addressees, pursuant to postal regulations, to decline to receive mail to which they objected. In each case, the Court dismissed the rights of the speaker, arguing that "nothing in the Constitution compels us to listen to or view any unwanted communication, whatever its merit."[54] This "right not to hear," like the "right to know," is not wholly intelligible. It seems to refer to the constitutionality of government capturing an audience for private communications where members of the audience itself object to the message. In each case, moreover, the speech emanated from a private party and not from the government itself, and did not take place in a government institution. There are overtones of privacy interests—the privacy of the home and the private relationship between parents and children in determining what the children may read, view, and hear.[55]

The natural extension of this line of reasoning, arguably, is that there is a constitutional right to absent oneself from a captive audience where the government is the speaker. The leading case standing for this proposition is *Yoder* v. *Wisconsin*,[56] in which the Supreme Court held unconstitutional the Wisconsin compulsory-attendance law as applied to Amish children after the eighth grade. The decision was explicitly grounded in the free-exercise-of-religion clause of the First Amendment and not on a general right of citizens to be free of the socializing influences of the state in public schools. Mary-Michelle Hirschoff has argued that *Yoder* should be extended to permit parents to absent their children from particular portions of the compulsory school curriculum. The argument rests on a number of related factors: the need for pluralism, the dangers of state indoctrination, the potential for state interference with the consent of the governed, the rights of parents to socialize their children as they see fit, and the power of teachers as communicators, given the respect with which they are treated.[57]

52. *FCC* v. *Pacifica Foundation*, 438 U.S. 726 (1978); cf. *Butler* v. *Michigan*, 352 U.S. 380 (1957).

53. *Rowan* v. *U.S. Post Office*, 397 U.S. 728 (1970); cf. *Consolidated Edison Company* v. *Public Service Commission*, 477 U.S. 530 (1980).

54. 397 U.S. at 738.

55. See, generally, Thomas Krattenmaker and Lucas Powe, "Televised Violence: First Amendment Principles and Social Science Theory," 64 *Virginia Law Review* 1123 (1978).

56. *Yoder* v. *Wisconsin*, 406 U.S. 205 (1972).

57. Hirschoff, "Parents and the Public School Curriculum."

Presumably, the same sorts of claims could be made for prison inmates, mental patients, and military personnel on military bases. The
argument, however, is flawed once the role of the state in these activities is perceived as legitimate. The mission of the schools is to teach and
train students for later life, and this inevitably involves socialization.
The process of training military recruits, rehabilitating prisoners, and
treating mental patients similarly involves socialization. A general
constitutional rule that the clients may exempt themselves from particular communications activities denies the central mission of these
institutions. For example, public education exists precisely because
parents frequently cannot perform the necessary education functions
and because of the need to instill a sense of political, social, and economic community. An unbridled capacity to choose to walk away from
a portion of the curriculum cuts too deeply into these significant state
interests. Hirschoff argues that the right of exemption should not apply
to basic skill courses (reading, writing, and arithmetic?), but there is no
reason to believe that such courses do not involve substantial indoctrination.[58] And who is to say which is more important, a course on civics
or a course on English literature? An arithmetic course may promote
capitalism as much as a civics course may promote democracy. As
Justice Douglas noted in another context, "a continuous auditing of
classroom instruction" would be needed—and with unclear standards
and judicial results.[59]

Even recognizing the dangers of indoctrination, the dilemma of
selective absenting of governmentally captured audiences in public
schools and other legitimate government institutions is at the cutting
edge of the distinction between government action expanding choice
and autonomy and government action contracting them. As Justice
White noted in his concurring opinion in *Yoder*, the Amish children
may be enriched by courses in modern dance, piano, or vocational
education.[60] Frequently, curricular offerings may expand the career
and other options open to students. If a parent pulls a student out of
class, this may have the effect of limiting the child's horizons, substi-
tuting the actual indoctrination of parents for the potential indoctrination of the state. Continued attendance would give the child an additional perspective and more information, thus enhancing his prospects
for autonomy and self-control.[61] Denying him access to the information—depending, of course, on the subject—may aid in the creation of
another intolerant citizen whose responses are compelled by a value
system which is his for no better reason than that it was his father's.

58. *Id.* at 926-941.
59. *Lemon* v. *Kurtzman*, 403 U.S. 602, 640 (1971) (Douglas, J., concurring).
60. *Yoder* v. *Wisconsin*, 406 U.S. 205, 239 (1972) (White, J., concurring).
61. See, generally, Isaiah Berlin, *Four Essays on Liberty* (New York: Oxford University Press, 1969).

Two other factors are also relevant to the analysis. Parents have the option, at least where they can afford it, to send their children to private schools. In this context, the states decide what must be taught, and there is usually great leeway in allowing private school authorities the discretion to determine the remainder of the curriculum. Additionally, state legislatures have frequently responded to the socialization problem by voluntarily granting different types of exemptions from compulsory-attendance laws.[62] Instruction at home is sanctioned in many states. Parental control over attendance in particularly controversial courses, e.g., sex education, is also commonly embodied in statutes. Thus, in part, the political system has already been responsive to the captive-audience problem.

The limits of these arguments should be kept in mind. As in *Yoder*, where infringement on religious beliefs can be shown, the right to absent oneself from the captive audience may be compelling (as it may be for the conscientious objector called to military service). The interest is not a generalized one in resisting any form of state indoctrination deemed objectionable; rather it is one grounded in the overarching constitutional commitment to religious freedom. The specific content of the message that is objectionable on religious grounds must be identified: there is no general assault on the socialization function of governments. Furthermore, the context of the argument relates to total or semi-total institutions in which there is general acceptance of the necessity of state indoctrination. Other centers of communication remain free to counter the state's messages. Finally, the argument goes only so far as to indicate that there is no constitutional right to selective absence from a captive audience: legislatures remain free to allow such exemptions as they see fit.

62. See, generally, Lawrence Kotin and William F. Aikman, *Legal Foundations of Compulsory School Attendance* (Port Washington, N.Y.: Kennikat Press, 1980).

[13]

Government Subsidies of Private Speech, the Public-Forum Doctrine, and Government as Editor

Government Subsidies

Governments sometimes do not engage in speech themselves, but rather subsidize private speech. Such subsidies occur in numerous settings. When state or federal governments decide (and are constitutionally permitted) to give aid to private secular and nonsecular schools, they are promoting communications by those private centers for education. Much of the debate about "parochiaid" can be reduced to the question of whether and to what extent states are promoting secular communications or are promoting nonsecular communications by replacing funds that would otherwise be devoted to nonreligious purposes.[1] Surely the answer must be that government subsidies to religious institutions promote both types of speech. Another example is the public-forum doctrine. If the notion is that public streets, parks, and buildings (under some circumstances) must be open to all of those who wish to use them to promote their views (subject to reasonable traffic regulations), the forum itself is a subsidy in kind to private speakers.[2] So, too,

---

1. See, e.g., *Lemon* v. *Kurtzman*, 403 U.S. 602 (1971); *Roemer* v. *Board of Public Works in Maryland*, 426 U.S. 736 (1976); *Wolman* v. *Walter*, 433 U.S. 229 (1977); *Levitt* v. *Committee for Public Education*, 413 U.S. 472 (1973); *Everson* v. *Board of Education*, 330 U.S. 1 (1947); *Board of Education* v. *Allen*, 392 U.S. 236 (1968); *Meek* v. *Pittinger*, 421 U.S. 349 (1975); *Board of Education* v. *Allen*, 392 U.S. 236, 244 (1968); *Tilton* v. *Richardson*, 403 U.S. 672 (1931). See, generally, Laurence Tribe, *American Constitutional Law* § 14-9 (Mineola, N.Y.: Foundation Press, 1978); Jesse Choper, "The Establishment Clause and Aid to Parochial Schools," 56 *California Law Review* 260 (1968); Donald Gianella, "Lemon and Tilton: The Bitter and the Sweet of Church-State Entanglement," 1971 *Supreme Court Review* 147; Stephen Sugarman, "Family Choice: The Next Step in the Quest for Equal Educational Opportunity?" 38 *Law and Contemporary Problems* 513 (1974).

2. See, generally, Harry Kalven, "The Concept of the Public Forum: *Cox* v. *Louisiana,*" 1965 *Supreme Court Review* 1; Geoffrey Stone, "Fora Americana: Speech in Public Places," 1974 *Supreme Court Review* 233.

second-class mailing privileges for magazines may be viewed as a subsidy to the mass print media.

If, then, we view these as subsidies, the primary danger is that the government will subsidize views with which it agrees and not subsidize others. Government selectivity of message content in its subsidies would thus promote a self-serving consensus. In this light, the First Amendment equal-protection doctrine[3] that requires that government be evenhanded in subsidizing private communicators makes a great deal of sense. Governments should not be permitted to favor religious schools over secular, private schools, *Reader's Digest* over the *National Review*, conservative campus speakers over liberals, or to finance the political campaigns of Democratic and not of Republican candidates. Apart from notions of fairness and the rights of the speakers, the justification for First Amendment equal protection may lurk in the danger of government domination of communications through the utilization of private communicators.

Note that the subsidy cases do not mean that governments have a constitutional obligation to subsidize private speech. Universities may be as free to deny podiums to all speakers as local governments may be not to allow anyone to utilize a public facility for purposes of expression.[4] This does not deny a point urged earlier that access to public institutions should be constitutionally required, or that people take their speech rights with them wherever they go subject to a substantial disruption test. Where it is difficult to distinguish the economic costs of ordinary or general use (pedestrians on sidewalks, for example) and use for expression (standing on a sidewalk to make a speech) of the forum, and the communications activity does not substantially impair the functioning of government, any distinction between the uses is motivated by a desire to limit expression. The right to deliver a speech in a particular place does not, however, necessarily imply the right to use the city's sound trucks where this substantially prevents the city from using them for their designated governmental purpose. Perhaps the line also involves some notion of *de minimus* subsidies versus those of a more substantial nature. Some "parochiaid" cases appear to turn on this distinction.[5]

The subsidization question has historically been worked out in an intriguing fashion. The conventional wisdom is that government is not required to devote its resources to amplifying the voices of private speakers, albeit it can choose to do so on a nondiscriminatory basis.[6]

3. See, generally, Kenneth Karst, "Equality as a Central Principle in the First Amendment," 43 *University of Chicago Law Review* 20 (1975).

4. See Charles Wright, "The Constitution on Campus," 22 *Vanderbilt Law Review* 1027, 1050 (1969).

5. See Tribe, *American Constitutional Law* 840.

6. *Id.* at 689.

Conversely, with respect to certain forums—particularly parks and streets—there is a tendency to ease into the idea that government must tolerate free expression. Yet the latter sometimes involves a substantial public subsidy.[7] Taxpayers are bearing the cost of providing marchers with police protection and of picking up the litter after the parade is finished. The difference perhaps lies more in traditions of providing services in kind rather than direct grants in aid than in constitutional law. In some circumstances, moreover, equitably allocating costs may involve transaction expenses higher than the amounts collected from speech and nonspeech users of the forum.

In *Cox* v. *State of New Hampshire*,[8] the Supreme Court expressly held that a reasonable user fee for government expenses in providing a public forum could constitutionally be taxed to the speakers:

> There remains the question of license fees [for the parade by Jehovah's Witnesses] which...had a permissible range from $300 to a nominal amount.... "The charge ... for a circus parade or a celebration procession of length, each drawing crowds of observers, would take into account the greater public expense of policing the spectacle, compared with the slight expense of a less expansive and attractive parade or procession, to which the charge would be adjusted." The fee was held to be "not a revenue tax, but one to meet the expense incident to the administration of the act and to the maintenance of public order in the matter licensed." There is nothing contrary to the Constitution in the charge of a fee limited to the purpose stated.
>
> There is no evidence that the statute has been administered otherwise than in the fair and non-discriminatory manner which the state court has construed it to require.[9]

Perhaps at some point user fees become so high as to preclude important groups of speakers from utilizing public forums in an effective manner.[10] Certainly courts have been quite attentive to the magnitude of charges and their reasonableness under the circumstances. Perhaps a waiver of fees for indigents is constitutionally desirable. On the other hand, the user fee is an effective device for insuring that taxpayers need not contribute their dollars to political or other communications with which they disagree. If they wish to promote the speech, taxpayers may simply make voluntary contributions to the speaker to defray the user fees.

7. See, generally, Vincent Blasi, "Prior Restraints on Demonstrations," 68 *Michigan Law Review* 1481 (1970).

8. 312 U.S. 569 (1941).

9. *Id.* at 576-577.

10. See Blasi, "Prior Restraints on Demonstrations" 1527-1534; Thomas Emerson, *The System of Freedom of Expression* 310-311 (New York: Random House, 1970). See, e.g., *Cox* v. *New Hampshire*, 312 U.S. 569 (1941).

Government Financing of Election Campaigns:
A Brief Note

In recent years, pressure has mounted for public financing of election campaigns. These pressures emanate from the desires to limit the influence of "fat-cat" contributors in government affairs, to lessen the amount of time elected officials spend on fund raising, and to reduce the magnitude of election expenditures and perhaps the degree of reliance on advertising in the mass media. While these goals are commendable, public financing of election campaigns poses substantial risks of government domination of political processes, including the risk that government will financially support only parties and candidates who espouse views acceptable to the government. The irony is that this effort to equalize the voices of voters and constituent groups (at least with regard to unequal abilities in the private sector to contribute to campaigns) may result in reinforcing the status quo, favoring those already in power. The Supreme Court has been markedly insensitive to such concerns.[11] And given the vested interest of executive and legislative incumbents, there is not much hope that these branches of government will stem the tide.

Congress enacted laws in 1974 that, in part, provided for public financing of presidential primary campaigns, party nominating conventions, and presidential election campaigns, revenue being obtained through a check-off provision on tax returns.[12] Individuals may designate one dollar of their federal income-tax liability for this purpose, and married couples may designate two dollars.[13] The critical point, of course, is who qualifies. Skipping the financing of primary campaigns, the allocations turn on whether a party is designated as "major," "minor," or "new." "Major" parties are those that received 25 percent or more of the vote received by all candidates at the preceding general election. "Minor" parties are those that received 5 to 25 percent of the popular vote, and "new" parties those that received less than 5 percent.[14] In general, only major and minor parties and their candidates qualify for federal assistance:

> Major parties are entitled to $2,000,000 to defray their national committee Presidential nominating convention expenses. They must limit total expenditures to that amount and may not use any of the money so allocated to benefit a particular candidate or delegate. . . . A minor party will receive a portion of the major

11. See *Buckley* v. *Valeo*, 424 U.S. 1 (1976).
12. See Internal Revenue Code of 1954, §§ 6096, 9001-9072 (1974), amending 26 U.S.C. § 9001 *et seq.* (1973). See, generally, J. Skelley Wright, "Politics and the Constitution: Is Money Speech?" 85 *Yale Law Journal* 1001 (1976).
13. Internal Revenue Code of 1954, §§ 6096, 9006.
14. See Tribe, *American Constitutional Law* § 13-31.

party entitlement determined by the ratio of the votes received by the party's candidate in the last election to the average of the votes received by the major parties' candidates. . . . No financing is provided for new parties. Neither is there any express provision for financing independent candidates or parties not holding a convention.

In the general election campaign, major party candidates are entitled to $20 million (plus adjustments for inflation). . . . Minor party candidates receive general election funding at a level proportional to their showing in the previous election and may also receive additional post-election monies if they improve their vote percentage over the last election. . . . New party candidates are entitled to post-election funding only if they achieve 5% or more of the vote in the present election. The amount they receive will be in proportion to their vote total relative to that of the major party candidates. . . . One further eligibility requirement for minor and new party candidates is that the candidate's name must appear on the ballot, or electors pledged to the candidate must be on the ballot, in at least 10 states.[15]

In *Buckley* v. *Valeo* the Supreme Court upheld these provisions in the light of a constitutional attack premised in part on the notion that government was attempting to establish particular political parties and activities.[16] By analogy to the establishment-of-religion cases, appellants argued that the law financed only particular political activities and organizations; discriminated against particular candidates; and created excessive government entanglement in political affairs.[17] The Court rejected the establishment-clause analogy, and, with it, the fear of government domination of presidential election campaigns. Justice Rehnquist noted in his concurring and dissenting opinion, however, that Congress has "enshrined the Republican and Democratic parties into a permanently preferred position, and has established requirements for funding minor party and independent candidates to which the two major parties are not subject."[18] As one commentator stated more generally,

> The public funding scheme . . . potentially regulates the number of political campaigns. If, as the Court postulated, money spent in a political campaign may be equated with speech, then the selective doling out of funds will have a significant impact on the

15. Comment, "*Buckley* v. *Valeo*: The Supreme Court and Federal Campaign Reform," 76 *Columbia Law Review* 852, 882 nn. 175 and 176 (1976).

16. 424 U.S. 1 (1976); see, generally, Tribe, *American Constitutional Law* 800-807.

17. Comment, "Supreme Court and Federal Campaign Reform" 884.

18. 424 U.S. at 293 (Rehnquist, J., concurring in part, dissenting in part). See also Tribe, *American Constitutional Law* 810-811.

marketplace of ideas. The ballot access cases may be viewed as narrowing the number of final choices according to the performance of candidates within the political marketplace; the public funding scheme narrows the marketplace itself.[19]

If the question is whether the federal government has sought to finance only those parties and candidates who express acceptable political positions, the answer is clearly no. By and large, the parties and candidates need only abide by certain total spending limits. But, in a broader sense, the federal law provides financing primarily to those already in power—that is, to those who represent mainstream political wisdom. In this way, the government is subsidizing some political voices and not others. The court in *Buckley* was unpersuaded by this First Amendment equal-protection argument, deeming the difficulties of administering a more evenhanded financing scheme to outweigh the inequalities inherent in the law. The Court, I fear, gave away too much of the game. The cold facts are that in most presidential elections the two major parties will be financed by the federal government, while all (or nearly all) others will be forced to fend for themselves in the private sector or to vie for support within the two major parties. Tribe puts the matter well:

> The Court [in *Buckley* v. *Valeo*] deemed it appropriate to deny aid to candidates with marginal public support in order that the Act not "foster frivolous candidacies, create a system of splintered parties, and encourage unrestrained factionalism." The Court thus endorsed the theme it had sounded in the ballot access cases wherein it had sanctioned the state interest in promoting the two party system and condemned only those schemes that effectively insulated particular political parties from all challenges by other candidates.
>
> Although Buckley comports fully with the ballot access cases in this regard, it is difficult to accept the Court's indication that suppression of minority parties may itself be a compelling state interest.[20]

Beyond these realities, Chief Justice Burger, writing separately in the *Buckley* case, is quite right in fearing the ultimate evolution of an "incestuous" relationship between government and party politics.[21] The establishment-of-religion-clause analogy is quite apt. As governments get more and more involved in financing campaigns, the temptation to regulate will grow. Reporting requirements and limitations on

---

19. Comment, "Supreme Court and Federal Campaign Reform" 888.
20. Tribe, *American Constitutional Law* 811.
21. 424 U.S. at 249 (Burger, C.J., concurring in part and dissenting in part).

the nature of expenditures may ultimately infringe upon the content of messages promulgated by parties and candidates. This would be true even if government were more equitable in allocating its revenues. Perhaps this risk would be acceptable if all voices were subsidized. But the risk grows inasmuch as the government is free to pick and choose among candidates and parties. It is as if the federal government agreed to support the religious activities of the three largest religious groups in the United States—Protestants, Catholics and Jews. The dangers would be (1) that government might come to circumscribe the religious freedoms of these three groups and (2) that government would promote their growth and well-being over that of other religious (and nonreligious) groups.

At a minimum, the *Buckley* Court should have adhered more closely to the First Amendment equal-protection doctrine. This might have advanced liberty and choice by promoting the flow of information and ideas during election campaigns. As it is, government is neither standing apart from the election process nor appreciably enlarging the capacity of the self-controlled citizen to make political choices. *Buckley* invites reconsideration and certainly the Court should be reticent about extending the *Buckley* holding to future statutes that may seek to secure public financing for congressional, state, and local campaigns.

Government as Editor: Reconsidering the Delegation Doctrine

The public-forum doctrine might well be thought to lead to every government communication activity being made subject to rules allowing reasonable and equal access by different speakers. For example, the Government Printing Office, government-sponsored newspapers (e.g., *Stars and Stripes*), and public broadcasting stations might be subject to such First Amendment requirements. This result would hinge on the same sorts of concern about government domination of communications networks as the equal-protection, academic-freedom, and other First Amendment doctrines. In *Columbia Broadcasting System, Inc.* v. *Democratic National Committee*,[22] Justice Douglas took this position:

> If these cases involved . . . [the] Corporation [for Public Broadcasting], we would have a situation comparable to that in which the United States owns and manages a prestigious newspaper. . . . The Government as owner and manager would not, as I see it, be free to pick and choose such news items as it desired. For by the First Amendment it may not censor or enact or enforce any other "law" abridging freedom of the press. Politics, ideological slants,

22. 412 U.S. 94 (1973).

rightist or leftist tendencies could play no part in its design of programs. . . . More specifically, the programs tendered by the respondents in the present cases could not then be turned down.[23]

Justice Stewart, in the same case, argued likewise that "were the Government really operating the electronic press [i.e., the national networks], it would, as my Brother Douglas points out, be *prevented* by the First Amendment from selection of broadcast content and the exercise of editorial judgment."[24]

The difficulty with the position is that it flies in the face of existing institutional arrangements, albeit those arrangements can be altered. As William Canby has noted, "Selectivity is inherent and essential to a number of governmental operations to which the public has grown accustomed, including public libraries and art galleries, public school newspapers and law reviews, and, perhaps, even public school offerings."[25] Unless these operations are unconstitutional, how can one square such editorial functions of government with the public-forum doctrine? If government cannot exclude a production of *Hair* from an auditorium that has been opened to other productions, why should it be able to exclude articles from a law review or exhibits from a public museum?[26]

The problem with the Douglas-Stewart position, a position never adopted by a majority of the Supreme Court, is that it rests on assumptions about the illegitimacy of government expression in a democracy. It ignores the need for even democratic governments to communicate effectively in order to advance public policies. It wishes away the vast communications powers and editorial functions already exercised at every level of government. Perhaps the best way to think about the problem of the public forum and the government as editor is to begin with the proposition that the nature of the public's participation in a forum depends on the nature of the enterprise and its governmental mission. A teacher may not subvert the curriculum under the doctrine of academic freedom, and marchers on a public street are not permitted to block the flow of traffic. Similarly, where the government's mission is to communicate and the scarcity of resources and the nature of the enterprise make editorial selectivity inevitable, the state need not tolerate or acquiesce in use of the forum that substantially destroys the communication and editorial processes. Canby puts the matter this way:

23. *Id.* at 149-150 (Douglas, J., concurring in the judgment).

24. *Id.* at 143 (Stewart, J., concurring). But cf. *id.* at 139 n. 7 (Stewart, J., concurring).

25. William Canby, "The First Amendment and the State as Editor: Implications for Public Broadcasting," 52 *Texas Law Review* 1123, 1124-1125 (1974).

26. *Id.* at 1130-1132. See *Southeastern Promotions Ltd.* v. *Conrad*, 420 U.S. 546 (1976).

As the Chief Justice observed, "... [E]diting is what editors are for; and editing is selection and choice of material."... To forbid the managers of ... [public communication] enterprises to select material for inclusion and, necessarily, exclusion would for all practical purposes destroy these endeavors.

When confronted with a claimed right of access to a governmentally-operated organ or facility of communication, a court must make several determinations. The first question is one with which the courts are familiar: whether the facility to which access is sought is an appropriate forum for speech. The mere fact that the state is operating a medium of communication, however, does not itself determine the right of access. The court must further determine whether the medium is one in which the state *necessarily* exercises an editorial function. Of course, many efforts at restricting a public forum might be posed in terms of an editorial function, as ... in the case of public high schools that exclude outside publications because they intrude on a desired atmosphere of civility or morality. But nothing in the nature of an auditorium or school plant requires the exercise of editorial judgment over the entire facility; the auditorium and much of the school can function as well or better as a truly open forum. ...
As long as alternative methods of expression are available, a right of access should be denied where the governmental enterprise cannot truly exist without the exercise of editorial discretion.[27]

The thrust of this argument is that government should not be disabled by the public-forum doctrine from communicating its messages through media over which it exercises editorial control. The critical point is that government seeks to accomplish its objectives through communication, and the creation of a public forum would frustrate those objectives. Thus, a rehabilitation program for prisoners need not be opened to the public, nor need a scholarly journal accept articles that do not meet the standards of the editorial board.[28] In these cases, the purpose is not to frustrate freedom of expression, but to guarantee the integrity of the enterprise. Where the communications activity does not inherently involve editorial judgments, and where, in the words of Laurence Tribe, a facility is deliberately used "as a place for the exchange of views among members of the public,"[29] the public-forum doctrine should apply. So, too, when the establishment of a public forum would not impair the government's ability to communi-

27. Canby, "First Amendment and the State as Editor" 1124-1125, 1133-1134.
28. *Avins* v. *Rutgers*, 385 F.2d 151 (3d Cir. 1967).
29. Tribe, *American Constitutional Law* 690.

cate, the government should not be permitted to seek refuge in the editorial-judgment exception.

Finally, it should be noted that failure to allow a public forum in relation to some government communication activities does not leave the populace entirely unprotected from government overreaching. The nature and extent of government communications, as discussed in chapter 7, frequently result in the delegation of some or all editorial responsibility to a lower echelon government agency thought to have special expertise (e.g., psychiatrists in public mental hospitals, teachers in public schools, museum directors, and the editorial boards of journals). Such delegatees are less likely to be influenced by partisan political concerns, and, in any event, their existence makes orchestration of a uniform government communication program more difficult, as the elements of centralization and hierarchy are absent. Where such delegation has voluntarily taken place, courts ought to treat its *ad hoc* withdrawal in order to censor particular communications as a violation of the First Amendment. Essentially, government agencies should be held to their own institutional arrangements in this sensitive area. For example, there is nothing constitutionally amiss about a university placing the editorial functions of a college newspaper entirely in the hands of the faculty or the central administration. The university could reserve editorial control over the editorial page but not over the news columns. Or it might delegate all editorial functions—over news, advertising, and the editorial page itself—to a student board of editors. Having made the decision to delegate, however, the university should not be permitted to revoke the delegation merely because it objects to the content of a single piece clearly within the established editorial authority of the board.

The constitutional justification for the irrevocability of a delegation of editorial judgment rests on the belief that interference with such delegation should not be permitted where the purpose is no longer editorial but only to eliminate "objectionable" ideas. The state's communication functions are not impaired, nor does the decision rest upon the scarcity of resources for communication. Canby demonstrates the operation of this constitutional rule in relation to public school libraries:

> State statutes . . . gave the [School] Board the authority to select instructional materials. The Board could presumably have exercised its editorial judgment on every book that went into, or was removed from, all school libraries. Apparently the Board was content to delegate this authority and only participated in the selection, or deselection, process when it wished to assert content control in a specific instance—a content control possibly based

on grounds apart from and even inconsistent with the editorial policies used to build the rest of the library collection. Arguably, this leaves the school system with the evils of content regulation without protecting the editorial judgment thought to necessitate it. Clearly, the Board may establish general policies governing libraries and exercise some supervision to insure the effectuation of those policies. The Board might reasonably make library acquisitions over a period of time the subject of policy discussions with the supervisory school officials with whom it normally deals. When it specifically overrules a librarian in an individual instance, however, it does not seem unreasonable to require the Board, when challenged, to justify the incursion in terms of its educational policy and the editorial structure that it has created. A court could then intercede . . . to insure that editorial judgment, once placed, is not obstructed for reasons outside the scope of the editorial function. This is particularly true when the editorial function has been delegated to a person with special expertise in the performance of that function.[30]

In short, the courts, within a constitutional framework, should hold authorities to the original allocation of control over the selection of material for government communication enterprises. By compelling such adherence, the political and legal processes combine in a fashion that limits the ability of government to speak, without compromising the integrity of its communication efforts.

From this vantage, the irrevocability of delegation-of-editorial-authority doctrine can be seen to be operating in many First Amendment cases. The doctrine helps explain the cases involving public broadcasting, academic freedom, student newspapers, and a variety of other instances where higher government authorities are pitted against subordinate bodies with varying degrees of editorial responsibility. But implicit in the doctrine is the notion that government is not locked into existing institutional arrangements, and barring a restructuring effort growing out of an effort to censor, government agencies are free to undo their delegations. Thus, it may be one thing for the governor of a state to prohibit the editorial board of a law review from publishing a particular article to which the governor objects on grounds of content, and quite another for the governor to assume editorial responsibilities because he is generally dissatisfied with the law review's performance. Certainly, a state legislature may decide not to fund a journal on the grounds that it is an inappropriate activity for taxpayer funding. Ob-

30. Canby, "First Amendment and the State as Editor" 1135. See, generally, Robert O'Neil, *Classrooms in the Crossfire* (Bloomington, Ind.: Indiana University Press, 1981).

viously, tradition, professionalism, and lack of interest on the part of politicians make it unlikely that many delegations will be revoked except where there is dissatisfaction with a particular article, broadcast, book, or museum exhibit. This means that, where litigation actually occurs, the delegation doctrine may be extremely significant in limiting government's ability to dominate communications networks.

[14]

Rights to Gather State-Held Information and Freedom of Association

Introduction

Democracy in a complex world requires that messages flow both from governments to the people and from the people to their governments. Government can regulate the flow in both directions in numerous ways. This chapter examines (1) how government can reduce the flow of information to the people by controlling access to information it possesses, and (2) how people-to-government communications can be rendered less effective by interfering with citizens' associational rights and preventing them from mustering sufficient volume to be heard. Traditional individual-rights litigation provides an opportunity for the judiciary to counter these dangers by increasing the information flow in both directions. Courts can increase government-to-people communications by taking a much more expansive view of constitutional rights in the framework of information gathering vis-à-vis governments, the subject of the first part of this chapter. The second part discusses the use of the right of association by the judiciary to facilitate people-to-government communications by increasing communication *among* citizens, which then allows them to coalesce in groups to speak loudly enough so that government hears and responds.

Rights to Gather Information

A substantial amount of litigation and discussion in recent years has involved efforts to limit the access of the public and mass media to information held by governments.[1] Such litigation takes a variety of forms. It may involve access to government facilities not, or at least

1. See, generally, Note, "The First Amendment Right to Gather State-Held Information," 89 *Yale Law Journal* 923 (1980) (hereinafter "State-Held Information").

not primarily, for the purpose of communicating with a captive audience,[2] but to gather information about how the institution operates, and about those who work or are "incarcerated" there.[3] This reportorial function is an attempt to learn more about government, to be in a position to publish facts and opinions about the shortcomings and strengths of government policies and programs. The institutions involved may be prisons, mental hospitals, military bases, institutions dealing with sensitive military and other matters, and others which are largely closed to public scrutiny. Closely related to access to institutions are those instances in which reporters or others seek access to government deliberations, be they administrative proceedings, legislative debates or committee hearings, or judicial proceedings.[4] Facts about such proceedings are necessary prerequisites for public debate about government operations. Finally, there are simply direct requests for information that government officials and bureaucracies may honor or refuse to honor on national security, privacy, executive privilege, or other grounds.[5] All of these cases involve access to an involuntary government source, not the right to receive information from a willing private source.[6]

Concern about government secrecy and withholding of information is long-standing.[7] For example, article II, section 5, clause 3 of the Constitution requires each house of Congress to keep a journal of its proceedings, "excepting such Parts as may in their Judgment require Secrecy":

> The whole idea, of the publication of the journal was a good deal
> of an innovation, for the State legislatures did not publish theirs,
> neither did Parliament, but the recognition of the right of the

2. For cases in which private parties sought access to a government facility for the purpose of disseminating their own messages, see, e.g., *Brown* v. *Glines*, 100 S.Ct. 609 (1980); *Greer* v. *Spock* 424 U.S. 828 (1976); and *Brown* v. *Louisiana*, 383 U.S. 131 (1966).

3. See, e.g., *Houchins* v. *KQED, Inc.*, 438 U.S. 1 (1978); *Saxbe* v. *Washington Post*, 417 U.S. 483 (1974); and *Pell* v. *Procunier*, 417 U.S. 817 (1974).

4. See, e.g., *Richmond Newspapers, Inc.* v. *Virginia*, 100 S.Ct. 2814 (1980); *Gannett Co.* v. *DePasquale*, 443 U.S. 368 (1979); *In re Oliver*, 333 U.S. 257 (1948). See, generally, James Wiggins, *Freedom or Secrecy* chs. 1-3 (New York: Oxford University Press, 1964); "State-Held Information"; and Comment, "The Right of the Press to Gather Information after *Branzburg* and *Pell,*" 124 *University of Pennsylvania Law Review* 166 (1975).

5. See, e.g., *Nixon* v. *Warner Communications*, 435 U.S. 589 (1978); *United States* v. *Nixon*, 418 U.S. 683 (1974); *EPA* v. *Mink*, 410 U.S. 73 (1973); *Frankel* v. *SEC*, 460 F.2d 813 (2d Cir. 1972). See also Privacy Act of 1974, 5 U.S.C. § 552a (1974); Freedom of Information Act, 5 U.S.C. § 552 (1976); and, generally, Norman Dorsen and Stephen Gillers, eds., *It's None of Your Business: Government Secrecy in America* (New York: Viking Press, 1974).

6. See, e.g., *Virginia State Bd. of Pharmacy* v. *Virginia Citizens Consumer Council, Inc.*, 425 U.S. 748 (1976). See, generally, Emerson, "Legal Foundations of the Right to Know," 1976 *Washington University Law Quarterly* 1; "State-Held Information"; and Note, "The Right to Know in First Amendment Analysis," 57 *Texas Law Review* 505 (1979).

7. See, e.g., a letter from James Madison to W. T. Barry, Aug. 4, 1822, in Gaillard Hunt, ed., 9 *The Writings of James Madison* 103 (New York: G. P. Putnam and Sons, 1910).

people to know the proceedings of Congress was generally con-
ceded, and doubtless also distrust lest Congress might become a
secret body led in part to the adoption of the requirement. . . .
Mason remarked, that if the legislature was made a conclave, the
people would be alarmed. Moreover, the old Congress had published a journal and to omit the requirement might give the
adversaries of reform a pretext for misleading the people.[8]

The openness of criminal trials to the public was recognized in colonial
times, and such trials are generally "open to all who care to observe."[9]
More recently, state and federal legislatures have made enormous
strides toward allowing greater access to government proceedings and
information. Federal and state open-records acts, freedom-of-information acts, laws governing student records, open-meeting laws, and so
on, have been enacted.[10] Under Executive Order 12065, progress has
been made toward preventing government officials from classifying
documents as secret to avoid embarrassment and admission of wrongdoing rather than to serve some legitimate public purpose.[11] And in
Nixon v. *Warner Communications*, the Supreme Court recognized a common-law principle of public access to documents in a judicial proceeding, absent a compelling reason to withhold them (pendency of a
criminal prosecution or defamation, for example).[12] Government tax
and land registers have long been open to inspection by some or all
citizens.[13] Many of the access doctrines have proven difficult to enforce, but the historical trend is unmistakable.[14]

8. Francis Thorpe, 1 *Constitutional History of the United States* 501 (Chicago: Callaghan,
1901); see also Wiggins, *Freedom or Secrecy* at ch. 1, and, generally, Vincent Blasi, "The
Checking Power of the First Amendment," 1977 *American Bar Federation Research Journal* 521.
9. *Richmond Newspapers, Inc.* v. *Virginia*, 100 S.Ct. 2814, 2821 (1980). For a history of the
public nature of criminal trials, see *id.* at 2821-2826. But cf. *Gannett Co.* v. *DePasquale*, 443
U.S. 368 (1979).
10. See, e.g., 5 U.S.C. § 552a (1974); 5 U.S.C. 552 (1976); and generally, M. L. Stein,
"The Secrets of Local Government," in Dorsen and Gillers, *Government Secrecy in America*
151; Constance Y. Singleton and Howard O. Hunter, "Statutory and Judicial Responses to
the Problem of Access to Governmental Information," 1979 *Detroit C. Law Review* 51.
11. "Executive Order 12065, National Security Information," in 14 *Weekly Compila-
tion of Presidential Documents* 1157 (June 28, 1978).
12. 435 U.S. 589 (1978); see, generally, Alan Westin, "The Technology of Secrecy,"
in Dorsen and Gillers, *Government Secrecy in America* 290.
13. Westin, "Technology of Secrecy."
14. "There is ample evidence that local government carries on much of its business
in secret, even in states where laws forbid or restrict the practice. So far, the fight
against closed meetings and records has been waged almost entirely by the more courageous and tough-minded elements of the communications media. There has been little
help from the public, which, for the most part, is either apathetic or actually sympathetic to the government" (Stein, "Secrets of Local Government," in Dorsen and
Gillers, eds., *Government Secrecy in America* 175). Stein recommends a "public-relations
campaign" by the mass media to "define clearly" access issues for the public.

The Supreme Court has not expressly recognized a broad individual right to gather information from an unwilling government entity.[15] And Justice Stewart has written that "[t]he Constitution itself is neither a Freedom of Information Act nor an Official Secrets Act."[16] But one commentator has argued that "the notion of a citizenry's right to self-government necessarily implies a right to gather information from one's government, even when that government resists disclosure." If the individual is to participate in democratic decision making, if he is to have the opportunity to influence the selection of leaders and the making of policy, access to information that enriches the ability to make informed choices is vital. Otherwise there is no assurance that preferences will be accurately expressed. "To maintain the validity of its own system of determining the public will, the government in a representative democracy must facilitate the individual's preference formulations, and, as required, make state-held information available."[17]

The thrust of the argument, then, is that a right to government-held information is necessary to the creation of the self-controlled citizen. But the emphasis on government's obligation to facilitate the expression of informed preferences is only half of the picture. Beyond the need to verify consent, the unidentified author overlooks the point that governments may not only inhibit the processes of consent, but may also seek to falsify consent. A constitutionalized right of access to government-held information undercuts the ability of governments to conceal ineptness, to withhold inconvenient facts, and to engage in processes of persuasion that deny vital information to those who would advance contrary positions. And it is these dangers, combined with the unique ability of governments to gather some types of information, that distinguish a "right to know" vis-à-vis government from a "right to know" vis-à-vis private individuals and entities.[18]

15. "State-Held Information" 927; but cf. *Richmond Newspapers, Inc.* v. *Virginia*, 100 S.Ct. 2814 (1980).

16. Potter Stewart, "Or of the Press," 26 *Hastings Law Journal* 631, 636 (1975), quoted in *Houchins* v. *KQED, Inc.*, 438 U.S. 1, 14 (1978) (Burger, C.J.).

17. "State-Held Information" 927-931.

18. Compelled disclosure of privately held information raises grave concerns about privacy interests. And although such private information may be reached by compulsory legal processes (e.g., subpoenas and valid search warrants), "There is no private right to compulsory process or to execute lawful searches of private property attached to the individual's First Amendment right to acquire information" ("State-Held Information" 928 n. 32). On the other hand, when government gathers information from the private sector, its disclosure may compromise the privacy of those who provided the information in the first instance. In this regard, however, the Supreme Court has not granted individuals the right to enjoin the government from disseminating information it has gathered from them (see *Chrysler Corp.* v. *Brown*, 441 U.S. 281 [1979]). The Congress or state legislatures may choose to afford such protection to individuals by declining to allow government agencies to collect the information or to disseminate it once gathered (see, e.g., 5 U.S.C. §552a [1976]). See, generally, "State-Held Information" 928 n. 32.

The Supreme Court's treatment of the issue of access to state-held information has been confusing in recent years. In prison cases, the Court has equated the rights of the mass media to gather information with those of the public, and has by and large been reluctant to articulate the issue clearly or resolve it.[19] The question has been further clouded by the tendency to treat prisons and military bases as special enclaves with limited rights of access, and by a conceptual confusion in the treatment of those who seek access for the purpose of gathering information and those who seek access to disseminate information.[20] It may well be the case that the gathering of information is less likely to be disruptive of the institution's mission than the dissemination of information that may cause the captive audience to rebel. Obviously, prison authorities have a substantial interest (as does the public) in avoiding disruption by an influx of reporters or other visitors. Equally obviously, they have an interest (not shared by the public) in keeping inmates from airing their grievances on television and in the newspapers. Investigations on the premises are necessary if the public is to make informed judgments about penal institutions and about how prison authorities perform their jobs.

The focus on the rights of the press has taken the Court even further afield. Some justices have posed the difficult question of whether the mass media should have greater access to public facilities and proceedings than other members of the public.[21] In fact, a good case could be made out for this.[22] Given the resources necessary for investigation of large-scale government institutions and the fact that the mass media reach an audience no individual could hope to reach without enormous expenditures, the access rights of the mass media could be viewed as surrogates for the rights of the masses of relatively powerless citizens. This is particularly true if one views the mass media as more objective and neutral than other large-scale private institutions. On the other hand, there is no need for such asymmetry in First Amendment law. Even if one shares the chief justice's skeptical view that the press is no more worthy of our trust than a host of other institutions,[23] the logical conclusion is not to limit the information-gathering activities of the press; rather it is to enlarge those capacities for everyone. Depending on the nature of the institution and the countervailing interest in avoid-

19. See cases cited in note 3 above. See, generally, "State-Held Information"; and Note, "The Rights of the Public and the Press to Gather Information," 87 *Harvard Law Review* 1505 (1974).

20. See *Richmond Newspapers, Inc.* v. *Virginia*, 100 S.Ct. 2814, 2827 n. 11 (1980); *Adderley* v. *Florida*, 385 U.S. 39 (1978); and cases cited in notes 2 and 3 above.

21. See, e.g., *Houchins* v. *KQED, Inc.*, 438 U.S. 1, 3 (1978) (Opinion of Burger, C.J.).

22. See *id.* at 16 (1978) (Stewart, J., concurring); cf. *Richmond Newspapers, Inc.* v. *Virginia*, 100 S.Ct. 2814, 2827 n. 12 (1980).

23. *First National City Bank of Boston* v. *Bellotti*, 435 U.S. 765, 795 (1978) (Burger, C.J., concurring).

ing violence, invasions of privacy, and violations of other interests, Mobil Oil, the press, Nader's Raiders, and private citizens should all, subject to reasonable traffic controls, have a presumptive right to enter public institutions to gather information.[24] Perhaps only the press will take advantage of such opportunities, but this does not diminish the general principle.

Further uncertainties are generated by the different doctrinal positions of the justices. Chief Justice Burger believes that there is no "discernible basis" in the Constitution for a right to state-held information in the prison context, and apparently Justices White and Rehnquist share this view.[25] Justice Rehnquist, however, would go further and deny such a right under all circumstances.[26] Justices Stevens, Powell, and Brennan cautiously advance a right of access to state-held information.[27] And Justice Stewart fuzzily places himself somewhere in the middle.[28] Further ambiguity was introduced in *Gannett Co. v. DePasquale*,[29] where the majority upheld the exclusion of the press from a pretrial hearing in a murder case. The majority consisted of Justices Stewart (who wrote the opinion for the Court), Stevens, Burger, Powell, and Rehnquist, with Justices Blackmun, Brennan, White, and Marshall concurring in part and dissenting in part. Chief Justice Burger and Justices Powell and Rehnquist, while joining the majority opinion, also filed separate concurring opinions.

As Justice Stewart articulated the question for decision in *DePasquale*, the issue was "whether members of the public have an independent constitutional right to insist upon access to a pretrial judicial proceeding, even though the accused, the prosecutor, and the trial judge all have agreed to the closure of that proceeding in order to assure a fair trial."[30] Despite the language of the Sixth Amendment guaranteeing a "speedy and public trial," the Court held that the right to a public trial was personal to the defendant and that the "Constitution nowhere mentions any right of access to a criminal trial on the part of the public." With regard to the First Amendment claim of a public right of access to criminal trials, Justice Stewart declined to decide whether such a right existed. He then proceeded to assume, *arguendo*, that such a right existed, but held that under the circumstances of the case the right was (would have been?) outweighed by competing societal interests. The circumstances included the failure of spectators to object to the closure motion, the likely prejudice to the defendant of a public

---

24. *Houchins* v. *KQED, Inc.*, 438 U.S. at 19 (Stevens, J., dissenting).

25. *Id.* at 3.

26. *Gannett Co.* v. *DePasquale*, 443 U.S. 368, 403 (1979) (Rehnquist, J., concurring).

27. *Houchins* v. *KQED, Inc.*, 438 U.S. at 19.

28. *Id.* at 17 (Stewart, J., concurring).

29. 443 U.S. 368 (1979).

30. *Id.* at 370-371.

trial, and the availability of a transcript of the hearing to reporters and the public. Chief Justice Burger concurred to add that only a pretrial and not a trial proceeding was involved in the case.[31] Justice Powell would have held that the public did have a First Amendment right of access to the pretrial hearing, but that the right was presumptive and not absolute. He agreed, however, that the likelihood of prejudice to the defendant justified the closure of the hearing.[32] Justice Rehnquist opined that there was no right of access to criminal trials under the First Amendment.[33] Justice Blackmun, writing for the four remaining justices, concluded that the Sixth Amendment broadly protected a right of access and that the accused must establish that "it is strictly and inescapably necessary" to close the hearing "in order to protect the fair-trial guarantee."[34] Without reaching the First Amendment question, the dissenters found that there was insufficient evidence, as a matter of law, to satisfy this demanding test for closure.

The *DePasquale* decision was widely attacked and its scope hotly debated. Was it limited to pretrial proceedings? Was there a First Amendment right of access to trials? Was the case largely limited to its own facts, as judges would need to weigh the possible prejudice to defendants in each case against the public's right of access? How would the dissenters vote if faced with a case in which they chose to consider the First Amendment issue? Did *DePasquale* represent an extension of the access-to-prison cases, indicating that the Court was drifting toward the position that the Constitution provided no right of access to government institutions and proceedings (and presumably records)? Or was the Court thinking only in terms of criminal proceedings and penal institutions, rather distinct sources of government-held information? These questions were clarified a bit—but not answered—in *Richmond Newspapers, Inc.* v. *Virginia*,[35] a case decided the very next term.

The *Richmond Newspapers* case, not surprisingly, produced no majority opinion. A majority of the justices, however, held that the closure of a criminal trial, under the circumstances of the case, violated the First Amendment rights of the public and press to observe criminal trials. Chief Justice Burger, announcing the judgment of the Court and speaking for himself and Justices White and Stevens,[36] disingenuously distinguished *DePasquale*, asserting that the Court had not in that case reached the question of whether the First Amendment created a presumptive right of access to criminal trials. *DePasquale*, in his view, was a Sixth Amendment case; *Richmond Newspapers* was a First Amendment case. But despite this gloss, the Burger opinion reads very much like a

31. *Id.* at 394.   32. *Id.* at 397.
33. *Id.* at 403.   34. *Id.* at 406, 440.
35. 100 S.Ct. 2814 (1980).
36. *Id.* at 2818.

Sixth Amendment repudiation of *DePasquale*. His summary of the evidence went largely to questions surrounding the criminal process, reasoning that "From this unbroken, uncontradicted history, supported by reasons as valid today as in centuries past, we are bound to conclude that a presumption of openness inheres in the very nature of a criminal trial under our system of justice."[37] While reading the First Amendment to embody the notion of protection of "the right of everyone to attend trials," the Burger opinion goes to great lengths to limit its scope and to reaffirm the earlier denial of access to prison and military-base cases. Indeed, the chief justice emphasized the lack of findings by the trial judge on the question of whether closure was necessary to insure fairness to the defendant. While disclaiming the need to set forth general rules, he clearly indicated his sympathy for closure to preserve fairness to the defendant, to keep order, and to regulate the flow of traffic in the courtroom. The Burger opinion is thus far from a ringing endorsement of a right of access to government proceedings and information. And Justices White and Blackmun stated as much in their concurring opinions, castigating the *DePasquale* majority for closing off the Sixth Amendment route to the result in *Richmond Newspapers*.[38]

From the perspective of government expression, the most interesting opinion in *Richmond Newspapers* is that of Justice Brennan, writing for himself and Justice Marshall.[39] The opinion claims to be based on a structural analysis of the First Amendment and identifies a presumptive right of access to government-held information. If this is the case, and if the Brennan opinion reveals the underpinnings of the Court's judgment, then, in the words of Justice Stevens, *Richmond Newspapers* is a "watershed case," in which, "for the first time, the Court unequivocably holds that an arbitrary interference with access to important information is an abridgement of the freedoms of speech and of the press protected by the First Amendment."[40] Brennan's structural argument, rooted in the writings of John Hart Ely and Alexander Meiklejohn, is that the First Amendment protects communication; that communication is essential to self-government; that communication and debate must be informed if it is to serve this vital democratic function; and that debate will be informed only if there is a presumptive right of access to government-held information.[41] Brennan, however, appreciates that this structural principle is so open-ended and abstract that

37. *Id.* at 2824.
38. *Id.* at 2830, 2841.
39. *Id.* at 2832 (Brennan, J., concurring).
40. *Id.* at 2830, 2831 (Stevens, J., concurring).
41. *Id.* at 2833 (Brennan, J., concurring), citing, *inter alia,* John Hart Ely, *Democracy and Distrust* (Cambridge, Mass.: Harvard University Press, 1980); Alexander Meiklejohn, *Free Speech and Its Relation to Self-Government* (New York: Harper & Row, 1948). See also *Saxbe* v. *Washington Post Co.,* 417 U.S. 843, 862-863 (1974) (Powell, J., dissenting).

access to virtually any information could be sought within its terms. He therefore appears to limit the right of access to government-held information, and, somewhat confusingly, relies on the history and tradition of access to particular proceedings to justify its application in any particular case. He also weighs the state's interest in secrecy and confidentiality against the individual's interest in gaining information about the particular governmental process to which he seeks access. This suggests that a generalized claim to government-held information, not related to the mission the governmental entity is charged with performing, would not be sustained under the Brennan approach.

The caveats in the Brennan opinion, combined with the fact that more than half of it is devoted to a discussion of the history of public trials, belie the structural First Amendment approach which he avowedly takes. Little effort is made to reconstruct the access-to-prison cases or other lines of authority in the light of a right to government-held information. Indeed, his efforts to erect a structural principle of access are so limited that it is not entirely clear why he bothered to write a concurring opinion. The distance between him and the chief justice, at least as expressed in the *Richmond Newspapers* case, is not great. And none of the justices refer explicitly to the need to place constitutional limits on the ability of government to manipulate consent by selectively revealing or withholding information. *Richmond Newspapers* is thus a step in the right direction, but it does not establish a right of access to government records, meetings, and institutions other than in the context of a criminal trial. As is so often the case, the meaning of *Richmond Newspapers* will be made clear only as it is actually relied upon as a precedent and the courts determine the extent to which analogies should be drawn from it in other types of access cases. The next twenty-five years will tell us whether this precedent is an important Sixth Amendment case in other garb or a "watershed" First Amendment case with enormous implications for democratic government in the United States.

In current case law, it appears that government has all kinds of rights of access to information about individuals, ranging from information about personal income to the right to search the premises of a third-party newspaper for evidence relevant to a criminal prosecution.[42] This has been blunted by an increasing recognition of rights of privacy, and by intra-governmental safeguards on the dissemination of information.[43] A world in which citizens can keep few secrets from governments but governments can keep many secrets from them is, however, inconsistent with the democratic aspirations of the self-controlled citizen. The question is always one of degree and of balancing of interests,

42. See *Zurcher* v. *Stanford Daily*, 436 U.S. 547 (1978).
43. See, e.g., Family Education and Privacy Act of 1974, 5 U.S.C. 513(a) (1974); Privacy Act of 1974, 5 U.S.C. § 552a (1974).

but the dangers of government speech argue for a much more expansive view of constitutional rights in the framework of information gathering vis-à-vis governments. As J. R. Wiggins has stated, "The right of citizens to know about the conduct of their government, to see for themselves the public records of the executive department, certainly seems implicit in all the theories of democracy and self-government upon which our system rests."[44]

Countering Government Expression: Pluralism and Freedom of Association

As the reader has doubtless surmised, virtually any constitutional decision vindicating the First Amendment rights of private individuals and groups strengthens the hand of centers of communication that have the potential to counter government's messages. The press cases are perhaps the best example.[45] If the Supreme Court invalidates a law requiring newspapers to afford a right of reply to political candidates,[46] obviously this has the effect of preserving the ability of newspapers to promulgate whatever messages they please. Indeed, private communicators cannot be required to transmit, and thus amplify, the messages of public officials or would-be public officials. To the extent that government enforces fairness or equal-time rules or bans on particular types of messages transmitted by the broadcast media, the power of those media has been diminished by their inability to retain control over what is broadcast.[47] In general, the practice of not permitting government to restrain the speech of the mass media, though grounded in a theory of rights of individual expression or freedom of the press, serves the purpose of promoting systemic pluralism in the communications network. What is true of the mass media is also true of protecting the speech of labor unions, corporations, and individuals. The Court has declined to embrace the view that government may "restrict the

44. Wiggins, *Freedom or Secrecy* 66–67.

45. See, e.g., *Landmark Communications, Inc.* v. *Virginia*, 435 U.S. 829 (1978); *Nebraska Press Ass'n* v. *Stuart*, 427 U.S. 539 (1976); *Miami Herald* v. *Tornillo*, 418 U.S. 241 (1974); *New York Times* v. *United States*, 403 U.S. 713 (1971) (*per curiam*); *Mills* v. *Alabama*, 384 U.S. 214 (1966); and *Near* v. *Minnesota*, 283 U.S. 697 (1931).

46. *Miami Herald* v. *Tornillo*, 418 U.S. 241 (1974); but see Jerome Barron, "Access to the Press—A New First Amendment Right," 80 *Harvard Law Review* 1641 (1967).

47. See, generally, Lucas Powe, "Or of the [Broadcast] Press," 55 *Texas Law Review* 39 (1976); but see also *Red Lion Broadcasting* v. *F.C.C.*, 395 U.S. 367 (1969); *Capital Broadcasting Co.* v. *Acting Attorney General*, 405 U.S. 1000 (1972), affirming *Capital Broadcasting* v. *Mitchell*, 333 F. Supp. 582 (D.D.C. 1971); *Yale Broadcasting* v. *F.C.C.*, 478 F.2d 594 (D.C. Cir. 1973), *cert denied* 414 U.S. 914 (1973); *Paulsen* v. *F.C.C.*, 491 F.2d 887 (9th Cir. 1974); *Brandywine-Main Line Radio, Inc.* v. *F.C.C.*, 473 F.2d 16 (D.C. Cir. 1972). Compare *CBS* v. *Democratic National Committee*, 412 U.S. 94 (1973). The Court has historically afforded less protection to the broadcast media than the print media (see Benno Schmidt, *Freedom of the Press vs. Public Access* [New York: Praeger, 1976]).

speech of some elements of our society in order to enhance the relative voice of others."[48]

Perhaps the most notable addition to First Amendment doctrine that may have the effect of bolstering competing private centers of communication is the notion of freedom of association. Taken literally, the concept of a right of association embodied in the First Amendment is a peculiar one. The First Amendment makes no mention of association, speaking of "the right of the people peaceably to assemble and to petition the Government for a redress of grievances." But narrow entitlements to come together in assembly to discuss governmental (and perhaps other) matters and to communicate with the government to assert grievances are a far cry from a more generalized right of individuals to associate with one another. Moreover, all sorts of government-imposed limitations on freedom of association have been historically tolerated. The state may set down conditions for the formation of businesses, partnerships, and corporations; it may forbid marriage in some circumstances;[49] it may compel blacks and whites to associate with one another in private and public schools;[50] it may require one to join a labor union or pay fees in lieu of membership fees to the union;[51] and association rights apparently do not entitle one to a government job, to membership in the armed forces, or to a seat in a state-supported college classroom.

There is some tendency to view association, whether stated in terms of privacy "penumbras" from the Bill of Rights or substantive due process, as an affirmation of the basic right of the individual to participate in private or intimate relations with one or more other individuals.[52] This leads to arguments about a "right to marry," a right to homosexual marriage, a right to contraceptives and marital privacy, a right to raise children, or a right to fornicate with other consenting adults. Such notions, I believe, fall wide of the mark in describing the origins of the First Amendment right of association. The notion of a

48. *Buckley* v. *Valeo*, 424 U.S. 1, 48–49 (1976); see also *First National Bank of Boston* v. *Bellotti*, 435 U.S. 765 (1978). See, generally, Comment, "Buckley v. Valeo: The Supreme Court and Federal Campaign Reform," 76 *Columbia Law Review* 852, 869–871 (1976); but cf. cases cited in note 47 above; and Barron, "Access to the Press."

49. See, e.g., *Zablocki* v. *Redhail*, 434 U.S. 374, 396, 399 (1978) (Powell, J., concurring).

50. See *Runyon* v. *McCrary*, 427 U.S. 160 (1976).

51. See *Abood* v. *Detroit Board of Education*, 431 U.S. 209 (1977); *Machinists* v. *Street*, 367 U.S. 740 (1961); and *Railway Employees* v. *Hanson*, 351 U.S. 225 (1956). Cf. 431 U.S. at 245, 250 (Powell, J., concurring).

52. See, e.g., *Zablocki* v. *Redhail*, 434 U.S. 374 (1978); *Moore* v. *East Cleveland*, 431 U.S. 494 (1977) (plurality opinion); *Eisenstadt* v. *Baird*, 405 U.S. 438 (1972) (plurality opinion); *Department of Agriculture* v. *Moreno*, 413 U.S. 528 (1973); *Stanley* v. *Illinois*, 405 U.S. 645 (1972); and *Griswold* v. *Connecticut*, 381 U.S. 479 (1965). Cf. *Quilloin* v. *Walcott*, 434 U.S. 246 (1978); *Califano* v. *Jobst*, 434 U.S. 74 (1977); *Smith* v. *Foster Families*, 431 U.S. 816 (1977); and *Village of Belle Terre* v. *Boraas*, 416 U.S. 1 (1974).

right of association grew up only in the 1950s and 1960s as the federal government and some states sought to investigate and ferret out members of allegedly dangerous organizations—the communist party in the case of the federal government and primarily the National Association for the Advancement of Colored People in the case of southern states.[53] A leading case is *NAACP* v. *Alabama ex. rel. Patterson*,[54] decided in 1958, in which the Court unanimously held that the NAACP could not be required to divulge a list of its members to the state. And the point of that decision was not some personal right to associate physically or intimately with other persons; rather association was tied to freedom of expression: "Effective advocacy of both public and private points of view, particularly controversial ones, is undeniably enhanced by group association."[55] This holding was amplified in *NAACP* v. *Button*, in which the Court noted that the NAACP's litigation activities should be treated as a form of political expression.[56] This derivation of freedom of association was recently traced by Mr. Justice Stewart in a dissenting opinion:

> Freedom of association has been constitutionally recognized because it is often indispensable to effectuation of explicit First Amendment guarantees. . . . But the scope of the associational right, until now, at least, has been limited to the constitutional need that created it; obviously not every "association" is for First Amendment purposes or serves to promote the ideological freedom that the First Amendment was designed to protect.
>
> The "association" in this case [involving an ordinance limiting occupancy of certain dwelling units to certain combinations of blood relatives] is not for any purpose relating to the promotion of speech, assembly, the press, or religion. And wherever the outer boundaries of constitutional protection of freedom of association may eventually turn out to be, they surely do not extend to those who assert no interest other than the gratification, convenience, and economy of sharing the same residence.[57]

The point of this argument is not to refute or defend the expansive privacy-oriented version of freedom of association, nor to indicate that

53. Edward Corwin, *The Constitution of the United States of America: Analysis and Interpretation* 966 (Princeton, N.J.: Princeton University Press, 1973). Arguably, a right of association was implicit in earlier Supreme Court speech and assembly decisions (see, e.g., *Thomas* v. *Collins*, 323 U.S. 516 [1945]; and *De Jonge* v. *Oregon*, 299 U.S. 353 [1937]).

54. 357 U.S. 449 (1958); see also *In re Stolar*, 401 U.S. 23 (1970); *Baird* v. *State Bar of Arizona*, 401 U.S. 1 (1970); *United States* v. *Robel*, 389 U.S. 258 (1967); *Keyishian* v. *Board of Regents*, 385 U.S. 589 (1967); *Gibson* v. *Florida Legislative Investigative Commission*, 372 U.S. 539 (1962); and *Sweezy* v. *New Hampshire*, 354 U.S. 234 (1957).

55. 357 U.S. at 460.

56. 371 U.S. 415 (1963).

57. *Moore* v. *City of East Cleveland*, 431 U.S. 494, 535-536 (1977) (Stewart, J., dissenting).

the Court has been undeviating in pursuing a particular concept of association. Among other cases, *Moore* v. *City of East Cleveland, Ohio*[58] argues to the contrary. Rather, my purpose is to note that the narrower version of the right of association is an immensely reasonable gloss to place on freedom of expression once one recognizes the desirability of countering the communications power of governments in a democracy. As government grows, as the activities of the welfare state expand, private individuals may increasingly feel the need to band together if they are effectively to compete with the government. There is a need to pool resources—to turn up the volume as it were, to reach a larger audience. The lone speaker is frequently no match for the organized and sophisticated communications efforts of governments. It is essential that "whenever men may speak as individuals, they may speak in and through groups."[59] Public-interest litigation, advertising, mass mailings, lobbying, billboards, films, and meetings are examples of communications activities people may be able to undertake in groups but not as individuals. And the group may have more public stature and greater access to the mass media. A right of association is thus responsive to modern policy concerns about government dominance of the channels of communication.

58. *Id.*

59. Reena Raggi, "An Independent Right to Freedom of Association," 12 *Harvard Civil Rights-Civil Liberties Law Review* 1, 27 (1977).

[15]

Direct Judicial Controls
on Government Expression

Courts, as I have noted, are risky guardians of government expression that may falsify consent. And the risk is greatest when direct constitutional limits are imposed. The Supreme Court, especially, relies extensively on communication and persuasion for its substantial powers in our structure of government. Its own institutional characteristics may blind it to the realities of government communication and persuasion. Alternatively, if it is more attentive to the communications excesses of other branches than to its own abuses, the attempt to impose constitutional limits on the utterances of other branches of government may lead to the diminution of important checks on the Court's own ability to falsify consent. Judicial reshaping of the communications network to limit the impact of government speech may prove wide of the mark and perhaps disable government from implementing policy objectives that require communications with the public. Despite these objections, cases of egregious government expression make it difficult to advocate completely closing the door to direct judicial intervention. This chapter discusses some of the circumstances in which the potential abuse of government expression is so great that constitutional limits may be necessary. The issues are complex, and distinctions are crucial. The discussion here is thus necessarily more detailed and technical than in most of the previous chapters.

Government Incitement of Unconstitutional
or Unlawful Behavior

The First Amendment as applied to private speech has long been thought by all but absolutists to embody the notion that some communications are so dangerous that government may constitutionally silence the speaker. Under a "clear and present danger," or some more stringent incitement test, speech too closely connected with unlawful action may be prohibited. An example might be a disgruntled trucker leading a demonstration against high fuel costs and urging his audience to pick up wrenches and destroy nearby gasoline pumps. Such cases, particularly in the context of criticism of government policies, have been the subject of long debate and criticism. In strictly causal terms, how frequently do speakers incite listeners to do something they are not already inclined to do? Why is it not sufficient to distinguish clearly between expression and acts, punishing only those who engage in unlawful conduct? In what sense do time and place factors play a role? Is it not one thing to urge a group of students to assassinate a government official who is sitting near the speaker, and quite another to urge such action where the would-be victim is thousands of miles away? Can any statement in writing truly be characterized as an incitement, given the time that the reader has for reflection? Too often, the causal relationship between the speaker's words and the audience's reaction has been assumed. And, in some cases, courts have upheld convictions where no violations of law took place, but the speaker's words might have led to such violations. Punishment of the speaker actually occurs because those in authority disagree with the statement. And there is a tendency to treat the statement in isolation, ignoring the complex nature of communications processes and the innumerable mutually affecting relationships.

Consideration of incitement standards under the First Amendment leads me to believe that they should be applied with far greater stringency to the utterances of government. Whatever the power of an isolated individual to distort the judgment of an audience and to incite it to unlawful conduct, the potential power of government in this regard is far greater. It is one thing for a newspaper owned by an anti-Semitic publisher to lash out against Jews and call for violence against them, and quite another for official government agencies to make similar statements through their extended private and public media networks. Government *advocacy* of unconstitutional or unlawful behavior should itself be subject to restraint, even if there is not the close nexus between speech and action required in modern incitement cases involving private expression.

Government expression is more to be feared when it seeks to overturn the basic political structure of the nation. Whatever the vagaries of identifying government domination of communications networks, they are offset by the dangerous nature of this type of communication. There may not be time for private speech to counter the government's messages. Under these circumstances, the First Amendment should be employed as a substantive limit on what government says. Furthermore, it is destructive to the very idea of a constitution limiting government powers that it should be able to accomplish through incitement of the private sector what it cannot accomplish directly. It should be no more constitutional for government to advocate housing discrimination against blacks than it is for it to pass laws forbidding integrated neighborhoods.

The proposed standard is not without difficulties—as will be demonstrated when a number of important cases are analyzed below. Government officials, speaking in their private capacities, should have the same rights as everyone else to advocate unconstitutional or unlawful conduct. And certainly government entities and officials should not be restrained from advocating changes in existing laws and constitutional provisions. It would be destructive of democratic values to forbid state legislatures from going on record as favoring constitutional amendments to allow prayers in the schools, or to forbid federal courts from ordering racial integration. Frequently, the line between advocacy of change and advocacy of breaking the law will be fuzzy. Moreover, there is always the difficulty of what one means by nebulous words like *incitement*, *advocacy*, and *encouragement*. Government information, for example, may facilitate private discrimination if only because it identifies a class that may be victimized by private actions or by the actions of other governments. The test should be whether the primary purpose appears to be to encourage lawlessness, and whether other lawful, substantial purposes are being served by the government communications.

Most of the cases that would fall within the narrow category of government incitement to lawlessness have ostensibly been decided under the state-action doctrine. That is, the question is whether the state is sufficiently involved in some activity that would be constitutional if carried out by private parties but unconstitutional if the state itself engaged in it. For example, in *Anderson* v. *Martin*,[1] Louisiana had amended its election law to require the designation of each candidate's race on the ballot sheet. Clearly, the Constitution does not forbid voters from voting their biases in elections for public office. Voters are free to favor or disfavor blacks, women, atheists, or whomever they please, irrespective of what constitutional limits may be imposed on government in terms of disqualifying candidates from running for or serving in public office. But, as Laurence Tribe notes, Louisiana's mandatory provision of racial information took the case out of the realm of mere private prejudice:

> The Court found that "by directing attention to the single consideration of race or color, the State indicate[d] that a candidate's race or color [was] an important—perhaps paramount—

1. 375 U.S. 399 (1964).

consideration in the citizen's choice, which may decisively [have] influence[d] the citizen to cast his ballot along racial lines." Therefore, despite the labeling provision's superficially equal application to all races, and thus its superficially nondiscriminatory nature, the effect of the classification was inevitably discriminatory, "in the light of 'private attitudes and pressures' towards Negroes at the time of its enactment."[2]

While the likely effects of the disclosure of racial information are important, perhaps the real point of *Anderson* is that it is unconstitutional for the government to be in the business of advocating racial discrimination. This is particularly true when the communications emanate from the highest levels of government and not from lower echelons that have been delegated substantial editorial powers in the context of a medium of mass communication financed and operated by government.

Lombard v. *Louisiana*,[3] a 1963 lunchcounter sit-in case, supports this analysis of *Anderson* v. *Martin*. In *Lombard*, three blacks and one white were convicted for criminal trespass after they asked to be served at a refreshment counter at the back of a privately owned retail store in New Orleans. The counter was customarily patronized only by whites. Contrary to the facts in a number of companion suits decided the same day by the Supreme Court, however, New Orleans had no ordinance and Louisiana had no statute segregating the races in restaurant facilities. The difficulty for the Court, then, was that segregation of the refreshment counter could aptly be characterized as private action by the management falling outside the ban on racial discrimination embodied in the Fourteenth Amendment. This would be the case unless, as Justice Douglas asserted in a concurring opinion, the act of calling the police and the subsequent arrests and convictions themselves constituted sufficient state involvement.[4] But to adopt this stance might well mean that all private discrimination might be unconstitutional—at least where there was some resort to legal authority to protect private preferences from interference by others.

The Court resolved these problems by relying upon conversations between police officers and the store manager and upon statements issued by various New Orleans public officials. In response to an earlier restaurant sit-in, the superintendent of police had publicly stated that the sit-ins were "not in the community interest." The mayor issued a statement condemning the demonstrations and demanding their cessation.[5] While there was some debate over the actual degree of coercion

2. Laurence Tribe, *American Constitutional Law* 1025 (Mineola, N.Y.: Foundation Press, 1978).
3. 373 U.S. 267 (1963).
4. *Id.* at 278 (Douglas, J., concurring).   5. *Id.* at 270-271.

of the store's management by city officials, the Court concluded that the former were influenced by the various public statements and private conversations and that the city attempted to use its communications powers in lieu of its ordinance-making powers.

> There was evidence to indicate that the restaurant manager asked petitioners to leave in obedience to the directive of the city officials. He told them [the demonstrators] that "I am not allowed to serve you here. . . . We *have* to sell to you at the rear of the store where we have a colored counter." (Emphasis supplied.) And he called the police "[a]s a matter of routine procedure."
>
> The store manager conceded that his decision to operate a segregated facility "conform[ed] to state policy and practice" as well as local custom.
>
> As we interpret the New Orleans city officials' statements, they here determined that the city would not permit Negroes to seek desegregated service in restaurants. Consequently, the city must be treated exactly as if it had an ordinance prohibiting such conduct. We have just held [that such ordinances are unconstitutional]. . . . Equally the State cannot achieve the same result by an official command which has at least as much coercive effect as an ordinance. The official command here was to direct continuance of segregated service in restaurants, and to prohibit any conduct directed toward its discontinuance; it was not restricted solely to preserve the public peace in a nondiscriminatory fashion in a situation where violence was present or imminent by reason of public demonstrations.[6]

The point of *Lombard* is that the advocacy of segregation by public officials was virtually as powerful a force in bringing about segregation as legal sanctions would have been. The messages combined persuasion and incitement with the threat of government force. Their primary purpose was not to bring calm and prevent violence, but rather to resist integration of restaurants. Under such circumstances, the Court properly held that the state was sufficiently involved in discrimination to have violated the equal-protection clause of the Fourteenth Amendment.

Stigmatizing Government Expression and the Due Process Clause

Note that the finding of unconstitutionality in *Lombard* simply resulted in overturning the convictions of the demonstrators. City officials were not enjoined from speaking out on the segregation issue. In *Martin*,

6. *Id.* at 272, 273-274.

the state was effectively enjoined from revealing the race of candidates on the ballot. The threat to legitimate government communication interests in *Martin* was minimal, given the absence of any substantial justification for revealing the race information. Still another form of government incitement case involves a very different remedy: the requirement, imposed under the due process clause, that government must hold an appropriate fact-finding hearing before revealing damaging information or conclusions about individuals or organizations. The classic case in this regard is *Anti-Fascist Committee* v. *McGrath*, decided by the Supreme Court in 1951.[7] The case involved the authority of the United States attorney general to include particular groups on a list of subversive organizations without a due process hearing, and to publish that list in the *Federal Register*. The justices were unable to agree on a majority opinion, but Justice Burton (in an opinion joined only by Justice Douglas) announced the judgment of the Court. Burton found that the designation of the organizations was arbitrary and that it was outside the attorney general's authority to designate organizations "as totalitarian, fascist, communist or subversive, or as having adopted a policy of advocating or approving the commission of acts of force or violence to deny others their rights under the Constitution of the United States, or as seeking to alter the form of government of the United States by unconstitutional means."[8] Burton found that the petitioners were entitled to have the names of their organization stricken from the list under such circumstances.

Implicit in the judgment of the Court is that the power of the attorney general to list subversive organizations might well have been upheld if the attorney general had utilized investigatory and other procedures more likely to guarantee the accuracy of the fact-finding process. Justice Frankfurter, in a famous concurring opinion, expressly relied on this due process ground. Frankfurter began with the understanding that the injury to the petitioners flowed from the government expression embodied in the list of subversives, for the "designation works an immediate substantial harm to the reputation of petitioners." On the other hand, he was unwilling to embrace the notion that "every injury inflicted by a defamatory statement of a government officer can be redressed in court."[9] What was important was the process by which the designation had been made:

> Yet, designation has been made without notice, without disclosure of any reasons justifying it, without opportunity to meet the undisclosed evidence or suspicion on which designation may have

7. 341 U.S. 123 (1951).
8. *Id.* at 125.
9. *Id.* at 159, 160 (Frankfurter, J., concurring).

been based, and without opportunity to establish affirmatively that the aims and acts of the organization are innocent. . . .

This Court is not alone in recognizing that *the right to be heard before being condemned to suffer grievous loss of any kind, even though it may not involve the stigma and hardships of a criminal conviction, is a principle basic to our society.*[10]

Before government labels an organization as subversive, impedes its ability to attract and retain members, encourages public and private entities and persons to act against it, and threatens the job security of present or future federal government employees who might belong to or join it, it should have its facts straight. And this requires a hearing:

Secrecy is not congenial to truth-seeking and self-righteousness gives too slender an assurance of rightness. No better instrument has been devised for arriving at truth than to give a person in jeopardy of serious loss notice of the case against him and opportunity to meet it.[11]

The Frankfurter analysis then establishes another technique for dealing with government speech that may defame an individual or organization or intrude upon freedom of association and expression. He does not opt for the *Martin* principle that the government communication may be enjoined outright, but permits the government to express views which may incite unlawful actions (assuming, for example, that the dismissal of federal employees belonging to one of the organizations would violate their rights of expression and association) so long as it abides proper procedures. Laurence Tribe well states the general principles that underlie cases, such as *McGrath*, dealing with government expression affecting reputation, stigma, privacy, and perhaps loss of First Amendment entitlements:

At stake, therefore, is . . . the more general guarantee that liberty will not be infringed without due process of law. Government should be recognized to have a duty to provide reasonable assurance (1) that it is not needlessly, or in breach of the terms on which information was gathered, (a) maintaining or (b) releasing (or encouraging maintenance or release of) information about people, however accurate; and (2) that such information as government either maintains or releases (or encourages others to maintain or release) is indeed as accurate as it can reasonably be made.

Of course, where exposure of potentially derogatory information about an individual serves a significant governmental

10. *Id.* at 161, 168 (emphasis added).
11. *Id.* at 171–172.

purpose, such exposure is not automatically unconstitutional. The key point to note is that a valid and sufficient governmental purpose may not be presumed lightly.[12]

In *Martin*, no significant government purpose underlay government disclosures that might well incite racial discrimination in voting patterns, and enjoining the government expression was appropriate. In *McGrath*, on the other hand, government had a substantial interest in identifying organizations that were subversive, and therefore an injunction was not appropriate. Nonetheless, the individual interests in jeopardy in *McGrath* were so significant that government was required to follow reasonable fact-finding procedures under the due process clause before speaking; if it failed to do so, the speech might be enjoined until such time as the government pursued a more appropriate and efficacious fact-finding process. Justice Douglas, in his concurring opinion, put the matter this way:

> This is not an instance of name calling by public officials. This is a determination of status—a proceeding to ascertain whether the organization is or is not "subversive." This determination has consequences that are serious to the condemned organizations. Those consequences flow in part, of course, from public opinion. But they also flow from actions of regulatory agencies that are moving in the wake of the Attorney General's determination to penalize or police these organizations. An organization branded as "subversive" by the Attorney General is maimed and crippled. . . .
>
> No more critical governmental ruling can be made against an organization these days. It condemns without trial. It destroys without opportunity to be heard.[13]

The Frankfurter analysis in *McGrath* has been extended to other cases of stigmatizing government expression or action, including the dismissal of public employees.[14] The due process approach employed in the stigma cases is then part of a constitutionally derived structure of restraints on inappropriate government communication. The due process procedures are not designed to prevent government indiscretions absolutely, but rather to give the alleged offender notice of the action and an opportunity to convince the decision maker and perhaps others (friends, prospective employers, neighbors in the community, and so

---

12. Tribe, *American Constitutional Law* 967, 969.

13. *Anti-Fascist Committee* v. *McGrath*, 341 U.S. at 175, 178 (Douglas, J., concurring).

14. The remainder of this section draws heavily on research conducted by a former student for seminar credit at the University of Texas Law School. See Mark Zeidman, "On Liberty and Stigmas: Due Process Limits on Government Speech" (unpublished seminar paper, 1979).

on) that the government has erred. Underlying these cases is the implicit assumption that while stigmatizing speech may be necessary to government's proper functioning, defamatory utterances serve no legitimate government purpose.

The earliest comprehensive statement on the stigma doctrine is *Wisconsin* v. *Constantineau*,[15] decided in 1971. In that case, the chief of police of Hartford, Wisconsin, pursuant to a state statute, posted a notice in all the liquor stores of that city that sales or gifts of alcohol to Constantineau were forbidden for one year. The statute provided for such "posting" without notice or hearing for "excessive drinkers" who exhibited certain traits or brought about certain conditions.[16] Constantineau brought suit, and a three-judge federal court found the posting statute unconstitutional as violative of procedural due process. The Supreme Court's opinion, *per* Mr. Justice Douglas, saw the case this way:

> The only issue present here is whether the label or characterization given a person by "posting," though a mark of serious illness to some, is to others such a stigma or badge of disgrace that procedural due process requires notice and an opportunity to be heard. We agree with the District Court that the private interest is such that those requirements of procedural due process must be met.[17]

Douglas reasoned that by in effect charging Constantineau with chronic drunkenness and familial irresponsibility, Wisconsin had attached to her a "badge of infamy." The test offered by the opinion for evaluating government speech was as follows: "Where a person's good name, reputation, honor, or integrity is at stake because of what the government is doing to him, notice and an opportunity to be heard are essential."[18] The apparent holding of *Constantineau*, then, was that a liberty interest in reputation is denied when government publishes information with serious and adverse consequences for an individual without affording the individual the procedural protections guaranteed by the Fourteenth Amendment.

The *Constantineau* approach was amplified a year later in *Board of Regents of State Colleges* v. *Roth*.[19] Roth, a nontenured political science

---

15. 400 U.S. 433 (1971).

16. The statute was justified as helping to keep chronic alcoholics and their families from becoming burdens on the community; the posted person was specified to be in danger of leaving his family without support or exhibiting irrational behavior that could pose a danger to family and community (*id.* at 434, n. 2).

17. *Id.* at 436.

18. *Id.* at 437.

19. 408 U.S. 564 (1972).

professor at Wisconsin State University-Oshkosh, was informed by the college's president that his one-year contract would not be renewed. No hearing was offered, and no reasons were given for nonrenewal. The rules of the Board of Regents afforded procedural protection for tenured teachers, and for nontenured teachers during the terms of their contracts, but there were no regulations pertaining to nontenured instructors after their contracts expired. Roth filed suit in federal district court, *inter alia* asserting deprivation of a property right in his job and a liberty interest in his professional reputation. The district court granted partial summary judgment for Roth on this procedural claim.[20] The United States Court of Appeals for the Seventh Circuit affirmed.[21] Before the Supreme Court, the only question addressed in Mr. Justice Stewart's opinion for the Court was "whether the respondent had a constitutional right to a statement of reasons and a hearing on the University's decision not to rehire him for another year. We hold that he did not."[22]

While declining to find a liberty or property interest infringed by the bare nonrenewal action of the Board of Regents, the Court did discuss at great length the meaning of liberty, and the kinds of government speech that would implicate a liberty interest. Essentially, a liberty interest necessitating a due process hearing was involved where the government expression or act related to "any charge against him that might seriously damage his standing and associations in his community . . . for example, that he had been guilty of dishonesty, or immorality."[23] The nonrenewal, standing alone, would not suffice.

While the *Roth* Court had little trouble determining that due process standards applied to some reputational losses, the more controversial question has become what constitutes serious injury to reputation, i.e., what consequences must be proved. Apart from the generalized injury to reputation, Justice Stewart opined that had the state "imposed on [Roth] a stigma or other disability that foreclosed his freedom to take advantage of other employment opportunities," for example, "invok-[ing] any regulations to bar [him] from all other public employment in state universities,"[24] a constitutional claim would exist. Under this second degree of stigmatization, government utterances must be shown to result in a substantial adverse effect on employability.

Until the Supreme Court altered the *Roth* doctrine in *Paul* v. *Davis*,[25]

20. Roth's deprivation claim was that he was not afforded a hearing prior to the decision not to renew his contract. He also asserted that the dismissal was in retaliation for certain free-speech activities, but this issue was not before the Supreme Court owing to the district court's disposition of the case (*id.* at 568 n. 5).

21. 446 F.2d 806 (7th Cir. 1971), reversed, 408 U.S. 564 (1972).

22. 408 U.S. at 569 (1972).

23. *Id.* at 573. See also *Owen* v. *City of Independence*, 100 S.Ct. 1398, 1406 n. 13 (1980).

24. 408 U.S. at 573.

25. 424 U.S. 693 (1976).

courts of appeal were in general agreement that the due process test to be applied to government speech was twofold; if a plaintiff could show either significant damage to his standing in the community or a disability foreclosing future employment opportunities, due process must be satisfied.[26] Usually these cases have arisen in connection with statements made upon dismissal from government employment.

The "first-degree stigma" doctrine is applied in cases charging individuals with dishonesty or immorality.[27] Thus, when the board of a junior-college district charged the college president with "misrepresentations, supplying false information, and withholding important information," the resulting "attack on his veracity" was sufficient to meet the first *Roth* test.[28] So, too, a physician's general reputation was unconstitutionally injured by charges of "excessive utilization of certain [narcotic and dangerous] drugs."[29] Accusations of diverting aircraft for personal use were held to implicate an active reserve officer's liberty interest in his reputation for honesty, where the charges were made by his commanding officer.[30] And one court has held that the first *Roth* standard is met by an unexplained order to undergo a psychiatric examination.[31] On the other hand, not all accusations of illegal conduct will satisfy the test, as where public school teachers are alleged to have participated in an illegal strike.[32]

The second part of the *Roth* test, relating to the effect of the government communication on an individual's employability, has been a fertile ground for litigation. Generally, charges of mere incompetence as grounds for dismissal do not satisfy the *Roth* standard.[33] Simple dismissal or nonrenewal without explanation, under the facts of *Roth* itself, is never of its own force a disabling stigma.[34] And, in order to affect future employability, the charges must, of course, be made known to potential employers. Incorporation into an official employ-

26. E.g., *Buhr* v. *Buffalo Public School Dist. No. 38*, 509 F.2d 1196, 1199 (8th Cir. 1974); *McNeill* v. *Butz*, 480 F.2d 314, 319 (4th Cir. 1973).

27. See, generally, *Owen* v. *City of Independence*, 100 S.Ct. 1398, 1406 n. 13 (1980).

28. *Hostrop* v. *Board of Junior College District No. 515*, 471 F.2d 488 (7th Cir. 1972), certiorari denied, 411 U.S. 967 (1973) (*Hostrop I*).

29. *Saurez* v. *Weaver*, 484 F.2d 678, 679 (7th Cir. 1973). The charges were communicated to the Illinois Department of Registration and Education, which licenses physicians. Why the doctor's general reputation and not his employability was the basis for the decision is not clear. Presumably Saurez found another job.

30. *Rolles* v. *Civil Service Commission*, 512 F.2d 1319 (D.C. Cir. 1975).

31. *Stewart* v. *Pearce*, 484 F.2d 1031 (9th Cir. 1973). See also *Owen* v. *City of Independence*, 100 S.Ct. 1398 (1980).

32. *Lake Michigan College Federation of Teachers* v. *Lake Michigan Community College*, 518 F.2d 1091 (6th Cir. 1975), certiorari denied, 427 U.S. 904 (1976).

33. *Blair* v. *Board of Regents of the State University and College System of Tennessee*, 496 F.2d 322 (6th Cir. 1974); *Abeyta* v. *Taos*, 499 F.2d 323 (10th Cir. 1974); *Clark* v. *Holmes*, 474 F.2d 928 (7th Cir. 1972), certiorari denied, 411 U.S. 972 (1973).

34. *Burdeau* v. *Trustees of California State Colleges*, 507 F.2d 770 (9th Cir. 1974).

ment record coupled with actual dissemination to at least one employer has usually been sufficient proof of effect upon employability.[35]

The circuits were in some disagreement as to the standard to apply when specific charges alleged to create a "stigma or other disability" were made. Some courts thought that *Roth* required a "practical test" for employment foreclosure, necessitating a factual inquiry to determine actual employment disability.[36] Others thought that *Roth*'s line between liberty interests and other, nonprotected interests depended upon "the nature of the charges used as a grounds for termination and not the actual consequences of the charge."[37] This nice theoretical distinction was rarely of controlling importance, however, as it was unlikely that a court would find an employment-foreclosing disability on the nature-of-the-charges test unless the plaintiff could show actual difficulty in securing employment because of government speech. Thus, under either test, the second circuit was clearly correct in holding that a principal's charges of bizarre behavior, prejudice, and obscenity, made against a probationary public school teacher and distributed in circulars to other school principals, were stigmatizing, since several schools did, in fact, discharge the teacher upon learning of the claims.[38] Depending upon the *nature* of the charges, the requisite proof of the probability of employment foreclosure may, however, vary. When a medical student was accused of lacking the mental capacity needed to practice medicine, the *Roth* standard was satisfied without requiring a showing that every medical school in the country had rejected his subsequent applications.[39] And where charges against an employee indicated "disloyalty to his superiors," one court found the probability of employment disability sufficient to bring the government speech within the second *Roth* category.[40] Likewise, a policeman charged with suicidal behavior and mental instability had been deprived of his liberty to seek similar employment.[41]

The *Roth* tests, or something very much like them, have also come into considerable use in school discipline cases. As the Court, *per* Mr. Justice White, noted in *Goss* v. *Lopez*, when school authorities suspend students for misconduct, "those charges could seriously damage the students' standing with their fellow pupils and their teachers as well as

35. See *Cato* v. *Collins*, 539 F.2d 656 (8th Cir. 1976).

36. *Weathers* v. *West Yuma County School District, R-J-1*, 530 F.2d 1335, 1339 (10th Cir. 1976).

37. *Stretten* v. *Wadsworth Veterans Hospital*, 537 F.2d 361 (9th Cir. 1976).

38. *Lombard* v. *Board of Education of the City of New York*, 502 F.2d 631, 634 (2d Cir. 1974), certiorari denied, 420 U.S. 976 (1975).

39. *Greenhill* v. *Bailey*, 519 F.2d 5 (9th Cir. 1975).

40. *Wilderman* v. *Nelson*, 467 F.2d 1173, 1179 (8th Cir. 1972); see also *McNeill* v. *Butz*, 480 F.2d 314 (4th Cir. 1973).

41. *Velger* v. *Cawley*, 525 F.2d 334, 336 (2d Cir. 1975), reversed on other grounds *sub nom.*, *Codd* v. *Velger*, 429 U.S. 624 (1977).

interfere with later opportunities for higher education and employment."[42] Indeed, the holding in *Goss* was based upon two rationales: a "property interest in educational benefits temporarily denied" and "the liberty interest in reputation, which is also implicated."[43] Since the due process requirements for disciplinary suspensions are more stringent than for purely academic suspensions,[44] *Goss* may well be read to stand for the proposition that the liberty interest at stake, and not the property interest, is of paramount importance. As will be seen, however, this conclusion has not been true of other areas of government stigmatization; school discipline cases, at least with regard to what state action is permissible under the due process clause, have become *sui generis*.[45]

To restate the *Roth* tests in an overly simple fashion, all reputational losses inflicted by the government *except* academic dismissals from school and unexplained dismissals from employment must satisfy procedural due process. For the individual involved, these two actions may do as much to foreclose future opportunities and damage peer relationships as outspoken accusations. The court's reasoning behind refusal to apply due process standards to academic sanctions and nonrenewals or dismissals has primarily been that of judicial restraint. To review *all* such actions would necessitate extensive judicial intervention in education and personnel policies, and the courts uniformly disclaim the necessary expertise or inclination to embark on such a monumental effort.

Although the vast majority of cases after *Roth* concerned government speech in connection with actual dismissal from government employment, until 1976 it was widely assumed that the *Roth* principles were applicable to stigmatizing speech even in the absence of dismissal. This assumption was particularly true of claims arising out of the first part of the *Roth* test, i.e., cases like *Constantineau*. Sufficient damage to reputation is, of course, more difficult to prove without a showing of injury to employment or other important interests, but this factor went as much to remedy (what due process, once activated, would require) as to the existence of a cause of action.

The Supreme Court, in *Paul* v. *Davis*,[46] changed all of this. The Court had before it a constitutional reputation claim by Edward Charles Davis, a photographer for the daily newspaper in Louisville, Kentucky. Davis, a black man, had been stopped by a security guard for shoplifting. Charges were filed, but dismissed by a Louisville police

---

42. 419 U.S. 565, 574–575 (1975).

43. *Id.* at 576.

44. *Board of Curators, University of Missouri* v. *Horowitz*, 435 U.S. 78 (1978).

45. See, generally, Gerald Gunther, *Cases and Materials on Constitutional Law* 661–669 (Mineola, N.Y.: Foundation Press, 10th ed., 1980).

46. 424 U.S. 693 (1976).

court. Meanwhile, the Louisville Police Department, pursuant to a long-standing practice, had circulated a flyer to all the businessmen in the city containing a list of names and mug shots of active shoplifters, among which Davis's name and picture were included. The notice came to the attention of a newspaper's director of photography, Davis's department head. Davis was told that if he were arrested again for any reason he would be fired immediately, and that in any event he would no longer be sent on assignments that would require him to have contact with local retail stores. His relations with coworkers, never good, deteriorated until Davis felt himself required to resign.

Davis brought suit in federal district court, alleging an unconstitutional deprivation of liberty by the state's action in circulating an untrue and defamatory statement. The district court dismissed the complaint. The court of appeals reversed, believing on the authority of *Constantineau* that Davis had stated a cause of action under the Constitution. The Supreme Court granted *certiorari* to consider whether Davis's interest in his reputation, standing alone, would support his claim. The Court, *per* Mr. Justice Rehnquist, held that it would not.

The thrust of the Court's opinion was that "the court has never held that the mere defamation of an individual . . . was sufficient to involve the guarantees of procedural due process absent an accompanying loss of government employment."[47] *Constantineau* and *Goss* were construed to rest upon an alteration or extinguishment of a "right previously held under state law" owing to the defamation.[48] In *Constantineau*, the right was the ability to purchase liquor, and in *Goss* the right was to educational benefits in Ohio public schools.

As a piece of constitutional analysis, Rehnquist's opinion has been roundly criticized.[49] Of prime concern in evaluating *Paul*'s impact upon due process limits on government speech are the statements Rehnquist made concerning the scope of liberty and the purpose of federal civil-rights actions. On the first, Rehnquist was correct in concluding that in no factual context solely involving defamation (except, perhaps, *McGrath*) had the Court found a liberty interest. On the other hand, the Court had never been faced with such facts. Certainly none of the cases relied upon in *Roth* "held that defamation alone *is not* an adequate basis for invoking constitutional redress."[50] Rehnquist's observation that Davis had failed to allege the violation of any "specific" constitutional

47. *Id.* at 706.
48. *Id.* at 708.
49. See Mark Tushnet, "The Constitutional Right to One's Good Name: An Examination of the Scholarship of Mr. Justice Rehnquist," 64 *Kentucky Law Review* 753 (1977); Comment, "What's In a Name? Reputation, the Constitution and *Paul* v. *Davis*," 8-9 *Columbia Human Rights Law Review* 263 (1977-78); *Paul* v. *Davis*, 424 U.S. 693, 714 ff. (1976) (Brennan, J., dissenting).
50. Comment, "What's In a Name?" 275-276.

provision does not prove that the term "liberty" in the due process clause does not encompass reputational interests. And his comment that the recent privacy decisions of the Court, based on Fourteenth Amendment substantive due process, did not relate to Davis's interest in not having a mistaken arrest publicized seems wholly out of line with his own dissent in *Roe* v. *Wade*,[51] in which he emphasized the Fourth Amendment core of the privacy concept. Most glaringly, Rehnquist's requirement that the state action, in defaming an individual, must deprive him of a right or status under state law was held not to be met in this case without an examination of Kentucky law. Reputation is *explicitly* protected by the Kentucky constitution and common law.[52]

The second important aspect of *Paul* is its apparent misapprehension as to the scope of § 1983 actions. Rehnquist's characterization of Davis's suit was that "he apparently believes that the Fourteenth Amendment's Due Process Clause should *ex proprio vigore* extend to him a right to be free of injury wherever the State may be characterized as a tortfeasor."[53] Clearly this misstates the current scope of § 1983, and is not a prerequisite to jurisdiction in *Paul*. § 1983 does not require the specific intent to deprive an individual of his constitutional rights (as do the criminal counterparts, 18 U.S.C. §§ 241, 241), but volitional performance of a certain act the responsible official knew, or with due care should have known, to be unconstitutional.[54] Thus, Rehnquist's fear that "the survivors of an innocent bystander mistakenly shot by a policeman or negligently killed by a sheriff driving a government vehicle, would . . . have claims . . . cognizable under § 1983,"[55] is completely unfounded. Negligent homicides have never been held to state a constitutional cause of action, but certainly not because "life" is not protected under the Fifth and Fourteenth Amendments.[56] Rehnquist's real point seems to be that since imputation of criminal conduct would amount to a *per se* defamation under state law, there is no point in extending the jurisdiction of federal courts and incurring the risk of making "the Fourteenth Amendment [the] font of tort law."[57] In giving such significance to the hypothetical availability of state relief, Rehnquist ignored not only some venerable precedents, but the basic focus of § 1983 itself on "misuse of power, possessed by virtue of state

51. 410 U.S. 113, 172 (1973) (Rehnquist, J., dissenting).

52. See Comment, "What's In a Name?" and cases collected therein.

53. 424 U.S. at 701.

54. Wayne McCormack, "Federalism and Section 1983: Limitations on Judicial Enforcement of Constitutional Protections," 60 *Virginia Law Review* 1, 54–55 (1974); *Monroe* v. *Pape*, 365 U.S. 167, 187 (1961): cf. *United States* v. *Guest*, 383 U.S. 745 (1966) (interpreting 18 U.S.C. § 241).

55. 424 U.S. at 698.

56. William Prosser, *Torts* § 112 (St. Paul, Minn.: West Publishing, 1971).

57. 424 U.S. at 701. State officials are often immune from such suits in state courts (see *id.* at 715 [Brennan, J., dissenting]).

law, and made possible only because the wrongdoer is clothed with the authority of state law."[58]

There is no doubt that Rehnquist was trying to make some statement concerning the limits of federal remedial powers under the due process clause. Laurence Tribe has pointed out that this may well be the primary message of the case.[59] It may never be clear why the Court did not simply state that the existence of a state-law action may prevent every state-inflicted injury to reputation from being actionable under § 1983,[60] instead of going to the extreme of requiring an unprotected liberty interest to be coupled with some unprotected "property-like" interest before due process comes into play. Or, even more simply, under the facts of *Paul*, the same result could have been reached by assuming a liberty interest and holding that there was a sufficient state interest in protecting retailers against shoplifters to warrant summary action. Due process would thereby have been satisfied, and the results of a proper balancing test would, by *stare decisis*, help to close the "floodgates" on such claims.[61]

In any event, *Paul* set a new standard of what constitutes actionable government speech under the Constitution. Essentially, the first part of the *Roth* test was obliterated.[62] As for the second *Roth* test, the post-*Paul* standard is aptly characterized as the "stigma plus" doctrine. A severe reputational loss *plus* contemporaneous loss of government employment or some other tangible change in status is required. Subsequent cases show that the circuits clearly understand that something more than mere defamation, no matter how serious, is now required. Of course, *Paul* did not affect the outcome of most of these *Roth*-type cases, since government officials rarely defame employees without also firing them. For example, in *Owen* v. *City of Independence*, the Court "decline[d] to disturb the determination of the court below" that the plaintiff was deprived of a liberty interest.[63] The plaintiff had been dismissed as chief of police amid charges by a city councilman that he had misappropriated police department property and that narcotics and money had "mysteriously disappeared" from his office. The plaintiff was given no formal reasons for the discharge, and his request for a public hearing was denied.[64] The Court held that the city itself may be held liable for the violation of plaintiff's due process rights.

58. *United States* v. *Classic*, 313 U.S. 299, 326 (1941); see also *Home Telephone & Telegraph Company* v. *Los Angeles*, 227 U.S. 278 (1913); *Monroe* v. *Pape*, 365 U.S. 167, 183 (1961).

59. Tribe, *American Constitutional Law* 971.

60. See *Ingraham* v. *Wright*, 430 U.S. 651, 700 (1977) (Stevens, J., dissenting).

61. The guidelines for such a test are found in *Matthews* v. *Eldridge*, 424 U.S. 319 (1976).

62. *Mazaleski* v. *Treusdell*, 562 F.2d 701, 712 (D.C. Cir. 1977).

63. 100 S.Ct. 1398, 1406 n. 13 (1980).

64. *Id.* at 1406; see also *Colaizai* v. *Walker*, 542 F.2d 969, 971 (7th Cir. 1976), certiorari denied, 430 U.S. 960 (1977).

A few cases have told us something about the "plus" in "stigma plus." Based on the facts of *Roth*, which holding was approved by *Paul*, one circuit has authoritatively stated that dismissal from nontenured employment, coupled with stigmatizing speech, is sufficient to trigger due process.[65] And we can be fairly sure that stigma plus an internal transfer and stigma plus a demotion not amounting to effective loss of employment do not satisfy *Paul's* high standards.[66]

But the real impact of *Paul* is in the cases not brought, but which might have been under *Roth*.

> Conceivably, Wisconsin could now enact a law allowing the posting of the names and photographs of public drunks, assuming that those posted were not also deprived of the right to purchase alcohol. Ohio schools could charge their students with misconduct, as long as the stigmatized students were allowed to stay in school. Government employers could defame their employees, provided that the employees were not fired.[67]

Surely due process limits on stigmatizing government speech have been severely diluted by *Paul* and its progeny.

Since *Paul*, the Supreme Court has rarely spoken on the stigmatizing-speech issue. In *Bishop* v. *Wood*,[68] the Court was faced with the problem of a policeman fired by the city manager of Marion, North Carolina, on the recommendation of the police chief. The reasons for discharge were communicated orally to the policeman in private and were also disclosed in answer to interrogatories after litigation had begun. The reasons were "insubordination, causing low morale, and conduct unsuited to an officer." The Supreme Court, in a majority opinion written by Mr. Justice Stevens, held that the private communication of derogatory charges could not form the basis for a reputational loss. Justices Brennan and Marshall dissented on the ground that prospective employers of a policeman were bound to investigate the reasons for dismissal and that the reasons were sufficiently defamatory to affect future employment opportunities.[69] The main effect of *Bishop* is to require a showing of actual dissemination and employment foreclosure. This may not seem entirely logical, since the cause of action is

65. *Dennis* v. *S & S Consolidated Rural High School District*, 577 F.2d 338 (5th Cir. 1978).

66. See *Sullivan* v. *Brown*, 544 F.2d 279 (6th Cir. 1976) (teacher transfer to another school without reduction in compensation); *Moore* v. *Otero*, 557 F.2d 435 (5th Cir. 1977). In the *Moore* case a police corporal was demoted to patrolman; Judge Gee called this an "internal transfer" but noted that if he were "transferred" to janitorial duties, the outcome would be different (557 F.2d at 438).

67. Comment, "*Paul* v. *Davis*: The Taming of 1983," 43 *Brooklyn Law Review* 147, 152 (1976).

68. 426 U.S. 341 (1976).

69. *Id.* at 351–352 (Brennan, J., dissenting).

grounded on a lack of prior procedural fairness and in these cases justice would be better served by preventing dissemination than by remedying it.

The other major post-*Paul* case is *Codd* v. *Velger*.[70] Velger, a probationary New York City policeman, was dismissed by Codd, the city's police commissioner, on charges of mental instability, arising out of an apparent suicide attempt. This information was placed in his personnel file, and allegedly resulted in his dismissal from a job with the Penn-Central Railroad Police Department and also prevented his finding other police-related employment. The district court found against Velger's claim of stigma. The second circuit disagreed, holding that the finding of no stigma was clearly erroneous. The Supreme Court reversed on grounds that Velger had failed "to allege or prove one essential element of his case," namely, that the charges against him were false.

The Court's *per curiam* opinion stated that since the remedy for procedural due process violation of a reputational interest is a name-clearing hearing, no useful purpose would be served by the suit unless there existed "some factual dispute between an employer and a discharged employee which has some significant bearing on the employee's reputation."[71] As Mr. Justice Stevens observed, in dissent, the practical impact of *Codd* on identifying objectionable government speech is very small:[72] plaintiffs will simply allege falsity in the future. The primary impact of *Codd* concerns the range of remedies available for due process violations.

Three of the four dissenting justices, Marshall, Brennan, and Stevens, thought that the majority's discussion of remedy was simply wrong in placing the burden of introducing truth or falsity into the lawsuit upon the injured party. Stevens went on to assert that, on the basis of his opinion for the Court in *Bishop*, "the truth or falsity of the charge 'neither enhances nor diminishes [the employee's] claim that his constitutionally protected interest in liberty has been impaired.' If the charge, whether true or false, involves a deprivation of liberty, due process must accompany the deprivation."[73] By denying the availability of these remedies in cases like *Roth*, the Court assumed that a hearing was useless for "guilty" plaintiffs and therefore need not be held. There is little logic in this; fortunately only the most ignorant of attorneys will be affected by the express holding of the case.

Before *Codd*, three classes of remedies were available in *Roth*-type

---

70. *Codd* v. *Velger*, 429 U.S. 624 (1977) (*per curiam*).

71. *Id.* at 627.

72. *Id.* at 636 (Stevens, J., dissenting).

73. *Id.* See, e.g., *Lombard* v. *Board of Education of the City of New York*, 502 F.2d 631 (2d Cir. 1974), certiorari denied, 420 U.S. 976 (1975); *Stretten* v. *Wadsworth Veterans Hospital*, 537 F.2d 361 (9th Cir. 1976).

cases; injunctive relief, damages, and hearings. Injunctive relief might have included a simple order restraining the governmental unit or official from disseminating the assertedly defamatory material—for example, by expungement from student records of references to procedurally defective school suspensions.[74] District courts also possessed the authority to require temporary reinstatement until a name-clearing hearing was held in cases involving dismissals.[75] Once the determination that due process required a hearing was made, however, permanent reinstatement was generally unavailable, unless the order to provide such a hearing was not complied with.[76] Reinstatement was considered an extraordinary equitable remedy, and has been limited to situations involving violations of equal protection in racial discrimination[77] and dismissals in retribution for the exercise of free speech.[78] The availability of this form of injunctive relief in these situations appears to rest on the need not only to compensate private individuals, but to punish government misconduct.

Since *Paul*, plaintiffs have had to add together two harms the Court considers to be of questionable constitutional import to yield one harm that the federal courts will even consider. There is no constitutional restriction on dismissal of an employee without a vested property right in his job, unless he is also stigmatized. *Codd* says, in effect, that when plaintiffs prove "stigma plus," they get a chance to refute the stigma. The "plus" can be taken away for any reason; even though it is absolutely required by *Paul*, it does not figure in the remedy.

Codd's apparent rejection of any remedy other than a due process hearing is extremely questionable. The holding rests on a statement in *Roth* that in order to remedy a reputation-in-the-community injury, a hearing is required to allow the injured party to clear his name.[79] Three things are worth noting about this. First, this "first-degree" cause of action no longer exists. Only the second part of *Roth*, as modified, now constitutes a constitutional claim, and Stewart did not limit the range of remedies for an employability stigma. Second, nowhere did the Court in *Roth* indicate that a hearing would be the *only* remedy available, even for a purely reputational loss.[80] And third, the statement referred to the purpose of the hearing due process requires *before* the liberty deprivation occurs, and may have no application to post-deprivation remedies at all.

74. *Pervis* v. *LaMarque Indep. School Dist.*, 466 F.2d 1054 (5th Cir. 1972).

75. *Everett* v. *Marcuse*, 426 F. Supp. 397 (D. Pa. 1976).

76. *Greenhill* v. *Bailey*, 518 F.2d 5, 9 (8th Cir. 1975); *Burton* v. *Cascade School District Union High School No. 5*, 512 F.2d 850, 854 (9th Cir. 1975).

77. See, e.g., *Rolfe* v. *County Board of Education of Lincoln County, Tennessee*, 391 F.2d 77 (6th Cir. 1968).

78. See, e.g., *Stewart* v. *Pearce*, 484 F.2d 1031, 1032 (9th Cir. 1973).

79. 408 U.S. 564, 573 n. 12.

80. *Codd* v. *Velger*, 429 U.S. 624, 635 n. 6 (1977) (Stevens, J., dissenting).

The Court's most recent statement on liability for the deprivation of due process rights in a stigma plus case indicates that *Codd* does not limit post-deprivation remedies. In *Owen* v. *City of Independence*,[81] the Court held that a municipality was strictly liable for the failure to hold a hearing where a police chief had been dismissed in the context of stigmatizing charges by high city officials. While the law is not at all clear on this matter, this suggests that if a name-clearing hearing is required and the government agency fails to hold it, the Court will require that such a hearing be held. If it is held and the employee's name is cleared, then presumably the employee may sue for the injury to his reputation and for any emotional or other harms associated with the failure to hold the hearing before the stigmatizing action was taken.[82] If the employee is not cleared at the hearing, his only remedy would be the rather modest one of a suit for damages for the failure to hold a timely hearing (perhaps including reputational injuries associated with the delay). In either event, if it is permissible under state law, the dismissed employee could sue in state court for defamation.

For the individual litigant whose rights have been violated, judicial remand to a hearing that should have been held before the violation would be a rather empty remedy.[83] A due process hearing *nunc pro tunc* could not deter injurious government speech, if for no other reason than that *Paul* and *Codd*, read together, require a showing of actual injury before the plaintiff's request for a hearing is even considered. In effect, the postdeprivation hearing is a right-of-reply forum that is inadequate in several respects. First, there is no obligation to attach testimony of good character to an employment record upon discharge. Prospective employers are likely to accept a previous employer's judgment; in fact, should it become known that the government maligned and dismissed a worker even after a full adversary hearing, the stigmatizing speech may take on added credibility. Second, the extent to which a person may rehabilitate his standing in the community by a postdeprivation hearing is dependent upon a great many variables. If the government issues a press release, public attention may be focused on the matter. Will the news media care to publicize the victim's side of the story? If the hearings are public, will they be attended? Much may depend upon the availability and quality of plaintiff's counsel, and his knowledge of agency politics. Third, the postdeprivation hearing may never erase some kinds of stigmas, particularly if the accusation is true.

Even if Constantineau were a drunk, was it necessary to post this

81. 100 S.Ct. 1398 (1980).
82. *Carey* v. *Piphus*, 435 U.S. 247 (1978).
83. Donald Simet, "The Right to a Pre-Deprivation Hearing Under the Due Process Clause—Constitutional Priorities and a Suggested Method for Making Decisions," 11 *Creighton Law Review* 1201, 1225 (1978).

fact around her home town? This is a question that can be answered prior to the posting, but becomes somewhat rhetorical afterwards. And if she were not a public drunk, how could she ever erase the belief that she was? If a person were a homosexual, and were excluded from certain establishments as an "active homosexual," the stigma imposed would require a predeprivation hearing, at which he might be able to convince the government speaker that he should not publicize the admitted truth. Even if he were a public employee and could somehow circumvent dismissal for failure to state a disagreement as indicated by *Codd*, what good would a postdeprivation hearing do once the information, perhaps desperately kept secret for years, was out? This, of course, is exactly the rationale of *Codd*: it begins with the flawed premise that only *post facto* hearings are available and concludes that guilty plaintiffs have nothing to gain. In this the Court was correct, but failed to go far enough: even innocent plaintiffs have nothing to gain.

We are left, then, with the hypothetical deterrent effect upon government speakers by virtue of their awareness that hearings must be held before they may constitutionally make (1) false, (2) very derogatory statements about individuals, (3) while in the process of discharging them or depriving them of some other state-guaranteed status.[84] Certainly hearings do not guarantee fair treatment or wise policy results. But if fair procedures are followed, and unjust results obtain, due process may nevertheless serve important purposes. First, the procedure identifies the speaker: his position may be open to reevaluation by his superiors, or, if elected, by the people. Second, formality may produce impartiality, through bureaucratization, and consistency in the application of facts. Due process may constrain unbridled discretion.

But after all of this has been said, it may well be the case that due process procedures simply do not adequately protect an individual from stigmatizing government expression and that the recent shift in due process doctrines reflects this fact. The adequate remedy lies in defamation and privacy actions, whether brought under federal or state constitutional provisions or laws. The difficulty is that the Court appears to be narrowing the hearing remedy without any assurance that damage remedies will be available or sufficient. Certainly, there are many difficulties in suing federal and state officials in defamation (including proving the dollar value of the injuries),[85] and some may need to be corrected by legislative action—action which may not be perceived as in the best interest of government officials. Furthermore, the Court itself shows a strong inclination entirely to withdraw the federal courts from this area of stigmatizing government expression and acts, favoring conjectural state court and law remedies. In this

84. See, e.g., Tribe, *American Constitutional Law* § 15-17.
85. See *Carey* v. *Piphus*, 435 U.S. 247 (1978).

sense, Laurence Tribe is surely right in noting that recent cases are antithetical to the historical federal judicial role in vindicating constitutional entitlements.[86] The current Supreme Court's concern is less with the scope of due process or the adequacy of alternative remedies, than it is with the need to get the federal courts out of the business of policing excesses in government communication. Given the relationship of stigmatizing government speech to the more general problem of imposing limits on government expression, the trend of recent cases is unfortunate.

The Speech or Debate Clause

In a number of cases, private individuals have attempted to recover damages or prevent congressional committees or congressmen from publishing or gathering information that was alleged to be private in nature, that would undermine their associational rights, or that would defame or otherwise injure them.[87] This has required the federal courts to determine the scope and meaning of the speech or debate clause, which states that "for any Speech or Debate in either House, [members of Congress] . . . shall not be questioned in any other place."[88] By and large, the federal courts have sought to determine whether the publication or other activity is within the scope of legitimate legislative functions or somehow political or private in nature. If the communications activity falls within the former category, it is absolutely privileged.[89] Perhaps the most significant of these cases, for present purposes, is *Doe* v. *McMillan*.[90] In that case, the Supreme Court held that the disclosure of the names of specific students in a congressional report on the District of Columbia schools was protected by the speech or debate clause despite the alleged irrelevancy of the names to any legitimate legislative purpose. The plaintiffs had alleged, *inter alia*, that their constitutional and common-law rights (association, privacy, reputation) had been denied by the publication of the report, and they sought the recall of existing copies of the report, an injunction against future publication of the objectionable material, and compensatory and punitive damages. The Court ruled, however, that an absolute privilege

86. Tribe, *American Constitutional Law* 527-530.

87. See *Eastland* v. *United States Servicemen's Fund*, 421 U.S. 491 (1975); *Doe* v. *McMillan*, 412 U.S. 306 (1973); *Long* v. *Ansell*, 69 F.2d 386 (D.C. Cir. 1934); *Hentoff* v. *Ichord*, 318 F. Supp. 1175 (D.D.C. 1970); and *McGovern* v. *Martz*, 182 F. Supp. 343 (D.D.C. 1960). Cf. *Gravel* v. *United States*, 408 U.S. 606 (1972); *United States* v. *Brewster*, 408 U.S. 501 (1972); and *Tenney* v. *Brandhove*, 341 U.S. 367 (1951) (immunities of stage legislators).

88. U.S. Const., art. 1, § 6, cl. 1. See, generally, Tribe, *American Constitutional Law* § 5-18.

89. See, e.g., *Eastland* v. *United States Servicemen's Fund*, 421 U.S. 491 (1975); *United States* v. *Johnson*, 383 U.S. 169, 184-185 (1966); and *Kilbourn* v. *Thompson*, 103 U.S. 168 (1881).

90. 412 U.S. 306 (1973).

was applicable not only to the congressmen, but also to the committee staff, congressional aides, investigators, and others participating in the investigation, preparation, and discussion of the report.

One interesting aspect of the decision relates to the possible civil liability of those responsible for printing and disseminating the report, the public printer and the superintendent of documents.[91] The majority indicated that it could not determine the extent and nature of the distribution of the report by the Government Printing Office, but indicated that there were circumstances in which the speech or debate clause would not protect them from civil suits:

> The proper scope of our inquiry, therefore, is whether the Speech or Debate Clause affords absolute immunity from private suit to persons who, with authorization from Congress, distribute materials which allegedly infringe upon the rights of individuals. . . .
>
> We do not doubt the importance of informing the public about the business of Congress. . . . A Member of Congress may not with impunity publish a libel from the speaker's stand in his home district, and clearly the Speech or Debate Clause would not protect such an act even though the libel was read from an official committee report. The reason is that republishing a libel under such circumstances is not an essential part of the legislative process and is not part of the deliberative process "by which Members participate in committee and House proceedings.". . .
>
> By the same token, others, such as the Superintendent of Documents or the Public Printer or legislative personnel, who participate in distribution of actionable materials beyond the reasonable bounds of the legislative task, enjoy no Speech or Debate Clause immunity.[92]

The distinction between aides or functionaries acting on instructions within the legislative sphere and those same aides and functionaries acting in a nonlegislative or political capacity is a necessary formal rule, but a fuzzy one which the Court has frequently been disinclined to apply to members of Congress themselves.[93] It is reminiscent of the difficulties attendant on distinguishing something called government speech from something called the private speech of government officials. But what is significant about the majority opinion is the sugges-

91. Laurence Tribe notes that "in four of the eight speech or debate clause cases the Supreme Court has thus far decided, the Court has held legislative employees liable to suit but barred suit against members of Congress themselves." Tribe, *American Constitutional Law* 296 n. 24, citing *Doe* v. *McMillan*, 412 U.S. 306 (1973); *Powell* v. *McCormack*, 395 U.S. 486 (1968); *Dombrowski* v. *Eastland*, 387 U.S. 82 (1967); *Kilbourn* v. *Thompson*, 103 U.S. 168 (1881).

92. 412 U.S. at 314-315.

93. See Tribe, *American Constitutional Law* 295-296.

tion that the distribution of a congressional report beyond some judicially established limits will deprive those functionaries charged with
printing and distributing it of the absolute protection of the speech or
debate clause, and leave them only with whatever official, conditional
immunities they enjoy.

The majority opinion is ambiguous about what sort of remedies
might lie against the superintendent of documents and the public printer if, in some ill-defined manner, they disseminated the congressional
report more widely than the legislative function would require. In
terms of monetary damages, perhaps, the Court contemplated recoveries against functionaries as a way of getting around the speech or
debate clause's absolute immunities and avoiding a confrontation with
the Congress in situations where congressional reports defame or otherwise injure identifiable individuals. While congressional authorization
for such civil suits might be preferable, such a notion would be consistent with the erosion of absolute official immunity for executive officials who act unconstitutionally.[94]

But what is most disturbing is the suggestion made by Justice Douglas in a concurring opinion, joined by Justices Brennan and Marshall,
that "at the very least petitioners are entitled to injunctive relief."[95]
This gives too little weight to the informing function of Congress,
congressmen and other government officials,[96] and, indeed, too little
weight to the free-expression rights they retain even as private citizens.
Just as it is one thing for a federal court to enjoin the issuance of a
congressional subpoena and quite another for the courts to overturn a
conviction for noncompliance with such a subpoena where there is an
infringement of First Amendment associational interests,[97] so, too, it is
one thing to enjoin the distribution of a congressional report and a
different matter only to allow recovery of damages from functionaries
after publication and distribution.

The federal courts should be reluctant to enjoin the speech of federal
legislative officials and the Congress, particularly given the informing
function of Congress, the difficulties attendant on disentangling government speech from private speech, and the principle of separation of
powers. Whether the speech occurs in a political campaign, in the halls
of Congress, or in books printed by the Government Printing Office, it
serves a valuable function. The court of appeals, on remand in McMillan,
grasped the matter well:

94. See *Butz* v. *Economou*, 438 U.S. 478 (1978).
95. 412 U.S. at 330.
96. See 412 U.S. at 332 (Blackmun, J., dissenting in part). See also *Gravel* v. *United
States*, 408 U.S. 618, 649 (Brennan, J., dissenting); Tribe, *American Constitutional Law* 295.
97. See *Eastland* v. *United States Servicemen's Fund*, 421 U.S. 491, 509 n. 16 (1975).

Distribution was solely to persons and agencies with standing orders for all reports. . . . Such routine distribution to federal government agencies outside the Congress serves to permit comment upon proposed legislation by the agencies that may be directly affected by it, and . . . we cannot say that such distribution is outside the legitimate legislative purposes of Congress.

Distribution [to private parties with standing orders] of such reports informs the public and permits them to comment on pending matters. It permits individuals and companies who consider their interests to be affected to take steps to exercise their constitutional right of petition [which is] . . . protected by the First Amendment of the Bill of Rights. . . . The right to petition would be meaningless if proceedings in Congress were not publicly available.[98]

While the portions of the opinion which appear to resurrect a sort of "right to know" constitutional protection for the report appear unwise (Congress could certainly choose not to publish it without violating the Constitution), the court of appeals is generally on the right track. Acting within the Supreme Court's mandate, it declined to decide whether a broader distribution of the report might have occasioned the issuance of an injunction or the awarding of damages,[99] but it seemed genuinely concerned with the question of judicially imposed restraints on government speech. Justice Rehnquist, dissenting in *McMillan*, also put the matter well, albeit he came close to the erroneous conclusion that government speech and private speech should be equated for First Amendment purposes:

We have jurisdiction to review the completed acts of the Legislative and Executive Branches. . . . But the prospect of the District Court's enjoining a committee of Congress, which, in the legislative scheme of things, is for all practical purposes Congress itself, from undertaking to publicly distribute one of its reports in the manner that Congress has by statute prescribed that it be distributed, is one that I believe would have boggled the minds of the Framers of the Constitution.

In *Kilbourn v. Thompson* . . . the Court reviewed the arrest and confinement of a private citizen by the Sergeant at Arms of the

98. *Doe* v. *McMillan*, 566 F.2d 713, 718 (D.C. Cir. 1977) (*per curiam*), affirming, 374 F. Supp. 1313 (D.D.C. 1974).

99. 566 F.2d at 719. The appeals court also held that the superintendent of documents and the public printer had been acting in good faith, in that they reasonably believed in the legality of their actions (*id.* at 719). They were thus also protected by their conditional, official immunities.

House of Representatives. In *Watkins v. United States . . .* the
Court reviewed the scope of the investigatory powers of Congress when the executive had prosecuted a recalcitrant witness
and sought a judicial forum for the purpose of imposing criminal
sanctions on him. Neither of these cases comes close to having
the mischievous possibilities of censorship being imposed by one
branch of the Government upon the other as does this one.

In *New York Times Co. v. United States . . .* this Court held that
prior restraints come before it bearing a heavy burden. . . . Whatever be the difference in the constitutional posture of the two
situations, on the issue of injunctive relief, which is nothing if not
a form of prior restraint, a Congressman should stand in no
worse position in the federal courts than does a private publisher. . . .[100]

The situation in *Doe* v. *McMillan* should be contrasted with the Supreme Court's 1979 decision in *Hutchinson* v. *Proxmire*.[101] In the latter
case, Senator Proxmire had awarded his "Golden Fleece" award to the
federal government agencies that had sponsored the research of Ronald
Hutchinson on objective measures of aggression in research animals.
The Navy and the National Aeronautics and Space Agency apparently
thought that the research might yield findings which would be useful in
resolving problems related to "confining humans in close quarters for
extended periods of time in space and undersea exploration." Senator
Proxmire did not agree, and the "award" was given "to publicize
what he perceived to be the most egregious examples of wasteful
governmental spending." The "award" was made in a senate speech,
and the text of the speech was incorporated in an advance press release.
Copies were sent to 275 members of the mass media in the United
States and abroad. Senator Proxmire also mentioned the award in two
newsletters, sent to about 100,000 persons, and referred to it in a
subsequent television appearance. Hutchinson sued Senator Proxmire
and his legislative assistant for defamation in making the award and
publicizing it.[102]

The case presented a number of difficult issues, but the most significant holding in the present context was that Senator Proxmire was not
wholly immune from damage recoveries for defamation under the
speech or debate clause. The Court held that his speech in the Senate
could not be the basis for a recovery in defamation, but the newsletters

100. *Doe* v. *McMillan*, 412 U.S. 306, 343-345 (1973) (Rehnquist, J., dissenting). Justice
Rehnquist's view is consistent with the traditional rule that the courts may not enjoin a
libel. See, e.g., *Wilson* v. *Los Angeles County Superior Court*, 13 Cal.3d 652, 119 Cal. Rptr.
468, 5232 P.2d 116 (1975); *ABC* v. *Smith Cabinet Manufacturing Co.*, 312 N.E.2d 85 (Ind.
App. 1974).
101. 443 U.S. 111 (1979).
102. *Id.* at 114-117.

and the press release were not so protected. The Court perceived no inconsistency between this result and the earlier decision in *Doe*:

> Neither the newsletters nor the press release was "essential to the deliberations of the Senate" and neither was part of the deliberative process.
>
> *Doe* v. *McMillan* . . . is not to the contrary. It dealt only with reports from congressional committees, and held that Members of Congress could not be held liable for voting to publish a report. Voting and preparing committee reports are the individual and collective expressions of opinion within the legislative process. As such, they are protected by the Speech or Debate Clause. Newsletters and press releases, by contrast, are primarily means of informing those outside the legislative forum; they represent the views and will of a single Member. It does not disparage either their value or their importance to hold that they are not entitled to the protection of the Speech or Debate Clause.[103]

The Court readily admitted that the communications from the senator might serve a broad public purpose in disseminating information about the performance of government agencies as widely as possible. But it declined to embrace the view that the information value of such communications should give a member of Congress complete and absolute immunity for defamatory statements.

Hutchinson is a significant decision in the balancing of interests with regard to imposing limitations on government expression. First, it is consistent with the notion that an absolute privilege for government officials may well lead private persons to refrain from criticizing their government. In the specific case, the fear of a defamatory attack from Senator Proxmire might well lead researchers to refrain from applying for the government grants necessary to sustain their research. Indeed, government agencies might hesitate to fund valuable research—a government function of the highest order—for fear that their funding decisions would be grossly distorted by members of Congress. This is not to say that members of Congress should abandon their oversight functions in the area of government-sponsored research, but only to say that reasonable efforts to get their facts straight should precede the publication of critical remarks outside the halls of Congress.

Second, the Court clearly embraced the idea that even defamatory remarks are protected by the speech or debate clause for communications more central to the legislative process, e.g., speeches on the Senate floor, congressional reports, etc. This is a reasonable accommodation of the interest in protecting government expression and the integrity of the legislative processes and the need to cabin injurious

---

103. *Id.* at 130, 133.

government speech. Indeed, the Court carefully drew a distinction between the views of an individual member of Congress, expressed in nonlegislative forums, and the member's or the legislative body's official communications in a legislative forum.

Finally, the Court opened the way for damage recoveries, while making no effort to give support to the view that Senator Proxmire could properly be enjoined from speaking. Since Hutchinson was not deemed a "public figure," he need not prove "actual malice" in order to prevail in his suit for damages. He need only meet the less burdensome fault standard articulated in other Supreme Court opinions. While the Court did not address the question of any official immunities that Senator Proxmire might have, the decision goes a long way toward extending *New York Times* v. *Sullivan*[104] to libel and slander by public officials. Thus, certain types of objectionable speech by public officials may lead to damage recoveries by those injured, thereby serving the important function of limiting what government officers may say— particularly as they rely on the prestige of their official positions. On the other hand, "vigorous debate on public issues" is not diminished by the drastic alternative of enjoining government and its officers from speaking out. The accommodation of the needs to promote and to circumscribe government expression reached in *Hutchinson* is both wise and workable.

Enjoining Government Expression: Legislative and Administrative Investigations

Legislative and administrative investigations may also provoke concern about constitutional limits on government expression. An excellent example is *Jenkins* v. *McKeithen*,[105] decided by the Supreme Court in 1969. The state of Louisiana had created an agency called the Labor-Management Commission of Inquiry. The stated purpose of the commission was to investigate and make findings of fact relating to possible violations of criminal law arising out of labor-management relations. In operation, it apparently sought to focus on the criminal misconduct of union officials. The commission had broad investigative powers in order to "supplement and assist the efforts and activities of the several district attorneys, grand juries and other law enforcement officials and agencies." It could proceed to hold hearings only upon referral by the governor, and it had the power to compel witnesses to attend, to examine them under oath, and to require the production of documents and other evidence. Individuals were not, however, afforded all of the constitutional safeguards to which they would have been entitled in criminal prosecutions. The commission was required to determine

104. 376 U.S. 254 (1964).   105. 395 U.S. 411 (1969).

"whether there is probable cause to believe violations of the criminal laws have occurred," and it was specifically empowered to make findings as to specific individuals and to make appropriate recommendations to the governor. The findings were matters of public record, albeit they could not be used for evidentiary purposes in civil or criminal proceedings. The plaintiff in *Jenkins* alleged that he was in danger of being convicted by an "executive trial agency," although he did not show that he personally had been or would be called to testify. The majority of the justices found, however, that there was a sufficient danger of future action with regard to him that he had standing to sue.[106]

Justice Marshall, joined by Chief Justice Warren and Justice Brennan, announced the judgment of the Court.[107] He emphasized that there was no indication that the commission's findings were to be used for legislative purposes or for civil or criminal litigation. Rather, the commission performed the function of punishing by public accusation:

> Everything in the Act points to the fact that it is concerned only with exposing violations of criminal laws by specific individuals. In short, the Commission very clearly exercises an accusatory function; it is empowered to be used and allegedly is used to find named individuals guilty of violating the criminal laws of Louisiana and the United States and to brand them as criminals in public.[108]

Justice Marshall then found that the procedures of the commission did not meet the minimal requirements of the due process clause of the Fourteenth Amendment, making the Fifth and Sixth Amendments applicable to the states, e.g., the right to confront witnesses and to present evidence on one's own behalf. The three justices then announced the judgment of the Court that the case be remanded for further findings as to the failure to meet due process requirements. In so doing, they explicitly stated "that we do not hold that appellant is not entitled to declaratory or injunctive relief. We only hold that he has alleged a cause of action which may make such relief appropriate."[109] This is consistent with the Court's earlier treatment of the *McGrath* blacklisting case. Justice Black concurred specifically on criminal-process grounds, and seemed inclined to grant injunctive relief:

> The Louisiana law here . . . is . . . nothing more nor less than a scheme for a nonjudicial tribunal to charge, try, convict, and punish people without courts, without juries, without lawyers, without witnesses—in short, without any of the procedural protections that the Bill of Rights provides.[110]

---

106. *Id.* at 415–418, 425.   107. *Id.* at 413.
108. *Id.* at 427–428.   109. *Id.* at 431.
110. *Id.* at 432–433 (Black, J., concurring).

This was also consistent with his separate opinion in *McGrath*. Justice Douglas essentially took the same position as Justice Black in a one-sentence concurring opinion.

Justice Harlan, joined by Justices Stewart and White, dissented both with respect to the standing question and the disposition on the merits.[111] With respect to the latter, he found that the commission's investigatory powers and its authority to report wrongdoing "to the proper federal and state authorities" distinguished its activities from those of agencies "whose sole or predominant function, without serving any other public interest, is to expose and publicize the names of persons it finds guilty of wrongdoing." He feared that the views of the justices joining in the Court's judgment would undercut the legitimate investigatory powers of such agencies as the Federal Trade Commission and the Securities and Exchange Commission. He was content to leave matters of what to disclose about investigations "in the sound discretion of the responsible public official."[112]

The issues of disclosure and procedural rights are inextricably intertwined in *Jenkins*. If the commission were enjoined from publicizing its conclusions or even making recommendations, presumably many of the justices would not be so concerned about protecting procedural rights through the investigations and hearings. On the other hand, some of the justices, consistent with *McGrath*, leave open the possibility that the government disclosures are permissible so long as constitutional due process protections are observed. Only Justices Black and Douglas stand firm on the conviction that the commission was conducting criminal trials in the guise of investigations, usurping the judicial function and abridging due process rights, and that this is unconstitutional. Even Justice Harlan, however, admits that there are cases where the agency's sole or primary purpose is exposure, and here he would apply constitutional limitations. He does not view *Jenkins* as such a case.

Viewed from the perspective of enjoining government speech, *Jenkins* presents interesting issues. In general, it would seem unwise in the extreme to put the courts in the business of silencing legislative committees and administrative agencies that cast particular individuals in an unfavorable light during the course of their investigations. The policy concerns are very much like those in the *Doe* and *McGrath* cases. Where exposure of associations or wrongdoing is a by-product, or even the thrust, of an investigation, the indirect route would appear preferable—i.e., allowing uncooperative witnesses to raise their First and Fifth Amendment objections as a defense when the legislative or administrative body seeks to hold them in contempt. There are a number of Supreme Court decisions supporting this approach. In an executive branch context, due process hearings may be required, following

111. *Id.* at 433 (Harlan, J., dissenting).
112. *Id.* at 441.

McGrath. In addition, witnesses have successfully argued, in a defensive posture, that legislative bodies have exceeded the scope of their authority, a kind of *ultra vires* doctrine informed by First Amendment policy.[113] But injunctions against holding hearings or publishing reports may too deeply interfere with the activities of government.

Having said this, however, *Jenkins* strikes me as one of those few cases in which injunctive relief becomes thinkable (albeit there are special problems in applying this approach to congressional rather than state investigations). If the commission's hearings and investigations were tantamount to a criminal trial—it was not just casting general aspersions, alleging violations of the civil law, or revealing false information injurious to reputation or business relations—then the plaintiff was seeking to vindicate an individual constitutional entitlement. It is as if the blacklist in *McGrath* labeled individuals, by name, as traitors. Specific provisions of the Bill of Rights grant criminal defendants rights as against the state. The group interest in limiting government expression, derived from the First Amendment, supports these individual claims deriving from other constitutional provisions, and may support an injunction against continuing this "quasi-criminal" process.

One should be acutely concerned about drawing the line between exposure for its own sake and exposure as part of legitimate legislative and administrative investigations and reports. These are weighty interests. And perhaps, at least in the context of legislative exposure, these matters could be dealt with by federal and state courts under doctrines of separation of powers—some legislative investigations are tantamount to criminal trials of individuals without the benefit of judges and juries. It may be permissible and wise to enjoin the government from indulging in such outrageous and blatant conduct and/or publicizing its conclusions. The due process approach of *McGrath* would not normally apply to legislative as opposed to administrative determinations, and hence an injunction may be the only viable remedy in such extreme cases.

There are also cases involving efforts to enjoin preadjudication publicity by regulatory agencies in which individuals or corporations are charged with violations of the applicable civil laws, e.g., securities regulations.[114] Sometimes the agency wishes to warn the public against

113. See, generally, Thomas Emerson, *The System of Freedom of Expression* ch. 8 (New York: Random House, 1970).

114. See, e.g., *FTC* v. *Cinderella Schools*, 404 F.2d 1308 (D.C. Cir. 1968); *Kukatush* v. *SEC*, 309 F.2d 647 (D.C. Cir. 1962) (no standing); *B. C. Morton* v. *F.D.I.C.*, 305 F.2d 692 (1st Cir. 1962); *Ajay Nutrition* v. *FDA*, 378 F. Supp. 210 (D. N.J. 1974) (press releases are privileged communications of executive officers); *Koss* v. *SEC*, 364 F. Supp. 1321 (S.D.N.Y. 1973) (case not ripe for judicial review); *Silver King Mines* v. *Cohen*, 261 F. Supp. 666 (D. Utah 1966). See, generally, Robinson Lacy, "Adverse Publicity and SEC Enforcement Procedure," 46 *Fordham Law Review* 435 (1977); Ernest Gelhorn, "Adverse Publicity by Administrative Agencies," 86 *Harvard Law Review* 1380 (1973).

buying allegedly dangerous products, entering into certain land or securities transactions, and so forth. The argument is that this amounts to an interference with property and business interests without observance of due process. Courts have occasionally granted such injunctions. These interests, however, are not as strong as those in the "criminal" exposure cases such as *Jenkins*. In this context, courts tend to be responsive (at least in terms of granting injunctive relief) only when the agency has exceeded its statutory authorization, and most courts have been generous in finding such authority.[115] As will be developed in the Conclusion below, perhaps it would be appropriate in the case of executive agencies to provide for a more exacting inquiry into the question of whether the agencies' communications activities were authorized by Congress.[116] Alternatively, subject to the standard sovereign and official immunity difficulties, perhaps damages for defamation or various business torts should lie where the agency communications are particularly punitive.[117]

Wickard v. *Filburn*: Misleading Speech by an Executive Officer

The judicial hesitancy to restrain government speech is also reflected in *Wickard* v. *Filburn*,[118] a 1942 case generally cited for the proposition that Congress has extraordinarily broad powers under the commerce clause to regulate private activities in the states. In that case, the Agricultural Adjustment Act of 1938, as subsequently amended, was upheld even as it applied to a farmer who grew only 462 bushels of wheat. But, as is so often the case, the Supreme Court paid scant attention to what appeared to the lower court to be the plaintiff's primary concerns. In the district court, the plaintiff argued that the vote on national marketing quotas by wheat farmers had taken place after they had planted their crops, and that the secretary of agriculture, Claude Wickard, had failed to inform farmers that the penalties for overproduction would be increased from their preplanting and prereferendum level of fifteen cents a bushel to forty-nine cents a bushel.[119] He alleged that the retroactive application of the higher penalties was an unconstitutional taking of his property. The lower court held for the plaintiff on this ground, and the Supreme Court reversed, with most of

115. Gelhorn, "Adverse Publicity" 1433, citing *FTC* v. *Cinderella Schools*, 404 F.2d 1308 (D.C. Cir. 1968).

116. See, e.g., *Silver King Mines* v. *Cohen*, 261 F. Supp. 661 (D. Utah 1966); *B. C. Morton* v. *FDIC*, 305 F.2d 692 (1st Cir. 1962).

117. Gelhorn has suggested an expansion of the Federal Tort Claims Act, 28 U.S.C. § 1291, *et seq.* (1970), to accomplish this result ("Adverse Publicity" 1437-1440).

118. 317 U.S. 111 (1942).

119. *Filburn* v. *Helke*, 43 F. Supp. 1017 (S.D. Ohio 1942) (three-judge court).

Justice Jackson's opinion being devoted to the commerce clause and not to the taking issue.

From the perspective of government speech, the key event was a radio address by the secretary of agriculture entitled "Wheat Farmers and the Battle for Democracy," in which he urged them to vote affirmatively for the wheat quotas. In the course of the speech, the secretary indicated that without the quotas, wheat prices would decline drastically and that farmers would not be eligible for wheat loans. What he did not tell them was that legislation pending in Congress would increase the penalties for overproduction. More than 80 percent of the eligible wheat farmers voted favorably on the quotas, and, in essence, the plaintiff alleged that they had been misled by the secretary's remarks. The lower court responded to this by simply saying "that the equities of the case . . . favor the plaintiff," but the judgment was based on the retroactivity argument, as the lower court held that the Agricultural Adjustment Act amendments regarding penalties were unconstitutional because of the retroactive increase in penalties for overproduction.[120] Justice Jackson misconstrued the holding by declaring that the lower court had held "that the speech of the Secretary invalidated the referendum."[121]

Whether Justice Jackson decided a real case or a hypothetical one, his remarks concerning the secretary's speech are quite interesting. He disposed of the issue in two paragraphs, disputing whether the speech would have misled anyone and whether anyone listened to, or was influenced by, it:

> The record in fact does not show that any, and does not suggest a basis for even a guess as to how many, of the voting farmers dropped work to listen to "Wheat Farmers and the Battle for Democracy" at 11:30 in the morning of May 19th, which was a busy hour in one of the busiest seasons.[122]

He also noted that the text of the pending act was readily available, and that the secretary's speech did not purport to be an explication of the provisions of the bill. Finally he was concerned with the practical implications of overturning the referendum on the basis of the speech:

> To hold that a speech by a Cabinet officer, which failed to meet judicial ideals of clarity, precision, and exhaustiveness, may defeat a policy embodied in an Act of Congress, would invest communication between administrators and the people with perils heretofore unsuspected. Moreover, we should have to con-

120. 43 F. Supp. at 1018-1020. The lower court enjoined the collection of the penalties.
121. 317 U.S. at 117.
122. 317 U.S. at 117-118.

clude that such an officer is able to do by accident what he has no power to do by design.[123]

Jackson's approach to the problem of government speech in the context of the case is quite sensible. While the remedy was fairly workable—invalidation of the referendum (perhaps like overturning a representational election in the employment context where the employer has resorted to threats and misrepresentation)[124] as opposed to enjoining the secretary from speaking—Jackson was essentially saying that high-level executive officers should not be held accountable for every misstatement or omission. If they were, government leadership on vital matters of national concern might well come to a halt. The text of the bill in Congress was publicly available, and it is up to the Filburns of the nation to organize, to inform, and to voice their opposition to the ratification of the quotas. In short, the preferred response to government "propaganda" is "counter-propaganda," and not the silencing of government officials.[125] Drawing the line in terms of what is "good" or "bad" executive advocacy; of what distorts judgment and what is public leadership; and of government versus private speech by a public official is so difficult that it is preferable to rely upon the pluralistic character of the system of freedom of expression. If the secretary, by virtue of his status and access to the media, is a difficult person to whom to reply, that is an inevitable consequence of pluralism; for, just as in the political system at large, there is no guarantee that all interest groups and individuals will be equally powerful and wealthy in pressing for political solutions favorable to their interests.

Government Speech and the "Right of Reply"

The Case Against a "Right of Reply"

Another response to government speech, such as that involved in *Filburn*, in cases of publicity by a federal agency and congressional speech or debate clause litigation is to focus on requiring government to be balanced in its communications or to afford a right of reply to the government's utterances. If the remedy for government propaganda is counter-propaganda, why rely upon the vagaries of the private sector or of opposing forces within government? Why not require the government itself to present both sides of the issue, or, better yet, allow

123. *Id.* at 118.
124. See Robert Gorman, *Labor Law*, chs. 6 and 7 (St. Paul, Minn.: West Publishing, 1975). See, generally, Julius Getman, Stephen Goldberg, and Jeanne Herman, *Union Representation Elections: Law and Reality* (New York: Russell Sage Foundation, 1976).
125. See William Van Alstyne, "The First Amendment and the Suppression of Warmongering Propaganda in the United States: Comments and Footnotes," 31 *Law and Contemporary Problems* 530 (1966).

opposition groups to respond utilizing approximately the same modes of communication?[126] The difficulties with this approach are immense. Is every government message to give rise to a right of reply? If not, how do courts distinguish among those that should and those that should not? Which groups should be given such a right, and who decides? What if there are not two positions on a question but a multitude of positions? Need the government pay for such replies—including purchasing time on television and radio? What if the private media won't cooperate? What is the "public" issue which triggers the government's obligation? If we require government to be fair and balanced in its own communications, how will governments be able to carry out their essential leadership and other functions? Won't there be a tendency toward blandness as a way of coping with fairness? Is Secretary Wickard required to present the position of the anti-wheat quota referendum forces? How will the courts police his speech and determine standards of fairness, and what shall they do with Wickard and the Roosevelt administration if they fail to comply?

Apart from the questionable constitutional derivation of a fairness doctrine applied to the utterances of governments, the suggestion is impractical unless Congress or other legislative bodies were to promulgate elaborate statutes to offer guidance to the courts. And, even under those circumstances, there are severe questions about the wisdom of such measures (and about their constitutionality if the private media were required to cooperate in providing access).[127] Massive subsidization, as opposed to tolerated countervailing speech, may go too far in weakening the exercise of government's legitimate communications functions. Further, there is an inherent paradox in holding governments to affirmatively fostering private communications that would weaken them. Would they not select those critics whose positions were closest to that of the government? Would governments give a right of reply to the Republican party, the Democratic party, organized labor, corporations, or the chamber of commerce? Or would they select the Communist party, the Ku Klux Klan, socialist parties, or libertarian parties? The very process of putting government in charge of pluralism, in the sense of moving from democratic tolerance to affirmative support for opposing centers of communications, raises the danger that pluralist theory will become nothing more than a guise for reinforcing the government's position or for confining the debate to narrow limits.

126. See Lacy, "Adverse Publicity"; Michael Lemov, "Administrative Agency News Releases: Public Information Versus Private Injury," 37 *George Washington Law Review* 63, 78 (1968). Cf. Jerome Barron, *Freedom of the Press, For Whom?* (Bloomington, Ind.: Indiana University Press, 1973).

127. See *Miami Herald* v. *Tornillo*, 418 U.S. 241 (1974). But cf. *Red Lion Broadcasting* v. *FCC*, 395 U.S. 367 (1969).

This is the classic case of setting the fox to guard the chickens, as opposed to simply allowing them to roam the farmyard.

The "Fairness" Doctrine

The "fairness" doctrine formulated by the Federal Communications Commission, applied to the broadcast media, and approved by the courts, has gained notoriety, and a good deal of criticism.[128] As the Supreme Court noted in *CBS* v. *Democratic National Committee*, the doctrine requires broadcasters (not the print media) to comply with "an affirmative and independent statutory obligation to provide full and fair coverage of public issues."[129] It does not require a broadcaster to give any particular person or group a right of reply or access to the radio and TV airwaves; for the obligation may be met through balanced presentations by the broadcasters' own personnel.[130] The traditional rationale for the doctrine has to do with the asserted scarcity of airwaves and the great power of the broadcast media; the primary enforcement weapon lurks in the power of the FCC to grant and renew broadcast licenses. Numerous questions have been raised about the doctrine in terms of what constitutes fairness, what the relevant market for achieving fairness should be (within a single station or across a community, for example), whether the broadcast media are more powerful than the press, whether the scarcity argument is stronger for the broadcast media than for the print media, and whether licensees tend to cope with fairness through blandness—that is, by failing to take up controversial public issues. Experience with the fairness doctrine is such that only the hopelessly optimistic would argue for its extension into other realms. Lucas Powe has also argued that the First Amendment freedoms of the broadcast media have been severely compromised by the fairness doctrine, and that few, if any, distinctions should be drawn between different modes of media presentation. The costs of any system in which the government makes decisions about what is true, fair, balanced, and controversial are too high.[131]

128. See *Red Lion Broadcasting* v. *F.C.C.*, 395 U.S. 367, 369-371 (1969); Federal Communications Commission, *Public Service Responsibilities of Broadcast Licensees* (Washington, D.C.: GPO, 1956). See, generally, Mark Franklin, *Mass Media Law* 744-793 (Mineola, N.Y.: Foundation Press, 1977); Newton Minow, John Martin, and Lee Mitchell, *Presidential Television* ch. 3 (New York: Basic Books, 1973).

129. 412 U.S. 94, 129 (1973). Lucas A. Powe describes the fairness doctrine as having two elements: "an affirmative side requiring stations to present controversial issues of public importance and a relative side requiring that overall presentations be fair." See Powe, "Or of the [Broadcast] Press," 55 *Texas Law Review* 39, 51 (1976), citing *In re Handling of Public Issues Under the Fairness Doctrine and the Public Interest Standards of the Communications Act*, 48 F.C.C.2d 1, 7 (1974), reconsidered, 58 F.C.C.2d 691 (1976).

130. See, e.g., 412 U.S. at 94; *Democratic National Committee* v. *F.C.C.*, 481 F.2d 543 (D.C. Cir. 1973).

131. See, generally, Powe, "Or of the [Broadcast] Press."

In any event, the obligation to be fair rests with the broadcast licensee and not the government. Furthermore, the fairness doctrine itself refers to public issues, no matter who the presenter is, and not specifically to media coverage of the speech of government officials. In this regard, it is clear that there is no automatic right of reply to a presidential address or speech by other government leaders, albeit there is still the underlying obligation to present contrasting points of view.[132]

The "Equal Opportunities" and "Political Party" Doctrines

Two outgrowths of the fairness doctrine are relevant to government speech. First, section 315 of the Communications Act, the "equal opportunities" doctrine, states that "if any licensee shall permit any person who is a legally qualified candidate for any public office to use a broadcasting station, he shall afford equal opportunities to all other such candidates for that office in the use of such broadcasting station."[133] Second, there is an inchoate doctrine dubbed the "political party doctrine" that holds that "if one of the major political parties is either given or sold broadcast time to discuss candidate or election issues, the other major party must be given or allowed to purchase time."[134] These doctrines differ from fairness rules in that they provide the opportunity for groups and individuals to obtain air time. The political parties rule applies only to parties and not to any individual or officeholder, including the president; the equal opportunities rule applies to candidates and officials who are candidates for reelection (as difficult as it is to figure out when an incumbent has decided to run again).[135]

A Perspective on "Fairness" and Related Doctrines

The significant point to be drawn from this brief discussion is that fairness and related doctrines do not directly deal with government speech, although some litigants have urged the FCC to so use them. Rather, the doctrines attempt to prevent the exclusion of the candidates of one party or set of parties from the broadcast media. It is only in the context of election campaigns and assertedly nonpolitical utterances by incumbents that government-speech issues are raised. No right of ac-

---

132. See, e.g., *Democratic National Committee* v. *F.C.C.*, 460 F.2d 891 (D.C. Cir. 1972), certiorari denied, 409 U.S. 843 (1972).

133. Communications Act of 1934, 47 U.S.C. § 315(a) (1970). The "equal opportunities" doctrine is rather complex and sometimes bizarre in its applications. See, e.g., *Citizens for Reagan*, 36 Rad. Reg.2d (P & F) 885 (FCC Mar. 8, 1976); *Paulsen* v. *F.C.C.*, 491 F.2d 887 (9th Cir. 1974). See, generally, Minow, Martin, and Mitchell, *Presidential Television* 75–80; Powe, "Or of the [Broadcast] Press" 50–51.

134. Minow, Martin, and Mitchell, *Presidential Television* 87.

135. See Franklin, *Mass Media Law* 786.

cess or reply is given to private individuals as opposed to parties and candidates, and nothing more than general considerations of fairness are applicable to other forms of government speech that utilize the private broadcast media. It would be difficult to derive a statutory or constitutional argument for an overall obligation of fairness or a right of reply to government speech across the spectrum of government communications activities from so limited a conceptual basis.

The Right of Reply and the Captive Audience

Consistent with the analysis of the fairness doctrine and the case law dealing directly or indirectly with government speech, federal and state courts have not created any general right of reply to government speech or any overall framework in which government speakers must be balanced in their presentations. State legislatures have occasionally entered the realm of balanced communications, as, for example, in the case of California statutes requiring textbooks in public schools to present fairly the contributions of certain minority groups and labor and industry.[136] The major exception appears to be a decision of the United States Court of Appeals, *Bonner-Lyons* v. *School Committee of the City of Boston*.[137] In that case the school committee adopted an official resolution authorizing the distribution of notices that urged the parents to support an anti-busing rally and march at the Massachusetts State House. The organizers apparently wished to express opposition to the state's Racial Imbalance Law and to the involuntary busing of school children to achieve racially integrated schools. The notice "encouraged" parents to support a state bill that would require written consent of the parents before a student could be bused, and was critical of a desegregation proposal pending before the State Board of Education.

The notices were distributed to approximately 97,000 students by requiring each teacher to deliver a copy to each student in his or her charge. The students were the intermediaries, as the notices were specifically addressed to the parents. The school committee refused to abandon the distribution plan when challenged by the Ad Hoc Parents' Committee for Quality Education, and refused to permit the dissemination, in a similar manner, of pro-busing notices. The district court denied the plaintiffs relief, and the court of appeals reversed:

> As we read the March 30 notice, it seems apparent that this message tended to lend support and to mobilize opinion in favor of the position of those private parties who sponsored the April 3 "Parents' March on the State House." Under these circum-

---

136. See California Education Code, § 9959 (West 1970). See, generally, David Kirp and Mark Yudof, *Educational Policy and the Law* 120–134 (Berkeley, Calif.: McCutchan Publishing, 1974).

137. 480 F.2d 442 (1st Cir. 1973).

stances, we conclude that defendants, by authorizing this distribution, sanctioned the use of the school distribution system as a forum for discussion of at least those issues which were treated in the notice. When defendants' refusal to allow plaintiffs access to this system is considered in light of this conclusion, the trial court's error becomes manifest since it is well settled that once a forum is opened for the expression of views, regardless of how unusual the forum, under the dual mandate of the First Amendment and the Equal Protection Clause neither the government nor any private censor may pick and choose between those views which may or may not be expressed.[138]

The court enjoined the defendants from distributing similar notices through their employees to students on school premises, "unless fair and reasonable timely opportunity is afforded to others having differing views to use the same channels to invite attendance at or call attention to rallies and activity in furtherance of such differing views."[139]

Read literally, the court's holding is unprecedented. The court gives private individuals and groups (though unspecified except in terms of their opposition to the school committee's position) an affirmative right to reply to the school committee's messages on racial-balance issues. The cases which the court relied upon do not support this position.[140] All of the cases cited refer to the public-forum doctrine and the notion that the equal-protection clause and the First Amendment do not permit a public institution to allow some groups and individuals access to a forum while denying it to others on the basis of the institution's sympathies and the content of the messages.[141] In some cases, the forum was made available to both public and private groups,[142] but in no case was a forum opened up because the public entity itself chose to communicate its own messages. Moreover, only the forum was provided in these cases: no right of reply was created with respect to specific messages that had been transmitted.

138. *Id.* at 443-444.
139. *Id.*
140. *Police Department of Chicago* v. *Mosley*, 408 U.S. 92 (1972); *National Socialist White People's Party* v. *Ringers*, 473 F.2d 1010 (4th Cir. 1973) (*en banc*); *Women's Strike for Peace* v. *Morton*, 472 F.2d 1273 (D.C. Cir. 1972); *People Acting Through Community Effort* v. *Doorley*, 468 F.2d 1143 (1st Cir. 1972); *United States* v. *Crowthers*, 456 F.2d 1074 (4th Cir. 1972).
141. See *Jones* v. *Board of Regents of the University of Arizona*, 436 F.2d 618 (9th Cir. 1970). See, generally, Kenneth Karst, "Equality as a Central Principle in the First Amendment," 43 *University of Chicago Law Review* 20 (1975).
142. See *National Socialist White People's Party* v. *Ringers*, 473 F.2d 1010 (4th Cir. 1973) (*en banc*) (use of school auditorium permitted for a variety of public and private groups pursuant to a state law allowing public schools to rent their auditoriums during nonschool hours); *United States* v. *Crowthers*, 456 F.2d 1074 (4th Cir. 1972) (Pentagon public concourse open to public and private expression, including a speech by Vice-President Spiro Agnew).

While the *Bonner-Lyons* case may have seemed easy on the basis of its facts—what business did the school committee have in trying to sway parents on volatile busing issues through its ability to communicate with a captive audience—the court never set forth principles to guide future, more difficult cases. If some people think that the established school curriculum promotes representative democracy, do those who disagree have a right to reply through the same channels (in the classrooms)? Presumably nearly everything that is taught in public schools may occasion opposition, but to allow a right of reply in every instance would likely disable governments from carrying on important socialization and communications functions. What principled distinctions can be made among different types of government communications? And if there is a right of reply in schools, why is there not such a right with regard to the military, prisons, hospitals, and other public institutions? A right of access to public institutions *consistent with institutional mission and the substantial-disruption standard* would contribute to the alleviation of the dangers of government communications to a captive audience. But this is a far cry from a tit-for-tat right of reply to every official communication. *Bonner-Lyons* may go too far in impeding important government activities, including communication activities.

Note that *Bonner-Lyons* could have been decided on far more defensible grounds. The court noted in a footnote that school authorities had permitted a "private" group, the Home and School Association, to utilize the school distribution system for anti-busing materials that the group itself had had printed.[143] Assuming that the characterization of the group as private was correct, the court would have been justified in declaring that a public forum had been created.[144] But, again, this would simply mean that in dispensing largesse the authorities cannot pick and choose among private groups on the basis of the content of messages. It would not mean, as the court's order clearly states, that opposition groups were entitled to reply to each anti-busing message communicated by public school officials themselves. Further, if there had been an outstanding desegregation order, the school committee's communications might be perceived as fomenting opposition and noncompliance with a lawful federal court order. Perhaps an injunction (or less plausibly, a right of reply) should lie under such extraordinary circumstances.[145] But the court did not treat the case in this framework.

143. 480 F.2d at 443 n. 2.

144. See, e.g., *Police Department of Chicago* v. *Mosley*, 408 U.S. 92 (1972). *Pickings* v. *Bruce*, 430 F.2d 595 (8th Cir. 1970); *Brooks* v. *Auburn University*, 296 F. Supp. 188 (M.D. Ala. 1969). Cf. *Healy* v. *James*, 408 U.S. 169 (1972).

145. Cf. *Caldwell* v. *Craighead*, 432 F.2d 213 (6th Cir. 1970), certiorari denied, 402 U.S. 953 (1971); *Melton* v. *Young*, 328 F. Supp. 88 (E.D. Tenn. 1971).

Captive Audiences and Enjoining Government Expression: *Bonner-Lyons* Reconsidered

While I am inclined to disfavor a constitutionalized right of reply in the circumstances of *Bonner-Lyons*, the type and context of government expression in that case raises profound concerns. First, there is no doubt that the message sent to the parents through the students was the product of official school board policies and directives and could be perceived as emanating from the governmental entity itself. We are not talking about the rights of school board members to express their own positions, even in a public meeting or against the backdrop of their being elected public officials. Second, the board wished to take advantage of its position of public trust to convey this official message to a captive audience, a situation that should make us particularly sensitive to government communications excesses. Third, and most important, the message was not only blatantly partisan, but clearly fell outside the institutional mission of public schools. The message was really not even addressed to the students; it was the parents that the board wished to reach. There was not even a pretense of the message being a part of the educational process.

At a gut level, one may be offended by the school board's action in *Bonner-Lyons*. Surely, political values are communicated in civics courses, in history courses, in the manner in which a school is operated, and in the rules children are told to obey in the school environment. And presumably individual teachers and administrators, either explicitly or implicitly, communicate their views on such controversial issues as school busing in desegregation cases. But somehow this speech was different in kind, more like the distribution of pamphlets listing the names of political candidates that the school system favored. Thus, while one may be reluctant to grant a right of reply to outside groups, *Bonner-Lyons* may be one of those rare cases in which injunctive relief was appropriate. The nature of the message, the nature of the audience, and commonly held perceptions about the legitimate role of public education lead to this conclusion. As always, there may be concern about the blurred line between "propaganda" and "education," partisan and nonpartisan speech, subtle and explicit indoctrination. One should be reluctant to expand the *Bonner-Lyons* holding on injunctive relief too much. But the dangers of such communications, when weighed against the nonexistent interference with the mission of the public schools under the facts of the case, reinforce the view that the case was properly decided.

Conclusion:
Enjoining Government Expression
under an *Ultra Vires* Doctrine

The preceding chapters have discussed two constitutional modes of judicial policing of government expression and raised concerns about the institutional competence of the courts to perform this function. The danger that, in attempting to recalibrate communications networks, courts will create more problems than they solve is greatest when judicial intervention is greatest—when the courts rely on the Constitution to provide direct limits on government expression. But the other approach—considering government speech and its impact as additional factors when vindicating traditional private rights—is unduly restrictive. My preferred technique for judicial resolution of government-speech issues is a variation of the "legislative remand." When grave issues of government expression and the First Amendment are involved, a court should be especially concerned that legislative bodies authorize the communications activity. This essentially statutory approach allows the courts to police government expression, while denying the judiciary the ultimate power to silence executive officers. Courts attempt to rivet legislative attention to alleged abuses and to reach a tentative decision themselves; but, in the end, the power of resolution lies with the legislature. This intermediate method of judicial control ties together the themes of institutional competence, the difficulties of distinguishing constitutional and unconstitutional expression, and the positive and negative implications of government expression.

The *Bonner-Lyons* case discussed at the conclusion of chapter 15 provides an example of the benefits of an *ultra vires* approach. The court in *Bonner-Lyons* chose the direct approach, holding that the First Amendment and the equal-protection clause gave private groups an affirmative right to reply to the Boston school committee's messages on racial-balance issues. I have proposed an alternative rationale, based on the public-forum doctrine, which would hold that in dispensing largesse the authorities cannot pick and choose among private groups on the basis of message content—a far cry from a tit-for-tat right of reply to every official communication. Perhaps a better way to resolve cases like *Bonner-Lyons* would build on the administrative-agency publicity cases, the legislative and administrative investigation decisions, and a small body of state court decisions. One might ask whether the legislature of Massachusetts had authorized local boards of education to act in this manner, and treat such highly offensive communications as *ultra vires* in the absence of explicit legislative authorization. Such a state-law approach, rather than the constitutional approach chosen by the court, leaves the last word with the legislature.

On an *ad hoc* basis, the legislature could decide for itself what constituted objectionable and unobjectionable speech by a school system, without compromising the state's educational program. And perhaps it could give assistance to the courts in distinguishing private speech of public officials—their constitutional due—from organized governmental communications activities.

The "suspensive veto" would not be grounded in the Constitution itself; for the *ultra vires* doctrine is a method of statutory construction which permits the avoidance of constitutional difficulties. I suggest this variation of the "legislative remand"[1] approach with great trepidation.

1. The phrase "legislative remand" is a shorthand reference to a statutory version of what has been described as structural due process or structural justice. In the words of Laurence Tribe,

> We may begin by observing that all ... of the constitutional models thus far examined have been concerned with ways of achieving substantive ends through variations in governmental structures and processes of choice.
> [A structural justice] ... model [is] concerned [with] ... match[ing] decision structures with substantive human ends. ...
> I mean [then] the approach to constitutional values that either mandates or at least favors the use of particular decisional structures for specific substantive purposes in concrete contexts, without drawing on any single generalization about which decisional pattern is best suited, on the whole, to which substantive aims. ["The Emerging Reconnection of Individual Rights and Institutional Design: Federalism, Bureaucracy, and Due Process of Lawmaking," 10 *Creighton Law Review* 433, 440, 441 (1977)]

See also Hans Linde, "Due Process of Lawmaking," 55 *Nebraska Law Review* 197 (1976). For discussion of the remand to legislative bodies and related concepts, see, e.g., Terrance Sandalow, "Judicial Protection of Minorities," 75 *Michigan Law Review* 1162, 1190-1193 (1972); *idem*, "Racial Preferences in Higher Education: Political Responsibility and the Judicial Role," 42 *University of Chicago Law Review* 653 (1975); Alexander Bickel and Harry Wellington, "Legislative Purpose and the Judicial Process: The Lincoln Mills Case," 71 *Harvard Law Review* 1 (1957); Alexander Bickel, *The Least Dangerous Branch* 111-198 (Indianapolis, Ind.: Bobbs-Merrill, 1962). Cf. Paul Brest, "The Conscientious Legislator's Guide to Constitutional Interpretation," 27 *Stanford Law Review* 585 (1975).

Tribe notes that structural concerns are inherent in cases in which the Court holds "that the challenged delegation had gone beyond the bounds of Congress' power to abdicate responsibility for substantive policy choice" (*supra* at 441). Thus, it is not just the substance of a law, rule, or activity that is constitutionally significant, but also the manner in which it is made or authorized that may count against its validity (*id.* at 442):

While the error of placing ultimate authority with the courts in a rigid constitutional framework has been avoided, it is not at all clear when it is appropriate for courts to intervene even on this more limited basis. Presumably, not all government speech should be subjected to a presumption that it is *ultra vires* in the absence of explicit legislative endorsement; for not all such speech arouses concern, and legislatures cannot be expected to sanction, or even think about, the endless variety of government communications. The propaganda/education distinction, for example, appears no less tenuous in the context of legislative remand than it is in its substantive constitutional garb. And even enjoining government speech on a temporary basis, pending legislative action (which is hardly inevitable) may have a crippling effect on governments' legitimate operations. And what if the legislature seeks to restrain executive speech as a way of gaining an advantage in the conflicts among branches of government? Or fails to act at all in blatant cases? I feel obligated to make the suggestion, in large measure, because state courts in a relatively large number of cases have utilized the *ultra vires* technique to grant injunctions limiting government communication activities without, apparently, precipitating any dire effects.[2] And state legislative bodies have almost invariably declined the opportunity to overturn the suspensive veto of the state courts.

An excellent example of the treatment of some forms of government speech in state courts is *Stanson* v. *Mott*,[3] decided by the Supreme Court of California in 1976. In that case, California voters were faced with a $250 million bond referendum, the bond monies to be used for

---

Both the *Panama Refining* approach and that of *Hampton put pressure on legislatures and/or agencies to reconsider the invalidated provision from a fresh perspective, and both approaches leave open the possibility that the Court may uphold a somewhat revised provision if such reconsideration leads to its enactment in an altered form or by a different body*. Thus both approaches bear some similarity to the notion of "remand to the legislature" often advocated by constitutional and common-law commentators. [*id*. at 442-443. Emphasis added]

The suggestion is that legislatures be required to consider the wisdom of certain types of government communications activities through the mechanism of enjoining the activity until such time, if ever, that the legislature chooses to authorize it.

2. See *Stanton* v. *Mott*, 17 Cal. 2d 206, 551 P.2d 1, 130 Cal. Rptr. 697 (1976); *Mines* v. *Del Valle*, 201 Cal. 273, 257 P. 530 (1927); *Harrison* v. *Rainey*, 227 Ga. 240, 179 S.E.2d 923 (1971); *Elsenau* v. *Chicago*, 334 Ill. 78, 165 N.E. 129 (1929); *Citizens to Protect Public Funds* v. *Board of Education*, 13 N.J. 172, 98 A.2d 673 (Sup. Ct. 1953) (Brennan, J.); *Stewart* v. *Scheinert*, 84 Misc.2d 1086, 374 N.Y.S.2d 585 (Sup. Ct. 1975); *Porter* v. *Tiffany*, 11 Or. App. 542, 502 P.2d 1385 (1972); *State* v. *Superior Court*, 93 Wash. 267, 160 P. 755 (1916). Cf. *Stern* v. *Kramarsky*, 84 Misc.2d 447, 375 N.Y.S.2d 235 (Sup. Ct. 1975). But see also *City Affairs Commission* v. *Board of Commissioners*, 132 N.J.L. 532, 41 A.2d 798 (Sup. Ct. 1945). For a parallel federal decision see *Mountain States Legal Foundation* v. *Denver School Dist. No. 1*, 459 F. Supp. 357 (D. Colo. 1978).

3. 17 Cal. 3d 206, 551 P.2d 1, 130 Cal. Rptr. 697 (1976); see also *Miller* v. *Miller*, 87 Cal. App.3d 762, 151 Cal. Rptr. 197 (Ct. App. 1978).

future acquisition of park land and recreational and historical facilities by state and local governments. The plaintiff, a taxpayer, alleged that the defendant Mott, director of the California Department of Parks and Recreation, had authorized the expenditure of $5,000 in public funds to promote the passage of the bond issue. The $5,000 was used for "promotional materials" written and published by the department staff or private groups, for the expenses of speaking engagements to promote the bond issue, and for a three-person staff to engage in similar activities. The court held that the expenditure of tax funds for such purposes had not been authorized by the California legislature, and further noted that

> every court which has addressed the issue to date has found the use of public funds for partisan campaign purposes improper, either on the ground that such use was not explicitly authorized . . . or on the broader ground that such expenditures are never appropriate.[4]

While not relying on the broader constitutional view,[5] the court noted that judicial reluctance to sanction such government communications activities as those in question had its roots in constitutional and democratic precepts:

> Underlying this uniform judicial reluctance to sanction the use of public funds for election campaigns rests an implicit recognition that such expenditures raise potentially serious constitutional questions. A fundamental precept of this nation's democratic electoral process is that the government may not "take sides" in election contests or bestow an unfair advantage on one of several competing factions. A principal danger feared by our country's founders lay in the possibility that the holders of governmental authority would use official power improperly to perpetuate themselves, or their allies, in office . . . ; the selective use of public funds in election campaigns, of course, raises the specter of just such an improper distortion of the democratic electoral processes.[6]

The state supreme court noted the difficulty in distinguishing "improper 'campaign' expenditures from proper 'informational' activities," but relegated this factual question to the lower court for determination in the light of a "careful consideration of such factors as the

---

4. 17 Cal. 3d at 217, 551 P.2d at 8-9, 130 Cal. Rptr. at 704-705. The court's statement is technically in error since I have found one case in which such authority was upheld (see *City Affairs Commission* v. *Board of Commissioners*, 132 N.J.L. 532, 41 A.2d 798 [Sup. Ct. 1945]). But see *Citizens to Protect Public Funds* v. *Board of Education*, 13 N.J. 172, 98 A.2d 673 (Sup. Ct. 1953).

5. See *Stern* v. *Kramarsky*, 84 Misc.2d 1086, 375 N.Y.S.2d 235 (1975).

6. 17 Cal. 3d at 217, 551 P.2d at 9, 130 Cal. Rptr. at 705.

style, tenor and timing of the publication." It could formulate "no hard and fast rule govern[ing] every case."[7] In terms of remedies, the court held that if the plaintiff succeeded in meeting his burden of proof, he would be entitled to a declaratory judgment that the expenditures were unauthorized and to an injunction against such activities if they were threatened in the future. The defendant public official, however, could not be held strictly liable for the unauthorized expenditures; rather he could be held liable only if he had failed to exercise "reasonable diligence, in authorizing the expenditure of public funds."[8] The court did not indicate that appropriate relief would include the overturning of the referendum result (the voters had approved the bond issue).

From *Stanson* and other cases, it appears that a number of factors enter into the calculus of whether particular government communications should be subjected to a strict test of legislative authorization. First, all of the cases involve government communications during the pendency of public elections or referenda. The courts feel that this is a critical point in democratic processes,[9] and that government attempts to influence election results are peculiarly suspect. Second, the objectionable speech involves something more than isolated instances of government involvement in partisan campaigns: the courts have not restrained individual officials from speaking out on public issues—albeit the question of who is footing the bill for the speech is often unclear. Third, almost invariably, the cases involve the dedication of a specific sum of tax monies to the communications activity. Fourth, it is usually abundantly clear that the messages are one-sided and seek to influence political results: these are not simply minor lapses in an objective and balanced presentation of the issues. Finally, the courts have tended to permit local governments to finance lobbying activities with the state legislature in terms of financing and presentation of their views to individual state legislators and legislative committees.[10] They are most hostile to the expenditures where they promote mailing and advertising campaigns directed explicitly to the voters.

Whether these criteria are satisfactory is an issue difficult to resolve. The information/partisan advocacy distinction remains elusive. There may be much to be gained by a *per se* rule that the legislative remand

---

7. 17 Cal. 3d at 221-222, 551 P.2d at 11-12, 130 Cal. Rptr. at 707-708.

8. 17 Cal. 3d at 226, 551 P.2d at 15, 130 Cal. Rptr. at 711.

9. See cases cited in note 2, *supra*. See, generally, *Monitor Patriot Co.* v. *Roy*, 401 U.S. 265, 272 (1971) (the First Amendment "has its fullest and most urgent application to the conduct of campaigns for political office"); and *Buckley* v. *Valeo*, 424 U.S. 1 (1976).

10. See, e.g., *Stanson* v. *Mott*, 17 Cal.3d 206, 218, 551 P.2d 1, 9, 130 Cal. Rptr. 697, 705 (1976); *Powell* v. *San Francisco*, 62 Cal. App.2d 291, 144 P.2d 617 (1944); *Crawford* v. *Imperial Irrigation District*, 200 Cal. 318, 253 P. 726 (1927). But cf. *Port of Seattle* v. *Lamping*, 135 Wash. 569, 238 P. 615 (1925). Compare also *Mulqueeny* v. *National Commission*, 549 F.2d 1115 (7th Cir. 1977).

should operate only during the pendency of elections; that, in itself, would greatly limit the scope of judicial interference with governmental communications activities. On the other hand, the distinction between electoral politics and, for example, interest-group politics seems to be an artificial one. Why is lobbying—an attempt to influence legislators—different in kind from an attempt to influence public opinion, which will in turn influence legislators?[11] Is the bond election in *Stanson* much different, in terms of the dangers of government speech, from the campaign in *Bonner-Lyons* to influence the state legislature? Certainly, one would be hard pressed to say that one issue was more or less partisan or controversial than the other, and the possibility of distortion of democratic processes is apparent in both cases.

The distinction between organized, publicly funded government communications and more sporadic utterances at virtually no public expense is also troublesome. The speech by the secretary of agriculture in *Filburn*, utilizing radio time for which neither Wickard nor the government paid, might be more likely to distort election or referenda outcomes than the three-person team in *Stanson* publishing and mailing out pamphlets at public expense. Perhaps this indicates that the state courts in the government-speech cases are more concerned with the misapplication of tax monies than with any other issue. Alternatively, perhaps some line is being drawn between types of government officials: high level, policy-making officials, both appointed and elected, are free to seek to influence political outcomes, whereas lower-echelon civil servants are to remain isolated from, or neutral toward, the political processes. Hence, Secretary Wickard might engage in a course of conduct and communications activities that would be forbidden to ordinary bureaucrats.[12] Indeed, this may be the real distinction between "isolated" speeches (which are generally made by higher level officials) and organized government communications activities (implying that many hands need participate in the enterprise, including those in non-policy-making roles).

The primary benefit of the legislative-remand approach is that it seeks to compel legislatures to grapple with government-speech issues. If the legislature is the one branch of government most likely to seek to address government-speech excesses, a judicial approach that seeks to focus legislative attention on such issues and encourages legislative debate and resolution of the role of government speech in a democracy is a desirable one. And, at least in part, it avoids the charge of an imperial judiciary, ruling in the stead of elected representatives.

11. See *First National Bank of Boston* v. *Bellotti*, 435 U.S. 765, n. 31 (1978); and, generally, Charles Lindblom, *Politics and Markets* (New York: Basic Books, 1977).

12. Cf. 5 U.S.C. § 1502(a), (c) (1976), which exempts governors, lieutenant governors, mayors, heads of executive departments, and so on, from the ban on state or local officers and employees working in federally financed programs taking "an active part in political management or in political campaigns." See also Hatch Act, 5 U.S.C. § 7324 (1976).

Index

Academic freedom, 215-218; history, 216

Access
—to administrative proceedings, 247
—to ballots, 239
—to committee hearings, 247
—to criminal proceedings, 248, 251-255
—to government facilities: information dissemination, 250; information gathering, 250
—to government information, 92, 94 *n9*, 246, 281-282; balancing test, 254; and falsified consent, 249; and self-controlled citizen, 249; and self-governance, 249, 253-254. *See also* Secrecy, government
—to government operations, 247
—to government printing office, 240
—to information, 90-91; Congress, 181; executive branch, 181; government, 254; mass media, 250-251; public, 251
—to judicial proceedings, 248, 251-255
—to local government records, 248 *n10*
—to media, 258; by public, 85; by students, 226
—to military bases, 227
—to prisons, 250, 254
—to private information, 247, 249 *n18*
—to public broadcasting, 240
—to public forum, 235, 240, 242. *See also* Public forum
—to schools, 225-227
—to total institutions, 247

Ackerman, B., 151 *n23*

Administrative agencies, 204; publicity, 203, 289-290

Administrative hearings: criminal, 286-288; due process, 287

Administrative investigations, 288-289

Administrative law, 204

Advertisement, 78, 114, 258; corporations, 98-99, 162-164; federal funding, 56-57, 62, 65; government, 7-8, 47, 48-50, 56-60, 113, 172-173, 203, 304, 305; misleading, 168-169

Advertising agencies, 56, 59

Advertising Council, 57-62, 114; business bias, 59; federal funding, 59; federal government, 59-61; preemption of time, 58-59; private funding, 59-60

Advocacy: controversy, 257; unconstitutional values, 219-220, 260-263, 296. *See also* Incitement

Affirmative liberty, 135

Aggression research, 284

Agnew, S., 130

Agricultural Adjustment Act of 1938, 290-291

Alcoholism, 267, 275, 278-279

Alienation, 103, 107

Aliens: democratic values, 222-223; teachers, 220-224. *See also* Fourteenth Amendment

Ambach v. Norwick, 220-224, 230

American Bar Association (ABA), 197

Amish, 231, 232

Anarchy, 39, 107; schools, 119

Anderson, C.: quoted, 98-99

Anderson v. Martin, 261-266 passim

Anti-Fascist Committee v. McGrath, 264-267, 287-289

Antimajoritarianism, 161, 178

Anti-Semitism, 260

Antiwar protest, 156

Apollo, 17, 131

Arrow, K., 154 *n30*

Art: complexity, 28

Associational rights, 43, 160, 202, 246, 256-258; history, 257; political speech, 257; regulation, 256; speech, 257-258; teachers, 220

Association of American Law Schools (AALS), 197

Attitudes: and behavior, 83; children, 83; formation, 112; instability, 83; reinforcement, 84

Audience, 74, 78-79; 119-120; captive, 165, 169-170, 173, 202, 204, 213-218, 220, 224, 226-228, 231-233, 247, 296-299; characteristics, 75, 76, 80-82, 217; defensive reactions, 80; inattentiveness, 79; maturity, 80; mental ability, 81; obstinate, 80; research on, 75; resistance, 77; selectivity, 77; self-esteem, 81

Authoritarian ideal, 20; flaws, 21

Authoritarianism, 20, 38, 102; asymmetrical power, 30. *See also* Totalitarianism

Authoritarian personality, 81

Authority, 119-120

Autonomy, 51, 52, 54-56, 73, 89, 101-102, 103, 106, 152, 155; institutional, 136-137; and mass media, 36; promoted by government, 33, 34, 40

Balkanization of government, 13, 115-116, 121-122, 137-138, 216. *See also* Decentralization; Delegation

Ballots: access, 239; race of candidates stated on, 261-262, 266. *See also* Elections

Bardach, E.: quoted, 120

Basic skills, 230, 232

Bauer, R.: quoted, 75

Benedict, R.: quoted, 53

Bickel, A.: quoted, 137, 147-148 *passim*

Bill of Rights, 44, 256, 287, 289; incorporation doctrine, 158

Bishop v. Wood, 275-276

Black, C., 158-161 *passim,* 217; quoted, 150, 159

Blasi, V., 147, 156-157; quoted, 160

Blum, J.: quoted, 64 *n48*

Board of Regents of State Colleges v. Roth, 267-271 *passim,* 274-275

Bonds, 113 *n5,* 303

Bonner-Lyons v. School Committee of the City of Boston, 296-299, 301-302, 306

Boorstein, D.: quoted, 31-32 *passim*

Bork, R., 106

Boulding, K.: quoted, 20-22 *passim,* 153 *n28*

Bowles, S. M.: quoted, 130-132

Boy Scouts, 64

Brainwashing, 88. *See also* Indoctrination

Brest, P.: quoted, 195

Bribery, 193

British Broadcasting Corporation (BBC), 136

Broadcast licenses, 27, 294

Broadcast media, 255; candidates for public office, 295-296; elections, 295; fairness doctrine, 294; First Amendment, 294; political parties, 295-296; regulation, 294. *See also* Mass media; Public broadcasting

Brown v. Louisiana, 227

Buchanan, J.: quoted, 149-150

Buckley v. Valeo, 237-240

Buckley, W. F., 131

Bureaucracy, 12, 119, 175; inertia, 122-123; public relations, 182. *See also* Organizations

Business. *See* Corporations
Busing, 296

Cabinet, 45, 291. *See also* Executive branch
Calabresi, G., 109
Camus, A.: quoted, xv
Canalization, 79, 82
Canby, W.: quoted, 130, 241-244 *passim*
Captive audience. *See* Audience, captive
Carnegie Foundation, 127-128
Carroll, L.: quoted, 108
Cater, D.: quoted, 108
Censorship, 18, 63, 156, 158, 159, 162, 189, 202, 206, 240, 243; public schools, 243-244; school newspapers, 218-220. *See also* First Amendment
Centralization: falsified consent, 179; government, 175
Checking power, 156-157
Child abuse, 193
Children, 51-53, 193, 213, 217, 224-227, 228-233, 256, 270-271, 296; attitudes, 83
Choper, J.: quoted, 177
Citizenship, 221-224
City of Boston v. Anderson, 43 *n22*
Civility, 108
Civil liberties, 145-146, 157, 176-177, 179
Civil rights, 162-163, 178; majoritarianism, 161; protests, 227; suits, 272, 274; state law, 274
Civil rights Act, 219
Civil Service Commission, 186
Classified documents, 248
Clear and present danger tests, 62. *See also* Advocacy; First Amendment
Coase, R., 93
Codd v. Velger, 276-279
Coercion, 33, 42, 73-74, 77, 79, 86, 195
Cognitive dissonance, 80-83

Columbia Broadcasting Systems Inc. v. Democratic National Committee, 240-241, 294
Commager, H.: quoted, 146 *n2*
Commerce clause, 203
Committee on Public Information. *See* Creel Committee
Communications Act of 1934, 295
Communications: centralization, 41; courts, 192-195; effectiveness, 113-114, 291; government, 16; marketplace, 92; monopoly, 77; pluralism, 200-203, 213, 219, 220; two-step, 296
Communications networks, 24, 117, 162-164; complexity, 72, 91, 164, 173; distortion, 164; domination by corporations, 163; domination by government, 158-159, 161, 164, 165, 201-202, 225, 245, 258, 260; judicial review, 204, 259; modern, 35; monopoly, 49; pluralism, 188, 230, 255, 258, 260; power, 28
Communications overload, 90, 117-118, 155
Communications research, 74-89 *passim*, 97, 114; complexity, 87; controlled experiments, 76, 78; inadequate, 87; polemical writings, 85-89; scientific evidence, 87
Communications revolution, 31-32
Communications Satellite Corporation, 128
Communications theory, 5, 74-89 *passim*, 113; audience characteristics, 80; "bullet" theory, 74-75, 81; cognitive dissonance, 81-82; complexity, 82; congruity, 82; simplification, 100-101; two-step, 76, 80
Communicator: characteristics, 77-78, 213, 224, 258; monopoly, 77; self-interest, 78
Communism, 180, 223, 257, 264
Communist Control Act of 1954, 176
Community, 103, 106-107; individuals, 89; mediating institutions, 107
Compelling state interest, 48, 201, 239

Competition, 92-93

Complexity, 101; art, 28; communication effectiveness, 180; communications, 87; communications networks, 72, 91, 164, 173; communications theory, 82; democracy, 100; government functions, 115-116; mass communications, 75-76, 84-85; pluralism, 95; public broadcasting, 133; time, 27

Compulsory education, 216, 229, 230-233

Conflict, 106-107

Confrontation of witnesses, 287

Congress, 123-124, 179, 191, 203; access to information, 181; civil liberties, 176-177; communications power, 179; Corporation for Public Broadcasting, 129; executive branch, 181-182, 185-188; falsified consent, 180-181; First Amendment, 174; fragmentation, 181, 184-185; hearings and investigations, 8, 184; information function, 282; journal, 247-248; legislative functions, 280; nonlegislative functions, 280; power, 180, 185; public relations, 182-185; reports, 283-284; speech, 282; speech or debate clause, 280-286; subpoena, 282

Congressional Record, 186

Congress, members of: personal liability, 281; speech, 282

Conscientious objection, 233

Consensus, 84, 149, 150, 154, 180-181, 193, 230; social cohesion, 87

Consent, 15, 20-21, 32, 42, 49, 89, 91, 135, 138, 148, 149, 152-154, 157, 158-160, 165, 175, 177-179, 186-189, 193, 200, 201, 249. *See also* Legitimacy

Constitutional interpretation, 19, 166, 191, 194, 205; courts, 177-178; framers' intent, 151; history, 160-161; judicial finality, 190; legislatures, 167, 174-175, 177; preferred interests, 178; structuralism, 148, 158-161, 178, 218, 253-254; textual

analysis, 159. *See also* Judicial review

Constitutional rights: derivative, 160. *See also* First Amendment; Fourteenth Amendment

Constitutional torts, 273

Constitutions: written, 150

Constrained volitions, 101-102

Consultation processes, 176, 178

Contempt, 288-289

Contraceptives, 256

Contract law, 34, 193

Cornwell, E.: quoted, 55-56 *passim,* 64 *n46*

Corporation for Public Broadcasting, 128, 133, 240; autonomy, 128, 136; Congress, 129; partisan politics, 129; political pressure, 130-131; president, 129

Corporations, 44, 161, 203, 251, 255, 256; advertisement, 98-99, 162-164; communications methods, 97; domination of communication, 163; government, 96-97; indoctrination, 100-102; mass media, 97; power, 95-100, 102-103; privilege, 98-100; public functions, 95-96; public opinion, 96-97; speech, 42-43, 45, 163, 164, 201-202; veto power, 99-100

Corrupt Practices Act of 1967, 163

Countermajoritarian difficulty, 147, 152

Courts, 175, 177; access, 248; civil liberties, 177; coercion, 195; communications powers, 179, 194; constitutional interpretation, 177-178; dispute resolution, 193; impact of decisions, 194; independence, 177; instrumental power, 193-194; judicial legislation, 147; law clerks, 197; leadership, 192; legitimacy, 190-191, 195; media access, 251-254; oral argument, 197; persuasion, 166, 189, 190, 192-195, 259; power, 166, 180, 185, 259; public relations, 195-199; published opinions, 195-197; restraints, 271; secrecy, 198; symbolic power, 193-199; unanimity, 196. *See also* Judicial review

Cox v. State of New Hampshire, 236

Creel Committee, 63-64, 121, 123

Creel, G.: quoted, 63, 64 *n64*

Criminal process: defendants, 289; law, 168; proceedings, 162, 251-255, 286-288; procedure, 180; trial, 248, 289

Curriculum, 217, 220, 229, 231-233, 241, 298; private schools, 233

Curtis, T.: quoted, 182-183 *passim*

Cybernetics, 22-23, 24, 72, 112. *See also* Feedback

Dahl, R.: quoted, 147 *n6,* 191 *n35*

Damages, 206-207, 279, 280, 282; due process, 277; nonlegislative functions, 282; against senators, 286

Davis, E., 122

Decentralization: delegation, 243; public broadcasting, 129-130; Public Broadcasting System, 130-131; schools, 118, 216. *See also* Balkanization of government; Delegation

Declaratory judgments, 205-206, 287, 305

Defamation, 26, 188, 207, 267, 272; burden of proof of falsity, 276; by government, 164; by public officials, 264, 284-286; civil rights suits, 274; deterrent effect of suits, 279; legislative function, 285-286; nonlegislative speech, 286, 287; publication, 275; public figures, 286; speech or debate clause, 285-286; state action, 273; state law, 272-274, 278, 279; traditional litigation, 279. *See also* Libel

Delegation, 135, 205; autonomous agencies, 138; decentralization, 243; editorial control, 243-245; partisan politics, 243; politics, 137; public broadcasting, 126, 133, 134; public schools, 243-244; revocable, 244; specialization, 136, 243, 244.

See also Balkanization of government; Decentralization

Democratic ideal, 102; flawed, 21-22

Democracy, 20, 38, 39, 41-42, 44, 51, 66, 74, 90, 91, 93, 98, 102-103, 112, 157, 160-161; communications networks, 22; complexity, 100; conflict with technology, 13; education, 54-55; legitimacy, 249; mutually affecting relationships, 21; pluralism, 108-109; public schools, 221-224; scientific method, 104-105; selectivity, 32; self-controlled citizens, 32; symmetrical power, 30. *See also* Polyarchy

Democratic values, 107-108, 111-112, 164; aliens, 222-223. *See also* Fundamental beliefs

Demography, 12

Department of Agriculture, 56

Desegregation, 192, 194, 256, 296. *See also* Segregation

Deutsch, K.: quoted, 5, 22, 202

Dewey, J., 54-55; quoted, 104

Dictatorship, 51, 56. *See also* Authoritarian ideal; Authoritarianism; Preceptoral state

Dignity, 43, 73, 89, 145, 152

Discipline, 270; public schools, 270-271

Disclosure of sources, 190. *See also* Press

Dissipative structures, 26

Distortion of judgment, 49, 66, 91, 117-118, 177, 201, 204-205, 225; advertisement, 168; by government, 168-169, 260; by individuals, 260; communications networks, 164; elections, 306; media, 93

Distrust, 114; of corporations, 98

Diversity, 108. *See also* Pluralism

Doe v. McMillan, 280-284, 285, 288

Due Process, 45, 158, 203, 256, 271, 275-276; administrative hearings, 287; burden of proof, 276; consistency, 279; criminal trial, 289; damages, 277; employability, 274-275; exclusive remedy for damage

to reputation, 277; government expression, 288; hearings, 277; impartiality, 279; injunctions, 277; liberty interest, 265, 267-268, 274, 276; nontenured professors, 268; personal reputation, 267; preadjudicatory publicity, 289-290; privacy, 273; property interest, 274; reinstatement, 277; remedies, 276-280; reputation, 272; "stigma plus" doctrine, 274-275, 277; stigmatizing government expression, 264-280
Dworkin, R., 164 *n17*

Education, 12, 40, 42, 51, 52, 53, 54, 88, 166, 189; by courts, 192; democratic, 54-55; pluralism, 230; public monopoly, 230. *See also* Parochial schools; Private schools; Public schools
Educational Television Broadcasting Facilities Act of 1962, 127
Elections, 7, 42, 48, 49, 159, 162-164, 176, 203; broadcast media, 295; campaigns, 84; candidates' race, 261-262, 266; compelling state interest, 239; distortion, 306; government domination, 237-240; government expression, 305; primaries, 237; private funding, 237-240; public funding 46, 170-171, 237-240; regulation, 239-240
Eleventh Amendment, 45
Ely, J. H., 253
Emerson, T.: quoted, 170
Employability: due process hearing, 274-275; public school teachers, 270; reputation, 269. *See also* Public employment
Employer speech, 168, 292
Enforcement: mechanisms, 150; power, 190
Entertainment, 85
Equal opportunity doctrine, 295
Equal protection, 221, 277; First Amendment, 225, 235, 239, 240, 297, 298, 301. *See also* Fourteenth Amendment
Equilibrium, 23, 82, 83, 101, 103; government communication power, 180; physics, 26; theory, 22
Espionage acts, 62-63
Establishment clause, 165, 173, 214-215, 234, 238, 239
Executive branch, 47, 56, 177, 179, 291; access to information, 181; and Congress, 94 *n9;* immunity, 282; influence on referendum, 291; misrepresentation, 291; power, 175; public accusation, 287; public relations, 64, 175, 181-182, 184, 185; speech, 291-292. *See also* Cabinet; President
Exogenetic heritage, 12, 53 *n10,* 54

Fairness doctrine, 62; balance, 294; broadcast media, 294; controversy, 294; government expression, 292-296; right of reply, 295-296
Falsified consent, 15, 42, 49, 90-91, 112-113, 138, 145, 152, 157, 159, 165, 175, 177, 178-179, 186-189, 193, 200-202, 204-205, 259; access to government information, 249; Congress, 180-181; government secrecy, 254
Family, 229-233, 257, 267; indoctrination, 232; private schools, 230; regulation, 229; socialization, 231-233. *See also* Mediating institutions
FCC v. Pacifica Foundation, 231
Fear arousal, 79-80, 82
Federal Communications Act of 1934, 126
Federal Communications Commission (FCC), 57, 62, 126-127, 133, 184, 294
Federal courts, 273-274; door closing, 280. *See also* Courts; Judicial review
Federal government, 44-45; Advertising Council, 59-61; limited powers, 44-45, 47, 159, 261. *See also* Administrative agencies; Cabinet; Congress; Courts; Government; Government expression; President
Federalism, 45
Federalist Papers, 190

Federal Radio Act of 1972, 126
Federal Trade Commission (FTC), 288
Feedback, 23-24, 76, 82
Festinger, L., 82
Fifth Amendment, 273, 287
Films, 122
First Amendment, 17, 22, 34-35, 90, 228, 240; broadcast media, 294; check on official power, 156-157, 160; clear and present danger test, 62, 168, 259-260; compelling state interest, 201, 239; Congress, 174; delegation, 243; equal protection, 225, 235, 239, 240, 297, 298, 301; government expression, 43-48; minorities, 146-147; private expression, 46, 63; public officials, 50; restriction of government, 159; school newspapers, 218-220; self-realization, 162-163; simplification, 145; structuralism, 253-254; students, 224-255; substantial disruption test, 219. *See also* Academic freedom; Associational rights; Broadcast media; Censorship; Establishment clause; Freedom of press; Marketplace of ideas; Petition; Press; Public forum
First National Bank v. Bellotti, 42-44 *passim,* 162-164, 201
Ford Foundation, 127-128
Ford, G., 60, 132
Foreign affairs, 10, 40, 94 *n9,* 113, 166
Fornication, 256
"Four-minute men," 63
Fourteenth Amendment, 219, 228, 263, 273, 287. *See also* Due process; Equal protection
Fourth Amendment, 273
France: public broadcasting, 125, 126
Frankel, C.: quoted, 153
Frankfurter, F., 194
Franking privilege, 8-9, 171, 181
Freedom of Information Act, 47, 166, 249 *n18*
Freedom of information acts, 162, 177, 188, 248
Freedom of press, 250, 255. *See also* Press

Freedom pf speech, 277; teachers, 215-218. *See also* First Amendment
Freund, P.: quoted, 198
Froehlke: quoted, 57
Fuller, L.: quoted, 204
Fundamental beliefs, 98, 101, 102. *See also* Democratic values

Gannett Co. v. DePasquale, 251-253 *passim*
General Accounting Office (GAO), 129
Gerrymandering, 176
Gilmore, G.: quoted, 191
Goebbel, J., 121
"Golden Fleece" award, 284
Goldstein, S.: quoted, 216 *n11,* 217
Goldstene, P.: quoted, 10
Goss v. Lopez, 270-271, 272
Gouldner, A., 119
Government: regulation of speech, 92-93; right of expression, 42-43. *See also* Federal government; Government expression; Local government
Government employees: political speech, 306. *See also* Employability; Public employment
Government expression: accuracy, 265-267; administrative agencies, 203; attitudes toward, 111-112; bias, 305; Congressional regulation, 186-188; Constitutional limits, 259-299; direct limits, 301; disclosure of private information, 288; due process, 288; editorial control, 240-245; elections, 305; fairness doctrine, 292-294, 295-296; First Amendment, 43-48; incitement test, 260-263; indirect limits, 301; injunction, 282, 288; institutional goals, 173, 299; judicial limitation, 189; judicial review, 280; justiciability, 165-173; labeling messages, 173; legislative authorization, 302-306; legitimacy, 241, 266-267, 282; limitation of abuse, 174-175; organizations, 116; partisan, 170-172, 304; to promote autonomy, 232-233; public fund-

ing, 173, 305, 306; public schools, 222-223; remedies, 44-45, 94, 190, 200-203, 215, 222, 226-227, 258, 263-265, 280, 299, 306; restraints, 266-267; right of reply, 294, 296-298; school prayer, 214-215; stigmatizing, 264-280; taxation, 170, 189; traditional litigation, 202-203; ultra vires, 188-189; unconstitutional values, 219

Government information: gathering, 10, 46, 254. *See also* Access to government information; Information; Mass media; Public service advertisement; Secrecy, government

Government operations: access to, 247. *See also* Access

Government Printing Office (GPO), 9, 113, 186-187; access, 240; good faith immunity, 283; publication of research, 187; remedies, 282; speech or debate clause, 281. *See also* Government publications

Government publications: injunctions, 289. *See also* Government Printing Office

Government secrecy. *See* Secrecy, government

Greer v. Spock, 227

Griffith, E.: quoted, 181-182 *passim*

Grodzins, M.: quoted, 115-116 *passim*

Gusfield, J.: quoted, 193

Hamilton, A.: quoted, 190

Hare, R.: quoted, 52

Hatch Act, 186, 306 *n12*

Health care, 229

Hierarchies, 45, 137; public schools, 216. *See also* Organizations

Hiring policies: judicial restraint, 271; private schools, 220-224, 230. *See also* Employability; Public employment

Hirschoff, M., 231-232

Hitler, A., 75

Holmes, O., 105-107 *passim*

Homet, R.: quoted, 126, 135

Homicide, 273

Homogeneity, 85; and private schools, 229-230; public schools, 221-224, 227

Homosexuality, 256, 279

Hooks, B. L. 133-135

House of Representatives: public relations, 183-184. *See also* Congress

Housing discrimination: government advocacy, 261

Hutchinson v. Proxmire, 284-286

Hypnosis, 73

Ideology, 117

Implementation, 71, 113, 116

Incitement: by government, 260-263. *See also* Advocacy

Indeterminacy, 82-83

Individualism, 33, 53, 54-55, 86, 103, 106, 161, 162-163; community, 89; conflict with technology, 10-11; preceptoral state, 34. *See also* Liberalism

Individual responsibility, 60-61

Indoctrination, 25, 42, 52, 88, 89, 94, 96-98, 112, 113, 152, 156-157, 160, 166, 169, 172, 186, 189; corporations, 100-102; effectiveness, 170; family, 232; military, 65, 227; public access to information, 15; private schools as a counter to, 229; public schools, 217, 224, 232; religion, 214-215. *See also* Persuasion; Propaganda

Industrialization, 12

Information, 42, 43, 66; distortion, 45; gathering by government,10, 46

Informing function: government, 282, 285

Injunctions, 206, 266, 280, 282, 299, 305; Congressional reports, 283-284; Congressional speech, 282; due process, 277; government expression, 282, 288; government publications, 289; libel, 284; nonlegislative functions, 282; public accusation, 287; "quasi-criminal" hearings, 289; senators, 286

Insko, C.: quoted, 78-80 *passim,* 82

Institutional goals: government expression, 265-266, 299; right of reply, 298

Institutions: routines, 120-121. *See also* Implementation; Organizations

Interest groups, 91, 92, 94, 98, 99, 103, 106, 114, 161, 251, 292, 306. *See also* Pluralism

Internal Revenue Service (IRS), 114, 237

Interpersonal communication, 76-77

Interstate commerce, 188, 290

Jehovah's Witnesses, 146, 236

Jenkins v. MacKeithen, 286-288

Johnson, L. B., 60, 64 *n47,* 128

Joyner v. Whiting, 218-220

Judicial. *See* Courts

Judicial review, 147-149, 150, 160, 166, 174, 175, 177, 179, 195; communications networks, 204; First Amendment, 173; government expression, 280; history, 190-191; legitimacy, 191-192; minorities, 146; reasoned elaboration, 191

Justiciability, 174; limits on government expression, 165-173

Kariel, H., 93

Kennedy, J. R., 60, 64 *n47*

Key, V.O.: quoted, 84-85

Klapper, J.: quoted, 83

Ku Klux Klan, 146

Labor laws, 229

Labor unions, 98-99, 161, 168, 180, 201, 226, 255, 256, 286, 290

Leadership, 15, 41, 42, 55, 56, 66, 76, 112, 166, 189, 292; courts, 192; opinion, 76, 80; schools, 118. *See also* Opinion leadership

Legal education, 62-63

Legal theory, 12, 15-16, 22; contracts, 35; distortion, 25; First Amendment, 19, 22; looks to the past, 19, 24; multi-disciplinary problems,

30; simplification, 24-25, 31, 34-35, 90-91, 145, 151, 155. *See also* Constitutional interpretation

Legislative remand, 188-189, 301-303, 305-306. *See also* Structural due process; Ultra vires

Legislature, 47-48; constitutional interpretation, 167, 174-175, 177; falsified consent, 179; investigations, 288-289; legitimacy, 176. *See also* Congress

Legitimacy: consent of governed, 160; Constitutional interpretation, 190-191; courts, 190-191, 195; decision making, 175; democracy, 249; government communication, 38, 39, 41, 44, 66, 241, 266, 282; institutional autonomy, 137; judicial review, 149, 191-192; legislature, 176; majoritarianism, 152-153; president, 195; public schools, 217; total institutions, 232. *See also* Consent

Levine, M., 154 *n30*

Lewis, C. S., 93

Libel, 275; injunction, 284. *See also* Defamation

Liberalism, 39, 41-42, 51, 92, 103, 113, 150, 157, 177; conflict with technology, 10-13; *See also* Individualism

Liberty, 54, 271; affirmative, 135, 213, 232-233; due process, 265; promoted by government, 39

Libraries, 227, 241; public schools, 243-244

Licenses: broadcasting, 57

Lindblom, C.: quoted, 14, 95-103 *passim*

Litigation: indirect effects, 203, 204; political speech, 257; public interest, 193-194, 200, 203, 204, 258, 301; social change, 204; traditional, 193-194, 200, 201-203, 207, 246, 301. *See also* Courts; Judicial review

Llewellyn, K.: quoted, 151

Lobbying, 185, 258; by corporations, 99; by executive branch, 182; by government officials, 291-292; by local government, 48, 49, 167, 261, 305; federal funding, 182, 185, 188; federal government, 182; public funding, 304

Local government, 48, 235; advocacy of unconstitutional values, 296; secrecy, 248 *n14. See also* Government; Municipal speech

Lombard v. Louisiana, 262-263

Loosely coupled organizations, 118

Loyalty oaths, 220, 221

MacArthur, D., 64-65

MacLeish, A., 122

MacNeill, R., 130

Madison, J., 90, 247 *n7*

Magnuson, W., 127

Mail, 231; second class, 235. *See also* Franking privilege

Majoritarianism, 47, 104, 106, 113, 146-148, 151, 152-154, 158, 160, 164, 176-177, 178, 189-201; civil rights, 160; consultation processes, 153-154; legitimacy, 152-153; pluralism, 108. *See also* Consent; Majorities; Morality of consent

Majorities: falsified, 155, 157; verification, 48, 49, 152-153, 154, 176-178, 201, 249. *See also* Majoritarianism

Malinowski, B.: quoted, 39 *n5*

March, J.: quoted, 118-119 *passim*

Marcuse, H.: quoted, 86

Marketplace of ideas, 163, 169, 204, 235; inequities, 164; market flaws, 164; private communications, 18; public opinion, 36

Marketplace theories, 92, 93, 102

Marriage, 256

Mass communications: audience, 78-79; complexity, 75-76, 84-85; content, 78-80; context, 78; communicator characteristics, 77-78; cumulative, 85; definition of effectiveness, 83; effectiveness, 72, 74-80, 82-85, 87, 97; fear, 79-80; indeterminacy, 82-83; pluralism, 84; rewards and punishment, 82; timing,

78, 79. *See also* Communications; Communications networks

Mass media, 38, 42, 51, 55, 60, 74, 161; access to government information, 8, 12, 250-251; and citizen autonomy, 36; consensus, 84-85; corporations, 97; education function, 163; focus issues, 84; government, 115, government secrecy, 248; government subsidies, 40; informed citizens, 250-251; information function, 163; interpersonal communication, 76-77; judicial proceedings, 251-254; pluralism, 255; private ownership, 114-115; public funding, 235; public opinion, 36; regulation, 16, 114, 125, 202, 255. *See also* Public broadcasting

Mass media markets, 37

Mass society, 36, 41, 86

McCarthy hearings, 184-185

McFarland, A. S.: quoted, 28-30 *passim*

Mechanical model, 22

Mediating institutions, 84, 107

Meiklejohn, A.: quoted, 32 *n38,* 155, 156, 253

Military, 56-57, 61, 62, 64-66, 78, 94 *n9,* 113, 122, 166, 169, 172, 185, 214, 228, 232, 233, 247, 250, 253, 256, 269, 284; indoctrination, 227; public forum, 227

Mills, C. W.: quoted, 13, 35-37 *passim,* 91

Mills, J. S.: quoted, 52 *n5*

Minorities, 146-147, 148, 153, 161, 164, 177; and First Amendment, 146-147; religions, 165. *See also* Desegregation

Modernization, 11-12

Monopoly: communications networks, 49; propaganda, 85-86, 169-170

Moore v. City of East Cleveland, 257-258

Morality of consent, 148

Morgan, D.: quoted, 174-175

Moyers, B., 131

Municipal speech, 43-44

Mutually affecting relationships, 38, 72, 83-84, 91, 100-101, 112-113, 116, 120, 153-154, 260. *See also* Cybernetics; Feedback

NAACP v. Alabama ex rel. Patterson, 257
NAACP v. Button, 257
National Aeronautics and Space Agency (NASA), 284
National Association for the Advancement of Colored People (NAACP), 257
National Educational Television and Radio Center (NET), 127-128
National School Service, 63
Natural law, 105, 149
New York Times v. Sullivan, 286
Nisbet, R., 107
Nixon, R. M., 60, 64 *n47*, 130-131, 132, 133
Nixon v. Warner Communications, 248
Nontenured professors: due process hearings, 268. *See also* Employability; Universities

Obscenity, 231
Office of Facts and Figures, 122
Office of Management and Budget (OMB), 187
Office of Technology Policy, 130-131
Office of War Information (OWI), 48, 58, 64; distortion, 123; political pressure, 123. *See also* Creel Committee
Official immunity, 282; public officials, 283; of senators, 284-285
Oligopoly, 92
Open meeting laws, 162, 248
Opinion leadership, 76, 80. *See also* Leadership
Oppression, 86, 88
Organizations, 23; loosely coupled, 118. *See also* Implementation; Institutions
Owen v. City of Independence, 274-278

Parental rights, 228-230, 231-232
Parochial schools: public funding, 234-235. *See also* Private schools
Partisan politics, 171-172, 181; delegation, 243; federal funding, 186-187, 237-240; government expression, 304; public broadcasting, 186; public funding, 235, 304; public service advertisements, 60
Partisan speech, 170-172; government employees, 172; public funding, 171
Partnerships, 256
Paternalism, 87. *See also* Self-paternalism
Patriotism, 222
Paul v. Davis, 268, 271-275
Peckham, M.: quoted, 27-28 *passim*
Pentagon, 47. *See also* Military
Personality development, 33, 52, 55. *See also* Autonomy
Personal reputation: due process hearing, 267-268. *See also* Defamation; Employability; Libel; Stigma
Persuasion, 6, 18, 33, 39-40, 42, 53, 55, 66, 73-74, 76-78, 84, 87, 92, 112, 168; and policy, 14; courts, 166, 189-190, 192, 195, 259; effectiveness, 71-72. *See also* Indoctrination
Petition: right to, 159
Physics: irreversible processes, 26; simplification, 25-27 *passim;* theory, 26; time and complexity, 26-27
Picketing, 225
Pierce v. Society of Sisters, 228-231
Plott, C.: quoted, 154 *n30*
Pluralism, 29-30, 42, 74, 77, 89, 91-92, 108, 114, 164, 180, 201, 230, 292; achievement of, 108; and alienation, 103; and community, 103; and relativism, 106; and science, 105; communications, 200-203, 213, 219, 220; communications networks, 22, 188, 255, 258, 260; complexity, 95; conflict, 106; constraints, 106-107; doubt, 106; education, 230, 231-232; ideal, 109; mass communication, 84; mass media, 255; promotion by

government, 93, 109-110; private communications, 256; public schools, 216, 221, 224, 225; "referee" theory, 92; right to reply, 293; social progress, 105; values, 104

Political campaigns, 75. *See also* Elections

Political dissent, 25

Political parties, 239; government dominations, 240; major, 237-238; minor, 237-238

Political party doctrine, 295

Political science, 38; reciprocity, 30; simplification, 38; time and complexity, 29-30. *See also* Political theory; Social science

Political speech, 155, 159, 160, 162-164, 223, 227; and associational rights, 257; litigation, 257

Political theory, 108-109. *See also* Political science

Polsby, N.: quoted, 183

Polyarchy, 97, 101-102. *See also* Democracy; Pluralism

Population density, 12

Pornography, 229

Positivism, 16

Post-deprivation hearing, 278-279. *See also* Defamation; Due process; Stigma

Powe, L. A.: quoted, 294

Power, 30, 92, 102, 160, 170-171; asymmetrical, 28-30; of communications networks, 28; of Congress, 180, 185; consent, 21; of corporations, 95-100, 102; of courts, 166, 180, 185, 190-192, 259; of executive branch, 175; of federal government, 159, 160, 175; of labor unions, 98-99; of president, 55-56, 185; of public school officials, 218; symmetrical, 28-30; of teachers, 232

Precedent, 194, 274

Preceptoral state, 14-15, 32, 33, 51, 86, 152, 159, 169, 213; individualism, 34; self-controlled citizen, 34.

See also Authoritarianism; Government expression

President, 45, 55-56, 75, 180; Advertising Council, 60; approval of government advertisement, 58-60; communication powers, 179; Corporation for Public Broadcasting, 129; domination of media, 187; elections, 237-240; falsified consent, 179; legitimacy, 195; power, 55-56, 185; public relations, 63, 122, 131, 181, 187; speech, 171-172. *See also* Executive branch

Press, 162-163, 240; access to information, 202; freedom, 240, 250; shield laws, 162. *See also* First Amendment; Mass media

Pretrial proceedings, 251-252

Prigogine, I.: quoted, 25-27 *passim*, 30

Primacy versus recency, 79

Primary elections, 237. *See also* Elections

Prior restraints, 45, 206, 255; government expression, 283, 284. *See also* Injunctions

Prisons, 71, 162, 169-170, 214, 232, 242, 247, 250-254

Privacy, 107, 231, 249 *n28*, 254, 256-257, 273, 279

Private schools, 41, 222; captive audience, 228; civil liberties, 228-230; curriculum, 233; criticism, 230*n51*; family choice, 230; government funding, 230; as a counter to homogeneity, 230; as a counter to indoctrination, 229; pluralism, 230; public funding, 234; regulation, 229-230, 233; religion, 230 *n51*; teachers, 230. *See also* Parochial schools

Private speech, 201, 223, 231; First Amendment, 63; pluralism, 256; public funding, 234-236; public officials, 206

Professors, 268

Propaganda, 5-6, 33, 47, 51, 63, 73-75, 87, 94, 97, 121, 124, 125, 131,

133, 155-156, 166-169, 171, 179, 182, 186-187, 189, 206, 299; federal funding, 188; government, 292; Nazi, 75; wartime, 64-66. *See also* Indoctrination; Persuasion

Property, 271, 277

Protest: antiwar, 156; civil rights, 227; conscientious objection, 233; picketing, 225; right to petition, 283; sit-ins, 262-263

Proxmire, W., 284-286

PSA. *See* Public service advertisement

Psychiatric hospitals, 214, 232, 247

Public access: government, 162; government information, 162, 253-254; information, 9-10, 15, 40, 46, 47, 49, 163, 202, 251; mass media, 59, 294. *See also* Access

Public accusation, 287

Public broadcasting, 124; access, 240; autonomy, 111, 125-126, 128, 133; centralization, 131-132; complexity, 133; courts, 131, 133; decentralization, 126, 129-130, 132-133; delegation, 126, 133, 134; editorializing, 240-241; elitism, 125, 133-134; executive branch, 64; federal funding, 125-128, 131-134; France, 111; history, 114, 125-126; minorities, 133-134; partisan politics, 134, 186; political pressure, 130-131, 133; private funding, 127, 133, 134; propaganda, 133; staff, 134; Western Europe, 135. *See also* Mass media

Public Broadcasting Act of 1967, 128, 129, 133

Public Broadcasting System (PBS), 130, 133; decentralization, 130-132; political pressure, 131; program development, 130

Public debate, 105, 163; democracy, 21; public opinion, 36

Public employment, 256, 266-271; universities, 269. *See also* Employability

Public figures: defamation, 286

Public forum, 40, 234-236, 240, 241, 301; access, 242; license fees, 236; military, 227; public broadcasting, 240-241; public schools, 225-227, 297-298; right of reply, 297-298; school newspapers, 218

Public officials: abuse of office, 170, 304; defamation, 286; defamation of, 284; First Amendment, 50, 170-173; fund raising, 237; immunity, 273, 282, 283, 285, 286; legislative speech, 281; misrepresentation, 291, 292; nonlegislative speech, 281; official speech, 299; personal liability, 206-207, 281-282; political speech, 306; private speech, 206, 261, 263, 282, 299, 302, 305; racial discrimination, 262; speech, 47, 50, 291; unconstitutional acts, 273

Public opinion, 6, 39-40, 60, 63, 102, 153, 154 *n30*, 266; marketplace of ideas, 36; mass media, 36, 37; political parties, 36; public discussion, 36, 37. *See also* Public debate

Public policy, 101, 113, 116, 152; communication, 14; debate, 155; formulation, 47; implications, 91, 204, 206, 241, 259

Public printer, 187. *See also* Government Printing Office

Public relations: courts, 195-199; local government, 48, 49; military, 65; president, 63

Public service advertisement (PSA), 57-62; air time, 57; beneficent government, 57, 61; content, 60; depoliticization, 60-61; effectiveness, 61-62; fairness doctrine, 62; partisan politics, 60

Public schools, 9, 17, 40-41, 63, 71, 112, 117, 120, 169, 172, 214, 232, 241, 242, 280, 302; academic freedom, 217; affirmative liberty, 213; censorship, 243-244; curriculum, 217; decentralization, 216; delegation, 243-244; democracy, 221-223; desegregation, 192, 194; discipline,

270; elementary, 217; goals, 214, 215, 217, 226-224; hierarchies, 216; hiring policies, 220-224; homogeneity, 221-224; indoctrination, 217, 224, 232; legitimacy, 217; libraries, 243-244; pluralism, 216, 221, 224, 225, 231-232; prayers, 214; public forum, 225-227, 297-298; religious freedom, 233; religious studies, 214; right of access, 225-227; right of reply, 226, 297-298; secondary, 217; socialization, 220, 222-223, 231; student suspension, 270-271; teachers, 118, 269, 270; textbooks, 296; totalitarianism, 224; values, 217. *See also* Education

Public trials, 251-255. *See also* Criminal process

Purcell, E., 104-106 *passim;* quoted, 108-109

Racial discrimination, 179-180, 218-220, 227 *n42,* 266, 271, 296; government advocacy, 261-263; private action, 263. *See also* Desegregation; Minorities

Radicalism, 88-89

Reapportionment, 176, 180. *See also* Elections

"Referee" theory, 92-93, 107. *See also* Pluralism

Referenda, 48, 49, 203, 291, 303-305. *See also* Elections

Reinstatement, 277

Relativism, 105-107, 149

Religious freedom, 159, 165, 167, 173, 214-215, 228, 231, 240; public schools, 233

Religious indoctrination, 214-215

Remedies, 24, 232, 263-265, 292, 303; courts, 190; damages, 206-207, 279, 280, 282; declaratory judgments, 205-206, 304; delegation, 205; due process, 264-266, 274; due process violation, 276-280; fairness, 205; Government Printing Office, 282; injunctions, 206, 266, 280, 282, 299, 304; personal liability, 206-207;

post-deprivation, 278; pre-deprivation, 277; proof of harm, 206-207; public accusation, 287; public interest litigation, 205-207; reinstatement, 277; state law, 274; taxpayers' suits, 205-206; traditional litigation, 202-203

Reportorial function, 247

Repression, 86-88

Reputation, 269, 272-273; community standing, 269; due process, 272; employability, 269; liberty interest, 267-268; post-deprivation remedies, 278; pre-deprivation remedies, 277; proof of injury, 268-270; public school teachers, 270; state law, 273. *See also* Defamation; Libel; Stigma

Research, 40, 166; government funding and oversight, 285

Restraints on government expression, 94, 266

Revolution, 51, 86, 88

Richmond Newspapers, Inc. v. Virginia, 252-254 *passim*

"Right not to hear," 231

Right of reply, 190, 255, 296-298; fairness doctrine, 295-296; government expression, 296-298; institutional goals, 298; post-deprivation hearing, 278; public forum 297-298; public schools, 226, 297-298; substantial disruption test, 298; to government expression, 292-294, 301-302; total institutions, 298

Rights, 201

"Right to know," 46, 49, 231, 248, 249, 283

Right to petition, 159, 283

Roe v. Wade, 273

Roosevelt, F. D., 64 *n47,* 121, 123, 194, 293

Rowan v. Post Office, 231

Rules, 119-120

Russel, B.: quoted, 53

Saint-Exupéry, A. de: quoted, 18-19

Schlesinger, A. M., 123

School newspapers, 241; First Amendment, 218-220; public forum, 218

School prayer, 167. *See also* Religious freedom; Religious indoctrination

Schramm, W.: quoted, 74-77 *passim*, 84-85 *passim*

Scientism, 104-105

Secrecy, government, 9-10, 18, 40, 42, 47, 92, 94, 152, 156-158, 160, 162, 166, 202, 246-248, 254, 265. *See also* Access to government information

Secret documents, 162

Securities and Exchange Commission (SEC), 288

Securities regulations, 289-290

Segregation, 218-220. *See also* Desegregation; Minorities; Racial discrimination

Selectivity, 38, 80-81, 90; audience, 77; democracy, 32; government, 241-242; media, 278; self-controlled citizen, 32. *See also* Communications overload

Self-controlled citizen, 37, 38-39, 41, 52, 89, 103, 135, 152, 157, 159, 164, 168, 178, 200, 204, 215, 232-233, 240, 254; access to government information, 249; democracy, 32; preceptoral state, 34; promoted by government, 112-113, 156; selectivity, 32. *See also* Autonomy

Self-governance, 154-155, 221, 231; access to government information, 249, 253-254

Self-paternalism, 149-150. *See also* Paternalism

Senate: public relations, 183-184. *See also* Congress

Senator: damages, 286; defamation, 284-286; injunction, 286

Separation of powers, 45, 94, 190, 259, 282, 284, 289, 303; communication, 180, 189, 200

Sex education, 233

Sexism, 86

Shapiro, M.; quoted, 146

Shearer, D.: quoted, 65

Shelton v. Tucker, 220

Sherman, E.: quoted, 65

Sherwood, R., 122

Shoplifting, 271-272

Simon, Y.: quoted, 73-74

Simplification: First Amedment, 145; communications theory, 100-101; human nature, 27; legal theory, 24-25, 31, 34-35, 90-91, 145, 151, 155, physics, 25-27 *passim;* polemics, 87, 88; political science, 38; social science, 72

Sit-ins, 262-263

Sixth Amendment, 251-255, 287. *See also* Criminal process

Skepticism, 105-106, 114

Social change, 88, 89, 105, 106; government, 261; stability, 54

Social contract, 104, 149-152

Social entropy, 120-121

Socialization, 39, 41-42, 52-55 *passim,* 86, 89, 101, 102, 111-112, 213, 215, 230; family, 232-233; government, 88; public schools, 220, 222-223, 231; total institutions, 232. *See also* Indoctrination; Persuasion; Propaganda

Social Science: simplification, 72. *See also* Political science

Social Security Act, 193

Source credibility, 77-78

Speaker's bureau, 63, 65

Specialization: delegation, 136. *See also* Delegation

Speech monopoly, 94

Speech or debate clause, 203, 284-285; defamation, 285-286; Government Printing Office, 281; legislative speech, 285; nonlegislative speech, 285, scope, 283

Standing, 165, 188, 202-203, 205-206, 288

Stanson v. Mott, 303-305

Stare decisis, 194, 274

State action, 47 *n39,* 219, 261-263; defamation, 273

State government, 44, 179

State law: civil rights suits, 274; def-

amation, 273-274, 278, 279; remedies, 274
Station Program Cooperative, 132
Stein, M. L.: quoted, 248 *n14*
Stewart, P., 217
Stigma, 276; publication, 269-270. *See also* Due process; Defamation; Libel; Post-deprivation hearing
Strategic weapons, 65
Structural due process, 302-303. *See also* Legislative remand; Ultra vires
Students, 296; access to media, 226; Congressional disclosure of names, 280; First Amendment rights, 224-226; records, 248; reputation, 270-271. *See also* Children; Education; Parochial schools; Private schools; Public schools
Substantive due process, 228
Subversive organizations, 264-266
Superintendent of Documents, 283 *n99. See also* Government Printing Office
Supreme Court, 175, 179, 188, 203; communication powers, 289, 192-195. *See also* Courts; Judicial review

Taxation, 170, 189, 237
Taxpayers' suits, 203-206
Teachers: aliens, 220-224, 230; associational rights, 220; diversity, 224; First Amendment, 220, 228; freedom of speech, 215-218; political speech, 299; power, 232; in private schools, 230. *See also* Education; Employability
Technology, 6, 12, 86, 175; conflict with liberalism, 10-13; education, 117, 119; officials' power, 11
Tenth Amendment, 45
Tenured professors, 268. *See also* Employability; Universities
Textbooks, 296
Thorpe, F.: quoted, 247-248
Threats, 79
Time, 23, 72, 78; and complexity, 26-27, 29

Tinker v. Des Moines Ind. Sch. Dist., 224, 226
Tolerance, 110, 215, 227, 233
Torts, 207
Total institutions, 9, 166, 169, 214, 227 *n43*, 232, 250; access, 247; goals, 232; legitimacy, 232; right of reply, 298
Totalitarianism, 38, 41-42, 51, 74, 86, 168; public schools, 224. *See also* Authoritarianism
Traditional litigation: defamation, 279. *See also* Courts; Judicial review
Tribe, L. H.: quoted, xvi, 17 *n50*, 225, 242, 261-262, 265-266, 281 *n91*, 302-303
Truman, H. S., 60, 124
Tussman, J.: quoted, 16-17, 38-40 *passim*

Ultra vires, 188-189, 289, 290, 301-304. *See also* Legislative remand; Structural due process
Unconstitutional values: advocacy, 219-220, 260-263
United States Information Agency (USIA),186
Universities, 136-137, 216-219, 235, 243, 256, 267-271; public employee, 269. *See also* Academic freedom; Education; Employability; Nontenured professors; Tenured professors

Values, 104-108, 112, 149-151, 164, 167, 175; consensus, 13, 149; democracy, 107-108, 111-112, 145; education, 230; electoral, 176; First Amendment, 176; participation, 176; promotion by government, 167; public schools, 217; unconstitutional, 167. *See also* Democratic values; Fundamental beliefs
Van Alstyne, W., 217; quoted, 156
Vanocur, S., 130
Verification of majorities. *See* Majorities, verification
Vietnam, 156

War Advertising Council, 58
Watergate, 131, 132, 156, 184, 195
Welfare state, 6, 49, 71, 86, 100, 107, 151, 157, 201, 257, 258
Western Europe: public broadcasting, 126, 135
Whitehead, A. N.: quoted, 11, 52 *n6*
Whitehead, C., 130
Wickard, C., 290-292, 293, 306
Wickard v. Filburn, 290-292, 306
Weiner, N.: quoted, 23
Wiggins, J. R.: quoted, 255
Wildavsky, A.: quoted, 95, 98-100 *passim,* 101-102
Wilson, W.: quoted, 63-64, 181
Winkler, A.: quoted, 121-124 *passim*

Wisconsin v. Constantineau, 267, 272, 278-279
Wolff, R.: quoted, 88-89, 91-93 *passim,* 103-104, 106
Women's International Year Commission, 188
World War I, 63-64
World War II, 58, 64-65
Written constitutions, 150

Yoder v. Wisconsin, 231-233 *passim*
Yudof, M., 138; quoted, 192

Zoning discrimination: government advocacy, 261